Heloise®

from

A TO Z

A PERIGEE BOOK

HELOISE is a federally registered trademark licensed exclusively to Heloise, Inc.

Perigee Books
are published by
The Berkley Publishing Group
200 Madison Avenue
New York, NY 10016

Library of Congress Cataloging-in-Publication Data

Heloise.
Heloise from A to Z.
p.   cm.
ISBN 0-399-51750-2 (trade paperback : alk. paper)
1. Home economics.   I. Title.
TX158.H434   1992   91-43955 CIP
640—dc20

Cover design by Mike Stromberg
Back cover photograph © by Michael Vasquez
Printed in the United States of America

20   19   18   17   16   15   14

This book is printed on acid-free paper.
∞

ACKNOWLEDGMENTS

To simply acknowledge is not enough, but to say thanks with a zillion hugs to Marcy Meffert, my always upbeat and reliable assistant/researcher/editor/helper and dear friend. Thanks for making my work life do-able and fun. Eugene Brissie, friend not foe. What a joy to work with a publisher who makes me laugh, not cry! Ted Hannah, Director of Advertising and Public Relations for King Features Syndicate who guides me through the maze of what and how with Southern charm. My office staff who are the worker bees who try to please: Ruth, Joyce, Kelly, Jinny Angie, and Janie; and our office managers, Fussy and Doolie. Never last or least, David, my husband, who is always here for me, even when I am not!

To: Sheba, our sweet, adorable Keeshond, who adopted us many years ago and now is in doggie Valhalla. You always had a ready "smile" and wagging tail for those you loved. You make us smile still. Woof!!

PREFACE

As I travel across the country, readers give me hints of all sorts but, in the past year or so, one hint began to pop up wherever I went. It was a hint to write a book of hints in dictionary form for people who are so busy they don't even have time to look in an index first. So, here it is—a dictionary of hints. You'll find some new hints, some old favorites, and some "new-old" hints—old favorites with a new twist.

Just for fun, I've added the "Letters of Laughter" sent to me by readers who sometimes got unusual results from using Heloise hints. For example, the man who sprinkled cat litter too deeply on his driveway to absorb motor grease and inadvertently created a kitty Valhalla—just about every cat in the neighborhood was happy to find a giant, driveway-size litter box!

Since my last book, *Heloise Hints for a Healthy Planet,* I've gathered more hints for helping to save our environment by recycling and using mild cleaning solutions and homestyle remedies that don't involve harsh chemicals. I've labeled those "Healthy-Planet Hints."

The very first hint in this book is the very first hint in my Heloise office files, ABRASIVE CLEANERS, and, as you've probably guessed, my two favorite non-abrasive cleaners are the same ones my mother recommended, baking soda and vinegar. These two safe and inexpensive household helpers have become synonymous with Heloise.

The last hint in the book is ZZZZ, 7 WAYS TO GET TO SLEEP. So many of us have so much to do that even with Heloise Hints, our activities are as abrasive to our nerves as harsh cleaners are to household fixtures and we lose our sparkle just like household fixtures cleaned with abrasives.

In between ABRASIVE CLEANERS and ZZZZ, you will also find some hints marked "Quick-Fix" which are emergency measures. For example, a "thread tail" of a machine-sewn shirt or blouse button is dangling on the button front; you know that means the button will soon pop off and you are on your way out the door to a meeting. You can avoid the button-pop embarrassment if you dab a drop of clear nail polish on the thread and "tail."

I have also included several "Checklists" of points to consider when you are avoiding allergens, saving energy (and energy dollars) in your home, winterizing cars, running a successful garage sale, avoiding mistakes on your taxes, questions to ask a Realtor before you list your house. Also, shopping to get best value, buying on layaway, and reading the fine print on an insurance policy or a warrantee agreement. The checklists can save money, energy (yours, too), and time for any consumer, but they are even more helpful to inexperienced consumers who too often pay more for less when they don't have enough information to make decisions.

And what Heloise Hints book would be complete without those "that's so simple, why didn't I think of that" hints from readers who have found a better way to do ordinary things? For example, a hint like grabbing a hot light bulb with the corrugated paper "box" from the new bulb instead of burning your fingers. Or, unusual how-to hints on feeding horses, snakes, and turtles, handling your pet salamander and keeping fishing worms from escaping. Look for hints on how to file the hints you clip from columns, too.

We are publishing this book in time to be given to new summer brides and grooms and students going away to school or graduating and moving from home to live on their own for the first time. The latter, for example, will find hints for making decisions at work and getting comfortable at the computer along with the ever popular Heloise Home Hints for cleaning, cooking, and yes, my most requested Spots and Stains Removal section. Believe me, most of the questions I get are about removing spots and stains from clothing, furniture upholstery, and carpets so I've tried to assemble as much information about this as I possibly can. The second most annoying problem seems to be odors—how to get rid of them and how to make rooms and things smell fresh.

I realize that Heloise hints can't solve all the world's problems, but they can help to make each person's individual world and daily life less stressed by the little things that are so aggravating. How often does one more little thing gone wrong become the proverbial straw that breaks the camel's back or the nudge that pushes us over the edge?

I've tried my best to alphabetize the hints according to the words most people would think of when looking them up. I hope you will use this hints dictionary often and as I've suggested in other books, working parents who delegate chores to children can copy sections of the book, such as laundry hints, and tape them up near the washer and dryer, or copy freezing food hints and tack them up inside a kitchen cabinet or near the freezer. The idea is to have the information where it's needed most.

If you have any hints you'd like to share, you can send them to me: Heloise, P.O. Box 795000, San Antonio, TX 78279-5000. Or FAX it: 1-512-HELOISE.

As always, hugs,
Heloise

A

• **ABRASIVE CLEANERS,** *Healthy Planet, Protecting Sinks and Tubs:*
Here are some reasons why I recommend cleaning with baking soda
and vinegar—two simple, gentle, environmentally safe cleaners. I
should note that my mother and I both recommended them because
they are cheap and safe, long before I even met my husband, David,
a plumbing contractor. David and I joke about having a premarital
agreement that if he finds a can of scratchy stuff stashed away
anywhere in our new home, it could be justifiable grounds for
divorce.
1. Most powdered cleansers on the market will scratch your sinks
and tubs and can cut the life of a new fixture by ten to fifteen years.
They also scratch kitchen fixtures, plastic-type surfaces like laminated countertops, fiberglass sinks and shower stalls. Once these
cleansers scratch surfaces they lose their shine, become dull, porous
and more easily stained.
2. If you prefer commercial products to plain, cheap baking soda
and vinegar, clean with spray-on, foamy-type bathroom cleaners.
Also, powdered dishwasher detergent has enough chlorine bleach in
it to clean like powdered cleansers, but protect your hands if they
are chlorine-sensitive. Sometimes a squirt of liquid dishwashing
detergent and a little extra elbow grease will do the job. *Letters of*

Laughter: I suggested using "elbow grease" in my newspaper column and found out later that many younger readers had never heard of the term. They asked supermarket managers where they could find "that elbow grease Heloise recommended in her column."

• **ACRYLIC PLASTIC DOOR PANES,** *Restoration:* Despite careful cleaning with various commercial products, one reader said that her storm door's acrylic panes stayed dull and cloudy most of the time. Then she applied liquid furniture polish with a soft, lint-free cloth and was amazed at how easily they became sparkling clean and clear.

• **ADDRESS BOOK:** Losing an address book is an incredible inconvenience. I keep a duplicate one in my safe in case of fire—the addresses are as important to me as any other valuable! Write the names in ink and the address and phone number in pencil. Then you can erase when the people move.

• **ADDRESS BOOK/FILE,** *Quick-Fix:* Cut the return address labels from envelopes and tape them to file cards or in address books with transparent tape.

• **ADDRESS CHANGE POSTCARDS,** *Time-Saver:* When you have a large family and circle of friends and move a lot, filling out change of address forms from the post office is a chore. (**Note:** These are FREE at your local post office for the taking, add a postcard stamp.) One reader gets one change of address form from the post office and fills it in appropriately. Then she has a local print shop copy the filled-out address form onto blank, plain 4 × 6 index cards—much faster and easier than writing in the information over and over! Don't forget to mail the cards!

• **ADDRESS FILES:** Instead of an address book, keep track of your mailing list in a 3 × 5 index card file, then you can replace the cards of people who move a lot. Add to the cards notes on birthdays, anniversaries, home and work phone numbers, and other helpful information such as a couple's children's names (if you see them infrequently), their food preferences/allergies, and directions to their homes. (My family was military and I remember how hard it is to keep track of such information when you have a large circle of friends who stay on the move.)

- **ADDRESS LABELS:**

1. Give extra address labels (like those you get from organizations soliciting donations) to your college students or elderly relatives to use when they write to you. (And in the case of students, hope they use them!)

2. Also, if addressing envelopes is a bother, either have labels printed for the people to whom you write most, get labels duplicated at a copy shop (ask for a "master" on which to put addresses), or ask people for their extra labels! Then, don't forget to write!

3. When you move, send a label with your new address to your friends and business contacts so they can just put the new label over your old address. **Hint:** Look for labels that will hold four lines so that the first line can be "We've Moved to:" or "Note New Address" and, if you can get five lines, have your new phone number printed on the label, too. To make sure there's no way not to notice, have them printed on yellow-green or other bright "Day-Glo" paper.

4. Stick one on your note or tablet paper for "custom-printed" stationery. Your address will always be legible.

5. Identification for Joggers/Walkers: Put an address label on the tongue of each walking/jogging shoe so that you will be identified in case of an accident on the road.

6. Halloween Trick or Treats: Stick your address labels on the treats you give away so parents know who gave them and that they are safe.

7. Stick one on your casserole dish and serving utensils when you take them to potluck affairs and you'll always get them back.

- **ADHESIVE BANDAGE,** *Removing Without Pain:* Soak a cotton ball with baby oil and apply it to the sides of the bandage. In about 10 minutes, the adhesive will be softened so much that the bandage will come off automatically and painlessly!

- **AFTER-CHRISTMAS SALES,** *Time-Saver, $aver:* Before you pack away those Christmas cards, wrapping paper, decorations, and all bought during the after-Christmas sales to save money, write down what you bought and make note of what you still need and then attach the list to the November page of your next year's calendar. It's easy to forget what's been bought and it's a chore to unpack early to find out what's needed.

• **ADVENT CALENDARS,** *Reminder:* If your family has the Advent calendar and/or Advent wreath tradition but forgets to get them started on time, pack the Advent things with Thanksgiving decorations as a reminder. Save by buying Advent calendars at post-Christmas half-price sales.

• **AFTERSCHOOL TALK WITH CHILDREN:** When all of the children arrive home from school and want to tell you about their day, feelings get hurt when they interrupt each other and some may feel left out. One mother of seven solves this problem by having the children draw numbers written on slips of paper when they come home from school. Each gets to talk in order from one to seven and they all feel fairly treated. It's easier on the mom, too!

• **AIRLINE TRAVEL,** *Seating:* Many frequent flyers agree that the smoothest ride is in the seats in the middle compartment over the wing's forward part. The quietest ride is in the front. There's more leg room if you get a seat next to the exit or at the bulkhead. A reader wrote that after he quit smoking and no longer had to sit in the back of the plane, he was surprised to find out how much more comfortable every other part of the plane was—one more good reason to quit, he said.

• **ALABASTER,** *Cleaning:* Alabaster is similar to marble (both are very soft) and so you can clean it with some marble-cleaning kits. Read the instructions on the label. You can also wipe alabaster items gently with mild detergent suds, rinse and dry with a clean soft cloth. Use this general cleaning method only occasionally; too frequent cleaning can damage alabaster. Commercial cleaning kits are available, too.

• **ALARM,** *Finding Snooze Button When You're Half-asleep:* Stick a self-gripping fabric dot on the snooze button and you'll find the fuzzy button with your eyes closed and one hand still gripping your pillow.

• **ALBUMS AND SCRAPBOOKS,** *When Old Pages Begin to Crumble:* Place pages between clear plastic protector sheets; protect odd-size page with clear protective covering from hobby shops.

• **ALLERGY,** *Checklist of ABCs for Relief:*

A—Air-condition your home.

B —Bathroom mold and mildew can cause allergy symptoms; scrub sinks and fixtures regularly.

C —Cats and dogs can cause runny eyes and sneezing. Avoid pets or restrict them to certain areas of your home.

D—Damp-mop hard surface floors at least once weekly.

E —Enclose your fireplace; stay away from smoke and fumes and don't store wood indoors.

F —Fluff-dry drapes and small rugs in your dryer to keep them dust-free.

G—Go see your allergist regularly, on schedule.

H—High-efficiency, non-electronic, ozone-free air cleaners can remove up to 99 percent of airborn contaminants from circulation. Get one for home or office.

I —Invest in an efficient kitchen exhaust fan.

J —Junior's fabric toys can trap dust and other irritants, so stay away from them; keep them clean.

K—Keep emergency medication handy but out of reach of small children.

L—Leave trees and plants alone during allergy season. (Or wear a surgical mask to reduce the pollen you inhale.)

M—Mattresses should be vacuumed regularly and pillows and other bedding should be non-allergenic synthetic fibers.

N—Notify school nurse and teacher of children's allergies and symptoms. Provide emergency phone numbers if your child has a serious problem.

O—Outdoor activities should be minimized during allergy season. Stay indoors in an air-conditioned area whenever possible.

P —Proper relative humidity during the winter furnished by a central humidifier will alleviate itchy skin and skin allergies.

Q—Quit smoking; it's needless extra irritation for eyes, nose, throat, and lungs.

R—Replace or clean air cleaner, air conditioner, and furnace filters as needed.

S —Stay away from odorous chemicals and heavy perfumes. Avoid industrial areas and high-traffic areas, too.

T —Tile your kitchen and bathroom floors; rugs trap allergens.

U —Use wood or vinyl furnishing rather than those with heavy upholstery fabrics.

V —Vacuum your whole house every week.

W—Windows and door should be shut and sealed tight.

X—X-tra care is needed during summer months.

Y—Year-round attention is important to allergy relief.

Z—Zip right through the allergy season with symptom relief, using common sense and these preventive tips.

• **ALMONDS,** *Roasting In Microwave:*
1. Toss almonds with oil to coat them lightly. Arrange them in a single layer on a microwave-safe plate.
2. Heat on full power for two minutes. Toss again and let rest one minute. Heat two minutes longer, until almonds are golden brown.
3. Drain and cool on paper towels.

• **ALUMINUM CANS,** *Recycling:* Pick up aluminum cans when you walk; you'll be exercising and helping the environment at the same time. If you don't want to turn the cans in yourself, give them to a church or other fund-raising group.

• **ALUMINUM FOIL,** *Healthy Planet Recycling:* If you line cookie sheets with aluminum foil, use that same foil, unwashed, to cover up the plate of cookies or between layers of cookies if you store them in a tin. **Hint:** If everybody could use every disposable thing at least twice, we'd cut our daily trash output by a half. That's not really realistic, but we can try to use as many disposables as possible at least twice to decrease trash output and save landfill space in our environment!

• **ALUMINUM FOIL,** *Recycling for Reuse:* Clean with a damp sponge, wiping the foil from the center out to the edges—it smooths the foil as it cleans.

• **ANIMAL FOOD,** *Storage:* If you feed your pets outside or feed birds, squirrels, etc., it's convenient to store the food outdoors. Keep uninvited animal guests from eating it by storing it in a self-locking trash can. **Hint** for feeding stray cats and dogs: Unless you plan to adopt the animal permanently, get it neutered and its immunizations, it's really kinder to call your local animal rescue organization. Strays lead a hard life—fighting disease, each other, traffic on dark streets, and they usually lose the fight. Also, the animal you're feeding may be registered as lost with the shelter and its owner may be anxiously waiting for word about it.

• **ANIMAL REPELLENT,** *Keeping Cats and Dogs from Shrubbery and Porches:* Sprinkle mothball flakes on the area that needs protection. Flakes will settle into the grass and last for several days so that you only need apply twice a week or so (only once a week after a while). The animals may eventually avoid that place even if you don't put out flakes anymore. **Caution:** Sprinkle FLAKES not moth balls; children can mistake the balls for candy and they are poisonous; also mothballs don't settle into the grass like flakes do.

• **ANSWERING MACHINE MESSAGE TAPES:** Save the messages from grandparents to grandchildren and vice versa in your fond memories box to enjoy again.

• **ANSWERING MACHINE REMINDER:** When you think of "must do's" at work, call your home answering machine to leave yourself a message—no more lost self-notes!

• **ANTIFREEZE CAUTION:** Animals, especially dogs and cats, love the sweet taste and only two ounces can kill. Once ingested, there is little to be done for the animal. Keep all antifreeze containers away from pets and wipe up all spills thoroughly.

• **ANTS,** *Extermination:* Sprinkle boric acid or borax powder along the ant trails and entrances. Keep crumbs vacuumed and any other ant "treats" wiped up so you don't attract more.

• **ANTS, IN OUTSIDE PET FEEDING DISH:** Make a moat! Partially fill a shallow dish with water and place the pet's food dish in the center of it.

• **APPLES,** *Added to Food:* If you can't bite apple chunks because of dental problems, grate apple for adding to salads or fruit compotes. **Hint:** If you can't chew your food properly, proper nutrition is difficult. See your dentist for help; new techniques diminish pain and restore teeth for better overall health!

• **APPLES,** *Freezing Excess:* Peel, core, and slice. Sprinkle with lemon juice or ascorbic acid (sold at supermarkets and grocery stores) to keep them from turning brown. Store in freezer containers or plastic freezer bags in specific-use quantities like one-, two- or three-cup packs so they'll be ready for recipes.

• **APPLES,** *Storage:* Apples give off ethylene gas and will make carrots bitter if stored in the same crisper drawer with them.

• **APPLESAUCE,** *Healthy Planet, Making Homemade Sauce Rosy Pink:* Leave on the skins of red-skinned apples, such as Cortland or McIntosh, when you cook the apples, then press them through a sieve or run them through a food mill (bought in cookware departments or shops) to mash the sauce and remove skins and seeds.

• **APPLIANCES,** *Cleaning Coppertone Finishes:* Dampen an old terry towel with a solution of half vinegar and half water to wipe off smudges, smears and finger marks; the appliance will shine.

• **APPLIANCE SERVICE CONTRACTS/BOOKLETS:** Put them in a large envelope and tape the envelope to the back (or side, if inconspicuous) of the appliance. You'll always know where they are. Or punch holes in them and keep all of them in a large ring binder.

• **APPLIANCES,** *Unplugging When Not in Use:* This safety warning is often given but seldom heeded as we leave toasters, auto-shut-off irons, sewing machines, hair dryers, etc. plugged in feeling confident that they are not on. Readers have sent me examples of near-disasters caused by leaving appliances plugged in between uses. The "toast" button on the toaster oven accidentally got pushed down and wasn't noticed until the smoke detector went off just in time to prevent an electrical fire. A roll of paper towels fell on a toaster oven; it went on and then the towels overheated to the point of catching fire. A rolled-up rug got placed on the foot treadle of a sewing machine, which was threaded and plugged in. The machine ran for unknown hours with the thread tangled in the bobbin case and caught fire. The family woke up to a smoke-filled house from the burning machine. It only takes a few seconds to unplug an appliance—precious seconds that could save your life or property!

Always unplug unused appliances and check smoke alarms frequently to be sure the batteries are working.

• **APPOINTMENT NOTICES:** Tape or staple doctors, hairdressers or other appointment slips to your calendar as soon as you get home and then you won't forget. If you have to remember (or if you want to remind someone else) that they have an appointment (or errand to run) on the way to or from school or work, tape a note on the car steering wheel.

• **APPLIANCE BOOKLETS,** *When They Are Lost:* Dial information, 1-800-555-1212, to get the manufacturer's customer service or consumer information number. Most have 800 numbers, but if there is none, call your local public library's business information number and get the address and/or phone number to write or call for information and to get a new booklet.

• **APPLIANCES,** *Quick-Fix Touch-Up:* Small scratches on white appliances can be covered with white nail polish or white typewriter correction fluid.

• **AQUARIUM,** *Cleaning:*
1. Because detergents may leave harmful residue, scrub an empty aquarium with non-iodinized salt and a heavy-duty plastic pot scrubber (one without any soap in it).
2. To bleach green algae stains from coral, shells and other aquarium decorations, soak in a mild chlorine bleach solution until white, rinse well under running water, and then soak at least 24 hours (until the bleach smell is totally gone) in a plastic basin or clean waste basket filled with water (enough to cover the decorations) and about one small bottle of aquarium water chlorine remover— the clear liquid (anti-chlor) you add to water to dechlorinate it before it goes into the fish tank.

• **AQUARIUM BACKDROP,** *Homemade $aver:* Instead of buying a plastic backdrop from the store, tape to the back of the aquarium a sheet of wrapping paper in a design that pleases you.

• **AQUARIUM GRAVEL,** *Recycling:* Put in a terrarium or the bottom of flower pots before planting; substitute for florist foam in flower arrangements; pour into ashtrays; layer different colors in an apothecary jar. **Note:** Not all fish tanks require gravel; some newer filter systems are not under gravel. Also, some fish, like African Chiclids dig so much that you're better off with pebbles at the bottom of your aquarium. Ask a knowledgeable person at your local aquarium store for advice and get information from library books and books about the specific type of fish you plan to buy.

• **AQUARIUM WATER,** *Healthy-Planet Water-saver:* When you clean out your fish aquarium (not salt-water tank), water plants with this free non-chemical fertilizer solution.

• **ART,** *Letter of Laughter:* A mother who always taught her children that "God is the greatest artist there is" found out that children really do listen sometimes. After a dark and rainy day, the sun came out and so did a rainbow. When her three-year-old saw it, she said, "I'm so glad God likes to paint!"

• **ASPARAGUS,** *Quick-Fix, Microwave Cooking:* For variety, place asparagus in a shallow microwave-safe dish and pour chicken broth over it. Sprinkle cut-up shallots and a bit of lemon juice on top, then microwave for a few minutes (see your microwave book for times per amount of veggie) until the asparagus is hot.

• **ASPARAGUS,** *Storage:* The fresher asparagus is, the better it tastes, but if you have to store asparagus for a day or so, put the uncooked asparagus stalks in a deep pot, cut ends down, put ice water in the bottom and over with a plastic bag. Keep the pot in the fridge until you're ready to cook.

• **ASSEMBLY,** *Bikes, Furniture, etc.:* Take a long piece of masking tape and press the ends together with the sticky side out. Then attach the tape to work table or the carton in which the pieces came and you can stick to the tape all those bits and pieces of nuts, screws etc. They won't get lost while you try to figure out the "easy assembly" instructions. **Hint:** When assembly is required, don't destroy boxes or containers until you're sure all is well. Keep all extra hardware, instructions, and tags in an envelope or zipper bag labeled to identify contents.

• **AUTO,** *Hot Wheels, Hot Seats:* Summer sun can make the steering wheel and driver's seat hot even with a windshield sunshade. Try covering the driver's seat and wheel with an old flannel-backed plastic tablecloth "tent" draped over the wheel and seat back. Or, to Quick-Fix if your wheel's not leather, rub an ice cube over the steering wheel; it'll cool quickly and you won't have to drive with two fingers!

• AUTO, *Rental Use Agreements:* Don't lend a rental car to anyone because the collision damage waiver agreement can be made invalid if damage is caused by a driver who's not listed on the rental agreement. Other reasons for invalidating the agreement can be an accident that doesn't occur on a highway, or if the rental company believes you were the careless driver in an accident (even if the other driver is clearly at fault). The deductible for most collision damage waivers is $100–$250, to be paid by the auto renter if the car is in an accident.

• AUTO, *Safeguarding Against Theft:* Purses have been stolen from car seats at stoplights when thieves break the passenger window and reach in. Either keep your purse hidden on the floor or, before snapping your lap seat belt in place, run it through your purse handle so that you and your purse are safely belted in. Of course, you do lock your doors, especially when driving in unfamiliar places. Please see AUTO THEFT.

• AUTO, *Summer Driving Care:* Overheated cars can spoil summer travel. When the temperature-warning light flashes or the heat gauge registers in the hot zone, try the following hints.
1. Turn off the air conditioner to give your car's cooling system a rest. Turn on the heater to drain some of the heat away from your engine.
2. If your car continues to be overheated, pull out of traffic to a safe parking place. Put the transmission into neutral and race the engine for a minute or two. This increases the fan speed and moves more air through the engine compartment.
3. If the car still says hot, turn off the ignition, raise the hood, and wait for the engine to cool off. Then get to a repair facility.

• AUTO, *Washing off Road Tar:* Spray spots with an oil-based pre-wash spray, let it set for a few minutes and then scrub with nylon net or a plastic scrubber. Repeat application to stubborn areas. Rinse and buff with soft cloth.

• **AUTO,** *Winterizing Checklist:* The following are potential winter trouble points:

1. Battery: Watch for corrosion on terminals and have a mechanic replace loose or frayed cables.
2. Windshield Wiper Blades: When they screech a lot or don't clean properly in the rain, they won't work in the snow either. Replace them. They are relatively inexpensive.
3. Belts and Hoses: Frays, cracks and bulges are warning signs. When the engine is turned off and cold, check for proper fan-belt tension by pressing down on the middle of the belt. It shouldn't give more than half an inch.
4. Lights and Turn Signals: Replace all bad bulbs.
5. Tires: See owner's manual for recommended cold weather air pressure. (Temperature affects pressure—generally, it's one pound for every 10 degrees of temperature.)
6. Radiator: Clean with a garden hose, spraying from front to back so fins are cleared of grease, dirt, and debris. Radiator caps and thermostats should be replaced after four years or 60,000 miles. Coolant should be changed every two years or after 30,000 miles.

• **AUTO,** *Winter Emergencies:* If you're stranded in a car during a snow storm, stay calm and stay put.

1. Don't leave your car unless you can see another shelter close by.
2. While you wait for help, alert passing vehicles with flares, reflective triangles, or even a brightly colored piece of cloth tied to your car antenna.
3. Keep warm in the car by running the heater once an hour, or every half hour in extreme cold. **Caution:** Be sure the area around your exhaust pipe and outside heater vents is not obstructed by snow or anything else to avoid carbon monoxide poisoning.

• **AUTO,** *Winter Emergency Items Checklist:* Keep the following in your trunk:
Flares or reflective triangles; jumper cables; abrasive material for traction (sand, salt, cat litter stored in recycled, clean, dry, plastic gallon jug); flashlight; sleeping bag or blanket.

• **AUTO ASHTRAY,** *Discouraging Smoking In Your Car:* If you aren't bold enough to put a no smoking sign on the ashtray, fill it with coins for parking meters or with potpourri, which smells nice, too.

- **AUTO EMERGENCIES:**

1. Make it easy to get helped. Place an envelope in your glove compartment marked "In Case of Accident" that contains the name and phone number of a person to notify in case of emergency, doctor's name, blood type and allergies.

2. Keep a "throw-away" camera in your glove compartment so that you can photograph damages, license-plate numbers, street signs and configurations, construction work or other obstacles, and anything else that gives you information for filing and proving an insurance claim if there's been an accident.

3. Keep an old blanket in the truck for picnics, for warmth in case you get stranded in the cold, and to drape over the back of the trunk and the bumper when you are loading or unloading a dirty car and don't want to mess up your clothes.

Letters of Laughter: Have you noticed that when you drive your spouse to work so that you can have the car for the day, you always get the flat tire? One reader, who has trouble remembering which way to turn lug nuts (left to loosen and right to tighten) when changing a tire, offers this rhyme which sounds just silly enough to be remembered: "Lefty Loosey, Righty Tighty."

- **AUTO INSURANCE,** *Checklist for Liability Coverage:* Make sure you get the best rate for the amount of coverage that you need.

1. Newer cars purchased with a car loan are required to have full coverage.

2. Older cars of minimal value can get by with liability coverage alone.

To get a free single copy of a pamphlet titled "Oops," send your request with a stamped, self-addressed, business-size envelope to the Insurance Information Institute Consumer Affairs, 110 William St., New York, NY 10038.

- **AUTO INSURANCE,** *Discounts:* Check your insurance to see if you get a reduction in rate for installing an anti-theft device, for having certain safety features such as anti-lock brakes, and so forth. Don't just pay without questions.

• **AUTO KEYS,** *Leaving Them in the Ignition:* Tie your keys to your purse or briefcase with a long leather boot lace so that when you pick up your purse or briefcase to leave the car, you can't go without removing the keys. The thong also helps prevent rummaging around in the bottom of a purse for keys—just pull the thong.

• **AUTO LITTER BAGS,** *Recycling:* Hook the handles of a plastic grocery bag over a floor-mounted gear shift to keep the litter bag handy. When it's full, just remove, tie the handles shut and discard.

• **AUTO MAINTENANCE,** *Simple Do-It-Yourself Checklist $aver:* Keeping your car in tip-top shape will get you a better price when you trade it in and will made it more pleasant to ride in while you own the car.
1. Keep a small bottle of matching color touch-up paint, bought at auto supply stores or dealers, to cover up small scratches, chips and minor nicks before they become rust spots.
2. If you live where road salts are sprinkled to deter ice, wash your vehicle as often as possible to prevent damage and corrosion.
3. Wash your car only with soap formulated especially for car washing. Dishwashing and other cleaners are too harsh for the finish and will eventually dull it.
4. Protect the paint job by waxing your car at least three times a year. Wax protects against grime and sunlight to keep paint shiny. Remember to always apply wax in a shady area. Car wax applied in full sun gets "baked on" and is very hard to remove.
5. In the interior, protect vinyl with a cleaner/protector to keep it from drying out and cracking; it also helps prevent color fading. Vinyl car tops are especially prone to these problems. Maintain cloth upholstery by removing dirt and dust before it gets ground into the fabric. A quick brush or vacuum will do the trick. Foam upholstery cleaner will remove dirt from cloth seats.

• **AUTO-MATICALLY FINDING YOUR CAR IN A MALL LOT:** Some years ago, my column had a hint to put a plastic flower or bicycle safety flag on your radio antenna to make it easier to find your car in mall parking lots. Afterward, I received lots of *Letters of Laughter* telling me that the best way to find your car in the lot was not to follow the hint—it seems that almost everyone attached something to radio antennae and it was easier to spot an undecorated car in mall parking lots.

• **AUTO SAFETY:** Get the habit of saying "Hands Up" to child passengers before you close the door to avoid hand injuries and make "Hands Up" a rule without "Captain May-I" discussions. *Letter of Laughter:* One member of my editorial staff got so used to saying "Hands Up" to her children during years of carpooling that she still says it to adult passengers even though she hasn't carpooled children in ten years!

• **AUTO SEAT BELTS:** When there are three seat belts in the backseat it's hard to figure out which parts go together—unless you color-code the belts with colored Christmas tape or colored "dots" so that riders can just match buckle parts according to color. *Letter of Laughter:* One kids' carpooling reader awards Seat Belt Olympics gold, silver and bronze medals to wear in the car as an incentive to buckle up their seat belts quickly.

• **AUTO THEFT,** *Prevention Checklist:*
1. Always lock your car, even for short absences.
2. Keep car keys separate from house keys. Don't put your name and address on key chains. Don't leave house keys in your car. If you leave keys with a parking valet, leave only the car key, never house keys, and don't tell when you will return.
3. Park your car as close to a building as possible with the front end toward the street to make it easier to spot anyone tampering with the car. At night, always park in well-lighted areas.
4. When parking, always turn the wheels sharply to the curb; it makes towing difficult. Put the emergency brake on.
5. Install an alarm system that turns on light, car horn, or siren if someone tampers with the car.
6. Install a locking gas cap or fuel switch that cuts off the fuel supply when the car is parked.
7. Buy a "crook lock" or "club lock" which locks the steering column to the brake pedal or which prevents the steering wheel from being turned without breaking the windshield. These devices make stealing a car so difficult that they are excellent deterrents— thieves don't want to bother with them.

• **AUTO TRUNK,** *Checklist for Emergencies:* Flashlight with extra batteries; ice scraper; road salt or cat litter; extra windshield-washer fluid; set of jumper cables; flares or reflective devices, extra container of antifreeze; blanket; sweat shirt or jacket; pair of gloves and hat; sandpaper to clean corroded battery terminals; plastic sheeting or garbage bag to kneel on in case you have to fix a flat on wet ground. In the glove compartment, keep spare change and emergency phone numbers, including one for road services.

• **AVOCADO,** *Rooting Plants from the Pits for a Free Plant:*
1. The usual way is to poke toothpicks in the sides and let the flatter rooting end rest in water until roots form and the plant is about four inches tall; then plant it in dirt.
2. Another method is to remove the outer (brown) skin from the seed, then put it in a zipper-type plastic bag with two tablespoons of water. Place bag in warm place. After about a week, the seed splits; after about two weeks, there's root growth; after about a month, there's enough root to plant in soil.
3. You can start seeds in dirt, too. Plant the seed with the pointed end up in a pot full of dirt; place in a sunny spot with no direct sunlight and keep soil moist.
4. I always trim my plant back to keep it from being spindly tall. When it grows to about six inches tall, I cut it in half and it branches out with new growth. I have several that are 10 to 12 feet tall.

B

• **BABY BATHTUB "PLAYPEN":** When a baby is just learning to sit up, let the baby sit in a little plastic bathtub to play with favorite toys. Of course, even if there's no water in the tub, don't leave baby unattended; accidents do happen.

• **BABY BIB,** *Quick-Fix:* No bib? Place a clean dish towel around baby's neck, and let it hang in the front like a bib, secure in the back with a plastic clip or clothes pin.

• **BABY BLANKET,** *Recycling:* Two baby blankets will equal one twin-size mattress pad on a child's bed.

• **BABY BOOK,** *Shower Gift:* Collect Heloise baby hints, cartoons about parenting, and magazine articles about child-rearing and put them into a book for the parents to read and save.

• **BABY-BOOK TAPE:** One mother who's too busy to write cute baby things in the baby book every time they happen, makes notes by talking on tape and then recording the notes when she has time. She saves the tapes, too.

• **BABY BOTTLE,** *Identifying at Day-care Facilities:* Since even permanent marker tends to wear off plastic bottles after a few washings, try sanding an area on the bottle with fine sandpaper and then writing your child's name on the roughened place with permanent marker and cover with clear nail polish. The marker gets absorbed into the scratched area and lasts for months.

• **BABY BOTTLE,** *Washing Baby-bottle Nipples and Caps:* Place them in a small hosiery bag (made to wash hose in the washing machine) and secure them by tying the bag to the top rack of the dishwasher. The heat from the water and drying cycle will clean them.

• **BABY-BOTTLE BRUSH,** *Recycling, Time-Saver:* The pointed tip and flexibility makes these brushes ideal for cleaning crevices and corners, such as the holes of cheese graters or the space around faucets.

• **BABY/BRIDAL SHOWER,** *Addresses for Thank-you Notes:* Save the guest list and note the gift next to the name as gifts are opened; then the showeree will have all the information she needs when she writes her thank-you notes.

• **BABY CAR SEAT,** *Keeping Cool in Summer:* The metal center of the harness can get very hot; place an old sweatshirt or towel over it for shade while you're out of the car to avoid risking a burn.

• **BABY CEREAL,** *$aver:* If baby decides to refuse baby cereal just after you've bought a supply (and that's usually when), mix some adult cereal with the baby-textured ones to keep breakfast-in-a-bowl from being too runny for a baby-held spoon; then you can use it all up.

• **BABY CLOTHES,** *Storing Outgrown Ones:* Store them in empty disposable diaper boxes—you'll always know at a glance which are baby clothes. Mark the outside with the sizes and descriptions so you don't have to play hide-and-seek.

• **BABY CRIB,** *Changing Sheets in the Middle of the Night:* When making the bed, layer rubber mattress protectors with sheets so that you can just pull the top one off if it's wet—without waking baby.

• **BABY CRIB,** *Substitutes When Traveling:* Toddlers—Pad a bathtub (if you can tape faucets so that toddlers can't turn on the water), a plastic toddler wading pool, or other SAFE container. Or try a mattress on the floor in a safe, protected room. Infants can sleep in a padded dresser drawer (removed from dresser, of course!), suitable clean box, or plastic infant bathtub. **Caution:** When using substitute cribs, always make sure there are no lids or loose padding to suffocate the child!

• **BABY EXPANDABLE GATE,** *Healthy-Planet Recycling:*
1. Expandable doorway gates used to keep children and pets out of rooms can be stretched width-wise across the bathtub for sweater-drying. Be sure the gate is plastic-coated or has no metal parts to put rust marks on the sweaters.
2. When your toddler grows up, nail two wood strips inside a closet to support the tension of the gate and make a "closet dam" to hold out-of-season blankets, comforters, extra pillows and children's sleeping bags for overnight guests.

• **BABY-FOOD JARS,** *Quick-Fix Opening:* Instead of wrestling with vacuum-sealed jar lids, place the end of a spoon handle under the rim of the jar lid and pry it open just enough to break the seal and pop the "safety button." The lid comes off more easily and the bonus is that you make sure the safety button was down on each jar and the food is safe for your precious little one.

• **BABY NIGHT FEEDING:** Instead of dashing up and down stairs to get a new baby's bottle for that 2 A.M. feeding, try putting a few bottles of formula in a small cooler with a frozen reusable ice pack and keeping a bottle warmer in baby's room. Then you can feed the baby without long-distance travel.

• **BABY NIGHT-LIGHT:** Install a dimmer switch for a baby's room overhead light and baby won't be startled when you switch on the lights for that 2 A.M. wake-up call session.

• **BABY PHOTOS:** Take photos each month on baby's birth date and include a sign in the pictures that says "Jane is 3 months old today." You can add information on baby's height and weight to the sign, too. Later you won't be confused about which pictures are of whom and when.

• **BABY POWDER CONTAINER,** *When It's Too Generous:* Cut the amount sprinkled out at one time by putting a piece of tape over a couple of the container's holes.

- **BABY'S COMFORT-BLANKET:** Because her first child suffered so much when her favorite "blankie" was in the washer, one mother made a point of buying two identical "blankies" for her second child so that one could be cuddled while the other was in the wash. Some children are comforted by a cotton gauze diaper, all of which look the same, and then there are lots of comforters and laundry time isn't a time of anxiety.

- **BABY SHOWER,** *For the Baby Whose Mom Has Everything:* If mom-to-be has already had a shower or has lots of hand-me-downs from other children, try a theme shower focusing on the one essential all babies need—diapers. Buy large boxes of diapers and containers of baby wipes, or buy gift certificates for diaper service for several weeks if that's mom's choice. Don't forget to clip diaper coupons to add to the gift cards. This hint is especially good for an office shower when co-workers don't know what the mom-to-be has for baby.

- **BABY SNAP BEADS:** Snap together a circle big enough to frame a clock, mirror, or picture and glue in place for a baby room decoration.

- **BABY SOCKS,** *Recycling Lacy Ones:* After washing outgrown lacy girl's socks, fill them with potpourri and sew the tops closed or tie them shut with a ribbon. Grandma or Godmother especially would enjoy having such sentimental sachets for lingerie drawers.

- **BABY-SITTING SOLUTION:** When an older child is the family sitter and younger siblings give their sib-sitter a hard time, try telling the younger ones that if they don't mind and cause trouble, the sib-sitter's baby-sitting fee will come from THEIR allowances. One mother said this solved her problem quickly and quietly.

- **BABY'S ROOM,** *Keeping Cats Out:* Replace the bedroom door with a light wooden screen door. You can see and hear anything that goes on in the room but the cat can't get in to snooze with baby or on baby's bed.

- **BABY, TAKING TEMPERATURE:** When you take a rectal temperature, let baby watch the egg timer you use to keep track of time. Watching colored sand fall or listening to the ticking can keep a small baby occupied during the process.

- **BABY TOWELETTE CONTAINER,** *Recycling:* Store children's crayons and pens; nails, screws, etc. in the garage; rubber bands and safety pins or other bits and pieces in the kitchen; hold plastic utensils and napkins at campouts or picnics. After removing the label, wash thoroughly; the cover fits tightly and small items don't fall out.

- **BABY TRAVEL,** *Taking Supplies in the Car:* Instead of a diaper bag, put baby's diapers, wipes, food, even toys in a plastic basket on the floorboard. It's easier to get to than a diaper bag when you're on the road.

- **BACK SCRUBBER,** *Homemade:* Get a strip of nylon net the length of a bath towel. Put a bar of soap in the middle, wrap the net around it a few times, then tie a knot at both ends to keep it in place. When showering, pull the net "towel" back and forth across your back as if you were drying it.

- **BACON,** *Storing:* If you don't use up a package quickly, try freezing individual strips; the bacon stays fresh and you can take out as many slices as you need. Place individual slices on a cookie sheet and freeze quickly. Then stack the frozen strips in a freezer-safe container with waxed paper between layers. Recycle: Use the waxed paper from cereal boxes for this.

- **BAGS,** *Healthy-Planet, Recycling Idea:* Carry your own mesh or other bags to the store when shopping to avoid collecting grocery bags at home. Europeans have done it for years; we can do it, too!

- **BAGS,** *Storing Plastic Grocery Bags, Healthy Planet Recycling:* Cut a hole about the size of your fist in the side of a clean plastic one-gallon milk or water jug and stuff bags inside; it'll hold more than you think. Then, you can pull one out at a time.

- **BAGS, PLASTIC DRY CLEANERS:** Knot the "hanger" end and line small wastebaskets with them. The bags will hold light paper trash and can be doubled for extra strength.

- **BAGS FOR PRODUCE:** Instead of wrestling a bulky head of leaf lettuce into a plastic bag, put your hand into the bag as if it were a glove, then with your "bagged" hand, grasp the bottom end of the lettuce and invert the bag up and over the head. No more shop-torn salads!

- **BAKING,** *With Honey, Corn Syrup, Molasses, Other Sticky Things:* Spray cups and spoons with non-stick spray before measuring for easy clean up.

- **BAKING DISHES,** *Measuring Capacity:* When you can't tell if a new dish will hold as much as your old one did, pour water to the level your recipe filled in the old dish and then pour it into the new to test for overflow. Or, if you know the quantity your recipe makes, measure that quantity in water and pour it into the new dish to make sure there'll be no overflow. (For example, a nine-inch pie plate holds four cups of liquid exactly.)

- **BAKING FISH STICKS, POTATO NUGGETS, ETC.,** *Fat-saver, Time-saver:* When baking, place food on a wire rack and the rack on a foil covered cookie sheet so that extra grease drips out while food cooks. The sticks and nuggets will be crisper, too, and there's no need to turn them over.

- **BAKING WITH LESS SUGAR:** Replace half the sugar in the recipe with half heat-stable diet sweetener. It will work in most recipes.

- **BAKING SODA,** *Healthy Planet, Recycling:* Baking soda safely cleans many things around the house. Sprinkle on baking soda, wipe or scrub with a damp sponge, rinse well. Sinks, countertops, you-name-it will sparkle. Keep baking soda in an empty plastic jar with a shaker top, like those that dried herbs come in, for easy access.

- **BALCONY,** *Childproofing:* Buy the widest available heavy plastic webbing (for lawn chairs) and then weave it in and out of the railing bars until all spaces are completely closed. Secure the ends and make sure the webbing is close together and strung tightly. Test by pushing on it. This doesn't replace adult supervision because a determined child can get through any barrier. This method can also help confine pets and give a bit of privacy if you like to sunbathe on your balcony.

- **BANANA BREAD,** *When Someone Throws Out the Bananas You've Saved for It:* Substitute canned peaches or experiment with other fruits.

• **BANANAS,** *Storage:*
1. To hasten ripening, store in plastic bag.
2. Once at the proper state of ripeness, you can place bananas in the fridge. The skins will darken but the fruit will be good for about two weeks.
3. Bananas frozen on a stick or in hunks make delicious and nutritious treats, especially for dieters because they take longer to eat.
4. Overripe bananas are perfect for banana bread or other baked goodies. You can freeze them until you have enough for a recipe. But then, use them, don't save them forever! *Letter of Laughter:* Someone once told me that the road to hell is paved with bananas saved for banana bread!

• **BANANA TREATS,** *Homemade:*
1. Freeze peeled bananas, then dip them in chocolate syrup and refreeze until the syrup hardens.
2. Cut peeled bananas into quarters and put peanut butter on the cut sides, wrap in plastic wrap and freeze.

• **BANDAGES FOR PETS,** *Keeping Them On:* Tape usually won't work, especially for dogs; they pull bandages off their legs and elsewhere.
1. Try slipping an elastic wrist sweatband or an elasticized terry ponytail holder (for a small animal) over the bandage to hold it in place. Be sure it's snug but not too tight.
2. If your dog just won't leave an injured area alone, ask the vet for a plastic collar. The dog won't like it, but the collar will prevent it from reaching a sore place and healing will be faster in the long run.
3. The leg from a child's knit footed sleeper can cover a neck sore. Cut enough sleeper leg on the upper side of the ankle elastic to gather (about 3 or 4 inches) and cut just above the heel on the lower side of the elastic, then place the gathered "leg" on the animal's neck with most gathers toward the animal's shoulders.

• **BANK DEPOSIT SLIPS,** *Recycling Excess:* Unfortunately, most of us don't make bank deposits as often as we write checks so we often have leftover deposit slips. Cut out the square area printed with your name, address and phone number and then glue or tape this "address label" to forms for in-store giveaways, on envelopes for

return address, and on other forms that require this information. You've already paid for them, you may as well use them! Keep some in your wallet, handy when someone you've just met wants your phone number.
Or slip them behind the window of a luggage tag.

• **BARBECUE,** *Identifying Food for Scouts, Others:* Clip plastic bread tabs with the person's initials to their clothing and write initials on each foil dinner with permanent marker so that the leader/cook can distribute cooked dinners with less commotion.

• **BARBECUE AUTO-GRILL,** *Letter of Laughter:* I get lots of barbecue hints but this one's ingenious! On a camping trip to the mountains, a family discovered that they'd forgotten their barbecue grill. They took the hubcap off their spare tire, covered it with foil, punched holes in the foil for grease to run out and used it for a grill. The heavy metal worked so well that now they always use the spare tire hubcap for a camping grill! Perhaps a used hubcap from a wrecker yard would do, too.

• **BARBECUE FIRE STARTER,** *Healthy-Planet Recycling:* Half-fill each section of a cardboard egg carton with dryer lint; pour melted wax over it and allow to harden. Cut apart segments for fire starting. **Caution:** Do not use plastic foam egg cartons; they won't burn away and they give off toxic fumes!

• **BARBECUE GRILL,** *Storage for the Winter:* Before storing your grill, be sure to wash the grate well. An unwashed grate sitting all winter can build up bacteria that can contaminate your food and make you sick when you cook on it in the spring.

• **BARBECUE GRILL FIRE STARTER,** *Healthy Planet, Recycling, Making a "Chimney" to Avoid Using Charcoal Lighter to Start the Fire:*
1. To Make the "Chimney"—Wash and dry a one-gallon paint can with a wire handle. Then, take the triangular end of a can opener and make about a dozen triangular openings around the bottom of the outer side of the paint can. **Note:** That's side, not the flat bottom end! Then cut off the flat bottom with a manual can opener so that both ends are open; now, it's a "chimney."
2. To Light a Fire—Place the can in the bottom of the barbecue pit and ball up about six half-sheets of newspaper; put them at the

bottom of the can. Fill the rest of the can with charcoal. Light the newspaper in several places through the holes in the bottom of the can. Because everything is contained in the can, there will be very little flame, just smoldering paper to light the coals. The chimney effect of the can decreases the fire starting time.

3. Before You Grill—When the coals are good and hot, use metal tongs to lift the can out of the grill by the wire handle. **Caution:** Protect your hands and arms with fireproof barbecue mittens and be very cautious when removing the hot can. The can will cool quickly once removed from the grill; it can be reused many times.

• BARBECUE GRILLING: When you grill something that cooks only a short time, like fish, have portions of another meat ready to cook on the coals to use up the heat. You can reheat the second meal in your microwave the next day.

• BARBECUE GRILL PLANTER, *Recycling:* Drill a few holes in the bottom of an old barbecue grill, remove rust with wire brush, spray inside and out with rust-retarding paint. After the paint dries, put a layer of stones or broken pot pieces on the bottom, fill with potting soil and peat moss, add plants and you have a nice planter.

• "BAR-LE-DUC," *Recipe, Quick-Fix Breakfast or Snack:* Top three-fourths cup cottage cheese or cream cheese with one or two table-spoons of preserves and serve with toast or crackers.

• BARRETTES, *Storage:* When you have long hair, usually the combs, barrettes, etc. are a mess in the bathroom. One reader tacked (horizontally) eight separate lengths of one-inch ribbon with fancy tacks to the back of her bathroom cupboard door. She attaches all combs, barrettes, and other hair accessories to the ribbons and can tell at a glance where each of them is.

• BASSINET SHEETS, *Substitute $aver:* Slip the bassinet mattress into an inexpensive king-size pillowcase. The bonus is that after baby is no longer in the bassinet, you have extra pillowcases in your linen closet instead of a bunch of bassinet sheets stored in the attic.

• BASEBALL CAPS, *Repairing:* If the plastic adjustable strip on the back breaks, sew a piece of three-fourths-inch elastic on one side, measure for the right fit, and then sew the other end in place. Often these caps are one of a kind and are as precious to their wearers as a blanket or teddy bear is to a toddler so repairing them is an absolute necessity!

• **BASEBALL BAT GIFT BOX:** If you want to disguise a baseball bat so that it's a surprise gift, buy a florist's box normally used for long-stemmed flowers. You won't even have to wrap it.

• **BATH,** *"Kitchen" Remedies for Soaking in the Bath:* A reader suggests that you shower first, then fill the tub with lukewarm water, squeeze juice from sliced lemons into the water and throw the slices in, too. Then soak in refreshing, lemon-scented, natural astringent water. I like to put lemon juice in my hair rinse water. It removes all the soap film and oil and smells great all day. (Also, please see SKIN, "Kitchen" Remedies for Soaking in the Bath and BATH SALTS.)

• **BATH ACCESSORIES,** *Handy Storage:* Hanging a three-tier wire "egg basket" near shower or tub, where you can reach without getting out, gives you a perfect holder for shampoos, conditioners, bath oil, washcloths, and extra soap.

• **BATH MAT,** *Drying:* Instead of leaving a rubber bath mat in the tub after you bathe where it stays wet and is more likely to mildew, push an edge of the mat gently to the wall so it sticks on the tile by its suction cups and water drips into the tub.

• **BATH MAT,** *Washing to Remove Mildew:* Toss in washer with hot, soapy water and bleach, add a couple of bleach-safe towels for "scrubbing action."

• **BATH PILLOW,** *Substitute:* Partially inflate a plastic beach ball.

• **BATHROOM,** *Painless Cleaning Without Bending:* Instead of leaning over to scrub bathtubs and tile walls, put a few inches of soapy water in the tub, add some bleach and scrub all with a sponge mop. After tiles are clean, drain the water and mop the tub.

• **BATHROOM,** *Healthy-Planet, Quick-Fix Cleaning:* Using up toothpaste squished into the sink to clean it and the fixtures is an old favorite hint. An update is to use shampoo which has dribbled in the shower or tub for the same purpose.

- **BATHROOM COUNTER CLUTTER,** *Eliminating:* Attach a wicker hanging basket from the ceiling about 10 inches above the counter-top to hold brushes, toothpaste, combs and other bits and pieces. There's no rule against using wire mesh kitchen hanging "egg" baskets either.

- **BATHROOM MIRROR,** *Preventing Fog:*
1. Put a bit of shampoo on a dry cloth and wipe the mirror with it before you bathe.
2. When taking a tub bath, run cold water only for the first inch or so, then add the hot water.
3. To "de-fog" quickly without smears, blow the mirror dry with a hair dryer.

- **BATH SALTS,** *Homestyle:* Pour three cups of Epsom salts into a metal or glass bowl. In a separate cup, mix 1 tablespoon of glycerin (available at drugstores), a few drops of food coloring (optional), and some of your favorite perfume. Blend well and slowly add it to the Epsom salts, stirring until thoroughly mixed. Store in a sealed decorative container and add it to your bath water for a treat.

- **BATH TOWEL,** *Pleasure:* Just before you get out of the tub, ask a nice person to warm your towel in the clothes dryer so that you can jump into a warm "cozy" when you get out. (Check out discount linens for bargains on "bath sheets" to wrap in.)

- **BATHTUB DECAL RESIDUE,** *Homestyle Remedy for Removing:* Apply prewash spray and scrub with nylon scrubber; or, when the tub is dry, sprinkle the residue with dry cornmeal and apply elbow grease with a nylon-net scrubbie. *Letters of Laughter:* I used the term elbow grease in one of my columns and found out later that many younger readers had never heard of the expression. They asked supermarket managers where they could find "that elbow grease Heloise recommended in her column."

- **BATHTUB DRAIN PROTECTOR:** Place a one and one-half-inch diameter kitchen sink strainer cup upside down over your bathtub drain to catch bobby pins and other dropped things that can go into the drain. You can still open and shut the drain.

- **BATHTUB/SHOWER DRAIN,** *Quick-Fix, Cleaning Hair from It:* Hate to stick your fingers into the hairy drain? Whisk it clean with a swish of a cotton swab. You touch only the other end of the swab!

- **BATHTUB OR SINK DRAIN QUICK-FIX STOPPER:** A rubber racquet ball (usually blue) will plug the hole of most non-grated drains.

- **BATHTUB OR SINK STAINS,** *Removing:* Scrub with paste made from cream of tartar and hydrogen peroxide.

- **BATHTUB SAFETY,** *When a Toddler Is in That "Me-do-myself" Phase:* Here's one reader's idea. To avoid scalding with hot water, paint a bright line (with model-car paint or fingernail polish) on the faucet handle and on the wall where the two should line up if the water is at the proper temperature for a bath. Then when your toddler insists upon drawing bathwater, the temperature should be safe. **Caution:** The lines are a guide. Never ever let a child prepare to bathe or bathe without adult supervision.

- **BATTERED WOMEN'S SHELTER,** *Helping:* When you clean out your closets, give women's and children's clothing, bedding and towels to your local battered women's shelter. Same for those mini-shampoos, rinse, lotions, shower caps you accumulate from hotels if you travel a lot like I do. If the phone number is not listed, you can usually get the drop-off location from a local volunteer agency, pastors of churches, your local newspaper, and other sources. Also, the next time you are sale shopping, especially at a discount or close-out store, consider buying up some of those bargains on clothing—often good garments that are off-size, or have missing bows etc. and are marked down to less than $5, an amount that's not too hard on the budget. Eventually, you can accumulate a nice wardrobe to donate to a women's shelter to cheer up one of its residents.

- **BATTERIES,** *Storage:* It's no longer advised to store batteries in the refrigerator. Store in a dry place at room temperature. Exposure to extreme heat, such as in attics or garages, can reduce battery life. If kept loose in a purse, coins or keys could cause them to short out.

- **BEANS,** *Dry, Cooking:* Perplexed about changing cooking times for dry beans? The higher the mineral level in your water, the longer it takes to cook beans. Since the mineral content varies from day to day, your cooking times also vary. Also, the older the beans, the longer the cooking time; that's why it's not a good idea to mix bags of beans. **Hint:** Dried beans are less likely to be "gaseous" if you soak them overnight, then discard the water in which they've soaked and cook with fresh water. Also, adding a pinch of ginger works well to remove "gaseousness" of home cooked or reheated canned beans.

• **BED-BOUND PATIENT,** *Back-Saving Helps for Caregivers:*
1. Rolling Over with Ease—Fold a twin flat sheet lengthwise and tuck it in across the center of the mattress on both sides of the bed. When you need to move a bed patient, untuck one side and roll him to the side of the bed where you want him.
2. Getting out of Bed, off and on a Chair, Getting in and out of the Car—Place a big plastic trash bag under the person so that sliding out of bed, in and out of chairs and car seats is easier on both patient and caregiver.

• **BEDDING,** *Reviving Faded, Making "Designer" Sets for Kids Beds from Hand-Me-Downs:* Tie a strip of old fabric around the center of a bed sheet and keep wrapping it around and around until you get to the outside edges. Fasten it tightly, then dye in the washing machine with fabric dye.

• **BEDDING,** *$aver:* If you can't find matching pillowcases at a sale, or if you want to save some money and sew, one twin flat sheet has enough fabric for at least two king-sized pillowcases and usually costs less than a set. So buy top and bottom-fitted sheets plus one twin.

• **BEDDING,** *Storing Extras:*
1. Store in an unused laundry hamper.
2. Put extra shelves above the ones already in your closet.
3. Put extra pillows in shams or corduroy zipper cases and pile them on unused beds or use them on the sofa. Fold or roll extra blankets and put them in pillow shams.
4. Make up unused beds. Toss a fabric softener sheet under the blanket or bedspread to keep sheets smelling fresh.
5. Fold a blanket so that it fits between a mattress and box spring. Store the mattress pad used on a couch under its pillows.

• **BED-MAKING,** *Time-Saver:* If only one person sleeps in the bed and/or if the bed is against the wall, tuck the sheets and blankets in snugly on the unoccupied side so that bedmaking in the morning is just a pull and a tug.

• **BED ROLLERS,** *Replacing When You Have No Helper:* Hold the bed up with a scissor-type car jack. Put a piece of plywood under the jack to keep it from damaging the floor. Also, be sure you know how to operate the jack safely before attempting this.

• **BED SHEETS,** *Fitted Bottoms That Don't Fit:* Newer mattresses are thicker than many old ones; look for "deep pockets" or those that give the depth in inches on the package. Some queen-size fitted bottoms fit thick double-bed mattresses and suspenders can help, too. Adjust suspenders to fit the bed width, slide them between mattress and box springs about a fourth of the way from each end and clip an end to each side of the sheet. You can also buy elastic "garters" to place on each corner from several catalogs.

• **BED SHEETS,** *Pilling:* Sometimes defects in milling cause pilling on sheets; shaving with a fabric shaver is usually not satisfactory. Best idea is to return the sheets to the store along with the receipt that proves purchase, or contacting the manufacturer of the sheets; readers have reported getting replacements.

• **BED SHEETS,** *Quick-Fix Decorating Uses:*
1. Pre-hemmed curtains and drapes (sew pleating tape at top for drapes, gather on rod for curtains, drape over pole for swags).
2. Super-size tablecloth.
3. Sew two together to make a super-size pillowcase to cover a worn/tired comforter (add self-gripping tape to the open side if you feel ambitious or leave as is).

• **BED SHEETS,** *Recycling Old Ones:* Old sheets can be dust covers for furniture, a tablecloth for picnics, tents for children's rainy day activities and can be made into pillowcases, curtains, or costumes.

• **BED SHEETS,** *Saving Money on Water-bed Sheets:* King-size or queen-size flat sheets will fit on a water-bed mattress if you tie each corner of the flat sheet into a knot and slip it under the mattress corner, tucking in sides securely. If you sew, you can sew corners. Then a second king- or queen-sized flat sheet can be the top sheet.

• **BEDSPREAD,** *Finding the Center:* Sometimes an all-over pattern is hard to center when you are making the bed; try marking the top center with a safety pin or a few stitches in a color that blends into the pattern and you'll save time shifting the spread around.

• **BED TABLE/TRAY,** *Temporary, for Sick-a-bed:* Try an adjustable ironing board placed perpendicular to the bed so that the legs slide under it. Cover with a plastic sheet or bag and a cheery tablecloth for meal serving.

• **BELT TAB,** *Securing:* When a belt is too long and sticks out in front, a single pierced earring will secure the end in place. Coordinate the earring stud with buttons or other decorations on the outfit so it's an extra accessory as well as functional.

• **BEEF JERKY,** *Homemade Without Preservatives:* Jerky is best made with lean beef flank steak and cut easily when partially frozen.
Step 1. Cut off visible fat, then cut into thin strips across the grain, making the strips as thin and uniform as possible for even drying. The steak can be dried as is or marinate it overnight in a shallow baking dish in the fridge. If you marinate it, drain it well before starting the drying process.
Step 2. To dry, lay strips close together but not touching on a cookie-cooling rack and place in the oven. If you have a gas oven, the pilot light will give off enough heat to dry them, but if your oven is electric, turn it on at the lowest setting. Prop the door open for good air circulation. Dry the jerky for twelve to forty-eight hours, testing it every so often. It's done when a piece snaps in half if you bend it.
   The drier the jerky, the longer it keeps without refrigeration, but if you don't like it too dry, store it in the freezer until you're ready to eat it.

• **BEREAVEMENT GIFTS,** *Gifts from the Heart:* Sometimes the death of a spouse causes a drop in income that turns things we consider necessities into luxuries. But even if the remaining spouse is not suffering loss of income, a small gift can help knowing there is a special someone who cares. Some helps are a book of stamps in with the sympathy card; gift certificate for a food store in the area, beauty or barber shop, or department store; a check for gas, oil change, or tune-up at a nearby garage (call to find out the cost). And, most of all, an invitation to dinner out which is special because it provides companionship in addition to food. Eating alone is difficult for widowed spouses.

• **BICYCLE,** *Fitting the Right Size to a Child:* Riding a poorly fitted bike can result in an accident.
1. Have your child stand barefooted and measure her/his inseam from crotch to floor.
2. Take this measurement, subtract 10 inches for a boy's bike and 9 inches for a girl's model to get the proper frame size. (Adult bicycles generally measure from 19 to 26 inches.)
3. Buy a bicycle helmet when you buy a bike; consider the helmet and bike as going together like seat belts and autos. Thousands of deaths and head injuries from bike falls could be prevented if bikers wore properly fitted helmets—they should protect without obscuring vision.

• **BICYCLE,** *Checklist for Protection from Thieves:*
1. Most bicycles have serial numbers. Record this number and keep it along with a picture of the bike and the sales receipt in a safe place. This information will help police if your bike is stolen.
2. When you leave your bike at a destination, lock it to a solid object like a telephone pole, and use a heavy-duty bike lock. Light chains, cables, or locks are easily broken by thieves.
3. At home, never leave your bike on the front lawn or porch. Keep it in a safe locked place like your garage. **Hint:** Another reason to store your bike out of sight was given me by a door-to-door salesperson. A house with lots of bikes is a house with lots of children and parents who may be good sales targets for encyclopedias, insurance, and other family-oriented items!

• **BIKE RACK,** *Mind-Saver:* Tripping over children's bikes lying askew on the front lawn? Make a bike rack from a large uniform log. Treat the wood with wood preservative and then dig a shallow ditch and place the log in it. Using a saw, cut equally spaced grooves—one for each bike in the log—and make each groove the proper width to hold the front tire of a bicycle.

• **BIKING,** *Safety:* See JOGGING, Safety at Night for Joggers or Bikers.

• **BIKE SAFETY COLOR:** Hot pink clothing, even if you hate the color, is the safest, most visible color to get you noticed by motorists. You can also sew bands of fluorescent material around sleeves and legs of your biking outfit. Fluorescent bands sewn on hot pink would be double safety! A good idea if you ride in heavy traffic!

• **BILL PAYING,** *Keeping Your Financial Balance:* You don't have to own your own business to have a business account. If your company reimburses you for business expenses that you put on your credit card, such as lunches or trips, deposit your reimbursement checks into a separate account so that the right amount of money is always available when your credit card bills come in. Pocketing the reimbursement money could lead to spending it and being "short" at the month's end! You'll have better records for tax preparation, too.

• **BIRD CAGE,** *Bottom Liner:* Stack seven or eight pages of an old phone book or catalog in the bottom and remove one at a time as they get soiled.

• **BIRD CARE HINTS:**
1. Buy a bird only from a reputable pet store or dealer to make sure the bird has been brought into this country legally. Illegal birds may be diseased. Have pet birds checked by a vet who specializes in birds; many don't offer bird care.
2. Buy a cage large enough for the bird to fly from one perch to another and place it away from air-conditioning and heating ducts, out of drafts, and away from direct sunshine. Keep the cage out of the kitchen and clear of kitchen fumes, which can be deadly to birds. Also, cooking oil and grease settling on birds' feathers can destroy their natural insulation. Birds are sensitive to fumes of any kind, such as insecticides, paint and varnish, deodorants and hair spray.
3. Birds don't need immunization shots like dogs or cats but should have regular checkups and diagnostic exams if they appear ill.
4. A bird will accept a wide variety of food for a balanced healthy diet if it is hungry at feeding time. Don't keep food dishes filled all day. Instead, set up feeding times and give it fewer seeds and more fruit and vegetables. Feeding time is also a special bonding time

with your pet and is also a time to observe changes in eating habits or health.

• **BIRD FEEDER,** *Keeping Squirrels Away:*
1. Hang the bird feeder from a straightened wire coat hanger. It will hang far enough from the tree branch to keep squirrels and other unwanted guests from eating the bird food.
2. Hang the feeder with heavy filament fishing line; squirrels can't climb up or down. **Note:** I keep a separate feeder for squirrels on the same tree with my bird feeder in an attempt to keep all of the critters happy.

• **BIRD FEEDER,** *Pinecone:* Spread a thin layer of peanut butter or honey onto a pinecone, roll it in birdseed and tie it to a tree with a piece of string.

• **BIRD FINDER,** *Letter of Laughter:* A reader wrote that when her neighbor lost her parakeet, she put out a neighborhood flyer describing the bird and telling people to listen carefully because "He will give his phone number." He did; the finder called, and the parakeet was returned to his owner! He sure was no "bird-brain!"

• **BIRDS,** *Scaring Them Away from Fruit Trees:* Readers have said hanging mirrors from old compacts in the trees, suspended with string or rope, work like a scarecrow. Also, hanging a few rubber snakes in a fruit tree scares birds—and sometimes the neighbors, too!

• **BIRD SEED,** *Healthy-Planet Recycling:* If you dry watermelon and cantaloupe seeds during the summer, you can feed them to the birds in the winter. **Hint:** If you begin to feed birds in the winter, they will come to depend upon you and may perish if you stop feeding. So don't start if you don't intend to continue feeding until the weather allows "your birds" to find their own food.

• **BIRD SEED,** *Recycling:* If you have pet birds who don't always eat every seed, when you empty their food dishes, save the leftovers and put them where outdoor birds can sift through and get the seeds missed by your pets.

• **BIRTH ANNOUNCEMENT,** *When Friends Keep Calling to Ask If This Is THE Day:* Tell your friends to watch your mailbox. Put a big white bow on it when you leave for the hospital to deliver and, after the baby arrives, place a pink or blue bow on the box to signify the sex. You can also put the vital statistics on your answering machine and then, after Mom comes home, friends can get information even when Mom and baby are napping and not taking calls. My editor's daughter made a message from baby and Mom that said, "Tell them we are napping (baby coos and gurgles), tell them to leave a number and we'll call back later (baby coos again)," etc. Everyone loved it!

• **BIRTHDAY/ANNIVERSARY,** *Remembering:* Mark them on your calendar at the beginning of the year and if you have colored highlighters handy, color-code birthdays with one color and anniversaries with another. Some people like to address all cards at the beginning of the month and then send them out at intervals so that they arrive in time.

• **BIRTHDAY BOOK GIFT:** When one Heloise reader took birthday cake and decorations to her daughter's day-care center, she also took a book in which she wrote the child's name, birth date, and a brief note saying that the book was a gift from the child to the school on her birthday. Teachers liked the idea; so did other parents, and now birthday children are proud of their books each time they are read in class.

• **BIRTHDAY CARD CENTERPIECE:** To make sure children remember who sent them birthday cards and to get more enjoyment from the cards than just a momentary glance, make a dinner table centerpiece. Lay the cards facedown, side by side, on a flat surface, and tape them together. Then tape the last and first cards together to form a circle. Place the circle in the center of the table and by the end of the week, children will remember who the cards are from and the birthday person will feel honored all week long!

• **BIRTHDAY CELEBRATION,** *For Child Born on Christmas Eve:* Having a birthday during the holidays can make a child feel not-too-special. One reader solves the problem by having a "Half-Birthday" for her Christmas Eve child in late June. She sends all guests an invitation on a half sheet of paper; serves half of a sheet cake and freezes the other half for Christmas Eve; wraps presents with half birthday paper and half Christmas paper. If a gift the child wants is very large, she gets part of it in June and the rest at Christmas. For example, on the "half-day" she got a doll and a few clothes for it, then on Christmas Eve, she received the rest of the doll's clothing and other accessories.

• **BIRTHDAY GIFT,** *For a Friend Who Has Everything:* Give the friend a calendar at the beginning of the year and mark a promised lunch date near the birthday date. Don't forget to mark your own calendar, too!

• **BIRTHDAY PARTY,** *Substitute for Competitive Games for Young to Young Adult Children:* Tape a long piece of white shelf paper over waxed paper and lay it out on a floor or lay out a white poster board and provide lots of crayons. Have all the children at the birthday party write their wishes for the birthday child; they can also draw pictures if they wish. Even very shy children can participate in this activity along with the more outgoing ones. After the party, date the art work, roll it up (the waxed paper prevents smudges on the "art" side of shelf paper), and put it into an empty cardboard wrapping roll for storage. Taking the rolls out after years of collecting them is a fun nostalgia trip for the whole family.

• **BIRTHDAY "POPCORN" CAKE,** *To Mail:* To send a birthday cake to a student or overseas military person, make your favorite popcorn ball recipe and pack it into a well-greased bundt or angel-food pan; let cool. When it's hardened, remove and decorate like a regular cake. Popcorn cakes travel well and stay fresh.

• **BIRTHDAY SURPRISE:** Blow up about twenty or so balloons and decorate the bedroom after the birthday child has fallen asleep so that the special day can start off with the child awakening to a colorful surprise.

• **BIRTHDAY TABLECLOTH,** *Happy Memories:* On a solid color tablecloth, have birthday party guests sign their names with embroidery paint or fabric markers for a "keepsake cloth." Use a different color each year and be sure to include the date and year. The names and dates could be embroidered over the fabric marker, too. **Caution:** Protect the table top from ink "bleeding" through with appropriate padding.

• **BISCUITS:** Brush lightly with butter or margarine as soon as they are removed from the oven to make them look like an ad and taste extra delicious.

• **BLANKET BAGS,** *Recycling Zippered Ones:* Blankets, mattress pads, and bedspreads often come in heavy-duty zippered bags that you can recycle for storing all sorts of linens, clothing, and just plain stuff. One reader keeps old picnic and football game blankets in the zippered bags and hangs them in the garage so that they are handy to grab when the family goes on an outing.

• **BLANKETS,** *Laundering Washable Woolen Ones:* If the care label says the blanket is machine washable, here's how to get a comfy, clean renewed blanket.
1. Fill the washer with warm water, add detergent, and agitate to completely dissolve the detergent. Stop the washer and load the unfolded blanket evenly around the agitator. Soak for 10 to 15 minutes, then agitate on the gentle cycle for one minute. Stop the washer and advance the timer to the drain cycle and spin for about one minute.
2. Rinse by filling the washer with cold water for a deep rinse. Add fabric softener and allow the washer to complete the rest of the cycle automatically.
3. To dry in the dryer, set the temperature selector to the high setting. Place three or four bath towels in the dryer and turn the dryer on for a few minutes. Heated towels help absorb moisture so that the blanket dries more quickly. Place the blanket in the dryer and set the timer control to 20 minutes. Check after 10 minutes and remove the blanket while it's still damp. Overdrying and excessive tumbling may cause shrinkage. Place the blanket on a flat surface or stretch over two lines to complete drying. Gently brush up the nap with a nylon brush. Press the binding with a cool iron if needed.
4. To line dry, hang the blanket over two parallel lines and straighten to shape. As the blanket dries, change the position and straighten. Then brush up the nap gently with a nylon brush.

• **BLANKETS,** *Recycling Electric Ones:*
1. If an electric blanket no longer works, unplug it; feel for the wires at the end of the blanket; make tiny slits there; snip the wires;

pull them through the slits. (You may have to enlarge some slits to remove thermostats.)

2. After removing the wires, sew up the slits, reattach the loosened bindings and you have a usable blanket.

3. If you don't feel like sewing up the slits, put the blanket in a comforter cover that coordinates with the colors in your bedroom. These covers are sold in some linen departments and catalogs and can be used as cover-ups when blankets are moth-eaten, worn, or just don't match anything.

• **BLANKETS,** *Recycling Old and Worn Ones:*
1. Old baby blankets can be sewn together for a memory blanket a young child can cover up with—especially at grandparents' house; it's extra nice to curl up under the blankets which have comforted the child's parent, aunt and/or uncle in the past.

2. Cut rounds or squares from old worn blankets for pads to place between non-stick coated frying pans, china and other stackables that might scratch each other.

• **BLANKET,** *When It Shrinks in the Dryer and Is Too Short:* Sew a strip of matching-color fabric to the bottom of the blanket. You can tuck this section under the foot of the mattress and your bed will still look nice.

• **BLENDER,** *Washing:* Tried and true is to fill the blender about halfway with water, add a couple drops of liquid dishwashing detergent and put the lid on. Blend for a few minutes, rinse and dry.

• **BLOUSE SIZE,** *Letter of Laughter:* A woman wrote that the husband of another secretary in her office called her to ask for his wife's blouse size. When she said "medium" or "size 36," he just couldn't believe it. He said he wore a 33 sleeve and his wife's arms were not "that long." He was relieved to know that women's blouse size 36 doesn't mean sleeve length.

• **BLT WITHOUT THE "B":** Substitute imitation bacon bits for real bacon when you make a bacon, lettuce, and tomato sandwich and you'll get the flavor without the fat calories.

• **BOOK MARKING,** *Passages, Quotes, Recipes You Want to Find Again:* If you can't bear to dog-ear or pencil mark pages of a book, attach a pocket to the inside flap (made from an envelope—bend back the flap and glue the flap to the book cover) and write the page numbers you want to check later or just place a small sheet of paper in the front that lists page numbers and notes subject or names of recipes.

• **BOOKCASE,** *Portable Student "Model":* The traditional brick (or concrete block) and boards student bookcase can be dressed up if you cover the bricks with cloth, felt or wallpaper scraps, or paint the whole thing. If you spray-paint the parts, put them one-by-one inside a box when spraying so that you avoid mess. **Hint:** If the shelves are made from pressed wood, they will absorb lots of spray-paint unless you brush paint them with a primer before painting on the final color.

• **BLINDS,** *Cleaning Mini-blinds and Others:*
1. To dust, put old socks on your hands (inside out terry is good) and spray them with dust attracting spray, then dust each slat separately as noted below for washing.
2. To wash, put old socks on your hands and spray them with window cleaner. Close the blinds and starting at the top, go over them side to side, then do the back side.
3. To wash, take them down and put them flat on a surface you can get wet and soapy (sidewalk, driveway). Wash with a soft brush or nylon net (or old panty hose scrubber) dipped in a solution of mild dishwashing soap and water. Rinse well and dry immediately. **Caution:** Be very careful when you clean blinds; they are easily scratched and mini-blinds can break if handled roughly. **Hint:** Prevent heavy dust buildup by frequent vacuuming; the upholstery attachment works best.

• **BOAT BAILER,** *Recycling:* Cut off the spout of a plastic milk jug, leave the handle on, and you have a good bailer.

• **BOBECHES,** *Substitutes:* Make foil bobeches to catch dripping candle wax. Cut a square 1½-inch piece of heavy foil, then cut a slit in the center. Carefully slip the foil over the tapered candle and flute or turn up the edges so that they catch the wax drips. No more scraping wax from tablecloths!

• **BOOKENDS,** *Substitute, Recycling:* Decorative tins (especially those from fancy gourmet teas) filled with sand will keep books standing at attention in your bookcase.

• **BOOKMARKS,** *Recycling, Time-Saver:* That leftover strip of wrapping paper—too narrow to wrap anything—can be cut into shorter pieces for bookmarks. Take all of the strips and put them into the front of a cookbook so that as you use recipes, you can put a gift-wrap bookmark at the page to make it easier to find the recipe the next time. If you want to get even more organized, mark holiday recipes with appropriate holiday paper or colors. Make note on the bookmark if you changed the recipe in any way with different spices or other additions. **Note:** I have a friend who really needs this hint. She usually forgets which recipe she fixed and often adds other spices and ingredients to change recipes. When one of her innovations turns out to be good, her children say, "Gee, this is good. Too bad we'll never have it again!"

• **BOOKMARK,** *Sentimental:* Press leaves or flowers between two sheets of clear laminated plastic to make a bookmark. Flowers from your wedding in your family Bible or a photo album are a nice sentimental remembrance.

• **BOOK MEMORIAL:** When a dear friend passed away, a reader donated books to the library in her friend's name because she and her friend both enjoyed their local library's selections. The library gave her a list of wanted books and put a memorial sticker to honor the friend in the ones she bought.

• **BOOKS,** *Getting Yours Returned When You Lend Them:*
1. Stick your extra address labels inside each book or cover the book with brown paper (recycle grocery bags) and write on the cover your name and the date you lent the book.
2. In your calender or in a card file make note of who borrowed the book and when. (Ring-bound index card packs sold with school supplies make good small index files for just about any information. Also, you can carry one in purse or briefcase and make notes on cards at business meetings or when traveling. The cards are perforated so that you can remove them and put them in a permanent file (addresses, books, recipes, etc.).

• **BOOKS,** *Packing for Moving or Transporting to a Fund-Raiser Book Sale:* Books are heavy all by themselves; packing in cartons adds more weight. Try sorting books according to subject (or by price for a book sale) and then packing them in paper or plastic grocery sacks. Seal bags with masking tape; mark as to contents for easy sorting at your destination. To move bagged books from one place to another without straining muscles or tempers, stack the bags on a hand truck (dolly) or a sturdy luggage carrier.

- **BOOKS,** *Removing Price Stickers:* Heat the iron to Medium, put a pressing cloth over the book and press the sticker for a couple of seconds. The warmth softens the stickers enough to let them be pulled off easily and shiny covers aren't damaged.

- **BOOSTER CHAIR FOR YOUNG CHILD:** Tape together several catalogs or old telephone books. Or, if you don't want them so permanently joined, place them in a pillowcase, wrapping the "tail" around the stack to hold them together.

- **BOOTS,** *Drying, Storing:* Stuff boots with newspapers to keep their shape while drying and for storage. Newspapers also help absorb odors.

- **BOTTLE STOPPER,** *Unsticking Stuck Ones:* Pour a bit of THIN lubricating oil or mineral oil around the stopper and let it sit for a while (some take a day or two), then gently pull it out. Lubricating oil is thinner than cooking oil and will slide down quicker and more easily.

- **BOTTLES,** *Recycling Baby Food and Sample Jelly Jars:* If you do crafts with beads, sequins, wiggle-eyes, bits of jewelry, tiny bottles are super see-through storage containers. They also hold sorted buttons.

- **BOWL SCRAPER,** *Recycling Plastic Lids:* Cut off the rim about halfway around lids from dips, sour cream, and cottage cheese; leave the rim on the other half-side for a handle. These scrapers clean a bowl in seconds and they are free!

- **BRA SIZE,** *Determining with Measurements:*
1. Bra Band Size—First measure your chest (just under your bustline); add five inches to this figure and if the total is an odd number, round it off to the next higher number to make it an even number. This is the band size. For example, if your chest measures 32 inches, adding five will give you 37, so round up to 38 for the correct band size.

2. Cup Size—Measure the fullest part of your bust while wearing a bra. This total, compared to the band size, will give you the cup size. For example, if the bust measurement is one inch more than the band size, your cup size will be an A; two inches over the band size is a cup size of B; three inches over the band size is a C; 4 inches over the band size is a D; and so on.

Not all bras in the same size fit the same so it's important to try bras on for a good and comfortable fit.

• **BRASS,** *Cleaning Door and Other Hardware:* Clean hardware on doors, drawers, etc. with a good brass cleaner, then to prevent tarnish, rub on paste wax, let dry, and polish to a shine or spray with a clear lacquer finish. **Note:** Sometimes it's easier to remove the hardware (street numbers, etc.) to clean it without messing up the area with brass polish. Or, knobs can be poked through a slit in cardboard or posterboard so that the door or drawer finish is protected. (This is a good idea when you clean brass buttons, too.)

• **BRA STRAP PAD ON C-CUP SIZES,** *Keeping Them in Place:* If you pin the pads in place, then run a machine stitch across the front and back ends, they will be anchored and won't twist to make bumps under the shoulders of lightweight blouses.

• **BREAD,** *Dough Rising:* To prevent plastic wrap from sticking to rising dough, spray one side of the wrap with non-stick vegetable spray and put that side against the dough. The wrap will peel off easily.

• **BREAD,** *Quick-rising Dryer Method:* A reader tried the dryer method in which you heat the clothes dryer first and then balance the bowl of dough on a cookie sheet inside to quick-start the rising process. But, she forgot to turn the dryer off and so when she closed the door, the drum revolved one full turn before she could stop it. The good news was that it all went so fast that the dough bowl and cookie sheet didn't even move and ended up exactly as they had begun—a real circus act. However, she suggests that an unbreakable stainless steel bowl would be best when using this hint, just in case!

• **BREAD,** *Recycling Stale Slices:* Use the slice for a spoon rest while you cook and then toss it out for the birds to eat.

• **BREAD,** *Setting Dough to Rise:* If the hints readers send me are an indication, getting bread dough to rise is one problem that has as many solutions as there are bread bakers. Here are just a few:

1. Put the rack in your microwave oven, place a pan of very warm water on the bottom of the oven and the dough bowl on the rack. (You don't turn on the microwave for this.) If your microwave has no rack, use a cake-cooling rack.

2. Turn the oven on "warm" for just five minutes, then turn it off, leaving the door closed. Cover the dough and pop it into the oven. The temperature should stay about right if you don't open the door too often.

3. Turn the oven light on and it will usually maintain just enough low heat to work.

4. Place a pan of hot water in the oven on a lower shelf; change the water if it cools off.

5. Heat a slow cooker only to its lowest warm setting; then unplug it, put the dough in and keep the cover on it during rising.

6. Turn the clothes dryer on for a few minutes, turn it off, set the bowl of dough in it and close the door. Be sure to let people know that the dryer is being used for bread raising! See BREAD below.

7. Put the dough where the sun will shine on it, cover the bowl with a black plastic bag and let solar heat do the work. How about this for new-tech solar energy-saving?

• **BREAD,** *Storing When You Don't Eat Much of It:* To prevent bread from getting stale or mouldy, double bag the loaf (with a bag from the previous loaf) and store in the freezer. Close bags with twisties or a spring clothes pin. When you remove a serving, always leave the "heel" plus one or two slices frozen together; they're a "lid" to protect the remaining slices from drying out. To thaw, either toast or zap in the microwave (ten to twenty seconds per one or two slices). Storing bread in the refrigerator may cause it to dry out.

• **BREAD CRUMBS,** *Quick-Fix:* Grate frozen bread if you don't have stale bread; it's easier to get "crummy" than fresh unfrozen bread.

• **BREAD CRUMBS,** *Substitute:* Crush commercially packaged croutons with a potato masher in the bowl you'll use for mixing meat-loaf or on the plastic foam meat tray you'll use for dipping meat to be fried, and you'll have a tastier entrée from the flavored crumbs and less mess, too. Substitute unprocessed bran, wheat germ, or dry corn cereal for a flavor change when you bread fish or meats.

• **BREAKFAST FRUIT,** *Heating on Cold Mornings:* If cold grapefruit is an unpleasant shock on cold mornings, heat it. Heat sectioned grapefruit halves in the oven at 350°F for about 10 minutes or in the microwave oven 30 to 45 seconds.

• **BRIDAL SHOWER KITCHEN MAID:** For fun, make a "kitchen maid" gift for a bridal shower. The main part of the "maid" is an ironing board. Tie a pretty apron around the middle of the ironing board to form the waist and put a dishtowel in the apron pocket. Attach a toilet plunger to one side for an arm and a bowl brush to the other side for another arm. A mop, attached to the back with the mop end over the top of the ironing board, will be the hair. For an extra touch, add a colander for a hat. Two scrubbies can be eyes, a small sponge for the nose and a nail brush for the mouth. Add a dustpan for the feet and a few personal final touches and you have the fun favorite "kitchen maid." Also see WEDDING SHOWER, For Couples Who Have Everything.

• **BRIDEGROOM "TROUSSEAU":** Since most brides have a shower and grooms don't, one mother buys each of her sons a "trousseau" when they get married that includes two nice dress shirts, a couple of work shirts, some T-shirts, socks, pajamas, slippers, and a robe.

• **BROCCOLI,** *$aver Saving Stems:* After removing the "flower" ends of broccoli, slice the stems thinly and toss into a green salad or add to stir-fry veggies for an extra crunch and food value.

• **BROOCH,** *Remembering to Remove:* To prevent loss or a brooch ending up in the washer when it's left attached to clothing, try pinning the brooch through a blouse and onto a slip or bra strap. Then, you can't undress until you take it all off.

• **BROOCHES,** *Storage, Recycling, Time-Saver:* Pin brooches on an old T-shirt and hang it in your closet. Then you won't have to dig through your jewelry box in the morning when you're in a rush to get dressed and gone.

• **BROOM,** *Storage:* Screw a magnet into your broom handle about halfway down and you can store it stuck to the refrigerator between fridge and wall.

• **BROWNIES,** *Remedy If You Overbake Them:* Place them in the microwave on "Low" for a few seconds right before eating and they'll get nice and soft.

• **BROWNING DISH (BROWNER), MICROWAVE:** This specially designed dish is treated with a metal coating so that the bottom absorbs energy from the microwave to make the surface hot enough to sear and brown foods. It has a non-stick surface that's easy to clean and can be submerged in water. Some are dishwasher safe. When you buy a browning dish, look for "browner" or "browning" to be printed on it or look for directions that say the dish needs preheating. Always follow directions for use and care.

Generally, the browning dish is preheated on "High" for a period of time that depends upon the food to be cooked. When you sear a piece of meat, the first side may brown more evenly than the second side and second batches may not brown as well as the first batch because the dish cools as food absorbs its heat. Browning dishes work best for one to four servings. Never cut anything with sharp utensils on the dish. **Caution:** The dish gets hot enough to melt plastic and can cause serious burns to your skin. Never touch it without pot holders or insulated gloves protecting your hands. When removing the dish from the microwave, set it only on a heat-proof surface.

• **BROWN SUGAR SUBSTITUTE:** This mixture will not have the same texture as store-bought brown sugar but can be substituted in a pinch. Mix together one cup of granulated sugar with four tablespoons of dark molasses. Mix with a fork to make sure the molasses is evenly distributed. (Molasses is one of the ingredients used in manufacturing brown sugar. The amount added determines light or dark brown sugar. You can substitute dark for light or light for dark in recipes. However, the dark has a stronger flavor due to having more molasses.)

• **BUBBLE FUN,** *Substitute for Store-bought:* Mix half water and half mild dishwashing (not dishwasher) liquid. Dip a ring from a canning jar or leftover ring from commercial bubbles and bubble away. **Note:** This is definitely an outside activity!

• **BUG COLLECTING CAGE:** When children want to study fireflies, grasshoppers, crickets, little lizards, and other "nature pets," place a half-gallon milk carton on its side and cut away two opposite sides leaving two sides intact along with the bottom and top of the carton. Slip an old nylon stocking over the container and tie a knot on the bottom, leaving about 6 inches on top. The top can be opened and closed when the child puts grass, food, or another critter into the container. To close, pull the stocking tight and tie a knot. The critter gets plenty of air and can be seen by your budding biologist, who will, of course, be kind enough to set insect-eating critters free after observing them for a few hours and never keep them overnight.

• **BUG REPELLING,** *Selecting and Experimenting With Healthy-Planet Homestyle Methods, Letter of Laughter:* A cafeteria manager tried cucumber peelings as a repellent for ants; they worked very well when left on the kitchen counter overnight. Then a friend said that watermelon was even better so they chopped some up and left it on the counter overnight. The next morning it was loaded with feasting ants. The manager decided to stick with the proven hint of cucumber peelings!

• **BULBS,** *Selection Checklist:*
1. Get planting instructions from the garden center if you are buying bulk bulbs. Packaged bulbs usually have printed instructions.
2. Select bigger bulbs for bigger blossoms.
3. Don't buy soft, mushy, moldy, or heavily bruised bulbs. But, you can buy bulbs which have loose or torn "tunics" (the outer papery skin like on onions). Loss of the tunic does not damage the bulbs and may actually promote faster rooting after planting.

• **BUMPER STICKER,** *Removal:* Heat the sticker well with a hair blow-dryer, then lift the corner with a sharp knife (be careful not to scratch the bumper!) and peel it off. If you don't get it all, repeat the process. **Hint:** Next time when you put a sticker on, remove only a 2-inch strip of the backing from around the edges and leave the center intact. Then removing it will be easier; just split the center and pull it off.

• **BUNK-BED LADDER,** *Recycling:* When the ladder is no longer needed, paint it to match the room, hang it on the wall and the steps can hold knickknacks.

• **BUNK-BED SPREADS:** For two spreads that fit without hanging over the sides, cut a king-size bedspread in half lengthwise and hem the cut edges.

• **BUNS,** *Leftover Hot Dog and Hamburger Buns:* Butter and add garlic and other spices as usual, broil for a few minutes and you have garlic bread to serve with spaghetti or other meals.

• **BUSINESS CARDS,** *Recycling Old Ones:*
1. Punch a hole in the edge, write a description of clothing placed in a storage bag, and put the card over the top of the hanger outside of the bag. Or, write on the back of the card and tape it to a storage box. No more guessing what's inside.
2. Write a brief description of a recipe on the back of a card's shorter edge and poke it into a cookbook so you don't have to look in the index.

• **BUTTER,** *Storage:* When you are counting fat calories, cut butter sticks into 24 same-sized pats and store in airtight container; you'll know exactly how much you use each "dose."

• **BUTTER (MARGARINE) "PATS":** While the butter/margarine stick is still cold, slice it into individual "pats" with an egg slicer. "Pats" are easier and less messy at the table and if you are dieting, you'll know how many pats to the stick and therefore how many you can take.

• **BUTTER (MARGARINE) STICK MEASURE:** Before you remove the paper from a stick of butter or margarine, score the stick on the measure lines provided then you can still get a measured "dose" when you need it without messing up a measuring utensil.

• **BUTTER WRAPPER,** *Healthy-Planet, Recycling:* When you unwrap a new stick of butter or margarine, fold it butter sides in and store in a zipper bag in the freezer. Then when you need to grease a pan, pull out a wrapper, grease the pan and then toss the wrapper in the trash. Imagine if you could use every disposable thing that comes into your house at least twice instead of once; imagine if everyone did likewise—our landfills would last longer!

• **BUTTON,** *Quick-Fix, Preventing Pop-offs:* Inexpensive blouse and shirt buttons are sewn on by machine; a thread tail usually hangs loose and if you pull it, the button comes off. Try putting a small dab of white glue on each button before wearing the garment. The buttons will stay on longer.

• **BUTTONS,** *Replacing:*
1. Can't find the color you need? Paint buttons with fabric-matching epoxy paint before sewing them on.
2. Sew on buttons with six-strand embroidery floss. It's stronger and matches any color.
3. If you have to sew on a popped white button at the office with colored thread because that's all you have, cover the thread after sewing with typewriter correction fluid.

• **BUTTONS,** *Sorting and Storing, Recycling Time-Saver:* Those extra twist-ties will hold similar buttons together in your button box and you'll save time rummaging through loose ones.

• **BUTTONS,** *Strays, Recycling:* When the container in which you keep stray buttons for emergencies is full, get creative.
1. Decorate sweatshirts and T-shirts or sew different colors of buttons on a white blouse for a designer fashion.
2. Glue buttons flat to thumbtacks to give them bigger heads and to make them "designer," too.
3. String buttons to make jewelry for children, or adults, too. Give them to children for rainy-day stringing of necklaces or bracelets. Two matching strays (or non-matching if you like) can be glued to earring backs for boutique-look earrings to match a certain garment.
4. Toss into the bottom of glass flower pots instead of rocks.
5. Copy boutique ideas—create a "garden" of button flowers on a sweatshirt or one flower on each mitten by sewing one larger button in the center surrounded by smaller ones for "petals." A bow can be the "leaves" beneath the "flower."
6. Sew stray buttons in designs on sweatshirts and down the seams of sweatpant legs to make a boutique workout suit.

C

- **CACTUS,** *Repotting Painlessly:* Repotting cactus when it outgrows it's original container can be a sticky situation unless you have some carpet scraps to handle the plants.

- **CAKE,** *Baking:* Instead of water, substitute the same amount of club soda when making a German chocolate cake from mix; you'll get a delicious moist and tasty cake.

- **CAKE,** *Baking, Heart-Shaped:* If you don't have heart-shaped cake pans, bake a two-layer cake as directed on the package.
1. But, instead of two round layers, bake one 8-inch square layer and one round 8-inch diameter layer.
2. To assemble heart shape, cut the round layer exactly in half across the diameter. Place the square layer on a doily-covered cookie sheet or tray in a position that lets you add the cut diameter-sides of the round layer on either side of the top corner to form a heart.
3. Frost to cover "seams." Decorate with Valentine candies or decorator frostings.

- **CAKE,** *Cutting Unfrosted Layers:* It's easiest to cut cake layers with a long piece of thread or dental floss held taunt than to mess around with a knife.

• CAKE, *Dinosaur Decorations:* After frosting a regular cake for a child's birthday, decorate the top with graham cracker dinosaurs, sold by the box.

• CAKE, *Dome-Shaped Layers Prevention:* Try baking at 250°F for one hour and 20 minutes; or, from cake-decorating supply stores, buy wrap for around the outside of the pan.

• CAKE, *Football-Shaped:* Grease and flour a roaster pan as you would a regular cake pan. After baking, take the pan out of the oven and place it on a wet towel. The cake will slide right out. Color coconut with brown food coloring to cover the cake icing and make "laces" with black licorice.

• CAKE, *Freezing:*
1. It's best not to frost and fill cakes before freezing; fillings can make the cake soggy. However, you can frost a cake with confectioners' sugar or fudge frosting (using frosting instead of cream fillings to join layers). Freeze the frosted cake, THEN WRAP, and place in a heavy carton or other protective container.
2. To freeze layers without frosting, wrap cake as soon as it's thoroughly cool, then freeze. Store in carton or other container to prevent crushing; cakes do not freeze solid.
3. To thaw: Thaw in wrapping to prevent moisture from forming on cake surface. Large cakes take two to three hours at room temperature; a cake layer, about one hour; cupcakes, about 30 minutes.
4. Storage time: Unfrosted cakes may be kept frozen up to three months but frosted cakes are best stored only a month or two.

• CAKE, *Layer Stuck in Pan:* If you forget and let the cake get completely cooled and then it's stuck in the pan, put the layer into a warm oven briefly to soften the shortening used to grease the pan. When the pan bottom is warmed, remove it from the oven and turn the layer out immediately onto a cooling rack.

• CAKE, *Packing Neatly in Lunches:* If you slice a piece of sheet-cake in half (lengthwise) and then "fold" the two pieces so that the icing is in the center (top to center), the icing won't stick to the plastic wrap or lid of a margarine tub or other container.

• **CAKE,** *Preventing White "Flour Dust" on Cake Layer Bottoms:* After greasing the cake pan, sprinkle some of the mixed dry ingredients of the recipe or some dry cake mix on the pan to "flour" it. Return the excess to the mixing bowl and proceed with mixing the cake recipe as usual.

• **CAKE BAKER HELPER,** *Letter of Laughter:* When they were baking a cake, a grandmother told her five-year-old grandaughter that it was time to grease and *flour* the pan. She said, "I'll get the scissors if you will tell me which flowers I need to cut." Now that she's older, they share a joke whenever they bake together about not forgetting to "*flower* the pan."

• **CAKE DECORATING,** *Quick-Draw with Spaghetti:* Drain cooked very thin spaghetti, cut to desired length, let sit in several drops of red or other food coloring while you decorate the rest of a cake. Then, after removing drips of color if there are any, use the colored spaghetti to outline shapes. You can "draw" Easter bunny whiskers and mouths, etc.

• **CAKE FROSTING,** *Getting the Color Black:* Add some blue food coloring to chocolate frosting. Experiment until you get the desired results.

• **CAKE FROSTING,** *Quick-Fix Decorating Bag:* Substitute a plastic sandwich or storage bag. Cut a corner out of the bottom of the bag, slip in the decorating tip and close the bag.

• **CAKE FROSTING,** *Quick-Fix, Time-Saver Substitute for Chocolate Drizzle Icing:* Instead of making drizzle icing, cut a chocolate bar in little pieces and put them on top of the cake while it's still warm.

• **CAKE PAN,** *Recycling, Greasing:* Keep a plastic sandwich bag in the shortening can so that you can insert your hand, grab some shortening and grease pans with the same bag over and over.

• **CAKE PANS,** *Odd-shaped:* If you need to measure the batter capacity of an odd-shaped pan (hearts, lambs, bells, stars, etc.) to equalize the amounts used in different-shaped layers, fill the pan with water and measure the amount of this water. To fill an odd-shaped pan half full of batter, use half that amount of batter.

- **CAKE·PAN SUBSTITUTE:** In a pinch, substitute stainless steel mixing bowls for cake pans. See CAKE PANS above.

- **CAKE TESTER:** A long thin piece of uncooked spaghetti will test angel food or other deep cakes for doneness, substitute for a toothpick when you're out of them, or just keep you away from oven heat by letting you test long-distance.

- **CALENDAR,** *Recycling Your Favorite:* If you don't want to part with a special calendar (school band picture, gorgeous scenery) leave it up. Then tear off pages from a freebie calendar to tape over corresponding months on the old calendar.

- **CALENDARS,** *Family Activities Records:* Have each family member post activities with different colored ink so you can tell at a glance who has to be where and when. (You can also color-code—color dot on label and so forth—each member's possessions accordingly so that you can tell quickly whose stuff is lying around the house and who owns which tube-socks, T-shirts, etc.)

- **CALENDARS,** *Healthy-Planet Recycling:* Don't toss out the "days" of desk calendars. Write notes, grocery lists, phone messages, etc. on the backs or send the cartoon "days" to people who might enjoy them.

- **CALENDARS,** *Recycling Linen Ones:* If you don't want to use them for towels, sew them together and turn them into children's quilts or tablecloths. If you crochet, you can crochet them together for children's summer coverlets.

- **CALENDARS,** *What to Do When You Get Too Many Freebies:* One reader tacks a small bookmark-size calendar near the front door to record newspaper payments so she can keep track of which weeks are paid for. Keep a booklet calendar in the car to record mileage if your job involves getting reimbursed per mile or if you need to report work-related travel miles at income tax time.

- **CAMPFIRE HEAT SHIELD:** Stick marshmallow or hot dog roasting sticks through aluminum pie pans to shield your hands from the heat of the fire while the food toasts.

- **CAMPING SHOWER:** With an inflatable pool for the bathtub, and a hose for water, you can balance a hula hoop with shower curtain attached in tree branches above the "tub" and have a private shower anywhere.

• **CAMPOUT COOKING,** *Time/Energy-Saver:* Coat the bottoms of pots and pans with a bar of soap before placing them over the fire. The black soot will wash off easily.

• **CANDIED FRUIT,** *Quick-Fix Mincing:* When a recipe calls for finely minced candied fruit, cut it into small pieces and run through the food processor to mince. No sticky fruit wads to deal with!

• **CANDLE,** *Bathroom Light:* Light a safely contained scented candle in the bathroom when you have a party and guests won't have to fumble for the light switch. Or light it when you are home without guests just to enjoy the scent. **Caution:** Always, for safety's sake, remember to put candles out before retiring for the night!

• **CANDLE HOLDER,** *Avoiding Stuck-on Wax:* Spray the inside of each holder lightly with non-stick vegetable spray before putting the candle in. The wax will pop right out for easy cleaning.

• **CANDLE HOLDER,** *Removing Wax from Metal Holders:* Run under very hot water and wax will rub off.

• **CANDLE LIGHTER:** Light one end of a piece of raw spaghetti and you can light candles, especially on a birthday cake when there are so many to light. Also, please see MATCH HOLDER.

• **CANDLES,** *Quick-Fix When They Wiggle in Holders:*
1. Paper "cups" from boxed chocolates put on the bottom of a candle can help it stay put in its holder.
2. Wrap the bottom of the candle several times with a thin piece of tape to make the bottom a little fatter and, if you wrap the tape sticky-side out, it really holds candles in place.
3. Thin foam sheets used for padding china and giftware can be cut in small squares or circles to put on candle ends before poking them into candlesticks. Cut the foam so that it extends up the sides of the candlestick hole but doesn't show.

• **CANDLES,** *Recycling:*
1. Gather partly used candles and melt them in a coffee can placed on an electric frying pan at low heat or in a double boiler made from a can placed in a pot of water. Remove all wicks with a fork.

2. Dangle a long wick in the center of a mold as you pour in the melted wax.

3. After the wax cools completely, remove from mold and trim the wick if it's too long.

Hints for molds: Easy-to-use molds (because you can cut them away from the candle after the wax hardens) include clean milk cartons and long, narrow potato-chip cans. Just be sure the mold will hold hot melted wax. If you use metal cans, you'll need to place them in hot water for a few seconds to get the candles out. To get translucent effects as the candles burn down, put ice cubes or hunks into large molds (like milk cartons or large shortening cans) and pour the wax over.

• CANDLES, *Recycling Yellowed White Ones:* You might be able to get the yellow off older white candles if you rub the candle with a soft cloth and rubbing alcohol or wash it in warm (not hot to melt), sudsy water, and rub gently. Polish with a pair of old panty hose.

1. If you can't whiten it, try creative "play"—melt colored crayons or old colored candles and let the soft wax drop onto the candle so that each candle has its own unique design. Harden wax by placing the candle overnight in the refrigerator.

2. Or just melt all your candles and make new ones. See CANDLES, Recycling below.

• CANDLESTICKS, *Removing Wax Drips:* Place them in the freezer for at least an hour. The wax will harden and will be easily picked off.

• CANDLE WAX, *Removal from Dishes:* Gently scrape off large pieces, rinse or soak in very hot water. Finish by washing in hot sudsy water and, if necessary, scrub with nylon scrubber. (Skin-buffing pads that have become too rough for your skin are good for removing wax, sticky goo from labels, etc.)

• CANDY, *Freezing Leftover Chocolate:* Should a miracle occur and leave you with uneaten chocolate candy—for example, if you were to get two boxes of Valentine chocolates—freeze the extra pieces in plastic freezer bags. An unopened plastic-wrapped box can go into the freezer as is. Many people freeze chocolates to avoid the temptation to overeat—they take out only the allocated treat allowance for any time period.

• **CANDY,** *Saving for a Rainy Day:* Label a jar "Rainy Day Savings," and have children put all extra candy in it (like from Halloween Trick or Treat or Birthday Party Favors) and then, when they are cooped up in the house during bad weather, they can take out the jar and have a snack. (Not all of it, but some!) You'll be monitoring their candy consumption and teaching them about "delayed gratification" at the same time; they may also learn the advantages of saving money for a rainy day by this example.

• **CANISTER,** *Quick-Fix for Campers or Home Cupboards, Recycling:* Cut off the top half of plastic one-gallon milk jugs, leaving the top of the handle on. Then you can place bags of flour or sugar into the remaining part of the jug—they don't spill and are easy to pull in and out of cabinets.

• **CAN LID,** *Safety Hint:* Drop the lid removed from canned food into the can before disposing and you won't cut yourself if you have to rummage through the trash to find a lost item.

• **CANNED FOOD,** *Size Number Equivalents to Weights:*
  • No. 1 can = 10 to 12 ounces
  • No. 300 can = 14 to 16 ounces
  • No. 1½ or No. 303 can = 1 pound, 17 ounces
  • No. 2 can = 1 pound, 4 ounces or 1 pint, 2 fluid ounces
  • No. 2½ can = 1 pound, 12 ounces to 1 pound, 14 ounces
  • No. 3 can = 3 pounds, 3 ounces or 1 quart, 14 ounces
  • No. 10 can = 6 pounds, 2 ounces or 7 pounds, 5 ounces

• **CANNING CAUTION:** If you want to reduce sugar and salt in your diet, it's not a good idea to reduce the amounts in canning recipes because ingredients such as sugar, salt, lemon juice, and vinegar control spoilage. Instead get the new recipes that allow less sugar and salt while still keeping home-canning safe. To get the new recipes and methods, contact your county home economist. Look in the U.S. Government section of the phone book, under Agriculture Department.

• **CAN OPENER,** *Quick-Fix for Stuck Hand-held Model:* Oil the parts with vegetable oil.

• **CANS,** *Storing Fruits and Vegetables in Them:* The United States Department of Agriculture says it's okay to leave leftover food in the can and store it in the refrigerator for a couple of days. However, don't store acidic foods (such as tomatoes) in cans because they may get a tinny taste. Don't buy dented or otherwise damaged cans or bulging cans; you can get food poisoning.

• **CAR CARD GAME:** Cut out pictures from newspapers and magazines of anything children will see while traveling—cars, trucks, animals, buildings, bridges, etc. Then paste the pictures on index cards. "Deal" the same number of cards to each child when you leave the house. As the children see the objects on their cards, they put the card down in a "seen scene" pile. The child who "sees" all his cards first is the winner.

• **CARE PACKAGE,** *Healthy-Planet Packing Goodies with Goodies:* To send fragile items or food in a "care package" to a student or overseas service person, pack with packages of popcorn or marshmallows or peanuts in the shell—all are edible!

• **CAR KEYS,** *If You Frequently Lock Them Inside the Car:* Make it a habit to lock the car doors only with the keys even if your car can lock automatically.

• **CAR KEYS,** *When Teens Drive and Driveways Become Parking Lots:* It takes organization to avoid stress and confusion in multiple driver families.
1. When teens start driving the family car, give each person a set of car keys so that the teens don't have to borrow the parent's keys.
2. When teens have their own cars, have each person's keys or key chain color-coded so that finding the right one is easy. Have one central place for hanging all the keys so that finding any of the keys is possible. Then, if several cars are in the driveway and someone has to make a quick trip to the store, the rule is that you drive the last car parked in the driveway. You'll know its keys by the color!

• **CARPET,** *Bathroom Carpeting, Making Patterns:*
Method 1: Lay the carpet out and press it against the sink cabinet. Put straight pins all around the area to be cut. Do the same around the commode. Straight pins with large colored heads will be easier to locate, and you'll need a good sharp razor knife and scissors for

cutting. After marking, lay the carpet on a flat surface and cut around the line of the pins. **Note:** Don't think you can put the carpet upside down and draw markings with a marker. You will end up with a reverse pattern of your bathroom floor and, of course, when the carpet is right-side up, it won't fit properly. Few commodes and counters are positioned with identical spaces on either side.

Method 2: Make a paper pattern to fit the entire bathroom floor then you can trace the pattern on the back side of the carpeting. (You can also make all your mistakes on paper before cutting on the carpet and save the pattern for the next time.) **Caution:** Be sure to reverse the pattern when laying it on the backside of the carpeting or it won't fit. See above **Note.**

• **CARPET,** *Protecting Areas Beneath Children's Chairs:* Put a flannel-backed vinyl tablecloth under the chair; it's easy to wipe up and liquids don't soak into the carpet.

• **CARPET,** *Recycling Old Pieces:*
1. Lay runners on garden paths between rows of vegetables to avoid walking in mud.
2. Staple or nail pieces to garage walls and ceiling for free insulation.
3. Wrap carpeting around a post to make a cat scratching post.
4. Cut circles to fit drink coasters (plastic lids from different containers), then the coaster won't be stuck to the bottom of a "sweaty" glass when you pick it up.

• **CARPET,** *Removing Crayon on Acrylic Carpet:* After you've scraped off as much crayon as you can (a spoon works well), place paper towels over the stain and then gently press the towels with an iron on low-medium heat setting. Move the towels to a clean spot as they absorb the crayon and change them as needed. If color remains (and red is very difficult to remove) try a good commercial spot remover specifically made for carpets.

• **CARPET,** *Removing White School Glue:*
1. Working from the outside in, use a damp sponge to wet the area and then blot dry with a paper towel. Continue doing this until you've cleaned the entire stain.

2. If some of the glue remains, wash the area by applying a solution of 1 teaspoon mild dishwashing liquid dissolved in 1 cup of warm water, being careful not to make the rug too wet; blot with a clean cloth. Remove the cleaning solution by rinsing well with a small amount of water, then blot until dry.

- **CARPET BURN HOLE,** *Repair:*
1. Cut patches the size or a tiny bit larger than the burn holes.
2. Clean all the burnt fibers from the carpeting by rubbing with a spoon or cutting with cuticle scissors.
3. Put a bit of transparent or fabric glue on the patches and along the edges, then push each one into a hole, cover with waxed paper and place a heavy book on top.
4. After the patches are dry (about twenty-four hours), brush with an old toothbrush to lift up the fibers.

- **CARPET INDENTATIONS,** *Removing:* When heavy furniture has left indentations in the carpet, put an ice cube in each indentation and let it set overnight. The ice cube will melt slowly into the carpet. In the morning, blot up any moisture with paper towels and fluff up the carpet fibers carefully with the tines of a fork.

- **CARPET PROTECTOR:** Before you decide to protect new carpeting from traffic pattern wear with scraps of the carpeting, check the bottom backing. If the underside is rough, it will wear down the carpet like sandpaper. Only rubber-backed rugs should be placed over carpeting to protect traffic pattern wear and soiling. Also, remove the rugs often to vacuum beneath them so that dirt doesn't get ground into the carpet below.

- **CARPET TAPE,** *Removing Adhesive of Double-faced Tape from Tile Floor:* The Tile Contractors Association of America suggests lighter fluid. Be sure to test an inconspicuous spot first because the fluid could dull some tile finishes. **Caution:** Lighter fluid is highly flammable; be sure to ventilate the area well. Also keep it away from small children and pets.

- **CARPET TEAR,** *Quick-Fix:* Place a strip of carpet tape beneath the tear and press down. A permanent repair is to sew up the tear with a heavy upholstery needle and strong nylon thread and then reinforce the tear with tape. If the tear is in new carpet, it could be a defect; check with the manufacturer or store about replacement or at least professional repair.

- **CARPOOL CODE:** Plan with your carpool that if you can't reach a driver by phone to say that you won't be riding that day, you will put a piece of colored paper in a front window of the house. The driver won't have to waste time stopping or annoy neighbors by honking a horn.

- **CASSEROLES/COVERED DISH,** *Taking to a Potluck:*
1. Prevent spills in the car from casseroles by putting them inside a plastic grocery bag or a plastic bag lined box.
2. If the dish has no lid, place plastic wrap over the top and sides, heat on "High" in the microwave for a couple of minutes and the plastic wrap will have a tight seal that avoids a mess. This hint is useful even if the dish has a lid; some lids leak.
3. To keep hot—Put a folded towel in the bottom of a small foam ice chest; cover the casserole with another folded towel. With the lid on the chest, the casserole will stay hot until serving time, even up to an hour. **Caution:** My sources say food shouldn't stand for more than two hours between preparation and eating and should be kept at 185°F or reheated to that temperature before serving.

- **CASTERS,** *Runaway Wheels on Tables or Chopping Blocks:* Insert wedge-shaped pieces of wood between the wheel and the frame on two wheels, diagonally across from each other. Remove the wedges when you need to move the furniture and reinsert for stability.

- **CASTS,** *Care:* Proper care of your cast will prevent extra doctor's office visits, new casts, and time away from work for unnecessary replacements.
1. Plaster Casts: These harden in five to ten minutes but take two to three days to dry completely and reach full strength. Don't stand on your cast or rest it against hard surfaces for two to three days and wait the same time before letting people write on it. Once a plaster cast contacts water, it gets soft and ineffective and you'll have to get a new one. Protect your cast with plastic bags when bathing. If it gets dirty, you can touch it up with white shoe polish, but don't ever paint it entirely because the cast needs to "breathe."
2. Synthetic casts: They harden and dry immediately and reach maximum strength and can bear weight in about twenty minutes.

They are water resistant and lightweight. But, even if the cast can get wet, your injury may not allow it. Check with your doctor before getting the cast wet. Dry the cast thoroughly to prevent skin problems; if your skin feels damp and clammy under the cast, it's still wet. Wrap the cast in a towel to remove excess water or dry the cast more quickly with a blow-dryer set on "Low." Sorry, you usually can't write on synthetic casts!

3. Don't scratch under casts with hangers or sharp objects. You can try sprinkling baby powder into the end of the cast to relieve itching.

4. Make a "toe warmer" for your cast with an oversized sock or an old knit hat.

• CAST COVER-UP: Buy colored knee-hi stockings to match or contrast with your outfit, or plain white to go with an arm cast and man's shirt. Then, cut the toe off and put the stocking on the cast, elastic on top. For an arm cast, cut a small hole for the thumb and tuck edges under the cast.

• CAT, *Adopting a Stray:* To save yourself heartache, before you get too attached to a stray cat, take it to a vet for a checkup and testing for feline leukemia. Often the strays of an entire neighborhood have passed the infection around, and it's just a matter of time before the cat dies; sometimes only a couple of weeks. If the cat isn't infected, you'd need to see a vet anyway so that it could get neutered and all of its immunizations, which include vaccination against feline leukemia. If you bring an infected cat into the house, you will have to wait six months before bringing another cat into that area to prevent infection of the new cat.

• CAT BOX, *Quick-Fix, No Mess Litter Changing:* Line the cat box with a large plastic garbage bag, using a homemade elastic band to hold the bag in place when the cat digs. Make the band from ½-inch to 1-inch elastic tied into a circle (or use the elastic from old men's undershorts). To clean, just lift up the bag. **Note:** If your cat digs vigorously, put a layer of newspaper in the bottom before adding litter so kitty won't scratch through the bottom of the bag.

• CAT BOX, *Remove Odors:* After you discard the used litter, pour in a half-inch or so of white vinegar, or generously dust the bottom with baking soda and add an inch or two of water. Allow to stand for a few hours; then rinse and dry. AVOID future odors by sprinkling a generous layer of baking soda on the bottom of the clean pan and covering it with a newspaper section before adding the litter. Then on the next change, you can easily dump the litter with the newspaper, add water to the baking soda in the bottom, let stand; then rinse, dry, etc.

• CAT CARRIER, *Quick-Fix Homemade:* Tie two small plastic mesh laundry baskets together, one upside down over the other. Don't forget to put some newspaper in the bottom basket and place newspaper or an old plastic shower curtain or tablecloth under this or any carrier. Some cats will protest being in carriers in their own certain way!

• CAT COLLARS: To bell your cat as a warning to birds and jumpy houseguests, tie a small bell on a homemade or commercial elastic collar. Climbing cats can catch collars quickly (say it fast five times) on tree limbs. Elastic stretches and lets kitty get loose safely.

• CAT COMPANIONS, *Adding a Second Cat to Your Family:* A young kitten may be a better choice and less of a threat to an older cat. Try to match sizes so that the older, larger cat doesn't harm the smaller, younger one in play. Also, match personalities so that both are playful or both are tranquil loungers. Some vets suggest getting opposite sexes to lessen territorial battles and recommend neutering both pets to make them more compatible. When you bring the new cat home, put each cat in a separate room, then gradually let them be together for short periods under supervision, extending the time as they get used to each other. Provide each cat with its own litter box, food dish, toys and sleeping place. Be sure to show each equal affection and attention and allow time for them to adjust to each other.

• CAT COZY: When you have a cat that just won't stay inside, you can make a warm sleeping box by turning an old foam ice chest upside down, placing it on top of the lid, and cutting a hole in one side just large enough for the cat to get in. Put some newspaper on the bottom and a fluffy towel over the paper. Kitty will be insulated and waterproofed by the foam.

• **CAT FOOD,** *Au Gratin:* If a finicky cat refuses the flavor of cat food you've bought, try sprinkling Parmesan cheese on it. While it's not usually good to give milk products to cats, a little cheese, once in a while, won't hurt and you won't waste the cat food.

• **CAT SAFETY:** If cats in your neighborhood lounge around on cars, you can bet that one can crawl under the hood looking for a warm engine "bed." I've received several letters from people whose cats were severely injured when motorists started their cars and instead of an engine's "purr" they heard the shriek of a cat caught in the machinery. Tap on the hood or toot your horn before you turn the key, wait a few seconds, and any kitty sneaking a cozy nap will be out of harm's way.

• **CAT SCARE,** *Letter of Caution:* A reader whose cat, like many cats, liked to play with string wrote a chilling letter. Normally, when her cat finished playing with a string, the reader would pick up the string and put it away. The one time she forgot, she found her cat with a string in its mouth. Unable to remove the string, she took the cat to the vet who also couldn't remove the string; it had worked its way through the cat's system and was wound throughout its intestines. Emergency surgery revealed 31 inches of string! The cat never gets string to play with anymore!

• **CAT SCRATCHING POST:** Buy one or cover a post with nubby carpeting, or for some cats, cover a piece of garden timber with carpeting and lay it on the floor.
1. Encourage the cat to scratch the post instead of furniture by sprinkling it with catnip or by attaching a small toy to it.
2. Lead the cat to the scratching post by dangling a toy on a fishing pole closer and closer to the post and let kitty catch the toy only when it's on or at the post. This training is fun for you and the cat.

• **CATS,** *Spraying:* Sometimes, even if neutered, a cat will continue to spray, usually in the spring when mating instincts occur or if a new carpet or piece of furniture is brought into the home and the cat decides to "mark it." Check with the veterinarian; prescription pills are available to correct this problem. *Letter of Laughter:* A friend of mine loved this hint because it let her continue to love her two old cats—a neutered tomcat who liked to spray his own image in the dresser mirror, much to the dismay of the person who used that dresser, and a spayed female who periodically sprayed the kitchen range burners to the disgust of the whole family. The positive about this was that nobody dawdled during breakfast to avoid going to school if the cat had sprayed the stove the night before!

• **CAT SPREAD:** If your cat likes to snooze on your bed and the result is cat hair on the spread, substitute a next-size top sheet for the bedspread, in a print that coordinates with your bedroom colors. You can more easily wash it than a heavy spread or quilt. Queen sheets cover double beds; king covers a queen mattress.

• **CAT TRAINING,** *Keeping Kitty Out of Dried-Flower Arrangements:* Spray the arrangement with hair spray and sprinkle with white ground pepper. One taste and kitty won't return to the scene of the crime.

• **CAT TRAINING,** *Keeping Kitty Out of Plants:*
1. Try putting lemon, lime, orange, or grapefruit rinds on the soil of planters; cats don't usually like the smell of citrus.
2. Try making a planter cover from lightweight pliable garden fencing. Cut to the right size with heavy scissors and bend to fit into the planter. The wire will still let air, water, and light in but will keep kitty out.
3. Place a layer of pinecones over the pot plant soil; it's unpleasant for cat walking. The bonus is that pinecones keep moisture in the soil while keeping "cat moisture" out of it and look nice, too.
4. Spritz your cat with water each time it goes near the plant.

• **CAT TRAINING,** *Keeping Away from "Forbidden Places":* When a cat is persistent, each time your cat goes to a "forbidden place" touch its lips with a cotton ball moistened with rubbing alcohol or vinegar. You need not use force, just a light touch—cats hate this. Then leave the scented cotton ball at the forbidden place. Later, you can put an alcohol or vinegar scented cotton ball at the forbidden place whenever kitty is near it. It takes patience, but eventually, the cat will avoid that place.

• **CAT TREAT:** Instead of discarding the liquid that comes in canned salmon, tuna, and sardines, give it to your cat—it's kitty champagne to most of them!

• **CEDAR CHEST,** *Renewing Cedar Scent:* Lightly sand the inside of the chest with fine grade sandpaper. (Wrap sandpaper around a big rectangular sponge so the heat of sanding doesn't bother your hands.) Vacuum up wood particles. You can also add cedar balls or blocks from closet stores if this doesn't renew enough of the scent.

• **CEILING,** *Quick-Fix Repair After Removing Swag Lamp or Planter Hooks:* After unscrewing the hook, plug the hole with a cork pushed flush with the ceiling surface; then paint the cork to match the ceiling. See WALLS, Repairing, for other ideas.

• **CEILING FAN,** *Telling Fan from Light Chains:* Put a large wooden or ceramic macramé bead on the light and a tassel on the fan or vice versa—anything that helps you tell one from the other. Cork or plastic fishing line floats or plastic lime/lemon juice squirters are good quick-fix chain pulls for lights or fans. A yellow lemon on a closet light pull makes it especially easy to find in semi-darkness.

• **CELERY,** *Restoring Limp Stalks:* Put stalks in cold water to crisp up again. They will keep in the fridge for a day or two. When there's too much celery to consume quickly, dice it, cook in a bit of water until just tender and then cool, divide into small amounts for soup or casserole recipes and freeze.

• **CELERY,** *Storing:* To make sure you have celery to munch on even if you have no time to cut it up for sticks, cut off the stalk end when you bring the celery home, rinse off the stalks and place them bottom-side down in water in a large wide-mouth vase (like the freebies in which florists deliver cut flowers). Save the heart of the celery for cooking either in the refrigerator or freezer. To further avoid temptation if you are dieting, put your celery "bouquet" on the table for before-dinner munching. A vase will hold the celery vertically and so it takes very little space in the fridge.

• **CEREAL,** *Keeping It Fresh:* If the cereal isn't in a resealable bag, pour it into gallon-size zip-closing bags and return it to the box. It will stay fresh longer. You can use the cereal-box liner to cover foods cooking in the microwave, to hold scraps when you peel veggies, to line drawers, and more.

• **CEREAL-BOX INNER BAG,** *Recycling Ideas:* Cover dishes when microwaving foods; wrap potatoes for microwave baking; base for rolling cookies and pie crusts; crush crackers or cereal in it for breading; open the bag for a flat surface to hold crumbs and flour for breading and a place to lay coated meat pieces as they dry for 20 minutes before frying. (If you let breaded meats dry, flip the meat so each side is exposed to air 10 minutes or so or place on a rack before deep or pan frying, and the coating will stay on better and be crisper.)

• **CEREAL DRIPS,** *Avoiding Them with Small Children:* When children begin to feed themselves dry cereal, mix it with vanilla or fruited yogurt instead of milk. It sticks to the spoon and the extra nutrition sticks to the ribs, too. Low-fat yogurt and milk are about equal in calories per amount.

• **CEREAL FAST FOOD:** There's no rule that says hot cereal must be served in a bowl. Put it in a cup; add a bit more milk so it's thinner; then, drink it. This idea is especially helpful when small children make a mess eating hot cereal with a spoon. Give them a straw and see them slurp up breakfast! If you get a late start, put the cereal in a lidded, insulated coffee cup, insert a straw in the lid-hole and sip breakfast en route to work or when you get there!

• **CEREAL SUGAR,** *When You Don't Want Sugar To Sink to the Bottom:* I've received hints to avoid this problem like dissolving sugar in the milk before pouring it on the cereal but the easiest idea is to pour milk on the cereal first and then sprinkle on the sugar. The sugar granules will stick to the moist cereal.

• **CEREAL SURPRISE,** *$aver:* Mix the last few ounces of different cereals for a "custom blend" that uses up all the leftovers and tastes good, too. **Hint:** When children prefer to eat cereals that have the nutritional value of a cookie, mix the sweetened favorites with "real food" cereals.

• **CEREAL TREATS,** *Without Sticky Mess:* To press rice cereal treat mixtures into the pan, place clear plastic wrap over the top and press away or use a frozen mug as a "rolling pin" to press the mixture down.

• **CERVICAL COLLAR (NECK BRACE) COVER-UPS:** Wearing a cervical collar can be dreary and after a while, you need to cheer it up.

1. Cover the collar with colored sandal-toe knee-hi stockings (or legs cut off panty hose) that match your clothing. Slip on so that the elastic end is inside the fold-over. The self-gripping fabric tape will hook through the stocking mesh, which is easy to wash, too.
2. Pin a brooch or small silk flower jauntily off center.
3. Wrap a silk or sheer nylon scarf around the brace, and pin ends in place if they slip out.

• CHAIRS, *Taking Sags Out of Cane Bottoms:* Wipe the surface of the seat with a cloth which has been dipped in hot water and wrung out. Scrub thoroughly, then place the chair outdoors in the sun to dry.

• CHAIRS, *Storing Folding Ones and Extra Table Leaf:* To prevent marring walls where they lean and to keep the chairs or table leaf clean and dust-free, put a pillowcase over each bridge chair or table leaf when storing it.

• CHAMOIS CLOTH, *Care to Make It Last:* Wash after each use in mild soapy water, leaving a little soap in the cloth to help keep it pliable between uses. After washing, wring it out gently and pull it to its original shape. Lay out to dry, but not in direct sunlight or near a heat source. Also, never use a chamois with strong chemicals, oil, grease, or as a sponge when washing the car.

• CHAMPAGNE CORK, *Catching Identified Flying Objects:* Place an oven mitt over the cork and bottle neck after you take off the foil and wire covering. Then holding the bottle and mitt with one hand, release the cork with the other. Exploding corks will fly into the top of the mitt. It's not very glamorous but beats hitting someone in the eye or taking pot shots at the chandelier!

• CHANDELIER, *Moving Within a Room:* Hang a swag hook in the new position for the lamp, add more chain to the lamp and make the fixture look like it was intended to be a swag lamp.

• CHANDELIER CRYSTAL, *Repair:* If crystals fall off because wires have broken, replace the wire with a twist-tie. Scrape the paper off the wire and put it through the opening of the crystal; hang it back on the chandelier.

• **CHANGE,** *Loose Change Uses:*
1. Put a large decorative bowl in a catchall spot so that all family members can easily contribute, then when there's enough money, take each other out to a restaurant.
2. Put parking-meter coins in your car ashtray so people won't put ashes in it or think twice before smoking in your car.
3. Collect loose change from laundry pockets until there's enough "pocket money" to buy something for the chief laundry-doer even if it's just an ice-cream treat.
Letter of Laughter: Someone I know calls coins left lying around the house or left in pockets "mad money" because it makes her mad to see her family treat money so carelessly.

• **CHARITY,** *Donations Guide:* When you are asked to give to charities, you want to give to those groups that use your money wisely. One way to check on any charity, national or local, is to call your local Better Business Bureau. BBBs have information on charities and how they meet the BBB standards for money usage, public accountability, fund-raising practices, solicitation, and informational materials (if they are truthful), how they are governed, and if they comply with laws and regulations.

• **CHECKBOOK ACCURACY:** When you write a check while shopping, collect the receipt and note the check number quickly on the receipt; then place it in your checkbook. When you get home, record all of your purchases at one time and balance the amounts. No more mystery checks that you forgot to record and therefore have no idea of the amount!

• **CHECK CHECK:** Place a small bookmark or piece of ribbon at the point in your checkbook where you have only five checks left. Then, you'll be reminded to put your next book of checks into your purse or checkbook case.

• **CHECK PRINTING,** *When Mother Remarries and Children Have Different Names:* Please see NAMES CONFUSION.

• **CHEESE,** *Preventing Mold:* If mold hasn't penetrated too deeply, scrape it off; you can eat the cheese. (But yogurt, cream or cottage cheese which has molded should be discarded.)

1. Moisture can cause cheese to mold. Place a few sugar cubes in a self-sealing plastic bag with the cheese. When the cubes become soggy in a few days, replace them.

2. To keep mold from forming on large hunks of cheese, the traditional way is to wrap the cheese in a cheesecloth (what else?) which has been moistened with vinegar (moistened but not dripping wet). Place wrapped cheese in a plastic bag and into the refrigerator. The vinegar doesn't affect the taste of the cheese, and you may have to sprinkle more vinegar on the cloth every now and then if you are storing the cheese for several weeks.

3. When buying "surface-ripened" cheeses like Camembert or Brie, make sure to "sniff test" if you can. If they have even a hint of ammonia scent, they are past their peak for eating. Don't buy them. It's a cheese-seller's myth that the ammonia scent is okay.

4. If you have a large hunk of cheese, instead of putting the whole thing out, cut off only the amount you expect to eat and allow it to come to room temperature (best for eating). Going back and forth from fridge to table dries out the cheese and speeds up spoilage.

• **CHEESE CUTTER:** Grasp each end of a piece of dental floss and slice away. Dental floss also neatly cuts cake layers horizontally.

• **CHENILLE BEDSPREADS AND ROBES,** *Recycling:* Cut 10 × 10-inch squares and hem them to make dishcloths. The chenille knots are terrific for removing stuck food from dishes and pans.

• **CHILD-PROOFING,** *Kitchen Checklist:*

1. Hang a knife rack on a cabinet door out of children's reach.

2. Put safety covers on electrical outlets.

3. Remove stove knobs if a child can reach them and keep them in a basket on your countertop. You can put a knob on when you turn on the burners.

4. Keep spices and other non-edibles out of reach. Instead of keeping cleaning supplies under the sink, put them in an upper cabinet out of reach.

5. Invest in safety locks for drawers and cupboard doors. A quick-fix is to put a rolled magazine in the cupboard door handles to keep a toddler out; older children will remove the magazine!

• **CHILDREN,** *Calling Them in at Night:*
1. Arrange to signal "time to come in" by flipping the porch lights off and on. It saves your voice for talking to children instead of yelling for them to come in.
2. Cut a plastic bleach bottle in half and use the bottom for plant clippings and the top for a megaphone so you only have to shout softly when you herd your family!

• **CHILDREN,** *Keeping Them Occupied in Doctor's Waiting Rooms:*
1. Put coloring books, crayons, stickers, and small toys in a large, self-sealing plastic bag and give one to each of your children when you arrive.
2. Give children a couple of pipe cleaners to twist and make things like stick people, alphabet letters, and anything else their imaginations can come up with.

• **CHILDREN,** *Safety on Outings:* A child can get lost in just a few seconds at such outings as the zoo or hiking.
1. Carry current photos and descriptions of each child and, if children's friends are guests on the outing, know their parents' names, addresses, phone numbers, and potential medical problems (allergies to stings, etc.) just in case of emergency.
2. Children should be taught to go to a park employee and say their parents' full names and phone number, to go to an easy-to-find meeting place in case of separation, and use the "buddy-system" to stay close together.
• Equip each hiker with a whistle and instructions to blow it if lost, but ONLY if really lost! Tell the story about the boy who cried wolf too many times.

• **CHILDREN,** *School ID:* Plastic pin-on name-tag holders like those we collect at meetings and conventions are handy name-tag holders for kindergartners or first-graders in a new school. Add your name and phone number to the back of the tag, too. Our precious ones can forget important information in the confusion of school buses, new classrooms, and all!
Or, buy a supply of stick-on name tags; you can put them on books, lunch bags, etc. as well as on your children.

• **CHILDREN'S FRIENDS,** *Parent-sanity Saver:* Often when children come to play, they've been told to return home at a certain time, and then they ask the houseparent for the time ALL OF THE TIME! To make life easier for everyone, ask the children when they must go home, then show them that you are setting a kitchen timer for the amount of time they can stay—actually set it for a few minutes earlier so they have time to gather their stuff and help pick up toys. Ah, peace!

• CHILD'S BATH, *Getting a Self-bathing Child To Wash All Parts:* One mother outlined a boy on a sheet of poster paper and colored it using her son's hair and eye colors. Then she wrote numbers with arrows pointing to the different body areas (ears, face, feet, etc.). In one hand she drew a red washcloth with an arrow pointing toward the washcloth and then she printed the word "SCRUB." She put the poster where he could see it as he bathed and even if he was too young to read, he would follow the arrows and then tell his mom what all he washed.

• CHILD'S GARDEN OF BEANS: To show a small child how plants grow, plant beans along the outside of a fishbowl or large jar filled with dirt. They can see roots go down and stems go up. *Letter of Laughter:* This hint came from a mom who thought of it after her preschooler dug up several of her plants "to see how they work."

• CHILD'S LAWN PARTY, *Summer Birthday Idea for Young Children:* On the invitations, make a note to the mothers to bring their children's swimsuits. For the party, hook up the garden hose to a rotating sprinkler and set it in the yard so the children can run through the sprinkler. Place lawn chairs out for the children to sit on. When the children tire of the sprinkler, they can dry off on the chairs while you serve refreshments.

• CHILD'S TABLE AND CHAIRS, *Curbing Childhood Curiosity for Safety:* One reader found a simple way to stop her toddler from dragging chairs from her child's table and chair set into other rooms so she could stand on them to reach forbidden things. Clever Mom tied one leg of each chair to one leg of the table closest to it. The chairs could still be pulled out to sit on but not removed for use as ladders!

• CHINA CABINET LIGHT: Instead of turning on the lights only when you have guests, plug the light cord of a lighted china cabinet into a socket timer and you can enjoy a few glowing hours each night without having to remember to switch them off.

• **CHOCOLATE,** *Dipping:* Place one or two pretzels (crackers, cookies, etc.) on a potato masher; dip in melted chocolate; pull out, and place on plate to cool.

• **CHOCOLATE MELTING,** *Preventing It from Getting Grainy:* If you are melting chocolate for fondue or other uses in a double boiler, don't let the water touch the bottom of the pan. It will scorch the chocolate and make it hard and gritty. Cooking the chocolate too fast or in a too lightweight saucepan can also make it gritty. The best way to cook chocolate is in a heavy saucepan over low heat and stir it often. I stir with a pancake turner so that the whole pan is scraped in a few swishes.

• **CHOCOLATE SYRUP,** *Good to the Last Spoonful:* When all that's left is a bit of chocolate syrup in the bottom of the container, make chocolate milk by adding milk and shaking until it's dissolved.

• **CHOPSTICKS,** *Recycling Disposable Ones from Restaurants:* They make sturdy plant stakes for indoor potted plants.

• **CHRISTMAS GIFTS,** *Extras:* Buy a variety of gifts, such as mugs, calendars, decorative candles, candy, etc. to keep under the tree and you'll have a surprise for unexpected guests. You can code them (for example, red or with bows for females; green or with crinkle tie for males) if you want to be more elaborate, but I just like to buy generic gifts.

• **CHRISTMAS LIGHTS,** *Annual Installation:* Install cup hooks about every 10 inches to the outside eaves of your house and leave them there as permanent anchors for lights. Then, you can cut a notch in the end of a yardstick and poke the lights' wires into place each year without a ladder. If you can't reach the eaves with a yardstick, screw a cup hook into a broom handle—the broom handle will be a useful "grabber" during the rest of the year and have a hanger so that it doesn't have to stand on end squashing its bristles.

• **CHRISTMAS LIGHTS,** *Healthy-Planet Recycling:* Here's how to make "lanterns" for lining your driveway or walkway during the holidays.

1. After spraying plastic jugs green or red, cut an opening in the top, leaving the handle on. Then, fill them with an inch or two of sand and insert a candle.

2. Save large 32-ounce juice cans and then with a nail, pound holes in the sides either in a random pattern or a design. (To keep the cans from bending when you pound nails into the sides, fill them with water, freeze until the water is a solid block, then pound away.) Spray with flat black paint. Pour in a couple of inches of sand and insert candle.

• **CHRISTMAS ORNAMENT HOOKS,** *Substitute:*
1. Unbend the middle "bend" of a paperclip so that you still have a loop on either end; one for the ornament and one for the tree.
2. Put a twist-tie through the loop of the ornament, twist the ends around each other, then make a hook and hang it over the branch, or just put the twist-tie through the decoration loop and wrap the ends around the tree branch and twist the ends together.
Note: My busy research editor has all of her ornaments permanently attached to her artificial tree. After Christmas, she covers the still-decorated tree with a plastic bag sold for disposing real Christmas trees and stores it in a spare room. Then each year, she brings out the tree, already decorated.

• **CHRISTMAS ORNAMENT RECIPE:** Store these from year to year in a tightly sealed container. In some climates, they can attract insects. One reader stores hers wrapped in tissue and placed in a box with a few mothballs or cedar shavings.

CHRISTMAS ORNAMENT DOUGH
   2 cups baking soda
   1 cup cornstarch
   1 ¼ cups cold water
   Mix cornstarch and baking soda in a saucepan and add the water. Cook over medium heat, stirring constantly, until the mixture is the consistency of wet mashed potatoes. Turn it out onto a plate, cover it with a damp cloth and let it cool.
   When cool, knead it until it's smooth. Seal it in a plastic bag and store in the refrigerator until you're ready to use it.
   Shape ornaments by hand or flatten the dough and cut out shapes with cookie cutters. Insert a wire hanger into the soft dough or make a hole in each ornament with a plastic drinking

straw so that you can hang the ornament with crinkle-tie or regular ribbon. Let ornaments dry overnight or heat them in a 250°F oven for 15 minutes. If not completely dry, continue to heat, checking at five-minute increments.

Dried pieces can be painted with water colors, poster paints, acrylic paints, or felt-tip pens. Finish the ornaments with a coat or two of clear nail polish or varnish and they'll last for years.

• **CHRISTMAS SOUVENIR ORNAMENTS:** Instead of buying dust-catching knickknacks as souvenirs, buy Christmas ornaments unique to the area you visit on vacation. You'll have a very personalized Christmas tree, wonderful memories of vacations when you decorate it, and not lots of stuff to dust throughout the year.

• **CHRISTMAS STOCKING TREE:** When one reader's family's new home had no fireplace for hanging their traditional Christmas stockings, they substituted a pole planter which had a hook for each stocking.

• **CHRISTMAS TREE,** *No-mess Watering:* Insert into the water pan a long funnel, the type designed for a car transmission, sold at auto parts stores. No more breaking ornaments and knocking things off when you're crawling under the tree to water it!

• **CHRISTMAS WREATHS,** *Hanging One on Each Side of the Door:* If both wreaths are about the same weight, try tying a sturdy ribbon from one to the other and draping it over the door. The weights of the wreaths will balance like a teeter-totter. Apply a heavy-duty tape, like duct tape, across the ribbon on top of the door to keep the ribbon from sliding when the door is opened.

• **CIGARETTE CASE,** *Recycling After You Quit Smoking:*
1. The extra-long snap purses that held cigarette packs and a lighter make good sun or reading glasses cases.
2. They can hold sewing supplies or jewelry when you travel.

• **CLEANING SUPPLIES,** *Carry-Around and Storage:* Leave the handle on, but cut out the top side of a large plastic milk jug and you'll have a container to store bathroom cleaning supplies, sponge, and scrubber.

- **CLOCK,** *Stopping an Annoying Humming Noise:* Try turning the clock upside down and leaving it that way for a day or so; it lets some of the small parts get "re-oiled."

- **CLOSET CALENDAR,** *Memory Jogger:* Mark a one-year calendar with birthdays, anniversaries and special events and then hang it up in your closet so that you will get a reminder each day when you get dressed. The reader who sent in this hint said his wife gave him a calendar like this one and wrote in their anniversary in big red letters. Very, very smart!

- **CLOSET CLUTTER SOLUTION,** *For Hats, Mittens, Gloves:* Attach spring clothespins with heavy duty staples or nails to the coat closet door so that hats, mittens, and gloves can be hung up and therefore found the next day.

- **CLOSET HANG-UPS,** *Healthy-Planet Recycling:*
1. Hang beads, chains, scarfs on a towel rack and hang belts on drapery hooks hooked to the rack.
2. Hang a plastic six-pack cover to a drapery hook or attach it to a hanger with twist-ties to hold scarfs.

- **CLOSET POLE:** Apply floor paste wax to the closet pole and hangers will glide more smoothly.

- **CLOSET ROD COVER,** *Time/Fingernail Saver:* Putting on a plastic closet rod cover is easier if you put a small bottle inside the plastic roll and then push it along in front as you fit the cover onto the rod. No more cut fingers, broken plastic, and broken fingernails!

- **CLOSET RODS:** Cover wooden closet rods with inexpensive (sometimes less than $2) plastic sleeves sold for shower-curtain rods. Hangers will slide smoothly and you can buy colors to match your room or to color-code each person's side of a shared closet.

- **CLOTHES,** *Organizing Work Clothes for the Week:* Instead of last-minute rushing at the ironing board, take 20 to 30 minutes on the weekend to plan your work-week wardrobe. Wash and iron whatever needs it and then hang everything in matching sets in the closet. No more suits without matching their clean and ironed blouses to start your day off with stress.

• **CLOTHES CLOSET SEPARATION,** *Quick-Fix for Family Peace:* When children or even adults share a closet, you can set boundaries for each person's clothing with plastic coffee-can lids. Cut a hole in the middle of each lid large enough to accommodate the wooden clothes rod in your closet and then make a slit from the center hole through the outer rim. Write each person's name on the lid with a permanent felt-tip marker and place on the clothes rod between "territories" to divide (clothing) and conquer (closet complaints).

• **CLOTHES HANGING IN THE CAR FOR TRAVEL:** Instead of a bar extended across the back seat which obscures vision, try placing two large key rings over the clothes hooks on either side of the back seat. The rings let you hang several hangers in each while the car's clothes hooks hold only two or three hangers each.

• **CLOTHESPIN HOLDER,** *Easy Fix:* When hanging a large spread or blanket outdoors on the line, clip clothespins to your shirt bottom and they'll be handy.

• **CLOTHESPINS,** *Recycling Spring-action Pins:*
1. Clamp them on to plastic bread or snack bags.
2. They will hold sheet music in place on a stand, even in the wind.
3. Keep one in the car to clamp on your keys when you switch lights on during the day so that you don't forget to turn them off. Of course, you'll have to remember to clamp on the clothespin when you put the lights on!
4. Clamp scarfs, skirts and other clothing onto a hangar.
5. Plastic-coated metal spring-pins can be attached to recipes, notes, phone messages and hung on a prominent cup hook to keep these things in plain view.
6. Clip together coupons when shopping. Clip a second pin to the cart or your shirt pocket to hold used coupons.
7. Remove mildew from wooden clothespins by soaking them for about an hour in a bucket with water, a bit of laundry detergent and about a cup of bleach. Then rinse and let dry before using.

• **CLOTHING,** *Outfitting School Children:*
1. Take advantage of back-to-school clothing sales, but with teens and pre-teens, it may be better to save some of the budget money for those things "everybody is wearing" that parents never heard of, especially if your child is attending a new school. Children need

not be slaves to fads, but it helps them fit in if they have some "everybody" clothes, backpacks, notebooks, lunch boxes, and so forth.

2. It may help to shop in stores located near the school your child will attend; they'll be catering to the local choices and school requirements.

• **CLOTHING CODING:** Before hanging a garment back in the closet, place a large bangle bracelet on top of the hangers to identify clothing that needs some sort of attention—take to dry cleaners (at the end of the week or after wearing one more time); replace button, fix hem, etc.

• **CLOTHING RECEIPTS,** *Keeping Track of Them:* When you go shopping for clothing, make a shopping list of planned purchases on the front of an envelope. Circle items you buy and insert the receipts. Write down purchases not on the original list. When you return home, put the envelope into a manila folder labeled "receipts" or other file drawer for that purpose only and you'll never have to search for receipts again.

• **CLOTHING SWAP,** *Recycling $aver:* Hold a clothing swap party for your friends to clean out outgrown, no-longer-liked or worn garments. Donate garments that nobody claims to a Women's Shelter or other charity. I'm still wearing a "swap" garment from ten years ago!

• **CLUTTER,** *Eliminating It:* Make it a rule of thumb or, more accurately, rule of hand, that when you leave a room, "don't go empty handed." Always pick up some clutter and take it to where it belongs. **Note:** It's cheating if you just take it to another room where it's still clutter!

• **COCOA,** *Storage:* Some cocoa cans have openings too small for measuring utensils. The solution is to sift the whole 8-ounce can of cocoa into a 2-pound plastic margarine tub with an airtight lid. You can scoop with any measuring utensils and the cocoa won't get lumpy either.

• **COCOA CAN,** *Quick-Fix Opener:* Pry open with a putty knife or clean paint-can lid opener.

• **COFFEE,** *Quick-Fix Flavors:* Add a sprinkle of cinnamon to the ground coffee before brewing. Or, add a drop or two of almond, vanilla or other extract to the ground coffee. For mocha, add chocolate syrup or cocoa mix to brewed coffee.

• **COFFEE CAN,** *Reusing:* When empty, wash and dry and reuse to store staples like pasta, flour, etc. on the pantry shelf. Great for storing items in the workshop, too.

• **COFFEE CREAMER,** *Homemade, Lower-Fat:* Combine non-fat dry milk with low-fat liquid milk; store in fridge and shake before pouring.

• **COFFEE CREAMER SUBSTITUTE:** A spoonful of sweetened condensed milk is both cream and sugar in your coffee.

• **COFFEE FILTER PACKS,** *Homemade:*
1. Place the coffee filter in a large margarine tub, measure coffee, add another filter and continue until the tub is full. Seal with lid to keep coffee fresh.
2. If you grind your own beans but hate the noise in the morning, grind away at night, place the filter in a margarine tub or other sealable container, add coffee, replace lid; then you can wake up and smell the coffee without hearing the noise.

• **COFFEE FILTERS,** *$aver Substitute for One-cup Cones:* To make filters for one-cup cones, fold a regular filter in half, then in half again. Open one side and you have a cone. Ordinary filters cost less than special cone ones.

• **COFFEE-FILTER SACHET:** Pour baking soda into a paper coffee filter, tape it closed (looks like an onion) and toss it into the clothes hamper to keep it odor-free. Replace the "sachet" every few weeks.

• **COFFEE FILTERS,** *Quick-Fixes:*
1. Cover bowl or dish in the microwave.
2. Grab one to clean window, mirror, or polish silver.
3. Place between plates, saucers, and good china or between non-stick cookware pieces to prevent scratches.

4. When serving tacos to children, place the taco in a coffee filter, fill it, and hand it to the child. Less mess!

• **COFFEE FILTERS,** *The Ultimate Way to Separate Filters:* Turn each layer inside out. The struggle is over!

• **COFFEE GROUNDS,** *No-mess Pouring:* To pour coffee into a canister from a can, cut a "spout" hole in the plastic lid and you'll save time not having to wipe up spilled grounds.

• **COFFEE MAKER SAFETY,** *Reminder to Switch It Off:* Is there anyone who has never ever left the pot on for hours and hours? Make it a habit to plug a night-light into the same socket with the coffee pot when you start the coffee and unplug the night-light when you switch off the pot. The extra light can be a reminder, especially if the "on" light of your pot is not very large or bright.

• **COFFEE MAKING,** *$aver for a Tight Budget:* Try making the first pot in a drip coffee maker with the regular amount of ground coffee. Then, for the second pot, leave the grounds in the basket and add half the normal amount of ground coffee on top of them. Brew as usual. For the third pot, throw it all out and start again. It's okay to pinch pennies but don't pinch so hard that Mr. Lincoln says "Ouch" or everyone who tastes the coffee says "Yuck"!

• **COFFEE MUGS,** *Healthy Planet, BYOM:* When your club has a party, have members bring their own coffee cups, marked for identification, and then your group won't need plastic foam cups that don't break down in landfills. You'll save money in the treasury, too. This can also work for casual group parties.

• **COFFEE MUG,** *Heater:* Place your coffee mug on top of the drip coffee-maker when it starts brewing. By the time the coffee is ready, your mug will be warm enough to keep your coffee hot longer as you sip those first eye-openers.

• **COFFEE OLE:** Readers often request this recipe so I'm including it in this dictionary. To a cup of regular coffee, add a little extra skim milk and a tablespoon of powdered skim milk. Add sugar or artificial sweetener to taste. Blend the mixture in the blender until it is foamy. Pour the mixture into a microwaveable coffee mug and heat it on "Warm" for a couple of seconds. Enjoy.

• **COFFEE POT,** *Cleaning Aluminum Percolators:* Fill the coffee pot with water, add a handful of baking soda or two or three teaspoons cream of tartar. Run through the full coffee-making cycle, let cool, then scrub with piece of nylon net. If the pot is badly stained, you may have to repeat this process to get it shiny bright and to get good-tasting coffee again.

• **COFFEE POT,** *Cleaning Burnt Bottoms of Glass Pots:* When you discover that an electric pot has been left on and the pot is burnt, pour table salt into the pot and let it stand for a few minutes. The burnt crust will come loose and you can wash the pot clean. (This hint came from an office worker who used salt because nothing else was handy; that's how most hints come into being!)

• **COFFEE POT,** *Cleaning Mineral Deposits in a Drip Pot:* Follow directions in the booklet that came with your pot. For most types, you can pour a full measure of white vinegar into the water well and run the pot through its cycle. Then run plain water through several cycle to rinse out the vinegar. Heavy deposits may require a repeat of the process. **Hint:** The vinegar can be stored in a jar to clean the coffee pot again. Let the minerals settle to the bottom and use the clear vinegar. Or, clean something with the used vinegar; pour it on weeds or grass in sidewalk cracks, or just pour the remains down the drain to deodorize it.

• **COFFEE THERMOS:**
1. Keep coffee in a thermos instead of on the heater and it will stay hot for a late morning cup without getting stronger.
2. When you have houseguests and need two potfuls quickly, pour the first pot into a thermos as soon as it's brewed so that you can start the second pot immediately.
3. Working people who are slow-starters can make a pot of coffee before retiring and keep it in a thermos so that the first "eye-opener" is ready and waiting. This is an especially good hint that first week of adjusting to daylight saving time or the beginning of the school year!
Hint: Don't forget to rinse out the thermos with hot water to heat it before you pour in hot coffee so that you aren't likely to crack glass inserts and the coffee will stay hot longer.

• **COLD,** *When You Have One:* Avoid putting messy tissues in your pocket or purse. Tuck a small plastic sandwich bag into either one and you can put nose tissues directly into the bag for disposal.

• **COLD-WATER WASHING:** The Association of Home Appliance Manufacturers says that although cold-water washing is energy efficient, detergents do a better job in warmer water. Whites and very dirty clothes wash best in warm to hot water. Also granular detergents don't dissolve well in cold water and so don't clean as well. When washing in cold water, use liquid detergents or dissolve granular ones in water before adding them to the load.

• **COLLEGE RECORDS,** *Storage:* When a child goes off to college provide a metal file and show how to organize files with folders. Then, if the student takes parental advice and files all receipts for tuition and books, dorm information, car expenses, etc. in the file, there'll be no confusion about records. If the student doesn't take advice, well . . . almost everyone grows up eventually! Parents can only do so much!

• **COLLEGE STUDENT HEALTH INSURANCE:** Send with your college student either an extra health-insurance card or copy of the card (both sides) and the student's Social Security number or card. This information is needed for billing in case of an emergency or hospitalization. Without pre-certification, the parent may be responsible for a large portion of a hospital bill.

• **COLOGNE,** *Spraying to Retain Scent:* Step into a walk-in closet when applying spray cologne and the extra fragrance will stay in the closet (to make it smell nice) instead of dissipating in the air. **Caution:** Don't spray on clothing because cologne can stain or damage certain fabrics.

• **COLOR COORDINATING,** *Matching Paint, Fabric, Wallpaper:* Get paint sampler color chips that match sofas, comforters, curtains, rugs, and other "unmoveables" so that you can take the chips shopping for wallpaper, paint, or whatever else you need to buy for redecorating.

• **COMBS AND HAIRBRUSHES,** *Easy Cleaning:*
1. Fill the bathroom sink with hot water and add a couple of squirts of dishwashing liquid or shampoo. Swish everything around

in the soapy water and let soak for 30 minutes or so. Then run the wide end of a comb through the brush bristles to remove hair and hairspray residue, etc. Drain water from the sink and rinse each item thoroughly under hot running water. Place on towel with brushes' bristles-sides down; let drip dry.

2. Put water into the bathroom sink, add a small glug of ammonia and then let combs and brushes soak for a while. Brush combs with brushes and clean both at the same time. Then whisk the brush or a sponge around the sink, let the water run out, and rinse all at the same time.

• COMICS, *Recycling:* Amuse children by letting them color black and white daily newspaper comics.

• COMPACT DISCS, *Cleaning:* Please see RECORDS, Cleaning.

• COMPLAINTS WITH CLOUT, *Checklist for Complaining About Faulty Merchandise or Service:* Be businesslike, not emotional, type the letter if possible and if not, make sure your handwriting is legible. Include all pertinent information, as follows.

1. Your name, address, work and home phone numbers.
2. Date and place of purchase.
3. Serial and model number of merchandise.
4. Name of the person who did the work if it's a service complaint.
5. Make and keep copies of all complaint letters and allow a reasonable amount of time for a response.

Sending complaints by registered letters gives you proof that the company has received your complaint.

• COMPUTER, *Checklist for Avoiding Back and Neck Tension on the Job:*

1. Place your terminal so that the top of the screen is at your eye level or just below.
2. Keep your feet flat on the floor.
3. Keep your elbows at 90 degrees—your fingers should just reach the keyboard comfortably.
4. Position your work station so that the screen receives the least amount of glare from windows or indoor lighting.
5. Take short breaks—at the least, stretch your arms for a few minutes each hour.
6. Make sure your chair provides good back support.

• **COMPUTER,** *Insuring a New One:* At time of purchase, check with your insurance company to make sure it's covered by your policy for theft or damage.

• **COMPUTER MONITOR SCREEN,** *Cleaning:* It's best not to clean the screen with wet cloths. You can wipe with a slightly damp cloth. Commercial anti-static cleaning pads are the best choice. Buy them in office supply or computer stores.

• **COMPUTER PAPER,** *Healthy-Planet Recycling:* Shredded office paper and the perforated edges of computer paper can be used for packing materials.
High-tech Hens: One reader uses shredded computer paper on the farm to line chickens' nests instead of hay and says she thinks the hens like it better!

• **COMPUTER-PAPER BOX,** *Recycling:* Many brands of computer paper come in lidded boxes that make perfect file storage.

• **COMPUTER PRINTOUT PAPER,** *Recycling:* You can run those long printouts back through the printer to print on the blank reverse side for a second time around. The quality is acceptable for test runs and informal jobs.

• **CONFECTIONERS' SUGAR SUBSTITUTE:** Mix one cup of granulated sugar and one tablespoon cornstarch in a blender at high speed for several minutes. As with most substitutes, the consistency and texture of the dish may be altered slightly.

• **CONSUMER INFORMATION:** If you can't find a number to call in the manual that comes with your appliance or on a product label, dial 1-800-555-1212 to get the 800 consumer information number of a company. If the company has no 800 number, main libraries of large cities usually have information services you can call to get addresses and phone numbers of national firms.

• **CONTACT LENS,** *Travel Kit:* A plastic soap case will hold all the accessories for cleaning your contacts when you travel.

• **CONTACT LENS CAUTION:** Don't clean contact lenses with generic/ regular hydrogen peroxide. It may contain additives or impurities that can cause soft-lens discoloration or irritate the eyes, even when this peroxide is safe for other uses. Instead, always clean and disinfect contact lenses with the cleaning solutions made especially for them.

• **CONTACT LENSES,** *Wearing Near Water:* Contact lenses let swimmers, snorklers, water skiers, surfers, and divers see better when they're in the water. To avoid losing lenses and the resulting inconvenience and expense of replacing them, here are some hints.

1. Soft contact lenses are less likely than rigid ones to get lost in or around water. Their larger circumference keeps them more stable in the eye.

2. Insert soft lenses at least 30 minutes before entering the water; reduce the risk of lens loss by using one or two drops of saline or, in a pinch, single-dosage containers of sterile distilled water.

3. Close your eyes if you expect a hard entry into the water; at least squint if you expect a splash.

4. Remove excess water in eyes with several fast hard blinks; avoid rubbing the eye.

5. If you get mild eye discomfort after water play, place a clean index finger on the lens and test-move it gently. If the lens slides easily, it can be safely removed, but if it doesn't move, the lens needs to be taken out immediately using sterile saline solution to help it come out more easily. However, it's best to wait 30 minutes after getting out of the water before you remove and disinfect your lens.

• **COOKIE BAKING,** *Time-Saver:* One reader wrote that she makes twenty-five dozen chocolate chip cookies at one baking session and to save time she scoops the cookie dough onto cookie sheets with a large melon ball maker. All the cookies are the same size and are just right for grandchildren and parties. **Note:** Save a teaspoon of chocolate chips when you are mixing the dough. Then when you get down to the last spoonful of batter and, as usual the chips are all gone with the first scoops of dough, you can add the reserved chips to make all of the cookies equally chocolatey!

• **COOKIE BAKING,** *Time-Saver:* Flatten cookies you roll into a ball, like peanut-butter cookies, with a potato masher.

• **COOKIE CRUMBS AND PIECES,** *From the Bottom of the Cookie Jar, Recycling:* Add them to bread pudding for extra Yum! **Note:** It's not true that the calories don't count when you eat broken cookie pieces instead of whole cookies!

• **COOKIE CUTTERS,** *Seasonal Plastic Ones:* Plastic cookie cutters come in many shapes and colors, such as for Christmas, Thanksgiving, Valentine's day, Easter; they can be festive but inexpensive napkin rings.

• **COOKIE DECORATING,** *Avoiding Mess (Especially When Your "Assistant Cook" Is a Small Child):* After preparing the dough and cutting out the cookies, place the cookie cutter around the cut-out cookies before sprinkling on colored sugars or sparkles. The cutter will corral the sprinkles and keep them from being scattered about.

• **COOKIE DOUGH,** *Quick-Fix Homemade Cookies:* When you make a batch of cookies, make double or more amounts and then freeze cylinders of cookie dough to slice and bake when you get an uncontrollable attack of the cookie munchies.

• **COOKIE JAR TRICK:** Fill the cookie jar with low-sugar dry cereal. It's a great snack and helps develop better eating habits!

• **COOKIES,** *Christmas:* This *Letter of Laughter* recipe appeared about twenty years ago in my mother's column and was sent to me by a reader when it was requested by another reader and I couldn't find it in my files. It proves that some recipes are timeless!

CHRISTMAS COOKIES

1. Light oven, get bowl, spoons, and ingredients, grease pan, crack nuts, remove ten blocks, seven toy autos, and one wad of chewing gum from kitchen table.

2. Measure two cups of flour, remove Johnny's hands from flour, wash flour off him, measure one more cup flour to replace flour on floor.

3. Put flour, baking powder, and salt in sifter. Answer doorbell. Return to kitchen. Remove Johnny's hands from bowl. Wash Johnny. Answer phone. Return. Remove quarter-inch salt from greased pans, grease more pans. Look for Johnny. Answer phone.

4. Return to kitchen and find Johnny. Remove his hands from bowl. Wash shortening, etc., etc., off him. Take up greased pan and take out shells from it. Head for Johnny who flees, knocking bowl off table.

5. Wash kitchen floor. Wash table. Wash kitchen walls. Wash dishes. Wash Johnny. Call baker. Lie down!

Perhaps the best way today's working mothers could use this recipe is to update it as follows.

CHRISTMAS COOKIE RECIPE, REVISED

1. Find Johnny, take him to the car and strap him in his car seat, go to the bakery.

2. Return home, sit down with Johnny to read his favorite Christmas story, and then have cookies and milk with him.

3. Lie down while Johnny naps.

Let's face it, some days you just can't do it all so you may as well seize the moment—friends and family have more value than homemade cookies. Make the cookies when Johnny is old enough to really help you!

• **COOKIES,** *Quick-Fix, Homemade, Small Batch:* For one dozen delicious fresh cookies, add to a box of store-bought muffin mix, two eggs and one-half cup oil. Drop by teaspoonfuls on an ungreased cookie sheet and bake. For extra flavor, add optional ingredients such as a spoonful of peanut butter, chopped nuts or raisins.

• **COOKIES,** *Quick-Fix for Peanut-butter Crisscrosses:* Make them with a plastic fork; the batter won't stick.

• **COOKIES,** *Quick-Fix for Too-browned Bottoms:* Rub the brown off with the coarse side of your vegetable slicer/grater.

• **COOKIE SNEAK:** To cut a few calories from chocolate cookies (or at least to feel as if you are trying!), substitute ½ cup of mini-chocolate chips for one cup of regular-size chips. Few cookie munchers will notice the difference.

• **COOKING,** *Substituting Low-fat or Nonfat Yogurt for Sour Cream:* When you do this for cooked foods, it may separate and get watery. Solution: Stir some flour into the yogurt before cooking or, if possible, add it to dishes after removing them from the heat.

• **COOL COOLER:** Instead of buying bagged ice which will just melt and be tossed away, buy frozen orange juice concentrate. Four cans of frozen concentrate will keep two cold six-packs of beverage cool in a small cooler and then you can mix up the juice for breakfast during the week after your picnic.

• **COOLER,** *For Party Beverages:* Ice down canned and bottled beverages for a party by lining the bottom of your clothes washer with a heavy towel and then filling up the machine with ice and cans. When the party is over, remove remaining cans and use the water for a cold water wash that includes the towel.

• **COOLER,** *Storing Without Mildew:* Place a spacer such as a piece of wood or folded cardboard between the lid and rim to prevent the cover from sealing tightly and to let air circulate. Don't forget to sprinkle in baking soda to prevent odors.

• **COPPER & BRASS,** *Quick-Fix, Brightening:* Sprinkle table salt on a wet sponge, rub off tarnish, rinse, and dry. Or, rub darkened places using a half-lemon with or without table salt, rinse, and buff dry.

• **COPY "MACHINE,"** *Quick-Fix with Transparent Tape:* When you are househunting or labeling videotaped movies with the descriptive paragraphs printed in the newspaper, try this:
1. Place a strip of transparent tape over the print area to be copied and rub well with your fingernail, then carefully lift the print from the paper.
2. You can then stick the movie description onto the side of the videotape or stick a house/apartment classified ad onto a sheet of paper or index card. Then, there will be space for writing your comments after seeing the apartment and other information you need to remember when deciding to rent or buy.

• **CORK,** *Removing When It's Been Pushed into a Wine Bottle That You Want to Save:* Pour ammonia into the bottle and leave it somewhere where air circulates. The cork will disintegrate in about a week. Wash the inside well with soap and water and the bottle is ready for display or to root a sprig of ivy in water.

• **CORKS,** *Recycling Those from Wine and Other Bottles:*
1. Use them to protect the points of knives, barbecue forks, ice picks and knitting needles.
2. They will hold safety pins, map pins, thumbtacks, etc.
3. They can be colored for craft projects with fabric or craft dyes.
4. Glue corks into frames of various sizes to make trivets and coasters.
5. Cut lengthwise so that there is one flat side and glue to a backing such as plywood, fiberboard or cardboard. (This project's gluing

phase could keep a vacation-weary child busy for a long time!) OR, glue on the side of a kitchen cabinet to make a message center.
6. Glue on backings for picture frames, Christmas wreaths, refrigerator magnets.
7. Make tiny sailboats with a toothpick-held sail to occupy a child.
8. Place in the bottoms of potted plants to help drainage and place around roots of orchids to stabilize them.

• **CORN,** *Healthy-Planet Recycling, Avoid Sharing with the Birds:* Cut off the bottoms of used beverage cans and place them on sweet-corn ears a week or so before they're ready to pick. It keeps the birds from eating the corn cobs before you can and doesn't harm the birds.

• **CORN-ON-THE-COB-ON-THE-GRILL:** After pulling off the corn shucks, boil the corn for about five minutes and then toast it over hot coals in the barbecue pit for several minutes.

• **CORN SYRUP SUBSTITUTE:** While you can substitute honey for corn syrup in a recipe, the flavor and texture may be altered and honey tastes sweeter. You cannot substitute corn syrup for granulated sugar and vice versa. With one being a liquid and the other a dry ingredient, it's difficult to adjust the recipe ingredients to get the same result.

• **COSMETIC CASE,** *$aver:* Buy a colorful zipper pencil case sold in school supplies departments of drug or variety stores.

• **COSMETICS,** *When You Travel in Warm Climates:* Instead of putting your cosmetic case in a hot car trunk, keep it inside the car where it's cooler. Even a thirty to forty-five-minute ride to the airport could damage face creams or melt your lipstick and make a big mess in the case.

• **COSTUME,** *Quick-Fix with Humor:* They're sold in catalogs but you can make them yourself with a magic marker and a plain over-size T-shirt, any light color or white.
1. Just write on the T-shirt "THIS IS A (Halloween, Tiger, Clown, New Year's Party) COSTUME" and if you can, do a "stickman" or other drawing on the back.
2. Or a T-shirt with, "MY (MOM, DAD) FORGOT TO GO SHOPPING SO THIS IS MY TRICK-OR-TREAT COSTUME" and/or "PLEASE FEED ME"

would surely get the biggest bag of Halloween goodies any child could want from the neighbors!

• **COTTON FROM MEDICINE BOTTLES,** *Healthy-Planet Recycling:* Don't throw this cotton away; it's great for nail-polish remover and cosmetic use. **Hint:** Cotton is placed in pill bottles to keep the pills from bouncing around and breaking in shipment. Once you open the bottle, remove it because it has no purpose anymore.

• **COUNTER SPACE,** *Temporary Cutting Space:* Turn a dish drainer upside down inside a sink and put your chopping board on top. Then you can chop vegetables and fruit with the easiest ever clean up. Just turn on the faucet and send the peelings down the disposal or collect them in the sink by hand and rinse the rest of the mess off.

• **COUNTERTOPS,** *When You Need Extra Work Space:* Open a drawer all the way and put a cookie sheet on it, then close the drawer until the cookie sheet fits tightly. **Hint:** A lower drawer can be an extra "table" for a child if you don't have enough space at the main table. Put a place mat over the cookie sheet after following the extra-space directions.

• **COUPON,** *Storage:* Instead of storing by category (dairy, meats, baking goods), file according to expiration date, leaving an extra envelope for those which have no expiration date. Make "file folders" by cutting sealed ends off used mailing envelopes.

• **COUPONS,** *Storage:* Clip together with a magnetic clip the coupons that correspond to items on your shopping list and keep on your refrigerator beside the shopping list so that both are handy when you go to the store. **Note:** Sometimes, my coupons ARE my shopping list!

• **COUPONS,** *When You Won't Use Them:* Give to charities when you donate clothing and other items; to senior citizen or other community centers; food banks for distribution to needy families and in some communities to coupon exchanges run by churches, libraries, and other social service projects. **Note:** I recently found a coupon taped to a product on the shelf by some generous donor. I don't know if the store manager would like to see flaps of coupons taped to items on all of the shelves, but I appreciated the 50 cents off!

• **COUPONS FOR A CAUSE:** Here's how one reader figured out a way to give several items weekly to her church "care bank" without breaking her budget and without raiding her pantry for donations. Instead of wasting good money-off coupons for foods that she doesn't usually eat but which are good staples, she allocates $1 per week to spend on coupon items to give to the church.

• **COVER,** *Plastic Wrap Tent:* Poke toothpicks strategically into cakes or other foods to be covered with plastic wrap to make a "tent" so that the tops won't get messed up. This works also if you are marinating meat and don't want the meat to touch the wrap.

• **COVERED DISH RECOVERY:** Getting plates and casseroles returned is often difficult and certainly a chore for the event chairperson. Readers have sent in many solutions.
1. Write your name on masking tape and stick it to the bottom of the dish or stick an address label to the bottom.
2. Cover several thicknesses of paper plates with foil or cover sturdy cardboard with foil, cover with a doily and send a cake on a disposable "plate."
3. Buy 12-inch square floor tiles, cover with foil and place cakes on them.
4. Buy casseroles, plates, salad bowls and other serving dishes and utensils at flea markets (sometimes for only 25 cents), run them through the dishwasher a couple of times to make sure they are sanitized and then don't care if they get returned.
5. If the covered dish event is at a friend's house, buy a dish that might match something in her house or a clear glass one and make it a hostess gift.

• **CRACKER CRUMBS:** Readers send in all sorts of shortcuts for crushing graham or soda crackers to crumbs from putting crackers in the blender; putting them in a sealable bag and substituting a glass when you don't have a rolling pin; putting them in a sealable bag and stepping on the bag until the crackers are crumbs. But one reader topped them all—she puts the crackers in a sealable bag and drives over them with her car. I don't think I would want to do this myself, but it makes a good story!

• **CRADLE,** *Recycling Doll or Antique Baby Ones:* Use them to store magazines, display older children's stuffed animals, hold throw pillows from the bed overnight, hold a folded bedspread overnight.

• **CRAFTS,** *Checklist for Selling Crafts in Consignment Shops:* Crafts are cottage industries for many women, who can remain at home but still supplement the family income. Selling in consignment shops in addition to the usual summer craft shows can be year-round income if you make the right connections.

1. Look for a consignment shop that displays a wide price range of varied crafts. Avoid shops that buy most of their products wholesale from other craftspersons or those that also sell lots of import or commercial gift lines. Seasonal orders are placed months in advance. It's probably too late to sell Christmas items in November.

2. If you exhibit at craft fairs, offer to distribute flyers to promote the shop or gallery that handles your work; make sure your retail prices are the same as those of the shop.

3. Keep careful records and get all agreements in writing. If the shop doesn't have a printed consignment form, print some of your own. The agreement should note:

   A. If the shop is insured against theft or other loss such as damage by fire or flood. (You may need your own insurance.)

   B. If you send your crafts by mail, who pays postage and insurance?

   C. The exact percent of commission the shop gets (store mark-ups are typically 100 to 150 percent). Whether payment is monthly or upon sale of a piece should be clearly stated.

   D. Will your crafts be displayed properly or will they be left in a storeroom or worse yet, in a window where they will get faded?

   E. How long will the item be displayed and if it's returned, will it be mailed or do you pick it up? Some agreements say items must be claimed after thirty to sixty days of display or thirty to sixty days after the craftsperson was notified to pick up.

• **CRANBERRY SUBSTITUTE,** *When Your Family Doesn't Eat Cranberry Sauce for Thanksgiving Dinner:* Please see PEACH SAUCE.

• **CREAM CHEESE,** *Quick-Fix Breakfast Perk:* Sprinkle flavored fruit gelatin on cream cheese after you've spread it on your English muffin or toast.

• **CREASES,** *Removing:*
1. To remove from let-out garment seams/hems, wash the garment first. There may be dirt on the crease that will leave a line if ironed. Apply white vinegar directly to the seam/hem line until it is thoroughly damp. **Caution:** Always test on an inconspicuous place before putting anything on fabric. Place a dry, clean cloth over the line and press with a medium-hot iron. Hang garment up to air; vinegar odors dissipate quickly.
2. To remove creases/wrinkles from wool garments, like those you get in the back of a pants leg, lay the pants (or other garment) out on the ironing board. Dampen a cloth with white vinegar; place it on the wrinkles to be removed. Iron over the cloth and the winkles should come out. Repeat this step if needed, but when repeating, leave more vinegar in the cloth the second time. Continue until wrinkles/creases are out. Then hang the garment in a well ventilated area so the vinegar odor can dissipate.

• **CREDIT CARD,** *When Your Application Is Rejected:*
1. The name of the agency which gave information to your prospective lender that caused your rejection should be included in the denial letter you receive. Write to this bureau and ask for a free copy of your report and the information that caused your application's denial.
2. If you find incorrect or out-of-date information in your file, you can write to the credit bureau and ask them to verify it for you. Also notify the creditor of the problem and try to resolve it yourself. You will need copies of bills, canceled checks and other papers to back your claim; send copies, not originals, to the creditor.
3. If you can't clear up the matter with the creditor, you may have a report of the problem placed in your credit file.
4. It's best to check with your local credit bureau to see if any negative information is in your report before applying. In fact, an

annual check is recommended by some of my sources. Making sure your credit file is up-to-date and accurate avoids problems when you need to borrow money. Credit-reporting firms charge a small fee to review your files; you get a free report only when a credit application is denied.

• **CREDIT CARD PURCHASES,** *Keeping to Your Limits:* Get an extra checkbook register and list your credit cards with the amount you are able to charge for the month on each. When you use a card, immediately write the purchase amount in the appropriate column in the checkbook and subtract it from the total amount you can spend. You will always know your exact balance and when "the well is dry." If you can't get a check book register, a small, lined notebook will do. Check out the spelling-test notebooks sold in school supplies departments; they are good for list making.

• **CREDIT CARDS,** *Safekeeping:*
1. Avoid rubbing the magnetic strips of credit cards against each other in a billfold. The cards can become demagnetized and then useless.
2. Carry cards separately from money clips with magnets, magnetized card keys used to enter buildings, and don't keep them in plastic which also can harm them.
3. Don't scrape ice from a car windshield with a credit card.
4. Leave them behind if you will be in a magnet field such as in an industrial area. The good news is that airport X-ray devices do not harm credit cards.
5. Make copies of all your credit and bank cards on a copy machine so that you have records of all the numbers and expiration dates on one sheet of paper in case you have to report a loss. **CAUTION**—Don't forget to take all of the credit cards out of the copy machine and keep the information in a safe place.

• **CROCHET/KNITTING PLACE:** Keep a pad of self-sticking notes near your chair, then when the phone rings as you are deciphering pattern instructions, you can stick a note on the line you were on when interrupted.

• **CROSSWORD PUZZLES,** *Corrections:* When you do your puzzles in ink, typewriter correction fluid keeps the puzzle neat and readable when you need to correct a mistake. *Crossword Myth Dispelled:* A reader wrote that when crossword fans do puzzles in ink instead of pencil, it's not that they are egotists; it's just easier to read darker pen letters than lighter pencil ones.

• **CUCUMBERS,** *When Your Garden Produces a Bumper Crop:* When you've eaten all the salad, made all the pickles, and cuked all of the friends you possibly can, try cooking cucumbers. Peel, cut into small quarter-sized slices and simmer in chicken broth for about 10 minutes. Drain, add a bit of butter and pepper and you have a tasty veggie dish. If you are cutting calories, cook in skimmed chicken broth and flavor with diet margarine.

• **CUPBOARD DOOR AND DRAWER HANDLES,** *Helping Hands:* People with arthritis often have trouble pulling drawers and doors open with their hands. One reader put fabric loops through her mother's kitchen cabinet handles so that she could open them by slipping her arm through the loop.

• **CUPBOARDS,** *Keeping Closed:* Re-reinforce the closures with self-gripping fabric tape. You can get stick-on dots and strips in neutral colors.

• **CUPCAKES,** *Baking Hints:*
1. Measure cupcake batter into pans with an ice-cream scoop or handled-measuring cup.
2. Pour cupcake batter into the tins with a pitcher.
3. Bake cupcake batter in ice cream cones for children's parties for no-mess eating.

• **CUPCAKE FROSTING,** *Substitute:* Place a small chocolate-covered mint on top of a cupcake, pop it into the microwave for a few seconds, then remove and spread the melted mint just as you would frosting.

• **CURLING IRON,** *Removing Hairspray Build-up:* Cool and unplug iron before cleaning. Then dampen a clean cloth with rubbing alcohol and wipe the wand several times until it's clean. Avoid build-up by cleaning with alcohol about once a month.

• **CURLING-IRON IRONING,** *Quick Fixes:* Run ribbons, dress sashes, some scarfs (depends on fabric), and even seams when you are sewing, through the curling iron.

• **CURTAINS,** *Make Them Crisp and Fresh Without Ironing:* Wash and rinse as usual. Add 1 cup of Epsom salts to a sink filled with water and rinse the laundered curtains in the solution; hang to dry—no need for ironing!

• **CURTAINS,** *Quick-Fix Recycling:* When you switch from window shades to curtains, you can make the curtain casing large enough to accommodate the shade rollers and save yourself the trouble and expense of curtain rods. The bonus is that you don't make more holes in the walls either!

• **CURTAINS,** *Removing Wrinkles Without Ironing:* When you wash sheers or similar fabrics, hang them back up damp and put heavy dinner knives in the hem openings. The added weight helps pull out wrinkles as the curtains dry.

• **CURTAINS,** *When Rods Show Through Colored Sheers:* Spray paint the rods with the appropriate color.

• **CURTAIN TIE BACKS,** *Quick-Fix, Placing the Hooks Exactly Even:* Pull the window shade up to the level where the nails or hooks are to be installed and you'll have a straight line marker for exactly the right place on either side of the window.

• **CUTTER,** *Non-messy for Children:* A pizza cutter will cut pancakes or waffles and other soft, sticky foods neatly.
Pizza cutters also cut homemade noodle dough quickly.

• **CUTTING BOARD HELPER:** Buy a brightly colored plastic dustpan so that after you chop vegetables for the wok, you can push them from the cutting board into the dustpan and from dustpan into wok without "flying veggies" all over the floor. Be sure to mark it "Vegetable Dustpan" so that it doesn't end up collecting dirt on the floor!

D

- **DAY CARE,** *Warm Fuzzy for Young Child:* Sometimes it's difficult for mothers and young children to adjust to the idea of day care. Here's one reader's solution. When her son entered a day-care program that required children to bring their own blankets for nap time, she and her son went to fabric and craft stores to pick out appliqués for the blanket—a Marine emblem because his dad was a Marine, a duck because he liked the story of the Ugly Duckling, and others. One of the final appliqués was a "warm fuzzy," a pink heart with a cotton ball in the middle that Mom sprayed with the perfume she usually wears. Each month when the blanket came home for laundering, Mom resprayed the heart. Mom's fragrance helped the tot take a nap, and Mom felt like she was still "connected."

- **DECANTER,** *Removing Stains and Mineral Deposits:* Fill the decanter with white vinegar and let stand overnight. Then add uncooked rice and shake to remove the stains on the inside that a sponge or brush won't reach. Rinse and dry.

- **DECORATING,** *Accents:* Dresser scarfs can cover "a multitude of sins" such as stains, nicks and scratches on a table-top, buffet or dresser; or substitute placemats or napkins (like the one remaining unstained member of a set), colorful serapes or fringed stoles for traditional dresser scarfs.

• **DECORATING,** *Living/Bedroom Pillow Perks:* Throw pillows always add new color and brighten a room. If you sew, you can make them from fabric remnants and stuff them with recycled panty hose, foam dryer sheets, foam packing materials, or bits of left-over-anything that's soft.
1. If your decor is "eclectic," make large TV-lounging floor pillows by sewing plush corduroy (back) and lightweight Oriental design throw rugs (front) together; stuff with old bedpillows and foam strips cut from carpet backing and other filler.
2. Make children's bedroom throw pillows by sewing shut the necks, sleeves and bottoms of favorite but outgrown T-Shirts and stuffing them. Use larger T-shirts as "decorator" pillow cases.

• **DECORATING,** *Silk Flowers and Plants:* "Dust" with cold air blown from a hair dryer or clean by shaking them in a bag with table salt.

• **DECORATING,** *Table Linen Cover-ups:* Discover a stain on the tablecloth and there's no time to change it? Make it look as if the cover-up is really your purposely placed decoration.
Cover-up with a centerpiece, hotplate-mat or trivet, a wide ribbon/serape/runner down the center, complementary colored napkins (placed diagonally), place mats (one in center or one on either side of the centerpiece) or doilies located so they will be beneath serving dishes or the centerpiece or candle sticks. Scatter holiday flowers or greenery so that spots are covered as part of your decoration scheme. (Cut stems off flowers so they'll lay flat; hold things in place with tape loops.)

• **DECORATING,** *Table Linens:* Colorful fringed "finger-tip" towels bought at white sales can be no-iron inexpensive placemats, especially at the "children's table" for family dinners where they'll also absorb spills.

• **DECORATING,** *Walls:* Group pictures and other hanging mementoes like plaques or plates to dramatize a wall or room area.
1. Avoid making extra nail holes in the wall—spread out a large sheet of wrapping paper or several taped-together newspapers on

the floor and experiment with frame positions. Then outline the frames on the paper, tape the paper to the wall, and drive hooks through the paper into the wall. Then remove the paper and hang the pictures.

2. Make small rooms look larger by installing wall mirrors or mirror tiles from hardware stores; instructions usually come with the products used for this project.

• **DENTAL FLOSS,** *Other Uses:*
1. String beads for necklaces.
2. Sew on buttons with white or new colored flosses; they'll stay on!
3. Faucets with clear plastic covers on the "Hot" and "Cold" knobs can be hard to clean. When you are in the mood to strive for perfection, dental floss cleans not only the nooks and crannies between your teeth but those of covered faucet knobs!
4. Cut cake layers (thread also works better and neater than a knife).
5. Lace up a chicken or turkey for cooking.
6. Household repairs, such as reattaching umbrella material to a spoke.

• **DENTURE CLEANSER,** *Homestyle Method:* Combine 1 teaspoon water softener, 1 teaspoon liquid bleach, and 8 ounces water and soak dentures in the solution for 10 to 15 minutes daily. Scrub with a denture brush and rinse well before replacing them in your mouth. **Caution:** Do not use this or any solution containing bleach if you wear a partial denture that has metal, wire clasps, cast chrome, or gold frame.

• **DENTURES,** *Identification:* Ask the dentist to put the denture owner's name inside the dentures of nursing home residents so that they don't get mixed up with those of other patients. Residents' possessions, including dentures, can easily get misplaced.

• **DENTURE SOAKER,** *Substitute When You Travel:* A resealable plastic bag fits easily in a shaving or cosmetic bag and dentures can soak overnight as easily in the bag as in a hard-sided container.

• **DEODORANT,** *Healthy Planet, Homestyle:* For a non-chemical deodorant, apply dry baking soda to the underarm area, then brush

off excess. It's not likely to irritate skin like some commercial preparations affect some people.

• **DESSERTS,** *Keeping Single Servings:* When only one or two people
live in a home, desserts can get stale before they are eaten. The
solution is to cut all freezable desserts into single-serving sizes and
freeze them in plastic freezer-safe bags. A few seconds in the microwave brings them back to freshness.

• **DETERGENT,** *Saver, Time-Saver:* When you empty a plastic squirt
bottle of dishwashing detergent, don't throw it away. Instead, fill it
with water and shake to dissolve the detergent that remains inside.
The resulting diluted detergent is powerful enough to squirt on
eyeglasses, your hands or on a sponge to quick-wipe dishes and it
will rinse off more easily than when you squirt full-strength detergent on washables. **Hint:** When washing eyeglasses with plastic
lenses, remember that paper towels, napkins, and tissues can
scratch—dry with a soft cloth.

• **DETERGENT BOTTLE CAPS,** *Recycling:* Caps from liquid laundry
detergent can be stacked like building blocks or for sand scoops
at the beach (please don't leave them there!) or in a child's sandbox.

• **DIAMONDS,** *Care:*
1. Don't wear while doing housework or gardening. Cleaning
products can harm diamonds and gold; a good knock can chip a
diamond.
2. Because diamonds can scratch other gem stones, store each piece
of diamond jewelry in a separate case or jewelry box section.
3. When you wash your hands, don't take your ring off and leave
it near the sink; it can fall down the drain or be forgotten when you
leave. I've seen people hold their rings between their lips while
washing their hands.
4. Powders, skin oils, soaps and lotions dull diamonds. To clean
them, try a squirt of mild liquid detergent in a small bowl of warm
water. Let the diamond jewelry soak a few minutes and brush with
an old soft toothbrush or eyebrow brush. Rinse well; pat and buff
dry.
5. Try dipping each piece in a bit of rubbing alcohol and buff dry.
It really makes diamonds sparkle.

• **DIAPERS,** *Laundering Cloth Ones:*
1. Pre-soak diapers in a diaper pail with mild sudsy solution and one tablespoon of bleach for each gallon of water or with borax in water. Rinse and unfold soiled diapers before placing them in the solution.
2. Wash contents (about eighteen diapers per wash load) every two or three days to avoid odors. To wash, dump the solution and diapers into the washing machine and run on the spin cycle. After the spin cycle removes the solution, launder as usual with hot water and cold rinse.
3. Add bleach every two or three washings to keep the diapers white and then run the diapers through a second rinse with one-half cup vinegar added to the rinse water to help remove soap and bleach residues. Fabric softener will make the diapers less absorbent so add it only occasionally, if at all.

• **DIAPERS,** *Recycling Disposable Diaper Boxes:* Store holiday decorations or outgrown baby clothes in them and they'll be easy to spot among the other brown storage boxes in your attic.

• **DIET DINING,** *Avoiding Restaurant-induced Diet Damage:*
1. Call the restaurant in the morning to find out what's on the menu, then if there's no low-cal meal offered, you can either eat somewhere else or eat the main course at home and plan to have a large salad while the others dine. (Ask for salad dressing to be served on the side so the salad isn't swimming in oil.) Good restaurants are happy to prepare a special vegetarian plate if you request it and will leave off fatty sauces, too—you need to ask for such special dietary needs, though. If you're embarrassed to ask at the table (though you shouldn't be), make a trek to the rest room as soon as you arrive and en route, talk to the table server privately.
2. If you know the portion of meat or pasta will be too large for your calorie count, ask for or bring your own "doggie bag" carryout container so that you can remove the excess before you are tempted to eat it "just because it is there." Don't make a fuss and don't feel self-conscious, just do it; people who care about you want your diet to succeed and remember, good restaurants care about pleasing their customers. (Check out the new microwave safe, tightly sealed plastic ware at supermarkets. You can carry them in your purse.)

3. Order first so that you won't be tempted to change your allowed selections by other people's choices.

• **DIET DIPS:** Substitute blended cottage cheese or yogurt for sour cream or check out the new low-fat or non-fat sour creams.
Dip 1. Mix cottage cheese in the blender with your favorite spices—pepper, paprika, onion/garlic salts, etc. or with low-cal Italian dressing.
Dip 2. Mix 16 ounces low-fat yogurt and a package of regular (not diet) Ranch Dressing mix in the yogurt container. A packet of sweetener is optional as are hotter spices to taste. Let set overnight. (You have to let this set overnight or it won't taste good.)

• **DINNER,** *Family Dinner Planning, Letter of Laughter:* One reader says fast-food has become so much a part of their lives that when she says, "Time to eat," the children all jump into the car.

• **DINNER,** *Quick-Fix When You Don't Want to Cook:*
First Spouse: What's for dinner?
Second Spouse: Fish (or other hated food), but it's not thawed yet.
FS: Oh, let's go out for dinner.
SS: Okay, I'll just put this fish (or whatever) back into the freezer.
The reader who sent this hint has used the same package of her husband's hated fish for five years. And he knows it! The package of frozen fish on the kitchen counter has become a signal that she wants to eat out. Now that's communication in marriage!

• **DINNER,** *Quick-Fix When You Forget to Thaw Something, Letter of Laughter:*
First Spouse: What's for dinner?
Second Spouse: Take out.
FS: Take out what?
SS: Take out me!

• **DINNER GUEST,** *File:* List the meals you serve at dinner parties on a 3 × 5 index card along with the names of the guests and keep in a file box. Then you won't serve the same menu over and over to the same people and you can note special likes and allergies, too. You won't serve your famous oyster bisque to someone who stops breathing after eating shell fish—a sure way to make your party memorable, to say the least! **Note:** My research editor once went to a party at which a guest, who didn't know she'd been infected with hepatitis, mixed the salad. The next day all the guests had to go for hepatitis immunizations. People are still talking about the party thirty years later!

• **DIP DISH,** *Healthy-Planet Edible Serving "Dishes":*
1. Cut off the top of a bell pepper carefully and stand it on end in the middle of a veggie platter to hold dip. The pepper can be red, green, or yellow depending upon the color you need to perk up the platter.
2. Put cocktail sauce in a hollowed-out cabbage then skewer a few shrimp on colored toothpicks and stick the opposite ends into the cabbage like antennae on a satellite. Place the rest of the shrimp around the cabbage.

• **DIRECTIONS:** Jot travel directions on pieces of self-sticking notepaper and then stick the note to the car dashboard so you don't have to hold it while driving.

• **DISH DRAINER, DRAINER TRAY, SINK RACK,** *Cleaning Gunk Off:*
1. Fill the kitchen sink with about 2 inches of hot water and add a couple of "glugs" of chlorine bleach. Place items in sink and let soak for about 15 minutes. If you can't put your hands in bleach and have no rubber gloves, after soaking is over, unplug the sink with barbecue tongs and let the bleach water drain away. Rinse items.
2. Best quality dish drainers can be placed upside down in the dishwasher ("Normal" or "Light" setting) for easy cleaning. Just be sure that all moving arms are not blocked by the rack.

• **DISHWASHER,** *Cleaning Hard-water Deposits and Removing Stains:* Citric acid, a main ingredient in powdered lemonade or citrus fruit drink, can be bought in pharmacies. To clean the dishwasher put about a tablespoon of the powder (drink or citric acid) in the detergent dispenser, no detergent, and run a cycle. You can also sprinkle the powder on a stain or blotch before running a cycle. If stains persist you may need to repeat the process.

• **DISHWASHER,** *Recycle Parts:* When a dishwasher can't be repaired, salvage the racks for use as organizers of wrapping paper and ribbons—rolls and ribbon spools fit on the upright progs and flat packages of tissue or gift wrap fit in slots. Also, some old dishwashers have silverware baskets with handles which can carry flatware to the picnic table and be used for informal outdoor buffet serving.

• DISHWASHER, *Silverware Basket "Leaks":* Put a piece of nylon net into the bottom of the dishwasher silverware basket if you have small-handled pieces that seem to poke through and possibly interfere with the rotating sprayer in the bottom of the dishwasher.

• DISHWASHER, *When Water-force Flips Lightweight Cups:* To stop cups from flipping over and getting filled with water and sediment, line up the cup handles and run a 1/4-inch dowel pin through them. Dowel pins are sold in most hardware stores.

• DISHWASHER DETERGENT, *Letter of Laughter:* Responding to one of my columns warning not to put regular liquid detergent in a dishwasher, a reader says that while she was in the hospital for surgery, her husband ran their dishwasher with liquid detergent. Her eldest daughter came home to find suds bubbling and flowing from the dishwasher so fast that they had to close all inside doors and open the back one—suds filled the kitchen and rolled out the back door, filling the porch and driveway. Her daughter's comment was "when Dad cleans, he cleans the kitchen and yard, too!" Dad was kidded about it, but he's not the first and I'm sure not the last person to clean the whole kitchen at one time this way!
Another *Letter of Laughter:* This story prompted a reader to tell how her sister decided to make wine and was feeling pretty successful until all the corks started blowing off, one after the other. Instead of a "cleaning mess" she had a real mess. Fortunately, the novice winemaker had a sense of humor and had a good laugh since it reminded her of an *I Love Lucy* episode!

• DISHWASHER RACK, *Repair vs. Replacing Rusty Ones $aver:* A commercial liquid plastic product made just for dishwasher rack repair is available from appliance or dishwasher service stores. It comes in several colors to match different brands.

• DISHWASHING FACTS, *Healthy-Planet Water and Energy Saving:* An efficient automatic dishwasher, properly used, consumes less hot water and less energy than hand-washing, according to the Texas Energy Extension Service at Texas A&M University.

1. You use a lot of water and energy if you wash dishes and rinse them in running hot water; less if you wash in one pan and rinse in another.

2. New dishwashers have "air dry" or "energy miser" buttons. These features save you money because they turn off heat during drying.

3. Dishwashers with booster heaters allow you to get hotter water for dishes than elsewhere in the house. You won't have to keep your water heater set as high.

4. Look for dishwashers that can dispose of food residue so that you don't have to rinse dishes before putting them into the dishwasher. Just take a used paper napkin or a rubber spatula and wipe off solids and let the machine do its work. **Note:** If your dishwasher consistently leaves residue on your dishes, check for blocked drainage along the line, including your main kitchen drain pipe/sewer line.

• **DISHWASHING SPONGE,** *Keeping Fresh and Clean:* Clip it to the top shelf of the dishwasher at the end of the day so that it won't fall to the bottom and damage the machine while the dishwasher's hot water and detergent deodorizes and cleans it.

• **DOCTOR SELECTION,** *Checklist:* The time to look for a physician or dentist is before you need one in an emergency when there's no time to choose. When you move into a new community inquire with a local medical or dental society or association for reference and ask neighbors, friends, and business associates. It's not easy to choose and remember that you can always change your mind if you don't like your first choice.

1. Check the doctor's background to find out the medical/dental school attended and if the doctor is a board-certified specialist in the area in which you need care.

2. Check the patient scheduling. Look for one that schedules enough time for visits so that you aren't rushed and have time to ask questions. Write down your questions and the answers, too. Also, if you want to avoid waiting, sometimes getting the first appointment of the day helps avoid delays from other patients'

unanticipated problems. **Note:** Also, if you have come to a physician for a cold, don't expect time for a complete all-encompassing physical examination. Different times are scheduled for different patient needs and procedures. (It's like calling the plumber over to replace a faucet washer and then asking for replacement of all the bathroom fixtures.)

3. Does the physician or dental surgeon have privileges in a hospital or surgical center that's close and meets your needs?

4. If you have special beliefs regarding medical care or medical preferences, find a doctor who will work with you. Often state or local laws vary on such subjects and you should put your last wishes in writing as well as tell your physician and relatives and give them copies of your written wishes.

• **DOG,** *Curing Car Sickness:* Common with puppies, car sickness can be outgrown more easily if you take your dog on fifteen-minute trips every other day or so, then increase the time gradually.

• **DOG,** *How to Tell If It's Too Fat:* At ideal weight, you should be able to feel a pet's ribs with your fingers without pressing. Generally, if you can see the pet's ribs, it is underweight. In either case, don't put your dog on a weight-loss or weight-gain diet with prescription foods or other schemes without your vet's advice.

• **DOG,** *Identification, Letter of Laughter:* The parents of a four-year-old son were passed during their walk by a man with a dog. "What kind of a dog is that," the child asked. "A bird dog," the mom replied. "Can it fly, Mommy, can it fly?" the child asked.

• **DOG,** *Introducing It to a New Baby:* Long before baby is born, teach the dog simple controlling commands like "sit" and "stay." While baby is still in the hospital, take home a blanket or article of clothing the baby has worn and let the dog get familiar with the baby's scent. Dogs will be curious about the crying sounds baby makes. It would help to have a tape of a crying baby to let the dog grow accustomed to that sound. **Caution:** Never leave a baby and pet alone. A dog or cat can jump a gate so one favorite hint is to put a screen door on baby's room so you can see and hear, but pets are kept out.

• **DOG BATH,** *Stopping "the Shakes":* Try firmly grasping the dog around his nose. For some dogs, "the shake" starts there—so, if they can't shake their noses, they can't shake anything else either. You'll stay dryer and have less mess.

• **DOG BIRTHING BED:** A child's small plastic swimming pool makes a good puppy-birthing bed. It's easy to clean, has no sharp edges; the dog can step over the side, but tiny puppies will stay in. *Letter of Laughter:* I considered suggesting this bed for mama cats, too, but I've heard so many tales of cats giving birth in peculiar places— dresser drawers, atop a neighbor's roof, under the bed, in a closet shoe-pile, in the backseat of a neighbor's car (he'll never leave windows open again!), I thought the suggestion might be futile!

• **DOG DISH,** *Keeping the Dog from Tipping It Over:*
1. For Outdoor Feeding: Buy a tube baking pan and put it over a stake you've driven into the ground. You can put food or water into the pan and the dog can't tip it.
2. Put dog food or water into heavy-based, widemouthed crocks.

• **DOG DRINK:** When you take your dog in the car, take also a small plastic water bowl or a bowl made by cutting off the bottom of a gallon milk jug and a jug of water. Then, you can "water" the dog when it's thirsty.

• **DOG EARS,** *Keeping Them out of Doggie's Dinner:* A reader wrote that she puts a stretchable headband over her cocker spaniel's head, tucking his ears under it, and he's so interested in eating that he doesn't notice.

• **DOG, HEARTWORM PILLS:** Heartworm pills are now given all year round instead of just summer as was the custom in the past. (Infected mosquitoes, carriers of the disease, have been found indoors when it was 7 degrees below zero outside!) If your dog hates the pill, wrap it in half of a cheese slice. (Wrap the cheese around the pill, then hold the wad in your palm for a minute and you'll have a pill-stuffed cheese ball that fools the dog into eagerly eating it.) Or coat the pill with peanut butter or liverwurst if that's what your dog likes. Pills are available in daily or monthly doses; ask your vet for advice.

• **DOGHOUSE,** *Winterizing:* A reader wrote that the first night's freeze made the leftover carpet placed on the floor of her dog's house wet and frosty—unsuitable for the dog to sleep on. So her husband built a platform about 10 inches high to elevate the house from the cold ground and removed the carpet. Instead, they put tar paper on the floor, covered it with layers of newspaper, then topped it all with a layer of hay. This insulation kept the dog warm and dry.

• **DOG SWEATER,** *Recycling $aver:* For a small dog, recycle an old ski mask so that the dog's front paws go through the eye holes and its head goes through a hole you open in the seam at the mask's top. The dog's tail wags from the neckhole, of course, to thank you for the warmth and kindness!

• **DOG TRAINING:** Praise is the key—pat, hug, and tell your dog "What a good dog!" when it responds properly to training, and reward it immediately with a treat. Hitting only teaches fear to an animal and is not training—it's abuse.

• **DOLL DISPLAY STAND,** *Recycling $aver:* Dolls with small bodies and full skirts can stand up in a widemouthed mayonnaise jar. The bonus is that the jar makes a good skirt hoop.

• **DOLLS,** *Cleaning Adoptable Ones:* **Caution:** While some people wash them in the machine, I must stress that you do it at your own risk and only when the doll is heavily soiled and all other cleaning attempts have failed.
Step 1: Remove all clothing, ribbons, and accessories. Pre-treat heavily soiled areas with pre-wash spray. Put the doll in a pillowcase and close it by tying a knot in the open end.
Step 2: Place the pillowcase in the washing machine, set on a gentle cycle, add warm water and regular laundry detergent. Add a few sheets or towels in with the doll to cushion the bumping.
Step 3: After the washing cycle is complete, remove the pillowcased doll and place it directly into the clothes dryer on low heat for about 10 minutes. After 10 minutes in the dryer, remove the doll from the pillowcase and place it in a well-ventilated area to finish drying overnight.

• **DOLLS,** *Special Clothes for Keepsake Dolls:* Buy a doll from a craft store and make doll clothes that resemble clothing worn for special occasions in the doll collector's life—First Communion, first day of school, etc.

• **DOMINOES CONTAINER,** *Recycling:* Wash and dry a white or colored (just not a see-through plastic) gallon-size plastic jug and cut an opening in the top-half opposite the handle large enough to admit an adult's hand. Then you can keep dominoes in the jug and pass it from player to player to draw from. Passing the jug also speeds up alphabet word games and the jug can also be safe storage so that you don't lose pieces.

• **DOORBELLS,** *For Children and Pets:* Hang a row of small bells on the doorknob so you can hear if children open the door to go out, especially if you have adventuresome toddlers. Also, if your pet scratches the door to go out, it will ring the bells so that you'll always hear the pet's pleas for relief and avoid pet "accidents." *Letter of Laughter:* These bells could be a problem if you have a cockatiel like the one belonging to one of my readers. "Clyde" thinks he's human and answers phone rings with "Hello, hello" and doorbell rings with "Come in." Strangers walk in if the door isn't locked!

• **DOORKNOB GUARD,** *For Toddlers:* Secure an old sock on the doorknob with a rubber band. Adults can open the door but when toddlers try to turn the knob, the sock slides around and prevents a child from getting a good grip on the knob. Or, buy a commercial device that fits over the knob and works the same way.

• **DOOR LOCKS,** *Deadbolt-Lock Checklist:*
1. The bolt should extend at least 1 inch from the edge of the door. (This is called a "1-inch throw.")
2. The connecting screws holding the lock together are on the INSIDE of the door.
3. The strike plate is attached to the door frame with screws that are at least 3 inches long.
4. The cylinder has a steel guard—a ring around the key section. The cylinder guard needs to be tapered or to rotate around the key section when twisted to prevent wrenching.

• **DOOR LOCKS,** *Outside Doors:* Deadbolt locks which need latchkeys inside and out to operate them are the most secure but those which can be opened from the inside without a latchkey are considered safer in case of fire; some communities have safety codes restricting inside/outside latchkey-only deadbolt locks. Check with local building inspectors or other suitable authorities.

• **DOOR LOCKS,** *Quick-Fix:* A lock may not be broken, just stuck. To unstick locks and to keep them working well, squirt the lock mechanism at the door's edge regularly with lubricant.

• **DOOR LOCKS,** *Safety:* Locks provide security only if you use them. Get in the habit of locking doors even if you leave the house for only a few minutes.

• **DOOR LOCKS,** *Types Available and Uses:*
1. Double Cylinder Deadbolt Lock: Placed on doors with glass panels or on all doors, they can be opened only with a key from either side. You can keep the key near the door but make sure it can't be reached from the glass panel; intruders won't be able to break the glass and get the key, but your family can get out in case of fire. Before installing these, check with local law enforcement agencies because some communities restrict use of these locks.
2. Police Lock: For rear and basement entrances and apartments, this is a metal bar bracketed against the inside of the door at an angle; it slides into a small hole on the floor and prevents burglars from jimmying the lock or kicking in the door.
3. Padlocks: Usually used for garages, sheds, and workshops; buy sturdy padlocks that don't release the key until the lock is locked. A padlock should have a rugged laminated case with ⅜-inch shackle so it can resist smashing. A padlock is only as good as its mounting hasp, which should be secured with bolts and mounted on a metal plate. Bolts must be concealed when the padlock is locked.

• **DOOR, LOUVERED PANEL,** *Quick-Fix, No-mess Cleaning:* If the louvered panel on a door to a hot-water heater, furnace, or air-conditioning unit is screwed in place, carefully unscrew the screws, remove the panel and wash it in a sink or tub of warm sudsy water with a soft scrub brush. Rinse, wipe dry, and replace. Trust me, removing the panel for cleaning is much easier than leaving it in place and then making a mess on the floor while you spray on cleaning solution and try to clean the louvers.

• **DOORS,** *Avoiding Frustration and Embarrassment:* Ever feel silly pushing on a door you're supposed to pull open? When you approach an unfamiliar door, scan the frame to see if the hinges are on the inside (PUSH) or outside (PULL).

• **DOORS**, *Recycling Old Ones:* Add legs and paint and you have a desk or table. The height is up to you.

• **DOOR SAFETY**, *Quick-Fix:* Prevent small children from slamming or closing doors on their little fingers—throw a thick folded towel over the tops of doors so they won't close completely.

• **DOORS & DRAWERS**, *Quick-Fix with Hardware:* New hardware gives your kitchen or bathroom a new look. Before you buy do the following.
1. Be sure to measure drawer handle spreads so that you can use the existing holes when attaching the new handles.
2. If you want to switch from handles to knobs, buy backplates to cover the old handle-holes and then drill a new hole in the center for the knob.

• **DOUBLE BOILER:** If you place a small jar lid into the bottom of a double boiler, the rattling sounds will warn you when the water is getting too low. Marbles work, too, but be prepared for quizzical looks if, when someone asks, "What's that noise," and you reply, "I'm boiling my marbles." They may think you've lost your marbles! **Note:** Someone once told me that your mind is like a cartridge and ideas are like marbles. When your cartridge (mind) gets too full with too many marbles (ideas) some of them start to spill out and that's where we get the expression, "losing your marbles." However, I haven't been able to verify this with my usual sources.

• **DOWN-FILLED GARMENTS**, *To Wash or Not to Wash, That Is the Confusion:* The International Fabricare Institute and most garment manufacturers recommend that down-filled garments be dry cleaned. As always consult the care label for exact instructions for your particular garment.

• **DRAFT GUARDS**, *Recycling:* Make draft guards for doorjambs and window sills by filling with sand double- or triple-thicknesses of newspaper bags; tie the open end securely with a twist-tie, and then put the "snake" into a long tube sock.

• **DRAPERY CORDS,** *Quick-Fix Identifying Open and Close:* Either put pieces of colored tape or a dab of colored nail polish on the cord that opens the drapes, or take the letters left over from video-tapes to stick "open" on one cord or "o" and "c" for open and close.

• **DRAPES,** *Easy Way, Removing Dust and Freshening:* When drapes need a good dusting but not actual cleaning, you can toss most washable fabric drapes into the dryer with a fabric-softener sheet. Set the dryer on "Air Fluff."

• **DRAWER KNOBS & PULLS,** *"Decorator" Substitutes:*
1. Toy blocks with holes drilled for the screws can go on a child's dresser. Some craft shops sell these already drilled.
2. Small wooden blocks and large beads used for macrame craft already have holes for screws and make novel pulls.

• **DRAWER ORGANIZERS,** *Quick-Fix When They Slide:* When plastic silverware organizers slide around in a kitchen drawer, keep them in place with double-sided adhesive tape. You can still remove them for cleaning.

• **DRESSES,** *Hanging Those with Spaghetti Straps:* Don't hang by the straps; they aren't strong enough to support the garment's weight, especially if the fabric is extra heavy like velvet or satin.
1. If the manufacturer has not attached long loops of seam binding to the upper side seams for hanging, make some with seam binding or woven hem facing. Be sure to tack them to the side seam allowance.
2. Or, hang over a pants hanger at the waist.
3. Or, clip the bodice to a skirt hanger. Be sure to put foam padding under the clips to prevent crushing or marring velvet, satin, or silk.

• **DRESSER DRAWERS,** *Identifying Which Drawer Holds What for Young Children:* Tape pictures of clothing (cut from catalogs) on the drawers to help young children put their laundry away in the right places. And, sitters can see at a glance where everything is.

• **DRIED FRUIT,** *Baking:* When a recipe requires cutting dried fruit, it's faster and easier to spray scissor blades with non-stick cooking spray and snip fruit into small pieces.

- **DRIVEWAY OIL STAINS,** *Quick-Fix:* Try spraying engine degreaser. Apply; let set about 10 minutes; wash away with a garden hose. Also, please see CAT LITTER.

- **DRY-CLEANER'S BAGS,** *Recycling:*
1. Tie a knot in the end, turn the bag inside out, and it will line a tall trash basket. You can insert a paper grocery bag to prevent things from poking through. Or you can double bag for heavier paper trash.
2. Put bags on clothing to be packed in hanging-type bags when you travel. It helps prevent crushing and helps prevent clothing from getting wet if rain should fall on the zipper area. You can also stuff bags into sleeve arms to prevent crushing.

- **DRYER,** *Quick-Fix, Cleaning the Lint Trap:* A baby-bottle brush sweeps the filter clean with one whisk.

- **DRYER,** *Quick-Fix When Seal Is Broken:* Self-adhesive weather-stripping will replace a broken dryer door seal if you can't get an "official" one from an appliance parts store.

- **DRYING RACK,** *Recycling Idea:* Please see FAN GRATE, Recycling and BABY EXPANDABLE GATE.

- **DUST,** *Removing from Corners and Crevices:* Secure an old sock on a yardstick with rubber bands and poke it into hard-to-reach places like under or behind the fridge. You can also reach cobwebs in corners with it.

- **DUST BRUSH:** An animal hair pastry brush or natural bristle paint-brush removes dust from the inside corners of picture frames, light bulbs and globes, chandelier chains, bric-a-brac, cloth lamp shades, pleated tops of draperies, and other nooks and crannies.

- **DUST MOP,** *Shaking Off Dust:* If the dust from your mop drifts onto your neighbor's porch or apartment balcony, you can help the environment and your neighbor's disposition by tying a paper bag around your mop before shaking it. The bag will collect the "dust bunnies."

- **DUST MOPS:**
1. When synthetic strands of yarn on your dust mop are all tangled from laundering, insert the mop into an old pillow case or make a

large "pocket" from an old towel. (Fold in half and sew up the sides, leaving the ends open.) You can spray the mop "pocket" with a dust magnet product before dusting and then launder it afterward so that you always have a clean mop.

2. To dust walls and remove cobwebs from corners, place an old pillowcase or your "towel case" over a broom or mop head.

• **DUST PREVENTION,** *On Party Crystal and Trays:* Cover them with plastic wrap when you put them away and they'll stay clean between parties. **Note:** This may seem like a waste of disposable wrap but the rule of thumb is that if water is scarce in your area, you use disposables at parties to avoid excess washing water waste. If water is abundant, you avoid disposables to save landfill space.

• **DUST RUFFLES,** *Keeping in Place:* Slipping, sliding dust ruffles can be kept in their place if you sew them on to an old fitted sheet or quilted mattress pad either by machine or hand-tacking. The fitted sheet will hold tight to the box spring.

E

- **EARRINGS,** *Avoiding Pain from Clip Backs:*
1. Place spongy nose pads sold in optical shops on the clip part and a piece of moleskin on the back of the earring.
2. Cut to fit small moleskin adhesive pads (those made for protecting corns and blisters) and stick them on the offending earring back and the front of the clip so that the pads "sandwich" your poor, suffering earlobe.

- **EARRINGS,** *Holding Them Straight, Recycling:* Cut small circles from plastic lids, such as from coffee cans, and place them behind your ear on the pierced-earring post before you put the back on. You can also buy clear plastic disks for this purpose at costume jewelry stores.

- **EARRINGS,** *Pierced:* Putting a bit of antibiotic ointment on the posts helps earrings go in easier and helps to prevent skin irritation.

- **EARRINGS,** *Prevent Loss:* If you take off your hook-style pierced earrings at the gym or doctor's office, poke them into a plastic foam "packing peanut" so the wires don't get bent or lost. When traveling, poke them through one-half of a washcloth and then fold the other half over them for protection.

• **EARRINGS,** *Recycling When You Lose One of a Pair:*
1. Poke posts through scarfs or knit ties to hold them in place.
2. A button-style pierced earring can be a stud for a missing button or a small lapel pin.
3. Turn an earring "dangle" into a small pendant and hang it like a charm on a bracelet or necklace.
4. If you have several leftover dangle earrings put them all together on a charm holder (sold at jewelry counters in silver or gold) and then put the holder on a chain or velvet ribbon for a multi-piece "pendant."
5. Poke large earrings through the screen door to prevent people from "walking through it" when it's closed—a special problem with sliding screen doors.
6. Break or cut off posts from the earring back; glue the earring "button" with a hot glue gun to a plain gold or silver ring and you have a new piece of jewelry.

• **EARRINGS,** *Recycling Single Clip-on:* If you clip a lone clip-on earring to a plain gold or silver chain it's a pendant.

• **EARRINGS,** *Storage:* Inexpensive, lightweight, clear plastic fishing tackle boxes will store many pairs of pierced earrings for easy selection. Some have twenty or more compartments, each with enough space for several pairs of similar earrings.

• **EARRINGS,** *Storing Pierced:* Poke them through anything—an old necktie, place mat, fabric belt, greeting card, strips of ribbon from gifts, a not-so perky scarf, a sock, a sentimental baby T-shirt, and on and on. The idea is to avoid losing earrings while recycling.

• **EARS,** *Cleaning Behind Children's, Letter of Laughter:* A reader whose sons "grow dirt behind their ears," and who complain that it hurts when she tries to rub or scrub them, found a solution. She dots baby fragrance petroleum jelly behind their ears and rubs it in—her sons smell sweet and their ears are spotless the next day.

• **EASTER BASKET GRASS,** *Substitute:* Instead of plastic/paper grass which seems to get everywhere before it's finally discarded, try a skein of rug yarn. Undo the wrapper, fluff it up, add eggs, bunnies, and other clean items. The bonus is that you can save it for next Easter or crochet or knit with it later in the year. Or, buy only green yarn instead of purple and yellow so that you can tie up Christmas packages with it later on.

• **EASTER BASKETS,** *Healthy-Planet $aver:* Instead of buying baskets which just get broken and thrown away, buy useful items to hold Easter goodies such as bicycle baskets, a football helmet or baseball cap, special milk mugs or cereal bowls, or anything else your imagination conjures up.

• **EASTER BASKETS,** *Substitutes for Adults and Older Children:* Fill a straw or other hat; a small trash can; a mug; collector glass; flying disk; nut bowl. For non-sweets eaters, substitute cheese and crackers, fruit and nuts, travel-size cosmetics, lunch snacks, cassette tapes, or a plant.

• **EASTER BASKETS,** *Using Them Year-round:* Fill with fruit and make a centerpiece; have it hold powder, lotion, and pins in the nursery; clippers, pins, scissors, etc. in the bathroom; spices and other small things on the kitchen counter; the remote control, TV-listing guide and your eyeglasses atop of the TV. Serve hard-boiled eggs in Easter baskets any time of the year.

• **EASTER EGGS,** *Healthy-Planet Dyes:* Boil eggs with onion peels to make them yellow, with spinach or turnip tops to make them green, with a fresh beet to make them red, or add a package of unsweetened powdered drink mix to the pot.

• **EGG,** *Quick-Fix When a Piece of Broken Shell Is in Food or Recipe Ingredients:* Tried and true is to scoop out the piece of shell with one of the larger pieces of the eggshell.

• **EGG,** *Quick-Fix When You Drop One on the Floor:* If you don't have an eager dog or cat to lick it up, pour salt over the broken egg, let it set for about 15 minutes. Cleanup is a cinch!

• **EGG CARTON,** *Recycling:* Place a cardboard or plastic foam egg carton, spread open, into the bottom of a plastic trash bag when you put it into the can. It will prevent the bottom from getting soggy and tearing.

• **EGG SUBSTITUTE IN CAKE:** If a cake recipe calls for two eggs and you discover that you have only one, substitute two tablespoons of mayonnaise for the missing egg.

• **EGGS,** *Cascarones "Confetti Eggs" Decorating:* Popular in my hometown, San Antonio, at Fiesta time, they are easily made.
1. Whenever you use a fresh egg, don't crack the shell in half; instead carefully poke a pin or thumbtack hole in the small end and with a spoon tap out a dime-size hole in the opposite larger end.
2. Hold the egg over a bowl and blow into the pin hole, forcing the egg out the dime-size hole or use a baby bulb syringe to "blow" it out. Gently run water into the empty eggshell to rinse it out, and place it on paper towels to dry.
3. Decorate the eggshells with dye or paint and fill the inside with confetti. After inserting confetti, paste a small piece of tissue paper over the larger opening to hold it in.
4. Have a Fiesta party and pop Cascarones atop the head of someone for a lot of laughs and a lot of flying confetti. At Fiesta, you know someone really cares when he or she cracks a cascarone over your head! Olé!

• **EGGS,** *Easy Semi-poached, No Broken Yolks:* Spray the pan lightly with non-stick vegetable spray, fry eggs until the whites are barely set, then add about one tablespoon of water. Cover tightly and turn heat down very low. It won't take long at all!

• **EGGS,** *Identifying Cooked:* There's no rule that says you can color eggs only at Easter. Add a few drops of food coloring or onion skins to the water when you cook them and the colored eggs will be the cooked eggs. P.S. Onion skins make a nice mottled marbled look!

• **EGGS,** *Identifying Cooked Ones by Spinning:* Hard-boiled ones spin and raw ones will wobble.

• **EGGS,** *Identifying Fresh:* Just mark the old ones with a pencil when you add new ones to the Fridge. The American Egg Board advises keeping eggs in their original cartons for best preservation and to keep them from absorbing odors.

• **EGGS,** *Rolling Down the Counter:* Stop run-a-way eggs when you are cooking—sprinkle a few grains of salt or sugar on the counter, place the egg on it and it will stay put.

• **EGGS,** *Separating Yolks from Whites:*
Method 1: Hold a funnel over a container and break the egg into it. The white slides into the container and the yolk stays in the funnel.
Method 2: Break the egg into a small bowl, then lift the yolk out with a large slotted spoon.

• **EGGS,** *Substituting Egg Whites for Whole Eggs in Baking:*
When two egg whites are substitutes for one whole egg, you need to add one tablespoon of oil and one and one-third tablespoons of liquid in your recipe to make up for the fat in the egg yolk. One reader saves all the yolks she removes from whole eggs in a plastic bag. When the bag is full, she cooks the egg yolks in a greased microwave dish and sets the "egg casserole" out for wild animals to eat. Raccoons, opossums and even foxes feast at her country home.

• **EGGS,** *White vs. Brown for Nutrition and Price:* The American Egg Board has the final word to dispel an "old wives' tale" that's been around as long as the "Which came first, the chicken or the egg" riddle.
Eggshell and yolk color may vary but color has nothing to do with the quality or nutritive value of an egg. The breed of hen determines the shell color. White breeds lay white eggs; brown or reddish-brown breeds (such as Rhode Island Red, New Hampshire and Plymouth Rock) lay brown eggs. Most Americans want white eggs but in some parts of the country, especially in New England, brown shells are preferred.
Generally, brown eggs cost more because the breeds that lay them are larger and require more feed, therefore the market price is higher. But why pay more for brown shells when you eat the inside of the egg not the outside?

• **EGGS, DEVILED,** *Expanding Filling:* To make the halves fuller, add about one-third cup of low-fat cottage cheese to six eggs' worth of yolk-filling. Mash all together, add usual seasonings and you'll have enough filling to make a nice mound in each half.

• **EGGS, DOUBLE-YOLK:** The American Egg Board says usually double-yolk egg yolks are smaller than regular yolks and so can be substituted one for the other.

• **ELBOW GREASE,** *Generation Gap Gaff, Letter of Laughter:* After I'd used the term "elbow grease" in a column, a reader shopping in the supermarket overheard a young woman asking the store manager where she could find the "elbow grease" she'd read about in Heloise's column. He thought she was kidding until a second shopper came up and said, "That's what I'm looking for too!" Neither shopper had ever heard the term before and thought it was a new product. When the first Heloise fan explained to them that it was a term meaning a good old-fashioned rubbing and scrubbing, they all had a good laugh, and so did I when I heard about this generation gap gaff. But, wouldn't it be wonderful if somebody would package "elbow grease" so you wouldn't have to use all of your own?

• **ELECTRIC BLANKETS,** *Washing:* If you've lost the instructions that came with the blanket, the following notes are usually safe.
1. Check care label for instructions and unplug the electrical control from the blanket before washing.
2. You CAN wash it in an automatic washer, but NOT in a coin-operated dry-cleaning machine. DO NOT dry in a dryer.
3. Long wash or spin cycles can damage the blanket. First fill the washing machine with warm water and add a mild detergent. Let the machine agitate on a gentle cycle until detergent is dissolved. Add the blanket and let it wash for three or four minutes. After the rinse cycle and the machine drains, set the load for a short spin cycle. Repeat the rinse cycle and a short spin cycle again.
4. Remove the blanket and press any remaining water out with your hands.
5. Lay over a clothesline (or a couple of lines if it is a king- or queen-size blanket) to dry in the fresh air and sun. *Letter of Laughter:* When a couple bought a dual-control electric blanket, they were disappointed because he complained that his side was too hot and she said her side was too cold. For a week they adjusted control knobs, he turning his down and she turning hers up until they decided that the blanket was defective. Then, when changing the sheets—you guessed it—she realized that his control was on her

side of the bed and hers was on his side. She had been "roasting" him and he had been "cooling" her. I'll bet that's not the first time this has happened!

• **ELECTRICAL EXTENSION CORDS,** *Healthy-Planet Recycling Storage:* Instead of rubber bands or twist-ties, bind cords neatly with toilet-paper or paper-towel rolls. Write the length on the roll so you don't have to guess.

• **ELECTRICAL SAFETY:** If you have turned off a circuit breaker to do electrical work at home, tape a sign on the circuit breaker that says, DO NOT TURN ON, to prevent people with good intentions from flipping the switch and causing you harm.

• **ELDER HELPER,** *In Apartments:* In apartment complexes where many elderly people live and watch out for each other, many have the custom of putting a red bandana or other marker on the doorknob at night and then removing it in the morning as a signal that all is well in that apartment. If the bandana is still on the doorknob by midday or afternoon, someone checks on the person who lives in that apartment to see if all is okay.

• **ELDER HELPER,** *When Eyesight Is Poor:* Write letters in large, bold print. Some eye conditions make red felt tip pen easier to see than black. Then include a self-addressed, stamped envelope with the letter so that the elder can write back with less trouble.

• **ELDER HELPER,** *When Fingers Fumble:* When fingers won't button shirts, sew a seam from the second button from the top down to the next-to-last button so that the shirt can be pulled on overhead.

• **EMBROIDERY FLOSS,** *Storing:* You can wrap floss on cardboard spools when it's long enough but, to store shorter strands, buy nine-pocket plastic sheets used to display baseball card collections and you can insert the label with color number along with the leftover pieces of floss. Keep pages in a three-ring binder and just remove the page when you need to take samples to the store for matching or coordinating colors.

• **EMBROIDERY THREAD HOLDER:** Wrap the thread around the post of a permanent wave roller—a separate roller for each color—and clip it in place. It's easy to remove the clip when you need more thread.

• EMERGENCIES, *Calling:* When you report an emergency or crime, you'll get faster results if you do the following:

1. If your city does not have a dial 911 emergency system, have the emergency number taped to your phone so it can't be lost or, if you have a programmable phone, program emergency numbers into it and clearly mark the emergency button.

2. When you call, try to remain calm and say "I want to report a (robbery, suspicious person, fire). You will be asked: Where, When, Describe person or situation? Weapons present? Injuries? Which way did the criminal run?

3. Get the number or name of the operator who took the information so that if you call again with more information you can give it to the same person and save time repeating what was originally reported.

4. Do call back if the situation changes or if you get more information. Remember, because of computerized communications systems, a police car can be on the way before you finish your first call; any additional information will be forwarded and can help.

5. Try to remember the description if a car is involved (color, make, any damaged parts) and if you can only get part of a license plate number, the first three numbers are more important than the last three.

6. Install lighting between houses if you live in a city neighborhood.

7. Place your house numbers on the rear of your home if you have a back alley to help police and firefighters identify your house.

8. Cooperate with local Neighborhood Watch organizations or help start one if your city promotes them.

9. If you are victimized, cooperate by going to line-ups and court.

10. Rehearse emergency procedures with your family and emphasize the seriousness of false alarms to children.

• EMERGENCIES, *Checklist for Getting Proper Medical Care:* When should we go to an emergency room, urgent care center, call the doctor for an appointment or just wait and see? With the different deductibles on medical insurances, cost of different facilities is as much a worry as the illness itself. The Mayo Clinic Health Letter advises the following.

Seek emergency care when you are ill or in pain if there is:
1. Chest pain or upper abdominal pain or pressure.
2. Sudden, severe pain anywhere in your body or sudden severe headache with no prior history.
3. Dizziness, sudden weakness or sudden change in vision.
4. Severe or persistent vomiting.
5. Difficult breathing or shortness of breath.
6. Fainting or feeling faint.
7. Suicidal or homicidal feelings.

Call your doctor for an appointment if there is:
1. Unexplained weight loss.
2. Lump in your breast.
3. Blood in your urine.
4. Abdominal cramps lasting two weeks.

Wait and see if you have:
1. Vomited once in six hours; no fever, pain or other symptoms.
Note: Age, past medical history, and other conditions change what is "wait and see" for one person as compared to others. Chances are that if you think your symptoms are an emergency, they are and you shouldn't delay getting medical attention. The sooner a doctor treats your illness, the better the chance for a good outcome.

• **EMERGENCY**, *Personal Affairs Checklist:* In case of an emergency, keep an up-to-date list for your family. Include:
A copy of will and trust agreements; doctor and hospital information; family records (births, marriage, divorce, social security, military service, citizenship); insurance policy information (numbers, agent, beneficiaries); funeral information (preferences, location of cemetery plots, deeds, etc.); safe-deposit box (key and location, person authorized to open it); bank account (number, locations); debts (your own and owed to you); pension plans, IRAs, Keoghs, financial/legal advisors' names and phone numbers, brokerage accounts (with brokers' name and phone number); all business records; all charge accounts. **Note:** Keep irreplaceable documents in a safe-deposit box but keep copies for your home records. Remember

that a safe-deposit box can be sealed when a person dies so that important information may not be available when it's most needed, such as funeral preferences, wills, etc.

• **ENERGY,** *Checklist for Saving on Cooling Costs:*
1. Leaving lights on, especially incandescent bulbs which furnish more heat than light, makes your AC run harder. Please remember to switch them off.
2. Change the AC filter at least monthly, or more often if you have shedding pets, to reduce the load on the AC unit and therefore cut costs.
3. Set your AC thermostat no lower than 78° F and in some climates, shut off the AC and open windows to use cool evening breezes.
4. Close off humidity-producing kitchen, bathroom and laundry areas to keep moisture from the rest of the house. You'll feel cooler in dryer air.
5. When you shower, open the bathroom window or turn on the exhaust vent if you have one to let moisture out.
6. Cover pots on the stove to confine heat and humidity. Covering the pot makes the contents heat up faster, too, so the stove won't be heating the room as long. (But then your mother told you that!) And, to save even more energy, if you turn off the electric stove 3 minutes before you're done cooking, it will stay hot for at least that long.
7. Warm air rises so open second floor and attic windows to let heat escape. In the evening when it's cool, you can let the cooler air into the house and close the windows early in the morning to keep the cool air inside.
8. A large window fan uses one-fourth the energy and costs one-fifth as much as an AC to operate. Placing one in an attic window can push hot air out and draw cooler air in through downstairs windows.
9. When buying an AC unit, bigger is not always better. Look for the Seasonal Energy Efficiency Rating (SEER)—the higher the number, the more cooling efficiency you'll get for electricity costs.
10. AC units work more efficiently when installed on the shady side of your house. Some people shade their units with awnings or trees.

Awnings, of course, also help to keep hot sun from shining into windows.

• ENERGY, *Checklist for Saving Cooling Costs for Apartment Dwellers:* For some apartment dwellers, window units are energy and utility bill demons.

1. If your apartment has a room AC unit, check the filter now and clean or replace it. Clogged filters make the unit run longer than needed and operate inefficiently. If you can do it safely, clean the condenser coils and fins (those grills on the outdoor side of the unit).

2. Set the temperature control no lower than 78°F and don't set the control to a cooler temperature at start-up. It won't cool the room faster and you may forget to set the control lower once the room is comfortable, thus wasting energy. Most window units don't have specific degree settings so place a thermometer somewhere in the room away from the AC air flow to get an accurate temperature reading.

3. Remember that lamps, TV sets or other heat sources placed near a window unit can cause it to run longer than necessary.

4. A window fan uses as little as one-tenth the energy of an air conditioner, so buying one to bring cool air into your apartment is good energy economy.

5. If your AC unit has an outside air control to bring in fresh air, you can use it without using the cooling mechanism. The unit's compressor motor guzzles the energy guzzler, not the fan. But remember to close the outside air control when you start cooling again.

• ENERGY, *Checklist for Saving on Heating Costs:*

1. Turn down the heat to 60°F in unoccupied rooms. Do this by closing duct covers, turning down radiators or the thermostat if the room has its own.

2. If you have the oven on in the kitchen for a long period of time (baking Christmas cookies, etc.) close off your kitchen hot air duct—you'll get enough heat from the oven.

3. If everyone will be away from home for eight or more hours, turn down the heat at least 8°F. The first one home can turn it back up.

4. When you are snug under a comforter at night, you can have the temperature reduced to 61° to 64°F.

5. If you have a programmable thermostat you can set it so the heat will go off and on when it's needed, resulting in lower heating costs and less fuel waste. Heating costs increase by 5 percent for each degree you set your thermostat above 68°F.

6. Cover all cracks in doors and windows to prevent heat from escaping. Get the children in on this project—they can be "air-leak police." Have them take a six-inch piece of ribbon or strip of paper and hold it near places at windows where air may be escaping, then make a map showing where these drafts are so that the family can stop them.

7. In newer homes, power ventilators cool the attic in the summer. Turn them off in the winter to prevent their drawing warm air up from the house. Such warm moist air can also cause frost buildup and damage in the attic.

8. If you don't like to sleep under an electric blanket or with a heating pad, use them to pre-heat your bed and turn them off when you get in—wearing warm PJs and socks, of course!

• **ENERGY RATING YOUR HOME:** In some cities public utility companies offer free energy-efficiency checks; others charge a minimal fee. If a utility company does an energy check for you, the results will be mailed along with recommendations for improvements, estimates of how much such changes would cost initially and what your long-term savings would be.

1. To be an energy miser, check if your home has adequate insulation in the attic and walls; weatherstripping and caulking in good condition; the proper insulation and temperature setting for your hot-water heater.

2. Check if appliances, heaters and air conditioners are operating efficiently. When you replace these items, look at the energy ratings on their tags before you buy.

Please see energy checklists above.

• **ENGAGEMENT CALENDARS,** *Recycling Pretty-covered Old Ones:* Convert them into specialized recipe collections. Copy recipes in bold print on appropriately sized blank cards and then paste the cards over used pages of past engagements. You can arrange recipes alphabetically or by general subject and put a tab on the first page of each category, if you wish.

• **ENTERTAINING,** *Buffet Table:* Make a long buffet table from two or more card tables placed side-by-side, and keep them from separating by having their "feet" standing, by twos (with a snug fit), in cans.

• **ENTERTAINING,** *Cleaning-up:*
1. Colored bulbs in lamps when you have holiday parties look festive and make dust invisible; they let you spend more time on the food and less on cleaning before the party. You'll have to clean after anyway!
2. Fill the sink with warm soapy water and toss flatwear into it as you pick up the plates, etc. so that it will soak clean.
3. Best hint is to say, "Yes, thank you" when guests offer to help bring food or clean up after.
4. Trade "maid-service" with a friend—you "do" her party and she "does" yours.
5. Get a sitter for young children if they aren't included in the party; pay older children as hired help.

• **ENTERTAINING,** *Family Parties:*
1. Place older children in charge of entertaining younger ones; provide board games and other playthings, such as "dress-up" clothing for "pretend" games and plays, in a room out of the food preparation traffic.
2. Offer a reward to older children of a movie or other entertainment for child care and clean-up after family dinner. Adults who remember their teens also recall that they were bored with adult-style visiting after the main feast is over.

• **ENTERTAINING,** *Quick-Fix for Spots and Stains:* Club soda is more than a beverage when you have a party; it can be used on many fresh spots and stains on clothing, carpets and linens, such as wine and foods. See SPOTS AND STAINS on page 398.

• **ENTERTAINING,** *Quick-Fix for Tablecloth Creases:*
1. Toss a tablecloth into the fluff cycle of the dryer with a damp towel; it may get some of the storage fold wrinkles out. After use, store the cloth for the next time on a coat hanger.

2. Prevent a centerfold: Make a lengthwise slit in a cardboard tube from a gift wrap roll (cut to hanger width), then put the tube on the hanger.

• **ENTERTAINING,** *Substitutes for Large Containers:* For family reunions and other large parties, buy new brightly colored plastic dishpans in which to mix and serve potato and pasta salads.

• **ENTERTAINING,** *Tablesetting:* To set the table before the party when you have toddlers, without fear of your child playing "magician" with the tablecloth, open the table as if to insert a leaf, poke about an inch of tablecloth into the crack with your finger, then close the table again. The tablecloth will stay put and your real friends will understand the reason for the crease across the table. Or use place mats.

• **ENVELOPE NOTE:** If the envelope is addressed and ready to go, but not yet, you can write notes to yourself on the upper right-hand corner about when to mail a birthday card, if photos or other items are to be included, when the bill is to be paid, etc. and then cover the note with the stamp at mailing time.

• **ENVELOPES,** *Recycling Junk Mail:* While they make good shopping lists, file holders for bits and pieces, receipts, and other things, DO NOT mail out your bill payments or letters in them. First, it is illegal to use postage-paid envelopes for anything other than the original intended use. Also, many reply envelopes are printed with bar codes that direct them to the intended address no matter what you write on them. Sticking on a label is no assurance of covering up addresses either; a reader wrote me that her label came off so her car payment went to a book club instead and, as a result, she got a late-payment charge on her car loan that would have bought a lot of new envelopes.

• **ENVELOPES,** *Sealing the Unsealable:* Dab the inside flap with a bit of clear fingernail polish and close it up. I use up the decorative stickers and return address labels that I get from various charitable organizations to reinforce the seals, especially on envelopes containing checks.

• **ENVELOPES,** *Steaming Open:* Set your iron on a hot setting, then place a slightly dampened cloth over the envelope seal and press with the hot iron for a second or two. This should open the envelope. To reseal, briefly touch the closed flap with the hot iron. If it doesn't want to stick, try a drop of household glue, tape or nailpolish, as noted above in ENVELOPES, Sealing the Unsealable.

• **ENVELOPES,** *Unsticking the Stuck:* Please see ENVELOPES, Steaming Open above. **Hint:** To avoid this problem in damp climates, place something between the flap and the envelope such as waxed paper, regular paper or just raise the flap of one envelope and place the next envelope under it. Or in really damp climates, don't buy the kind that need licking to seal; instead, buy self-sealers. Sometimes, spending a few pennies more saves a lot of aggravation!

• **EXERCISE,** *Letter of Laughter:* A granny-aged woman wrote that she found a way to keep aerobic and limbering up exercises from getting boring. She closes all the drapes, tunes up the jazziest music she can find on the radio and pretends she's a "go-go dancer" in a room full of panting Romeos. She says it gets her blood circulating!

• **EYE,** *Kitchen-style, Soothing Tired and Puffy Ones:* Working on computers or doing demanding needlework can be a strain.
Soother 1—Put wet used tea bags into the freezer for a few minutes. While they chill, dab olive oil on your eyelids. Place a tea bag on each eye and lie down for 15 minutes or so. Then carefully remove the oil by dabbing lightly with a clean tissue or cotton ball.
Soother 2—Soak a couple of cotton balls in cold milk, apply to closed eyes and lie down for 10 minutes.
Soother 3—Place a slice of cold cucumber on each eye and lie down for 10 to 15 minutes.

• **EYEBROWS,** *Darkening Light Brows:* If eyebrow pencil looks too harsh and fake, stroke a thin flat makeup brush across eye shadow (light brown or grey) and then apply it to your eyebrows. Also, try light upward strokes of mascara to color eyebrows.

• **EYEGLASSES,** *Emergency Repairs:*
1. If you lose the tiny screw from your eyeglasses use a twist-tie without the paper. When the point comes out the other side, cut off the ends you can see.

2. If the screw is just loose and you don't have a tiny screwdriver, try a pencil eraser. It works great, especially on metal-framed eyeglasses that seem to always have a screw loose!

• **EYEGLASSES,** *Removing Paint Spatters:*
1. Rub lenses gently with a soft cloth dipped in soapy water.
2. For glass lenses ONLY (not plastic, plastic coated, or other special coating), carefully apply acetone or mineral spirits with a soft cloth to remove paint. Then wash with soapy water, rinse, and dry.

• **EYE MAKEUP,** *Application:* Shading and color are the keys—dark shading adds depth and light shading comes forward. You can contour your entire face with makeup just like the stars do! **Hint:** If you have trouble putting on eye makeup because your lids twitch, open your mouth to the biggest "O" you can do comfortably and your face will stay put while you apply shadow, liner and mascara to your eyes.

• **EYE MAKEUP,** *Removing Waterproof Mascara, etc.:* Apply mineral oil or petroleum jelly and remove with cotton or a soft, natural sponge. (Note that mineral oil is listed on most commercial makeup remover labels.) Most cosmetologists agree that tissues are too rough on the skin.

F

• **FABRIC PURCHASE,** *Checklist for Upholstery and Drapery Fabrics:*
There are no returns or exchanges on these usually expensive fabrics so here are some guidelines to prevent costly errors.
1. Always be sure to buy enough fabric to finish the job completely. Dye lots vary; it's better to have excess than to run short. Leftover fabric can be used for repairs or to make pillows, etc.
2. Know the fabric you buy. Check for fiber content, repeating patterns, cleaning instructions, and stain or flame retardancy. These factors affect the amount of fabric needed, durability, and upkeep. Availability is also a factor. If you underestimate, make an error cutting, or decide to have more work done in the same fabric, know that there is more available and it's not a discontinued pattern.
3. Fabric and workmanship are related. Flawed fabrics, irregulars, or seconds will generally affect the outcome of your project. Inspect carefully before buying, especially markdowns. If there is a flaw near the end of a bolt of upholstery fabric, you may be given the remainder to compensate for adjusting the cutting but be sure that you can still cut out the large pieces you need for the project. For example, no extra yardage could compensate for drapery fabric flaws unless they can be concealed in the hems.

4. Get estimates if you are having the work done professionally because costs vary greatly. Ask to see samples of their work or for references.

5. When you go to buy fabric, swatches, paint chips, arm caps, cushions, fabric remnants taken with you are invaluable to selecting a good color match. Taking a tiny sample home is not as effective as seeing your swatches against a large piece in the store.

• **FACE POWDER,** *$aver, When It Hardens in a Compact:* Gently rub a piece of fine sandpaper or an emery board across the powder to loosen it. **Hint:** Makeup and oil from your skin gets on the powder puff and then gets absorbed into the face powder. Avoid caked powder by storing your powder puff upside down in the compact.

• **FACIAL,** *Home Remedy for Oily Skin:*
1. Make a paste of dry oatmeal and water; spread it on your face, being careful not to put it on the delicate eye area skin.
2. Let the mask dry and then splash your face with warm water to remove it or remove it with a washcloth.
3. After all is removed, splash a little cool water on your face for a delicious refreshed feeling. Your face will feel clean and smooth.

• **FAMILY NEWSPAPER,** *Letters to Grandparents:* Have children assemble family news in newspaper style—sports, editorial, world and local issues, advice column—and send a monthly family newspaper to their grandparents.

• **FAMILY WAKE-UP CALL:** *Letter of Laughter*—Tired of repeating children's wake-up calls on school days? One reader gives her children five minutes to get up after being called or she spray-mists them with a spritz water bottle. It took only a few spritzes and now she has no problems.

• **FAN GRATE,** *Recycling:* Save the grate from an electric box fan after the fan is worn out and it will be a good drying rack for sweaters and other garments that need to dry flat.

• **FAT FRYING SPATTERS,** *Quick-Fix, Time-Saver:* Place an inverted metal colander over a skillet. It lets steam escape and the meat brown without splattering fat all over the stove area for you to clean up.

• **FAT SUBSTITUTING,** *For Low-cholesterol Diets:*
1. Substitute vegetable oil for butter or lard in recipes other than bread or baked desserts. You will need one-third less vegetable oil—for example, 2 teaspoons of vegetable oil sub for 1 tablespoon of solid shortening (1 tablespoon = 3 teaspoons). Corn oil stick margarine works also.
2. When you substitute two egg whites per egg in a recipe, you may also add one teaspoon of vegetable oil for each yolk omitted so that the recipe has a better texture.

• **FAST-FOOD CONDIMENTS,** *Recycling:* Buying Fast Food usually means extra plastic-ware, ketchup, mustard, salt and pepper packets. Instead of throwing the extras away, save them for picnics and camping. They take less space in your food basket than whole jars of ketchup, etc. and there's no mess either.

• **FAUCET,** *When the Garden Faucet Is Too Low:* If leaning down to turn on the water is difficult for someone with a back problem or an elderly person, try raising the faucet to a more reachable height. Remove the faucet and put on an elbow fitting. Connect a two-foot length of pipe to the fitting and then attach the faucet to the pipe. Be sure the pipe is attached to the house so that it doesn't break or pop loose if jarred. If you aren't handy, have a plumber do the job.

• **FAX, COVER SHEETS,** *Healthy-Planet Paper-Saving, Time- and $-Savers:*
1. In my office, we made one standard cover sheet for all FAX transmissions. We put it into a clear plastic sleeve (the kind that lets you fax a cover sheet within it), and then write in all pertinent information with a dry erasable marker. When we finish transmitting, we erase the marker with a blackboard eraser and the cover sheet is ready for the next transmission. If several companies are using one FAX machine, each can have its own logo on a master cover sheet and then just change cover sheets in the plastic sleeve for transmission.
2. Have a "header" stored in the computer that has all the information needed to identify the FAX; then "Merge" it on top of correspondence and fill in the information blanks before printing it out.

3. Have a rubber stamp made with all necessary information—name, address, and person to whom the FAX is sent, number of pages, etc. and stamp the info in the margin of the page being FAXed.

4. If you frequently FAX information to one certain person or business, reuse the same cover sheet—just have several lines on which to write the date and subject of each FAX.

• FEATHERS, *Cleaning:* When ostrich or peacock feathers get too dusty for just a blowing with cool air from a hair dryer, gently swish them in a cold-water wash or in plain cold water, then gently blow-dry them with a hair dryer set on low cool setting. Hold the dryer at a safe distance from each feather so it dries gently. Don't try to reshape the feathers with your hands; a gentle swishing when dry would be enough to bring back the natural shape.

• FIBERGLASS SURFACE, *Cleaning Tubs and Showers:* Fiberglass is easily scratched with harsh abrasives. If you don't have cleaners specially formulated for fiberglass (sold in places that sell tubs and shower stalls), or a cleaner recommended for fiberglass from the supermarket, you can clean this surface with baking soda. Apply with a damp cloth, rub and rinse off residue well. I've also found that cheap shampoo "degunks" soap film on fiberglass.

• FIBERGLASS TUB AND SHOWER, *Cleaning:* Readers say they get good results if they wax fiberglass tubs and showers with car or boat wax. Clean with a non-abrasive cleaner and apply wax to the walls and sides and buff with an electric buffer for a super shine. **Caution:** Never wax the shower floor or tub bottom; it makes them too slippery for safety.

• FILE "CABINETS," *Homemade System:* Buy plastic milk-type crates in colors you like, then insert hanging files. The crates can be stacked easily and are lightweight if you need to carry them around.

• FILE SUBSTITUTE, *Recycling, For Newspaper Clippings, Coupons, etc.:* Please see JUNK MAIL ENVELOPES, Recycling.

• FILING IMPORTANT PAPERS IN A WALL SAFE: To avoid having to unfold each document to see what it is, fold papers so that the letterheads face out. You can just thumb through the files in a hurry.

• **FILM,** *Identification:* To prevent loss when having film developed, print your name and address on letter-size paper and take a picture of it when you start a new roll. If you are traveling, take a picture of a sign printed with the city's (or other location's) name so that you can identify your photos when you get home and your memory is fuzzy.

• **FILM CANISTERS,** *35mm, Healthy-Planet Recycling:* Don't pitch 'em. They can hold jewelry when you're at the gym, address labels and stamps, children's jacks, marbles, lunch/milk money, coins for the laundromat, sewing supplies at work or travel, styling gel in travel kit, and so on.

• **FINGERNAIL,** *Mending Broken or Split One:* A drop of instant glue will repair a split. For a bad tear or split, strengthen it by gluing on small torn bits of white tissue paper.
1. Glue a small piece of torn tissue (facial or toilet tissue or newspaper border, if you have no wrapping tissue) over the tear, then cover it with a larger piece.
2. After the glue dries, gently file the paper with the smoothest side of an emery board.
3. Add several coats of clear nail polish to smooth and, if you wish, colored polish to cover.
This mend will last long enough for a bad tear to grow out and save you a lot of finger pain!

• **FINGERNAIL FILE,** *Quick-Fix Substitute:* When a fingernail breaks and you don't have an emery board or file to smooth the rough edge, try the striking edge of a matchbook. One reader discovered this hint when she assumed that if the striking edge was rough enough to ignite a match it could file a fingernail—creative thinking!

• **FINGERNAIL POLISH,** *Keeping the Bottle from Spilling:* Put a droplet of polish on a scrap of heavy paper or piece of cardboard, then place the bottom of the bottle over it. The bottle will adhere to the paper and tipping is almost impossible. When you are finished with your nails, either remove the bottle from the paper with a drop or so of polish remover or leave it stuck for the next time.

• **FINGERNAIL POLISH,** *Marking Things with Red:*
1. Levels for measuring amounts in cups or buckets;
2. The start of the washer's rinse cycle on the dial;
3. The VCR stop (or other) button that's hard to find;
4. The light switch that's supposed to be left on;
5. Dab different colors (like white pearl and red) on the "On" and "Off" switches of the remote TV control to ID them without glasses.
6. Marking the line-up arrows on child-proof medicine bottles.

• **FINGERNAIL POLISH,** *Opening the Bottle:* Wind a rubber band around the bottle top to get a better grip on it.

• **FINGERNAIL POLISH,** *Repairing Things with Clear:*
1. Stop runs in stockings—an all-time favorite repair. I carry clear polish in my travel kit for this purpose.
2. Glue thread tail on a machine-sewn button so it won't pop off.
3. Spread some polish around the caps of cologne when you travel, replace the caps, and they'll stay firmly in place—no leaks.
4. Mend small holes in a window screen or door screen.
5. Mend a little hole in a window by building up a few layers of polish.
6. Paint on jewelry to keep it from tarnishing where it touches your skin.

• **FINGERNAIL POLISH,** *Thinning:* Add a few drops of enamel solvent (found in drugstores) to dilute thickened nail polish. Nail-polish remover will thin polish but it contains oil and fragrance and so is not recommended. AVOID the problem of buildup, which prevents a tight seal and allows air to dry out the polish, by wiping the neck of the bottle with nail-polish remover on a tissue or cotton ball.

• **FINGERNAIL POLISH BOTTLE,** *Recycling:* After cleaning thoroughly with polish remover, fill the bottle with white latex paint and you have a little touch-up bottle handy when you need to cover nicks in the wall or for correcting mistakes in your checkbook register. (Latex paint can be homemade correction fluid.)

• **FINGERNAIL POLISH REMOVER,** *For Travel or Office:* Insert a small piece of sponge into a small, plastic trial-size bottle and add just enough fingernail-polish remover to be absorbed by the sponge. Then when you need to remove polish, dip a finger into the container. There's no damage from leaky containers and the smaller one takes up less space.

• **FINGERNAILS,** *Quick-Fix, Keeping Clean:* Dig your fingernails into a bar of soap before starting messy chores like potting plants. The dirt will wash right off when you wash your hands.

• **FINGERNAILS,** *Whitening:* Nail polish can stain fingernails yellow. The trick is to apply a base coat of clear polish before adding color. To remove yellow, put your fingernails in a cut lemon half for a few minutes and they'll be white again. Cleaning things with baking soda also bleaches fingernails white, but it may dry some people's skin and nails so apply hand lotion after cleaning sessions.

• **FINGERNAIL SAVERS:** To make fingernails strong, apply white iodine (from drugstores) every day for seven days and then once weekly. Don't overdo or your nails will become brittle. You can polish nails over the iodine. The following hints help you save wear and tear on your fingernails.
1. Pry up the tabs of soft drink cans with the plastic fasteners from bread bags instead of fingernails.
2. Clip a steel-wool pad with a spring clothespin when scrubbing.
3. Wear rubber gloves to protect hands from cleaning solutions. Reinforce new gloves at the fingertips by inserting tips cut from old gloves.

• **FINGERNAIL TALES:** After reading a *Letter of Laughter* about a waitress whose "fake" fingernail caught on fire while she was lighting a restaurant customer's birthday cake candles, a reader sent in the story about her friend, also a waitress, who, after opening a baked potato for a customer, returned to the kitchen and discovered that one of her "fake" nails was missing. Had she driven a nail into the man's potato? He never complained so she still doesn't know!

• **FINGER PAINTS,** *Healthy-Planet, Homemade Non-toxic Formula:* Mix ½ cup cornstarch with two cups cold water in a saucepan.

Bring the mixture to boil and continue to boil until it thickens. Let cool slightly. Pour equal amounts into clean baby-food jars and color each with food coloring.

• **FIRE DRILL,** *Checklist for Family Safety:* Fire is always possible. It's important to have a home evacuation plan and practice it so that everyone knows what to do in case of fire.
1. What is the quickest, safest way out of your home and out of each room in case of fire? Plan an escape route for each room and plan alternate routes depending on the actual fire location.
2. Practice the fire drills so each person knows exactly what to do and where to go, especially children.
3. Instruct the family to feel any door before opening it to see if it is hot; if it is, don't open it. Heat means fire on the other side.
4. Instruct the family to crawl; don't walk upright. Air is safer near the floor. A major fire danger is smoke inhalation or inhalation of chemical vapors formed when man-made fibers and building materials burn.
5. Have a special place for all to meet outside so that you know immediately if someone is missing.
6. Show children a picture of a fire fighter with all his gear on. Very young children especially may be frightened when they see someone in a mask and the other equipment on and then hide. Teach children never to hide but to get to safety as soon as possible.
7. When fire breaks out, get out of the house and call the fire department from a neighbor's house. Time spent on the phone could be the difference between getting out in time or getting trapped.
8. Always remember that human life is more important than possessions. Don't risk your life for things.

• **FIREPLACE,** *Checklist for Maintenance and Winterizing:*
1. Inspection by a professional chimney sweep and cleaning if needed. If you seldom use your fireplace it may not need annual cleaning but frequent use may cause more creosote buildup inside which can ignite and cause fires.
2. If you have a fireplace insert, which is basically a wood stove fitted into a fireplace opening, the fans and blowers should also be serviced by a professional chimney sweep, and older models need to be checked to make sure they meet current safety standards.

• **FIREPLACE,** *Cleaning Soot and Smoke from White Bricks:*
Step 1. **Caution:** Cover the floor and hearth to protect them from bleach; wear gloves and make sure the room is well ventilated.
Step 2. Mix a solution of half laundry bleach and water and put into a spray bottle.
Step 3. Spray bricks with the mixture and scrub gently with a soft-bristled brush to remove soot and smoke stains.
Step 4. Rinse with plain water.

• **FIREPLACE,** *Energy-wise Modifications:* Despite expensive modifications (fireplace inserts can cost about $850 to $1500 and up, depending upon accessories), fireplaces are not considered to be efficient heaters by any of the experts on this subject. About 90 percent of the heat generated by a fireplace goes up the chimney. Glass doors and inserts not only prevent this heat loss, they prevent embers from popping out and starting fires.
1. Glass Doors: Having the doors closed during burning allows for more air control for combustion but cuts your fire's radiant heat output in half.
2. Fan-driven Heat Exchanger System: This can be built in or added to your fireplace to enable the fire to warm the room's air instead of merely radiating heat on objects in the room.
3. Fireplace Inserts: Basically wood stoves designed to fit into fireplace openings, inserts significantly improve heating efficiency and still retain some of the ambiance. These either fit into the fireplace or protrude onto the hearth. Protruding inserts are more efficient. A well-fitted fireplace insert also limits the amount of warm room air that goes up the chimney and the amount of air in the combustion chamber. Fans and blowers improve an insert's efficiency.

• **FIREPLACE,** *Summer Decorating:* Place several large candles in your fireplace and light them for a cheery glow instead of a dark, yawning hole.

• **FIREPLACE ASHES,** *Time-Saver Cleanup:* Take a tip from barbecuing; line the bottom of the fireplace with heavy duty aluminum foil so that the foil covers the bottom and extends a couple of inches up the sides. Then you can just roll the ashes up in the foil and pitch the whole mess.

- **FIREPLACE BRICKS,** *Removing Smoke and Soot:*
1. An art "kneaded" eraser, sold at art supply stores, lifts smoke and soot stains from some porous surfaces such as brick or stone. Knead the eraser until it's pliable, then press it against the smoke-covered bricks. Repeat the procedure until the eraser has removed the stains. When the eraser becomes soiled, knead it again and continue until the bricks are clean.
2. When a fireplace is surrounded by smoother brick or stone surfaces, a kneaded eraser may not work well to remove all of the stain. After cleaning with the eraser, you may need to wash the brick with a solution of one-half cup trisodium phosphate (sold in hardware stores) to a gallon of water. **Caution:** Always wear heavy-duty rubber gloves to protect your skin when cleaning with strong solutions such as trisodium phosphate and follow the box directions exactly.

- **FIREPLACE CAUTION:** Don't burn heavily oiled papers or chemically treated wood products such as railroad ties or outdoor lumber. Dangerous toxins can be released into the air when these woods are burned.

- **FIREPLACE STARTER LOGS:** Roll old newspapers tightly and fit them into empty cardboard paper towel tubes.

- **FIREPLACE TOOLS,** *Quick-Fix Shine:* Wipe with a kerosene dampened cloth. **Caution:** Allow to dry completely before replacing them near the fireplace or using them.

- **FIRE STARTER,** *In Fireplace or Barbecue Grill:* Light a "puff out proof" birthday candle and poke it into the barbecue coals or fireplace kindling. They'll light your fire because they don't go out!

- **FIRST-AID KIT,** *Checklist:* For camper or boat, put the following in a fishing tackle or old lunch box.
    Different sizes of adhesive bandages; gauze; medical tape; elastic bandage; antiseptic; rubbing alcohol; cotton; swabs, tweezers; ointments; sunburn pain reliever; sun block; small scissors; eye drops; special items needed by family members; a current first-aid book; a snake bite kit (from camping supply stores) if you are going to the wilderness; emergency ice pack (the kind that activate by tapping

them on a hard surface). Then tape some quarters to the lid so that you have change for emergency phone calls.

• **FIRST AID,** *Time-Saver:* Keep the tube of antibiotic ointment in the box with the adhesive bandages.

• **FIRST APARTMENT SHOWER:** If everyone's on a tight budget, including the person moving into a first apartment, hold a shower in which friends and relatives bring no longer needed household items—pots, pans, dishes, flatware, linens—still usable and in good condition. The organizer of the event can keep track of larger items like mattresses, furniture, etc. so that there aren't duplicates of such things. Any leftovers can be given to charity or sold at a garage sale with the money used for things the person still needs.

• **FISH FEEDING,** *No-mess, Especially for Children:* Transfer small amounts of fish food (small flakes or grains) into a shaker-topped spice jar so that food can be sprinkled in. It helps avoid spilled containers of fish food when children are in charge of their own aquarium.

• **FISH STEAMING:** Before placing fish in a steamer, place it in a coffee filter. Then you can lift out the fish whole instead of in a bazillion crumbled pieces.

• **FLASH CARDS,** *Recycling, Quick-Fix:* To make math flash cards, remove the face cards from a deck of new playing cards or one which has some cards missing or marked. To "play" math, shuffle the cards. Then, deal two cards face up and ask your child to add or subtract the numbers. These homemade flash cards also work for multiplication and division of small numbers. The math game can be played in an airplane, too; ask the flight attendant if cards are available.

• **FLASHLIGHT,** *Finding It in the Dark:* Stick on a strip of glow-in-the-dark tape (or paint a stripe with glow paint from a craft store) around the flashlight head, then you'll be able to find it when the electricity is off. **Note:** This is one of those so very practical hints that it's amazing nobody thought of it sooner—obviously you are most likely to need a flashlight when it's too dark to find one!

• **FLEAS,** *Controlling Them:* Persistence pays off. You need to interrupt the flea cycle because fleas multiply rapidly. Under good conditions (good for them, bad for us), ten fleas can produce 250,000 new fleas in less than thirty days! Flea bombs work; so does spraying; but you need to use these chemicals every couple of weeks in the beginning to kill the flea eggs as well as the fleas. Otherwise the eggs hatch and you're back to square one—or itch one!

1. Bathe pets and apply safe dips that control fleas at intervals according to directions. (If your pet is difficult to dip, mix the dip as directed and spray it on the animal.) Never apply several different insecticides at one time, like powder, dip, spray, etc. Never use dog products on cats unless the product label says it is for both animals. Improper use of insecticides can be toxic to animals. **Hint:** If a small cat or dog resists spraying, spray a towel and wrap the animal in the towel, holding it wrapped for about 15 minutes so the chemicals can work.

2. Vacuum your home frequently. Put a few mothballs in the bag and when you vacuum after spraying or flea-bombing the house, throw the bag away. Keep some mothballs in every bag you put in to kill the fleas vacuumed up.

3. Treat your lawn at the same time as you treat your pet and your house; otherwise the fleas just come back into the house. Follow insecticide directions exactly and do not allow children or pets to walk on the lawn while the insecticide is wet or fresh. Pets, especially, will lick the insecticide from their paws and it could be toxic.

4. Your best resources for ridding your home of fleas is your vet or your county extension agent.

• **FLEAS,** *Healthy-Planet Homestyle Remedies:*

1. Wash doghouses with salt water. Scatter fresh pine needles or cedar shavings under your pet's sleeping pad. Keep bedding clean.

2. Wash your pet and yourself with green soap; fleas supposedly don't like the dye that turns soap green.

3. Make a flea trap. Place a light-colored shallow pan filled with soapy water on the floor next to a 25-watt lamp. Position the bulb about 1 to 2 feet above the water. When the lamp is on, fleas are attracted to light so they will jump toward the lamp and fall into the pan. Rinse out the pan each morning and refill.

4. Fleas can jump as far as 12 inches or more in one leap, and can accelerate fifty times faster than the space shuttle—but you know that if you've ever tried to catch one! Wrap adhesive tape around your fingertips, sticky side out, to form a tape band for dabbing up the fleas when you see them. Fleas stick to the tape and can't escape as they do when you try to capture them with your fingers.

• **FLOPPY DISKS,** *Transporting:* Don't leave disks in the car during the summer, heat can warp them and cause other damage. When transporting floppy disks, put them in an insulated box such as a small cooler to protect them and take them indoors with you if you are making a lengthy stop.

• **FLOUR DUSTER,** *Time-Saver:* Place a brand-new powder puff in your flour canister so that it's handy to dust baking pans. Or, keep flour in a large-holed sugar/salt shaker for dusting pans with flour.

• **FLOWER POTS,** *Covering for Dry Arrangements:* Take a piece of fabric (remnant or one that matches the decor) and cut it a few inches longer and wider than the pot. Sew a casing along the top and bottom sides of the fabric. Insert string or elastic to ensure a snug fit. This won't work for a clay pot with real plants because water seeping through the clay can cause mold on the fabric.

• **FLOWERS,** *Arrangements:* If you've received a fresh flower gift arrangement, after the fresh flowers wilt, remove the dried baby's breath and straw flowers used as "filler" and save for your own arrangements of dried or silk flowers. (Look for seasonal sales on silk flowers at craft stores!)

• **FLOWERS,** *Cleaning Silk Flowers and Foliage:*
1. Silk-type Flowers—Usually made from nylon or polyester with plastic stems, can be washed in a basin with cool water and a few drops of mild detergent. Immerse flowers, gently swish around for a minute or so; rinse and air dry.
2. Most Fabric Flowers—Dust with a blow-dryer on cold-air setting. Or, put ¼ cup table salt in a brown paper bag and place the silk flowers stem-up in the bag. Gather the top shut and shake well; they'll come out cleaner.

- **FLOWERS,** *Cutting Stems:* Cut stems underwater and the flowers will last longer.

- **FLOWERS,** *Dye Carnations TWO Colors:* Popular when dyed in school colors, you can do this at home; it takes about two days.
1. Slit the stem in half lengthwise, about halfway.
2. Using two containers, put a cup of warm water in each and add different food coloring to each one.
3. Set the containers next to each other and put each half of the stem into each one. Leave in water for two days.
4. To dye a flower just one color, make a fresh cut at the bottom of the stem and place in a container of water to which food coloring has been added.

- **FLOWERS,** *Graveside Arrangements:*
1. Fill a coffee can with sand for weight; cut several small slits in the plastic lid and replace on can.
2. Arrange silk or plastic flowers and artificial evergreens by putting the stems through the small slits in the lid.
3. Cover the can with foil and add a ribbon for color.

- **FLOWERS,** *Keeping Cut Flowers Fresh:*
1. When you buy a bouquet, remove all leaves below the water level and cut off one-fourth to one-half inch of the stem. Change the water every other day and recut the stems each time.
2. Many of my readers say adding an aspirin or a teaspoon of sugar to the water prolongs the life of cut flowers.
3. Some say cut flowers stay fresh long if you put the arrangement in the refrigerator overnight when nobody is looking at them anyway.

- **FLOWERS/LEAVES,** *Preserving in Wax:*
1. Carefully melt paraffin wax, cool slightly, then dip each leaf or flower in it. Hold with tweezers or tongs to prevent burning your fingers. After dipping, lay the leaf or flower in the proper place directly on construction paper of a suitable color. No need to glue them, the wax sticks them to the paper.
2. The quick-fix way is to press leaves and flowers between two sheets of waxed paper and seal with a hot iron. Don't forget to put an old towel or cloth on the ironing board to keep the wax from getting melted into it.

• **FLOWERS,** *Preserving by Drying:*
1. Ornamental grasses and grains such as wheat or oats: Cut and hang upside down for a week.
2. Fruited branches like bayberry: Cut and arrange without water.
3. Strawflower, globeflower, thistle, statice, and silver dollar: Cut on long stems and arrange without water.

• **FLOWER SEEDS,** *Gathering Free Ones:* If you have cut flowers that you like, dry the flower and collect the seeds for spring planting. To get the seeds out easily, when the flowers are partially dry, put them into a large paper sack. When they finish drying, shake the bag to get the seeds to fall to the bottom. Then, pour the seeds into a clean dry jar and save for planting. Remember to label the jar so you'll know which seeds are which.

• **FLOWERS, SILK,** *Uses:* Use in flower arrangements to replace dead blooms, replace bed flowers in planters, attach to a comb and wear in your hair, pin on your lapel or blouse, scatter when setting table to cover spots on table linen, attach to a fan for a wall decoration.

• **FOAM MEAT TRAY,** *Recycling:*
1. Make a puzzle for small children—draw a picture and color it with acrylic paints. Then cut into puzzle pieces with a single-edged razor or wood-carving tool.
2. Place as pad between china and non-stick cookware to prevent scratching.
3. Place under iron skillets to prevent grease marks on cupboard shelves.
4. Wash and take on picnics for plates and trays.
5. Pad your knees when you are gardening by holding them on with the elastic top of an old sock.
6. Cover with foil and it's a tray for cookies to take somewhere; it doesn't have to come back. Hold the cookies on the meat tray with plastic wrap and add a bow.

• **FONDUE POT,** *Other Uses:* Melt chocolate in it when you make candy or dip pretzels, strawberries, etc.; the temperature is just right.

• **FOOD,** *Freezing:* You can get specific information on freezing garden surplus from your County Extension Agent or cookbooks, but here are some important rules for best results regardless of what you are freezing:

1. Select only best quality foods for freezing because what comes out will be no better than what you put into the freezer! It's like your computer instructor said, "Garbage in; garbage out!"

2. To control growth of bacteria, yeasts, and molds and to stop the chemical action of enzymes, you need to handle, chill, and freeze foods as quickly and exactly as directed for each food.

3. To keep food from drying out and to preserve its nutritional value, packaging should be moisture/vapor proof. Rigid containers and plastic bags need air-tight seals and wrapped foods should be stored in extra heavy aluminum foil, Pliofilm or polyethylene-lined papers. Use freezer tape around the edges of rigid container lids to ensure a seal. Squeeze air from bags before sealing. ALWAYS label containers with the name of the contents, the date of freezing, and, if you rent food lockers, include the locker number on the package.

4. Freeze fruits and vegetables quickly after packaging. Either put them in the freezer a few packs at a time as they are ready or keep packs in the fridge until all are ready. If you use a locker plant, transfer packs from your home freezer to the locker in an insulated box or bag.

5. Don't freeze too many items at one time; the heat given off by non-frozen foods can raise the freezer temperature. Try to place lukewarm products away from those already frozen to avoid heating up frozen products. (Many upright freezers have a special shelf designated for quick freezing non-frozen foods; see the book that came with the appliance.)

• **FOOD,** *Frozen, Storage Time:* How long you can store food before it deteriorates depends on its handling before freezing, packaging materials, storage temperatures, and the type of food. But, no food can be stored forever. (See chart.)

SUGGESTED STORAGE TIMES FOR FROZEN FOODS

- Beef: 6 to 12 months
- Cooked foods: Varies greatly according to product and preparation.
- Fish: Moderate to high oil content (like mackerel, mullet, croker), 1 to 3 months; Low oil content (like flounder, red snapper, redfish, trout), 3 to 6 months.

- Fruits and vegetables: 1 year or less
- Lamb: 6 to 9 months
- Liver: 1 to 2 months
- Oysters: 1 to 2 months
- Pork, fresh: 3 to 6 months
- Sausage: 1 to 3 months
- Poultry: 6 months
- Shrimp: In shell, 6 to 12 months (remove heads which contain fat that tends to get rancid); Peeled and deveined, 3 to 6 months.

• **FOOD,** *General Storage Guidelines:* Wrap airtight and ALWAYS identify and date purchases and make a list to post near the freezer that shows what's inside so that you save time digging around.

1. Processed meats such as pork sausage, luncheon meats, bacon, and hot dogs keep one to two months.
2. Crab, lobster, and shrimp keep one to two months; fresh fish keep six to nine months.
3. A whole turkey will keep for twelve months, a whole chicken for nine months and chicken or turkey pieces for six months.
4. Fresh pork will keep one to two months, pork chops, fresh hamburger, stew, and organ meats keep three to four months.
5. Roast pork and veal keep four to eight months; beef steaks or roasts, six to twelve months; lamb chops or roasts, six to nine months.
6. Leftover ham, either canned or cured, will keep one month; leftover lamb, beef, fresh ham and pork, two to three months; chicken for four months.

• **FOOD,** *Refreezing:* Fruits, vegetables, and meats which have not completely thawed, or those which have been thawed for a short time and have been refrigerated, can be refrozen but they will have lost quality and flavor. Refrozen vegetables toughen. Refrozen fruits become soft and mushy which makes them suitable for cooking but not for eating uncooked.

Low-acid foods like vegetables and meats spoil rapidly after thawing and reaching 45°F; it's not advisable to refreeze them. Acid foods, like most fruit and fruit products are likely to ferment after thawing and reaching 45°F. Slight fermentation of acid foods may change and spoil flavor but the food is not unsafe to eat.

- **FOOD,** *Storage in Freezer in Case of Power Failure:* A filled freezer will stay frozen for about two days; a half-filled freezer may not stay frozen more than one day. Prevent spoilage by packing the freezer with dry ice. About 50 pounds of dry ice will hold the temperature below freezing in a 20-cubic-foot home freezer for two to three days if you act quickly after the power is lost. **Caution:** Don't handle dry ice with bare hands; it burns.

- **FOOD,** *Storage, Freezer Temperatures:* Make sure your freezer stays at 0°F. Fluctuating temperatures cause frozen foods to lose moisture at a faster rate than normal and results in their becoming rough and dry. A full freezer maintains its temperature better than a half-empty one. **Note:** You can always fill up the freezer with ice if you don't have it full of food. Use bagged ice from the supermarket or recycle clean plastic milk jugs; fill with water and keep frozen. The bonus with the milk jugs (or 2-liter soft-drink bottles) is that you can take them camping or on picnics to ice down foods in your cooler and then as the water thaws, you have drinking water.)

- **FOOD,** *Storage, Recommended Temperatures:*
1. Recommended temperatures for preserving raw foods: 30°F to 50°F, depending upon the product. (Most fruit should be stored at 32° to 35° F; fish should be iced and kept at the same temperature.)
2. After processing or cooking, foods should be cooled quickly to below 60°F. If you can't cool the food immediately, it must be kept at a temperature warmer than 140°F until it can be cooled.

- **FOOD,** *Using Thawed Foods:* Use thawed food immediately after thawing. Not all bacteria are killed by freezing; bacteria become active as food thaws so food not used after thawing will begin to lose its nutritional value and spoil.
Foods which have reached temperatures of 40° or 45°F are not likely to be worth refreezing and may be unsafe to eat as well as deteriorated in quality. See FOOD, Refreezing.

- **FOOD PROCESSOR,** *Time-Saver, $aver:* Do all your grinding and chopping in a single once-a-week session so that you can cook creatively when you're short on time. Making your own bread crumbs and buying hunks rather than grated cheese saves money, too. To avoid lots of processor bowl washing, first chop bread crumbs, then grate Parmesan (or other hard cheese), then grate cheddar cheese (soft cheese), and then chop parsley and onions. You can freeze the chopped ingredients and they will still taste fresher than store-bought processed foods.

- **FOOTBALL BIRTHDAY CAKE:** Please see CAKE, Football Shape.

- **FOOTBALL FAN,** *Letter of Laughter:* A fellow Dallas Cowboys fan wrote me that since her husband isn't one, she usually watches her favorite team alone. She told her husband that she wanted to go to a Cowboy game before she died, and she wrote that so far, he'd taken her to two games. She asked if he was being extra nice of if he just wants her to "kick the bucket!" I think he's just nice!

- **FOOTPRINT FINDER:** One reader who often works at projects in her garage while her child naps has a way to make her child feel secure in case she awakens and "can't find Mommy." Mom cuts "footprints" from colored construction paper and lays them out in a path to where she is working so that her child can "follow the footprints to Mommy." The child thinks it's a "wake-up" game.

- **FOOT THERAPY,** *Reader's Solutions to Aching Feet:*
1. Pour baking soda into a pan, add warm water, and soak your feet. The bonus is that the soak softens rough skin. It also softens cuticles so that you can give yourself a pedicure.
2. Put dry beans in your tennis shoes and walk around to get a foot massage.

- **FORMAL DRESS LENGTHS,** *Which Is Worn When:* Just like reading labels at the supermarket to avoid raising your cholesterol level, you read party invitations to avoid raising eyebrows. Invitations usually give the dress expected for men. Different communities have different interpretations of "formal" and if you're new in town, it's best to ask someone who knows. The following are general "rules."
1. When men wear white tie and tails—women wear long or at least ankle-length dresses.
2. When men wear black-tie tux—the event is called "semi-formal"—women can wear short very dressy dresses. Black-tie/cocktail means women can wear strapless with or without beading and other glitter.

3. Men wear dark suit—women wear cocktail or dressy dinner dresses. A dressy dinner dress is less revealing than a cocktail dress and looks right at a restaurant after the cocktail party.

4. For dinner, theater, or symphony in most communities, women wear less revealing dresses made from rich fabrics such as silk. Revealing strapless dresses are appropriate at black-tie events but not at restaurants or dinner parties in someone's home.

• **FORMS,** *Filling Out on the Typewriter:* When each blank's instructions are under the provided spaces, they are easier to read if you begin typing at the bottom of the form and work your way up to the top.

• **FRAGRANCES,** *When You're Allergy Prone:* One reader solved her problem of sneezing when wearing perfume or cologne by adding a drop or two of her favorite perfume to her bath along with a few drops of mineral oil. She's not bothered by the fragrance when it's diluted by bathwater and still enjoys a bit of the scent when it's left on her skin in the mineral oil (which also softens her skin). **Caution:** When adding any oil to the bath, it can make the tub bottom slippery.

• **FREEZER,** *Quick-fix Defrosting Chest-type:* Turn an all-day job into a one-hour one.

1. Unplug the freezer and empty the food into newspaper-lined laundry baskets, cartons, or picnic coolers.

2. Place several large buckets of very hot water inside and shut the lid. Change the water in fifteen minutes. After a couple of changes, most of the ice and water will have dropped to the bottom. Use a wet/dry vacuum or bathtowels to remove it.

3. When clean, wipe up the residue, plug in the freezer, and load it up.

Caution: Always be careful using electrical appliances near water; never stand in a puddle. Make sure the vacuum is rated "WET." A regular vacuum won't work and is dangerous if used for this purpose.

• **FREEZER BOXES,** *Recycling:* Save cake-mix boxes so that when you put food in a freezer bag, you can put the bag into the cake-mix box; it will freeze in a block that will take less space in the freezer than various lumpy-shaped frozen foods. Either label and date the bags before filling them or remove them from the box when frozen hard and then label/date them. You can reuse the boxes throughout your food-processing season.

• **FREEZER LABELS:** Cut labels from foods and tape them to containers or packages when you freeze leftovers to make identification easier. For example, if you freeze spaghetti sauce, cut those words from the sauce jar label and tape to the leftover before freezing.

• **FREEZER MONITOR,** *While You Are Gone on Vacation:* Place a small clear bag of ice cubes in the top basket or shelf of your deep freeze when you go away, and if you find the ice cubes melted and refrozen into one chunk, you'll know that your freezer has been off for a considerable amount of time and that it may not be safe to eat perishable foods. Also, fill up all empty spaces with bags of ice or frozen water in plastic jugs to help keep your freezer cold in case of power outages. This is a good idea anyway because a full freezer uses less energy going on and off to maintain the right temperature.

• **FREEZER SPACE CONSERVATION:** Freeze soups and casseroles in bread tins or square pans. They will be easier to stack and fit.

• **FRENCH BREAD,** *$aver:* If not eaten the day it's baked, real French bread is nearly a brick the next day but wonderfully edible if you turn it into something else.
1. Do what they do in New Orleans; make bread pudding.
2. Slice it, then bake it until it's brown and hard. Then sprinkle the slices with your favorite grated cheese; let the cheese melt for a few minutes in the oven, then float the crispy, cheesy bread slice in a bowl of any kind of soup.
3. To make croutons for salads, soups, or snacks, bake French-bread cubes in a 275°F oven for thirty to forty-five minutes or until golden brown and crunchy. For flavorful croutons, before baking, drizzle over a spiced butter mixture.
Butter Mixture: For one-half loaf of French bread, simmer together one stick of butter or margarine, one teaspoon of minced basil (fresh is best), and two cloves of minced garlic while you cube the bread. Place the cubes in a roasting pan, drizzle spiced butter mixture over and bake as directed above. Store in a tightly sealed plastic container or jar.

4. For a quick breakfast or light supper, cut stale bread into cubes; mix with beaten eggs and fry in a small amount of butter or margarine as you would French toast. Serve with or without syrup.
5. Make French toast! Sprinkle with powdered sugar before serving.

• FRENCH TOAST: Add a dash of vanilla to the batter to perk up the flavor.

• FRENCH TOAST FOR CHOCOHOLICS: One reader mixes a bit of chocolate syrup to the egg coating for French toast and then drizzles a syrup of mixed maple and chocolate syrup on it before savoring it.

• FROZEN JUICE, *Quick-Fix Frustration Avoiding:* Does mixing frozen orange or other juices in the morning rank equally in your life with untangling wire coathangers? Try these ideas.
1. Break up the frozen juice chunks with a potato masher.
2. At bedtime, dump the frozen juice out of the can into a container, add the required amount of water, and place the container in the fridge. When you take it out in the morning, the juice will be thawed and you need only shake or stir.

• FROZEN TREAT, *Recycling, Avoiding Mess with Children (and Some Adults?):* Cut a slit in a clean margarine tub, then poke the stick through the slit so the tub will catch the drips.

• FROZEN TREATS, *No-mess Freezing:* Instead of dribbling sticky spills from a frozen treat "ice-pop" tray when you carry it from counter to freezer, fill the tray with a turkey baster.

• FRUIT, *Homestyle Candied:*
1. Wash and dice fruit peels to appropriate size. You can collect peels as you eat the fruit. Store them in the freezer until you have about four each of oranges, lemons, and grapefruit.
2. Slowly boil two cups sugar, one cup water, and one-fourth cup corn syrup over low heat for 30 minutes. Add peels and cook for 45 minutes to an hour. It's done when all the syrup is absorbed.
3. Sprinkle sugar on waxed paper, lay peels on it and toss to distribute, then allow to dry for a couple of days.
Keeps indefinitely in the refrigerator.

- **FRUIT, DRIED:** Please see DRIED FRUIT.

- **FRUIT JUICE TREATS,** *Frozen:* Pour the liquid "juice" from canned fruit (light syrup is best) into molds or paper cups, add Popsicle sticks and freeze. Enjoy!

- **FRYING-OIL TEMPERATURE GAUGE:** Drop a kernel of popcorn in it. If the popcorn pops, the oil is hot enough to begin frying the food.

- **FUDGE,** *Quick-Fix, Neat Cutting:* After homemade fudge is hard, cut it with a pizza cutter.

- **FUNNEL,** *For Filling Spice Jars:* Cut one corner of an envelope and you have a funnel for filling spice jars or creating designs with colored sugar on cakes.

- **FURNACE,** *Healthy Planet Maintenance:* Keeping your home furnace in good condition can decrease your fuel consumption by as much as 10 percent, which saves about fifty gallons of oil (multiply by oil costs in your area to get saving) and keeps 1,089 pounds of carbon dioxide emission a year from our air. In addition to keeping your filters changed winter and summer, have regular maintenance inspections and cleanings of your furnace by an authorized company. Often, by contracting for regular service (spring and fall each year) you can save on the overall service fee.

- **FURNITURE,** *Renovating:* You may not need to refinish marred and scarred furniture.
1. Scratches can be covered with colored markers, shoe polish, the meat of a pecan or walnut, or commercially prepared lemon or boiled linseed oil.
2. Renew a piece of furniture by cleaning it with mineral spirits (read container for directions and for surfaces it will not damage) or use my Heloise furniture polish. The recipe for Heloise Furniture Polish is: Mix together one-third cup vinegar, one-third cup turpentine, and one-third cup boiled linseed oil. Moisten a soft cloth with polish and rub over furniture, polish with a clean cloth. **Caution:** Never attempt to boil linseed oil; it's highly flammable. Buy it at the hardware store. **Also:** ALWAYS clearly label homemade cleaning compounds and keep them away from children and pets.

• **FURNITURE,** *Repair:* Cover the damaged top of a dresser, buffet, or coffee table with tiles. Look for tile kits in craft or hardware stores; tile is terrific for surfaces which are likely to be in frequent contact with cosmetics or liquids.

• **FURNITURE BOOTIES,** *Recycling Fabric Softener and Liquid Detergent Caps:* Basement furniture and storage cabinet "feet" can get damp (and even wet, if storms cause water on the floor). Putting on plastic cap "booties" keeps them dry and prevents rust stains on the floor from metal furniture or feet with metal "buttons" on them. Please see PLASTIC CAPS, Recycling for other recycling ideas.

• **FURNITURE FINISH,** *Determining Type:* Dampen a cotton ball with nail-polish remover and rub it across a small inconspicuous area like the underside of a chair.
1. If the finish gets gummy or sticky, it's either clear oil-base varnish, shellac, or lacquer. You can use liquid furniture refinisher.
2. If the finish remains intact with no damage, it's probably a plastic-resin base. It can be removed with paint remover.

• **FURNITURE MOVING:** Get a grip on this chore and the furniture by wearing rubber gloves and place rugs like bath mats (upside down if they have rubberized backing) beneath heavy furniture to make it slide across the floor without scratching the flooring.

• **FURNITURE POLISH,** *Healthy-Planet Homestyle Recipes:* Aerosol sprays, chemicals in personal and home products cause air pollution inside our homes. The following polishes are inexpensive and safer. **Caution:** Always test new polishes on an inconspicuous place.
Polish #1: Add 1 teaspoon lemon oil to 2 cups mineral oil for a lemon-scented oil polish.
Polish #2: Mix 1 teaspoon olive oil with the juice of one lemon, 1 teaspoon brandy or whiskey, and 1 teaspoon water. This must be made fresh each time.
Polish #3: Mix 3 parts olive oil with 1 part white vinegar.
Polish #4: For oak furniture, boil 1 quart of beer with 1 tablespoon sugar and 2 tablespoons beeswax. When cool, wipe mixture on wood, allow to dry and polish with a chamois cloth.

• **FURNITURE POLISH,** *Healthy-Planet Touch-up:* On some finishes, apply mayonnaise, rub in and then wipe off, buff with clean cloth to touch up scratches and/or remove white areas from heat. *Letter of Laughter:* When one reader tried mayonnaise to polish a low wooden chest, she applied too much, so she left the room to get a cloth to wipe off the excess. When she returned, she found her big old tom cat purring happily as he licked it off. She says she sat on the floor and laughed while he finished his snack. So, furniture polishing can be fun sometimes!

• **FURNITURE RENTING INSTEAD OF BUYING,** *Checklist:*
1. Most rentals are made with no down payment, no credit check, and you take the item home quickly. Ideal for a week or two until you can buy an item.
2. It's possible to have a part of the rental fee applied toward a purchase price if you have the item a longer time, but you may end up paying two to five times the true cost you'd have paid on a regular credit purchase plan. It's an expensive way to buy.
3. Terms must be disclosed in your rental agreement. Read all of the print very carefully. Also, don't get caught in the $11-a-month trap—how many months or years?

• **FURNITURE TOUCH-UP,** *On Black-Painted Metal:* Buying office furniture at an office supply store "scratch-and-dent" sale is a real bargain. Cover scratches on black-painted metal file cabinets, bookcases, desks, etc. with permanent wide felt-tip marker. Apply wax over the marker to finish.

• **FURNITURE, WATER "BLEACH" SPOT,** *Homestyle Treatment:* Rub the spot with equal parts of toothpaste (not gel) and baking soda, applied with a soft, damp cloth. Rinse out the cloth and wipe off any residue. When the finish is smooth, buff with a clean soft cloth. Restore color and shine by rubbing the spot with the meat of half a pecan, then buff.

• **FURS,** *Storage:* Never store furs in plastic bags; they need to breathe. Instead, make a protective cover from an old sheet or place a king-size pillowcase over the garment. You'll need about a three-inch deep or wide shoulder cover to keep dust off without crushing the fur.

G

• **GARAGE DOOR,** *Automatic:* Always disconnect your automatic garage-door opener when you go on a trip. One never knows when someone else's opener will have the same frequency.

• **GARAGE DOOR AUTOMATIC OPENER,** *Safety Checklist:* Older units don't have the sensitivity devices newer models have. These devices have an emergency reverse built in the motor that reverses the door when it hits something—when five to twelve pounds of pressure is applied.
1. Have all garage doors checked, adjusted, and reset each year. The clutch can stick if not reversed often or not used for long periods of time; doors can change during the years and get out of line.
2. To check if your garage door reverses immediately, put something solid (like a two-by-four) under the door that will stop it. When it touches the item, the door should lift up immediately.
3. If you have any doubt about your unit, get a garage-door company to inspect and adjust it. Non-functioning or improperly functioning automatic garage doors have caused many deaths and injuries.

• **GARAGE SALE,** *Checklist:* First, consider asking neighbors and friends if they want to join you; sales advertised as "several families" or "neighborhood" attract more buyers.

1. Check with your city to learn if there are any garage sale restrictions in your area, and if you need to get a permit.

2. Advertise in local newspapers, noting several of the best or most unusual items for sale in the ad.

3. Separate clothing by size and hang it up for easy pickings.

4. Mark prices on each item so that people don't have to ask. If you know you will have a sale when you are cleaning closets, stick prices on discards immediately so you won't have so many to price the week before the sale.

5. Price items objectively and reasonably. If several families are participating in the sale, use colored stick-on tags with a different color for each family. Then as you sell an item, remove the tag and stick it in a notebook; each family will know exactly how much it has earned.

6. Place large eye-catching items on the lawn or in the driveway to attract customers.

7. Have boxes, newspaper, and paper or plastic bags to package sold items.

8. Be ready for the "early birds" who show up an hour or two early to get the best bargains.

9. Keep someone at the money box at all times and arrange the tables so that buyers have to pass the "checkout" to get out. Of course, never leave the cash unattended.

10. Don't accept personal checks unless you know the buyer. Also, have plenty of change ready at the beginning of the sale. You can keep coins in muffin tins.

11. Since the object of the sale is to get rid of the stuff, be ready to bargain with buyers. There's no money at all if you give or throw away the items, so why not give discounts?

12. Give leftover items to a charity.

• **GARAGE WINDOWS,** *Security:* If you don't want to put old curtains or draperies on them, you can buy window-frosting paint or apply frosted adhesive-backed plastic for privacy. **Hint:** To apply plastic, hold a piece of the adhesive-backed plastic up to one of the panes and cut with a razor for a perfect fit. Remove the backing and apply carefully, smoothing out wrinkles. If you get a small bubble, let the air out with a tiny pin prick and press down.

• **GARBAGE DISPOSAL,** *Cleaning:* If your dishwasher drains through your garbage disposal, flip the unit on when hot soapy water is running through it so it gets a good cleaning.

• **GARBAGE DISPOSAL,** *How to Distinguish It from the Light Switch:* Is there anyone who has not switched on the disposal and got startling noise instead of the light you expected? Mark disposal switch with red nail polish, a stick on frown-face, a red stick-on dot, or colored tape—anything to stop the grating shock!

• **GARDEN,** *Making Indoor Gardens:*
1. Plant Display: Cover the floor with a heavy-duty plastic bag to protect it from water or soil stains. Cover the bag with ceramic tiles and set your pot plants on the tiles.
2. Indoor Winter Garden: If you have a sunny corner, make a pattern or take measurements to a sheet metal shop and have them make a planter deep enough to hold a ficus or other indoor-growing tree and other plants at the base. Fill the planter with a couple of large rocks for bottom-weight, soil and your favorite plants. If you need more light, install a grow light in the ceiling above.

• **GARDEN,** *Planning, Checklist:* Start small by first planning the area in which you spend the most time, then gather information about your yard before you go to your local nursery to get advice and buy bedding plants or shrubs.
1. Measure the space; draw a picture (graph paper helps you keep to scale) or take a photo that shows the plants already there. Note if a fence is near (for climbing or tall plants).
2. Determine if the area gets morning or afternoon sun and how much sun (shade, partial shade, full or partial sun).
3. Check drainage and type of soil (sandy, rich black earth, clay). Garden centers and your county agent can test soil if you bring them a coffee can full.
4. Consider plants native to your area; they will thrive with less effort than "imports."

• **GARDEN EDGERS/STRING TRIMMERS,** *Checklist of Cautions:*
1. Protect your eyes from flying debris by wearing a mask or goggles and protect your shins with soccer pads or pads made for that purpose.
2. The monofilament lines used to cut grass and weeds can damage shrubs, vines, and young trees by removing part of the bark. If you trim so closely that you remove parts of the bark, you can damage the cambium tissue just beneath it, thus preventing the flow of "food" to the root system.

• **GARDEN HOSE,** *Finding the End:* Use yellow paint to mark about 12 inches at the end of the hose. Then you can always find the end when the hose is tangled up.

• **GARDEN HOSE,** *Repair Leaks, Make Irrigation System:*
1. Repair: Lightly sand the area around the holes with sandpaper. Cut patches from an old rubber tube and sand the patch lightly, too. Apply contact cement to both surfaces, let dry to the touch, and press firmly over the hole. Keep the patch in place by wrapping it with black electrical tape or duct tape.
2. Make a Healthy-Planet Drip Irrigation System: With a large nail or ice pick, poke more holes into the hose at strategic intervals on one side. Then lay the hose between garden rows or in flower beds so that water dribbles through the holes into the ground without evaporating as it would with an ordinary sprinkler.

• **GARDENING,** *Growing Tomatoes in Pots:* Read the tags on bedding plants to find out the plant's mature size; larger plants (30 inches high) will grow in two gallons of soil and smaller ones (12 inches high) in hanging baskets. Get advice on growing conditions and methods in your area from local garden columns and your local Cooperative Extension Agent.

• **GARDENING,** *Herbs:* Herbs can grow in the ground, in hanging baskets, in window boxes, in pots (indoors in a sunny kitchen window or outdoors on patio, porch, or apartment balcony), even in a terrarium made from an old fish tank, large jar, or bowl. Remember, the farther away from the kitchen herbs are planted, the less they are used! Contact your local Cooperative Extension

Agent for best ways to grow herbs in your area. (See HERBS, Growing Your Own Herbal Teas.)

• **GARDENING,** *Plastic Mulch:* You can keep soil temperature and moisture constant by "mulching" plants with black plastic—plants are inserted in holes made in plastic sheeting or plastic sheeting is used to cover soil around them. Or, use organic mulch to reduce soil temperature and moisture fluctuations. (In some areas, heavy rainfall can cause rot when plastic mulch is used; check with your county agent or local botanical center/gardening experts.) Always plant in well-drained soil.

• **GARDENING,** *Pruning:* Spruce up your landscape by pruning trees and shrubs.
1. Cut crossed branches that rub each other; remove one to prevent damage to the other.
2. Remove dead or diseased wood. If a plant has been winter damaged, wait until new growth occurs so that you know what parts are really dead.
3. Prune spring flowering plants after they bloom. This includes climbing roses, which also are pruned after spring blooming. Other roses are pruned (in fall in most parts of the country) after their blooming period to a height of 18 to 24 inches, leaving four to six strong canes for the next year's growth.
4. If you have a tree or shrub that has outgrown its location, you can prune as much as one-third of the total plant. However, it's best to prune and shape plants each year on a schedule to avoid such major cutting.

• **GARDENING,** *Sowing Small Seeds, Healthy-Planet Recycling:* Pour seeds into an old spice shaker, put the lid on, and sprinkle over each garden row to evenly disperse small seeds. Cover seeds lightly with soil, water according to package directions, wait for results.

• **GARDENING,** *Watering Shrubs and Trees:*
1. Newly planted trees and shrubs need watering every five to seven days. When you water, apply a thorough soaking so that enough moisture gets to the roots and helps them become well-established.

But, don't water more often than every five days; roots will suffocate because too much water removes oxygen from the root zone.

2. Consider rainfall when making a watering schedule. Even well established trees and shrubs need water when less than one inch of rain falls during a one-week period. If your area hasn't had rain in 7 to 10 days, you'll need to water to maintain healthy plants.

3. Mulching the soil surface maintains moisture and prevents evaporation of water. It also regulates soil temperatures so that you get better root growth.

• **GARDENING,** *Winterizing Checklist:*
1. Mulches: In cold climates, mulches of straw, salt hay, evergreen boughs, pine needles, and non-packing leaves prevent the alternate freezing and thawing of the soil. In warm climates, mulches prevent soil from drying and crusting and keep it cool during hot weather. Before layering mulch on your garden beds, remove dead or diseased plants to ensure a healthy start in the spring. You can find out about winterizing trees and shrubs in your climate from your Cooperative Extension Agent (county agent), local gardening columns, and local garden centers.

2. Evergreens' Care: Evergreens grow in almost every state and they aren't just pretty shrubs. Planted strategically, they can be windbreaks, privacy screens, hedges, background plants, and foundation plantings. Plant evergreens adapted to your local climate so that you don't need to wrap them for protection against winter winds and freezing temperatures and can continue to enjoy seeing them year-round.

When heavy snow and sleet blankets shrubs in the winter, sweep or shake branches to relieve them of the weight as soon as you can because ice buildup can break branches and cause deformed shapes. Winter winds can dry evergreens and cause browning of needles in certain species; water evergreens right up to the freeze-up if your weather has been dry. Because they don't lose leaves in the fall like deciduous trees, evergreens continue to lose moisture by transpiration (through the green needles) all winter long.

3. Roses: If your area temperatures regularly drop below zero, you need to protect your roses.

A. *Climbers:* Remove canes from the supports and tie them together in several places. Place a round object, such as a plastic bucket, on its side at the base of the plant and then bend the tied canes over it. Keep them pinned to the ground by tying them to a notched stake. Then cover the whole plant with at least 10 inches of soil or soil-mulch mixture.

B. *Bushes:* Prune tops back to 6 inches, using slanted cuts at about ¼ inch above the strong outside buds. You should have three healthy canes remaining after pruning. Apply wound compound to the cuts as directed on product. Make a collar around the base of the plant with builder's felt and then mound soil over the stubs for winter protection. The mound should be 8 to 12 inches deep. In the spring, when new shoots are about ½ inch long, remove the mounds by spraying them with the hose.

4. Grass/Lawn, Fertilizer: Apply fertilizer in the fall to encourage root growth and help it build up nutrient reserves for the winter. Good organic fertilizers include cottonseed meal, castor bean pomace, blood meal, composted cow manure or even compost, if you can sift it fine enough for a top dressing. Before you feed the soil, it's best to have it tested by your county agent or local garden center to determine what it needs and the pH of the soil. Fescues and bent grasses grow best in a range of 6.5 to 7 pH; bluegrass, ryegrass and Bermuda grass like a slightly higher level. Most grass plants absorb nutrients best when the pH is 6.5 to 7 and when the lawn soil has been aerated. To aerate the soil, you punch out small cores of soil 2 to 4 inches deep with an aeration machine, which you can rent.

5. Grass/Lawn, Thatching: Early fall is the best time to have your lawn thatched so that the lawn has a chance to recover before growth slows down for the winter. Thatching means removing the thickly matted organic material such as old, dead roots and runners. If your lawn has a very thick layer of thatch, a rake won't do. It's best to rent a thatching machine from your local gardening-supply store or other source. You can toss the material you remove into your compost pile for next spring's fertilizing.

• **GARDENING CALENDAR:** On a gardening calendar, note what was planted when; when plants sprouted; when they were watered, fertilized, and harvested. Then, you can plan the next year by seeing what grew, produced well, and in how much time.

• **GARDENING TIMER:** Take a kitchen timer outdoors with you so that you won't get so absorbed with gardening that you're late for other activities.

• **GARDENING TRAY:** A rubber garbage-can cover will hold small plants, gardening tools and other necessities so that you can carry them around the garden and avoid back and forth trips.

• **GARDEN SEEDLINGS,** *Planting in Egg Cartons:* When planting seedlings in egg-carton cups, place an eggshell half in the bottom before adding soil; then, it's easy to lift the whole seedling at planting time.

• **GARDEN TIMBERS,** *Healthy-Planet Recycling:* Instead of buying garden timbers to border flower or vegetable beds, tie rolls of old newspapers with wire or old panty hose twine and place them end to end.

• **GARDEN TOOLS,** *Avoiding Loss:* Paint handles of your rake, shovel, and other garden tools bright orange so you can see them at a glance if they are left somewhere in the yard. Also, if you lend the tools to anyone, they'll be identified easily as yours (unless the borrower also has orange-painted garden tools). If you frequently lend tools, it's best to put your name on them! I even put my mailing labels on my books so that they get back to me instead of spending eternity on someone else's shelf.

• **GARDEN TOOLS,** *Storage:* Put rakes, hoes, shovels, etc. into a large garbage can and hang smaller tools on S-hooks around the rim. Then you can drag all of your tools along with you as you work.

• **GAS,** *Keeping the Smell Off Hands at Self-serve Stations:* Either carry a rubber glove or cheap, thin sandwich bags in your car's glove compartment (where else would you keep gloves?). Your hands will stay clean and odor-free.

• **GELATIN,** *Why You Can't Add Fresh Pineapple:* Fresh or frozen pineapple has not been processed and so it still contains the enzyme bromelain which breaks down gelatin and won't let it set. Canned pineapple has been processed so it can be added to gelatin.

- **GELATIN MOLD,** *Unmolding:*
1. Dip the mold in hot water to loosen the gelatin and go around the edge with a thin knife.
2. Place lettuce leaves on top of the gelatin with the leaves folded down around the edges of the mold.
3. Place the serving plate (upside down) on the lettuce.
4. Now, holding the mold and plate firmly, turn the whole thing over so that the mold is on top and the plate is on the bottom. Shake the mold gently in a circular motion while holding the plate and mold in place.
The salad should drop down and be centered on the lettuce.

- **GENEALOGY,** *Tracking Lost Relatives:*
1. Main libraries of most large cities have phone books of most major cities for reference use. Check different city's phone books for names and addresses of people with your family name (bearing in mind that spellings change as people move around), and then send out letters in which you explain what you are doing and what information you seek.
2. Whenever you travel to another city or state, look up your family name in the phone book and send more letters.
3. Get a book on genealogy that tells you how you can trace ancestors through citizenship papers and immigration records.

- **GEOGRAPHY,** *Teaching Children (and Reminding Us Adults):* Put up a world map in the television room and then whenever the news or other program goes on, point to where the action is taking place. Even very young children can learn shapes of countries. International Understanding, *Letter of Laughter:* In some countries overseas, people are taught to cross the number 7. I was taught to do this and so was a reader who helped a friend's child to do math homework. Afterward, her friend called to say that the child was worried about his homework because he thought there was no way it could be right—his mother's friend didn't even know how to write the number 7! *Related Letter of Laughter:* There aren't just differences from one part of the world to another; geography affects viewpoints in different parts of the U.S. A Florida child, who was playing outside when snowflakes started falling—a rare event there—ran indoors excitedly shouting, "Look, Mommy, it's raining grits!" She had never seen snow "in real life" before!

• **GERBIL TREAT,** *Recycling:* Give a gerbil cardboard tubes from paper towels and tissue to chew on and shred for its nest; you recycle, and the gerbil gets something to do. Also give a gerbil scraps from salads such as carrot tops, lettuce, and celery about once a week.

• **GET WELL CARD,** *To Cheer Long-term Hospitalized Person:* Provide one flat sheet (or posterboard) and permanent markers of many colors so that well-wishers can write messages on the sheet along with, if they wish, a drawing of something cheery, or something relating to hobbies or interests. You can write the recovering person's name down one side of the sheet and put an adjective describing him by each letter. The sheet or poster can then be a keepsake to remind the recipient that people do care! **Note:** If you decide on a sheet, put something under it when writing so that the markers don't bleed through to hospital bedding or to the patient's leg!

• **GET WELL CARD,** *Mailing to Hospitalized Person:* Put the patient's own return address on the card. Then, if the patient leaves the hospital before the card arrives, the card will follow the person home via the mails.

• **GIFT,** *Ideas for Long-term Hospital Patients:* A calendar and clock to keep track of days, which seem to get lost when you are confined; a personal radio with ear plugs so the patient can listen without bothering others; change for the telephone. Don't bring food unless you find out if it's allowed. If you bring cut flowers, bring a jar or inexpensive vase to put them in; but, you might check first about allergies before bringing flowers!

• **GIFT,** *Ideas for Nursing Home Residents:* Socks; washable and dryable slippers; toothbrushes; large print books; lap quilt or small afghan; soft candy like gumdrops or mints (ask if they should be sugar-free); cards, paper, or postcards with stamps; powder, perfume, and hand lotion for women; shaving supplies for men; family pictures put in plastic pages; a bulletin board for posting pictures and cards; bib made with hand towel and self-gripping tape; gift certificate for hairdo or cut; ride in the car to change the scenery; one fresh flower (or silk flower) and a visit.

Also, gift certificate for manicure/pedicure; coin purse of change for telephone and vending machines; reading materials, including large print magazines and books, if there's a vision problem, and newspaper subscriptions for long-term care patients; radio or tape player with headphones. (Check first if person will use them, some elderly people don't accept the concept.)

Sweaters are appreciated but all clothing must be machine washable and dryable and it's better to buy a size larger so that stiff limbs don't have to bend so much. Find out about the home's identification system and if the resident has labels to sew on garments to ID them; if so, sew them on securely; otherwise mark all possessions with indelible markers.

- **GIFT GUESSING FUN:** Place some loose, raw macaroni in the box with a gift so that those who like to shake before opening will have a harder time guessing what's inside.

- **GIFT IDEAS:**
1. For elderly person—installation of a second phone in a convenient place
2. For friends or relatives—a photo collage that remembers good times together
3. Person in hospital or nursing home—see above

- **GIFT QUILT,** *Wrapping:* Since it's so large and hard to wrap anyway, put it in an under-bed storage container so the recipient can store the quilt in its own box.

- **GIFTS,** *Mailing:* Protect bows in the mail by placing a clean margarine tub upside down over them before packing. Secure with a bit of tape.

- **GIFT OF THOUGHTS:** A reader whose younger brother was in the hospital recovering from a serious back operation wanted to give him something to show that she was thinking about him even if she couldn't visit him often. Recalling that he said he remembered little of his childhood, she bought a school composition book and wrote stories about things he did, about their family's history and about important people in their lives. After receiving the book in the mail, her brother called to say that if she'd sent him a million dollars he would not have been happier. She had included things he'd always wanted to ask his parents but didn't. I think this gift shows that not all treasures cost money!

• **GIFT WRAP,** *Healthy-Planet Paper-Saving:* Wrap a going-away present in a road map to the recipient's destination. Wrap a baby present in a baby blanket or diaper to which you've pinned a rattle or other toys with diaper pins.

• **GIFT WRAP,** *Recycling:* Foil party balloons, after they deflate, can be gift bags. Cut the little neck off the bottom, and staple or tape it closed. Then cut across the top, either in the shape it is or straight. Then insert tissue paper with the gift and tie it shut with a ribbon.

• **GIFT WRAP,** *$aver:* You'll have wrap handy for all occasions if you keep plain white paper, not glossy, on hand. Then decorate and personalize it with stencils and colored markers or crayons. Top your art work with a matching ribbon or bow.

• **GIFT WRAP,** *Storage:* To keep rolls of wrapping paper from getting mashed or mangled with torn edges, slide the roll into the good leg of old panty hose and hang the "leg" on a small nail inside your closet. I think that if you had several rolls to store, you could leave the panty hose whole, put one roll in each leg, let the legs straddle a hanger, and then put the hanger with three to five panty hose paper rolls in your guest closet. Then wait for comments from surprised guests!

• **GIFT WRAP,** *Substitute:* None in the house? Wrap the gift in aluminum foil, shiny side out, covered by a sheet of colored plastic wrap, then add a ribbon or yarn bow or a flower. The foil holds its shape so you don't even need a box. If you cut the plastic wrap larger than the foil and press both sheets together, you don't even need tape.

• **GIFT WRAP,** *When Item Is Large or Awkwardly Shaped:* Place the item in a colored plastic trash or department store bag and tie it shut. If the item is so large that it requires two bags, join the seam where the two bag open-ends come together and cover the joint with a wide ribbon.

- **GIFT WRAP BOWS,** *Healthy-Planet Recycling:* A curling iron will "iron" crumpled bow loops and make them look new in a few seconds.

- **GIFT WRAPPED IN A BOTTLE,** *Recycling:* When a two-liter soda bottle (with opaque bottom "bowl") is empty, run hot tap water over the outside to remove the colored bottom from the clear part. Then cut a hole in the bottom of the clear part and put a gift inside the bottle. Then stick the colored part of the bottle back on and tie a ribbon around the neck. Then, have fun as people try to figure out how you got the gift into the bottle! **Hint:** This also can be a terrarium for small plants, which can also be a gift!

- **GIFT WRAP RIBBON,** *Substitute:* Forget the ribbon? Cut strips of the remaining wrapping paper, curl them with scissors, and glue them to the package. These curls match better than ribbon!

- **GLASS,** *Quick-Fix Cleaning Up Shards of Shattered Glass:* After carefully picking up large pieces, wet a piece of newspaper and then put the paper on the tiny bits and pieces; lift it up and the glass will cling to the paper. Be sure to "blot" the entire floor—when glass shatters, it's amazing how far the pieces will fly!

- **GLASS CLEANER,** *Homemade:* Mix 2 ounces of rubbing alcohol, 2 ounces of non-sudsing ammonia, and 12 ounces of water and store in a clean spray bottle. **Caution:** Always mark containers of home-made solutions clearly to avoid accidents.

- **GLASS DECANTER,** *Removing Stains from the Inside:* Sometimes stains in antique decanters cannot be removed. Some dealers mix about ¼ cup dishwasher detergent compound with hot water. When the water cools, fill the decanter to the top and let soak for a few hours or overnight. A bottle brush may remove stubborn stains, too, but some may remain. **Note:** Since recent studies show that lead leaches from crystal containers into the contents, you may not want to store liqueurs or wines in the decanters for long term. One of my friends displays her favorite decanters with food-coloring tinted water and it covers up some of the stains.

- **GLASS DOOR ON STEREO SET:** If the stereo components are in a shelved cabinet with a clear, glass-only panel door, place a decal near the top so that people can see when the door is open.

• **GLASSES,** *When Two Stacked Ones Get Stuck Together:*
1. Put cold water in the top glass and dip the bottom one in warm to hot water. Gently pull the glasses apart.
2. Or, pour some baby oil or mineral oil between the glasses, allow to set for a while and then gently pull them apart. Wash in hot soapy water and rinse.

• **GLASSES, WASHING BY HAND,** *Avoiding Water Spots:* Wash with the proper amount of liquid dishwashing detergent and rinse in the hottest water safe for the glasses and your hands, and then dry with a soft, lint-free cloth. **Hint:** Wear rubber gloves to get a good grip and protect your hands from hot water. If your area has hard water, rinse the glasses in water to which a splash (less than a glug but more than a spritz!) of vinegar has been added.

• **GLASSWARE, CRYSTAL,** *Spot Removal:* Dip spotted glassware into water to which a splash of vinegar has been added, dry with lint-free dishcloth. Please see GLASSES, Washing By Hand.

• **GLUE,** *Healthy-Planet Ideas:* To avoid harmful chemicals, use staples or reusable metal paper clips and if glue is a must, use a glue stick (made from petroleum derivatives), white glue (made from polyvinyl acetate plastic) or yellow glue (made from aliphatic plastic resin). When using tape select aluminum or brown paper tape.

• **GLUE,** *Homestyle Healthy-Planet Recipes:* Here are some glues you can make yourself with ingredients from your kitchen and hardware or drug stores:
Glue #1 —*Paper, Glass, or Porcelain Glue:* 6 tablespoons gum arabic; 1 cup water; ½ cup plus 2 tablespoons natural glycerin. Dissolve gum arabic in water, add glycerin, and mix well. Apply to both surfaces with toothpick or tongue depressor, hold together for 5 minutes. You'll need to make a fresh batch each time, this doesn't keep.
Glue #2 —*Paper Glue:* 4 tablespoons wheat flour; 6 tablespoons cold water; 1½ cups boiling water. Blend flour into enough cold water to make a smooth paste, boil 1½ cups water and stir into mixture, stirring until mixture is translucent. Use when cold.
Glue #3 —*Paper Glue:* 3 tablespoons cornstarch; 4 tablespoons cold water; 2 cups boiling water. Blend cornstarch and cold water

to make a smooth paste. Stir paste into boiling water, continue to stir until mixture becomes translucent. Use when cold.

Glue #4 —*Paper Glue:* 1/4 cup cornstarch; 3/4 cup water; 2 tablespoons light corn syrup; 1 teaspoon white vinegar. Blend all ingredients above in medium saucepan. Cook over medium heat, stirring constantly, until mixture thickens. Remove from heat. In separate bowl, mix until smooth 1/4 cup cornstarch and 3/4 cup water. Add this to the first heated mixture, stirring constantly. This glue will keep two months in a covered container.

Glue #5 —*Paper Glue:* Blend 4 tablespoons wheat flour and 6 tablespoons cold water to make a smooth paste. Boil 1 1/2 cups water and stir in paste, cooking over very low heat for about 5 minutes. Use when cold.

• **GLUE GUN:** When you use a hot glue gun to glue trim on fabric, press the trim in place with the end of a chop stick (the cheap wooden ones that come in packages) and you won't burn the tip of your finger.

• **GOLD,** *Quick-Fix Polishing:* Wash in lukewarm, soapy water, dry and polish with a chamois cloth.

• **GOLF BALLS,** *Healthy-Planet Recycling Storage:*
1. Egg cartons will hold a collection of golf balls in neat stacks.
2. Rather than have them rolling loose, slip three balls into a tube from a roll of toilet tissue. Mark the outside with the brand of balls inside and then just peel off a portion of the tube to extract a ball.

• **GOURMET COFFEES,** *Quick-Fix Homemade:* The directions for all of them are: Blend ingredients in a blender or food processor until powdered. Substitute appropriate amounts of artificial sweetener for sugar and powdered creamer for powdered milk, if you wish. To serve, put 2 rounded teaspoons of coffee into a cup filled with hot water.
1. Orange Coffee: Blend 1/2 cup instant coffee, 3/4 cup sugar, 1 cup powdered milk, and 1/2 teaspoon dried orange peel.
2. Mocha Coffee: Just mix 1/2 cup instant coffee, 1/2 cup sugar, 1 cup coffee creamer, and 2 tablespoons cocoa.
3. Cinnamon Coffee: Blend 1/2 cup instant coffee, 2/3 cup sugar, 2/3 cup powdered milk, and 1/2 teaspoon cinnamon.

• **GRABBER:** To short? Can't reach? Make a "grabber" for picking up small items, pulling the oven rack in and out, and to hook on other unreachables by attaching a cup hook to one end and a coat hook to the other end of a ½-inch wooden dowel cut to a 3-foot length. (It also reaches that place in the middle of your back that itches!)

• **GRAHAM CRACKER CRUMBS,** *Substitute:* When she had no graham crackers to "crumb" for a dessert bar recipe, one reader substituted 1½ cups crushed ice-cream cone crumbs for one cup of graham cracker crumbs and loved it!

• **GRANDMA/GRANDPA GIFTS TO CHILDREN:** So that very young children who live far away can understand who sent the gift, take a photo of grandma/grandpa holding it and enclose it with the gift.

• **GRANDMA/GRANDPA VISITING:** To keep children occupied while adults talk and visit after dinner at the table, keep a bookcase in a nearby room filled with coloring books, picture books, storybooks, crayons, markers, games, bubble pipes, and plastic building blocks. Adults can excuse the children with some hugs and kisses and continue to talk while the children play. **Hint:** Cut puzzles and games from newspapers and save them for older children to work on. You could even paste them in a scrapbook or spiral notebook to make a puzzle book if you feel ambitious.

• **GRAPES,** *Frosted for Garnish:* Dip fresh seedless grapes in beaten egg white and then sprinkle them with gelatin. Put the gelatin in a salt shaker for easier shaking and use sugar-free gelatin if you are counting calories.

• **GRAPES,** *Frozen Treats:* Buy too many grapes? Freeze grapes in a plastic zipper bag or a well-sealed container for healthy sweet treats. Also, holding a frozen grape in your mouth for a while is a good dieter's trick for fighting an attack of the munchies.

• **GRATING CHEESE OR VEGGIES:** To prevent such "additives" as the tips of your fingers when you grate foods, put a thimble on the finger you usually abuse. For many people, it's the thumb.

• **GRAVY WITH "BLAHS,"** *When Chicken or Turkey Gravy Looks Pale:* Add a tablespoon of low-salt soy sauce or Worchestershire, depending upon your taste. Also, sprinkle paprika into the gravy as it boils to thicken and watch how it gets a nice warm brown color. Paprika doesn't affect the taste unless you add mass quantities of it. **Hint:** Sprinkle in paprika until the color improves, but don't sprinkle directly from the can or jar. Steam rising from gravy or sauces causes powdered spices to cake and loose their zip! Instead, sprinkle some in your hand, then, from hand to pan.

• **GRAVY WITHOUT LUMPS:** Always add powder to liquid not vice versa. Pour liquid (water, milk, bouillon) into a clean, empty jar with a tight-fitting lid. Add flour or cornstarch, screw on the lid, and shake until all is completely blended. Add mixture to casseroles, soups, gravies, etc.

• **GRAVY SERVER:** Try a large teapot for no mess gravy pouring at family dinner. It'll stay warmer, too, with a lid and tea cozy on it.

• **GREETING CARD DISPLAY:** Toss Christmas and other greeting cards into a pretty basket and keep it where it can cheer you up anytime.

• **GREETING CARDS,** *Having Spares:* When you shop for greeting cards, buy spares so that you have some handy when you can't go shopping. Watch for gift wrap sales, too, and stock up.

• **GREETING CARDS,** *Healthy-Planet Recycling Used Ones:* If you don't recycle them yourself by cutting off the fronts and using them for gift tags or postcards (draw a dividing line for message and addresses), call your local United Way and ask for information Referral Service (most have one) and they'll try to find a local organization that can use them. Sometimes pre-school or day-care centers and elementary schools can use the cards (and suitable magazines) for arts and crafts projects. **Hint:** If you include a handwritten note in your Christmas card, write the current Christmas message on last year's card fronts and each card you received will be used twice!

• **GREETING CARDS,** *Time-Saver:* When you buy extra cards, file them in an accordion record file or pattern file box according to "birthday," or "get well," etc. and you won't have to dig through them all when you want one. Toss a perfume sample from a magazine page in with them and they'll smell nice, too.

• **GRILLED CHEESE SANDWICH,** *Quick-Fix, No Mess, Less Fat:* Toast two slices of bread in the toaster, put cheese in between, zap in the microwave for 20 to 30 seconds (depends on type of cheese and your microwave wattage). No frying, less mess and fewer calories! **Hint:** If you like the toast to stay crisp, put the sandwich on a paper plate, which absorbs the moisture, before zapping.

• **GROCERY BAGS,** *Healthy-Planet Recycling for Kindling Wood:*
1. Put kindling wood in paper grocery sacks and then put sack and all into the stove or picnic bonfire as a firestarter.
2. When you buy charcoal for the grill, divide it into paper grocery sacks so that you have a "dose" ready for the fire without having to handle the charcoal again.

• **GROCERY SACKS,** *Easy Lifting:* If the handles of heavily loaded plastic grocery sacks cut into your hands when you carry them into the house, try hooking three to five bags on a boot hook (the kind used to remove cowboy boots). No more pain!

• **GROUT,** *Cleaning:* When bleach won't work, you may have to replace the grout. Oil that gets into grout of ceramic-tiled kitchen floors cannot usually be removed. You have to remove the stained area and regrout. An alternative can be to stain all of the grout, but that's a major project.

To avoid this problem, protect grout from stain, mildew and washing out by spraying a water-seal product on the area. Spray, then wipe excess from tiles while the product is still wet. Seal will remain in the grout and make it look good longer.

• **GUEST ROOM WELCOME:** This cute saying could be embroidered or printed on a plaque to make guests feel at home.
You are welcome here,
Be at your ease,
Go to bed when you're ready,
Get up when you please.

H

• **HAIR,** *Checklist for Choosing Shampoos:* Each shampoo seems to have some magic ingredient—wheat germ oil, aloe, collagen, jojoba, sheep's placenta, ammonium lauryl sulfate—that also makes the price "magic." I use baby shampoo or any shampoo that's on sale because I've found that the result is the same, no matter what I use. I often dilute my shampoos; they last longer and are easier to rinse off. Now, research reported by the University of California, Berkeley Newsletter confirms that many claims are meaningless and costly ingredients just go down the drain. Here's some help when you read those labels.

1. Washing Oil Out: You can wash your hair with bar soap but it leaves a film. Shampoos have detergent to remove oil and dirt. Oily hair shampoos just have more detergent. Most shampoos have foam boosters because suds make people feel clean.

2. Putting Oil In: After detergents take the oil out, people want conditioners to put it back in. Using a separate conditioner makes hair feel better to the touch. Conditioners include lanolin, balsam, glycerol, propylene glycol, and other oils.

3. Other Additives: Proteins such as keratin or collagen are supposed to make hair look fuller and botanicals like mint, chamomile,

or other "natural" herbals are supposed to add luster. These usually just add price and go down the drain when you rinse. Other additives are scents, colors, and preservatives. Citric acid is added to counteract the alkalinity of shampoos—the "pH"—but makes little or no difference to your hair's look.

4. Dandruff Shampoos: Contain active ingredients like pyrithione zinc, selenium sulfide, a sulfursalicylic compound or coal tar. They remove dandruff if used frequently but so do ordinary shampoos. Everyone has some dandruff; it's natural for the skin to shed its outer layers. If you have severe dandruff that causes crusting, itching or redness, see a dermatologist. The same advice applies to other scalp disease.

5. Hair shafts are dead tissue; the only cure for split or roughened hairs is to cut off damaged parts.

6. Price does not determine shampoo quality and most people can't tell one shampoo from another in blind studies. Try using less. Also, you don't need to lather up twice, especially if you shampoo frequently.

• **HAIR,** *Creme Rinse:* Laundry fabric softener diluted 1 teaspoon to 1 cup of water can be used for creme rinse after you shampoo. I've done it for years and it makes my hair manageable and soft.

• **HAIR,** *Dyes, Healthy-Planet Alternatives:* Many hair dye products contain potentially carcinogenic chemicals. They also contain chemicals which are absorbed through the scalp and which can cause problems for people who are allergic to them or have sensitive skin. These chemicals include coal-tar dyes, ammonia, detergents, hydrogen peroxide, and lead.

1. Henna is the safest commercial hair color product, henna can darken or highlight hair and it washes out gradually over a six-month period. Generally speaking with plant materials like henna, often sold at health food stores, you process the product as directed and then strain and cool before using. Pour the liquid through the hair 15 times, catching it in a basin so that you can rerinse with the same liquid. Then wring out excess, allow to remain in hair for 15 minutes and rinse with clear water.

2. To lighten hair: rinse with mixture of 1 tablespoon lemon juice to 1 gallon warm water.

3. To darken hair: rinse with strong black tea or black coffee.

4. To get red tones: rinse with strong tea of rosehips or cloves, or use strong black coffee.

5. To cover gray, simmer ½ cup of dried sage in 2 cups of water for thirty minutes, then steep for several hours. Apply tea to hair after it cools, allow to dry, then rinse and dry hair again. Apply weekly until you have the shade you want and then monthly to maintain the color.

• **HAIR,** *Healthy-Planet Homestyle Shampoos:*

1. Castile Soap: It's tried and true for shiny hair! Grate castile bar soap and mix it with pure water in a blender or food processor, then blend 1 cup of this liquid with ¼ cup olive, avocado or almond oil and another ½ cup distilled water. Store in properly marked squirt bottle. Use sparingly.

2. Baking Soda: Here's my baking soda again! This time it's a dandruff remedy. Wet your hair, then rub in a handful of dry baking soda, then rinse. This may make your hair seem drier than usual for the first weeks of use but soon your hair's natural oils will make your hair very soft.

(Many commercial shampoos are not as benign as they used to be; some contain ammonia, potentially harmful colors, cresol, detergent, EDTA, ethanol, formaldehyde, fragrance, glycols, nitrates/nitrosamines, plastic (PVP), sulfur compounds and a lot of other ingredients, such as the coal-tar solutions or recorcinol used in anti-dandruff shampoos, which can cause harm to internal organs if swallowed; some can be absorbed through the skin.)

• **HAIR,** *Making Thinning Hair Look Thicker:* After using the following methods, don't brush too much because you'll flatten your poufed hair.

1. Blow-dry in the opposite direction, starting at the roots, from the way you normally style or brush it.

2. Blow-dry your hair while bending forward from the waist.

• **HAIR,** *My Favorite Homestyle Conditioner:* Massage a dollop or two of real mayonnaise (not salad dressing) into your hair before shampooing; wrap your hair with plastic film, and cover all with a bath towel. Leave on for at least thirty minutes; wash hair as usual with warm or cool water, not hot. Rinse very well and enjoy great feeling hair.

• **HAIR,** *Removing Green Resulting from Pool Chlorine:* Try dissolving six to eight aspirins in a glass of warm water; saturate hair strands; leave on for ten to fifteen minutes; rinse thoroughly and shampoo. Also look for special shampoos formulated to remove discoloration caused by chlorine and minerals. They are usually referred to as swimmer's shampoo and can be found in beauty supply stores and some hair-care products sections in supermarkets.

• **HAIR,** *When the Perm Is Too Curly/Wavy:* Speak to the salon about the problem. If nothing can be done, styling with a hair dryer will straighten it out somewhat. Other ways to help the curl relax include applying a conditioner after each shampoo and controlling your hair with mousse or gel.

• **HAIR ACCESSORIES,** *Recycling for Other Uses:* If you cut long hair short, your favorite barrettes, ponytail rings and other hair accessories can be recycled as scarf rings and clips.

• **HAIR CONDITIONER,** *Other Uses:*
1. Smooth on conditioner after bath or shower and it's a nice body lotion.
2. Substitute conditioner for lather when shaving your legs; it won't leave your skin as dry as soap or shaving cream.
3. Put conditioner in warm water for a manicure/pedicure soak.

• **HAIR RIBBONS,** *Quick-Fix:* Iron them with the hair curler!

• **HAIR SHAMPOO/CREME RINSE,** *Slippery Containers:* Wrap a couple of fat rubber bands around your shampoo and creme-rinse bottles and they won't slip out of your hands in the shower.

• **HAIR SPRAY,** *Keeping It Off Earrings and Out of Ears:* Cover your ear on the side you are spraying with the spray-can cap.

• **HALLOWEEN,** *Trick or Treat Non-Sweets:* Instead of candy, buy small party-favor toys, balls, baseball cards, and other inexpensive items and let children pick some from a bowl.

• **HALLOWEEN PUMPKIN,** *Trick and Treat:* After carving, sprinkle the inside of the lid and inside bottom of the pumpkin with a bit of nutmeg and cinnamon. Then when you light a candle, "Jack-O'-Lantern" will look bright and smell nice, too.

• **HAMBONE BROTH:** Place the bone with leftover ham still on it into a large pot and cover with water. Bring to a boil and boil until all meat falls off. Cool and skim off the fat. Place the ham and broth into small individual containers and freeze. Then you can use the broth to season beans, vegetables, and more.

• **HAMSTER CATCHER:** When your hamster escapes, find a box with a lid and line the bottom with a small towel or crumpled newspaper. Make a hole in the lid large enough for the "escapee" to drop through, then lay a paper towel or hanky over the hole and put some food on it to entice the hungry hamster to the trap.

• **HAMSTERS, GERBILS, MICE AS PETS:** Rodent pets (Yes, they are rodents but nice ones!) are low-cost and easy upkeep pets, especially in apartments where dogs and cats aren't allowed.
1. Housing: One or two can live nicely in a ten-gallon aquarium with a wire screen on top or in any metal cage that same size—any "home" that they can't chew their way out of.
2. Needs: Small glass ashtrays make good feeding dishes. Food is usually sold in supermarkets or grocery stores. Treats include carrots or celery and unsalted sunflower seeds. A water bottle is a less messy way to give them water. They love to chew ice-cream sticks. An exercise wheel is important so they can run for health.
3. Maintenance: Cages need cleaning every couple of weeks and they will be almost odor-free. They are nocturnal—they'll do most of their running in the evening so a child can enjoy them after school but they can be noisy if kept in a child's bedroom overnight. Be sure to put some lubricant on the exercise wheel's moving parts!

• **HANDBAGS,** *Recycling Broken/Worn Ones:* They can hold craft items to work on when traveling or visiting, store small items in the closet, hold tools for odd jobs around the house, hold tools and other emergency items kept in a car trunk, organize temporary files, and more.

• **HANDBAG SHOULDER STRAPS,** *Prevent Slipping:* If one strap keeps slipping off your shoulder, join the straps by machine-stitching a

2-inch strip of self-adhesive tape to them; they will automatically stick together and you can still pull them apart when you want to. If the straps are too thick to stitch yourself, you can have a shoe repair shop do it.

• HANGERS, *Color-Coding to Organize Closet:* Durable plastic hangers in assorted colors can help you find your clothing quickly. One reader codes blue for blouses, red for slacks, yellow for skirts, white for dresses and so on and can always find blouses if they've been "misfiled" among the skirts or slacks.

• HANGERS, *Making Them Non-Slip:* When garments slip off their hangers, punch a hole in the center of a piece of fabric and slip the fabric over the hanger hook so that it hangs over and covers the "shoulders" of the hanger. Some fabrics can be old sheets cut to size, leftover yardage from sewing projects, an old diaper, terry-cloth towel, or just an old T-shirt hung normally.

• HANGERS, *When Wooden Ones Snag Clothing:* Sand them smooth with sandpaper then brush on clear shellac.

• HANGERS, *Recycling Wire Ones:* If your dry cleaner doesn't take them back, call local thrift stores, preschools, or Scouting organizations; they may be happy to have them for hanging clothes or for crafts.
1. Bend the wire into a circle, cover with old panty hose and you have a small leaf skimmer or paint strainer.
2. Remove the paper tube from pants hangers, bend the wire ends inward and you have a paper towel holder outdoors or when camping.
3. Straighten and hang a bird feeder from it; squirrels can't get to the food.
4. Unhook one end of a pants hanger, put rolls of gift ribbon on it and replace the end. You have a multi-roll dispenser.
5. Bend both "arms" of a wire hanger upward to hold spaghetti-strap garments in the closet or to hang bra straps on for drying indoors.

• HANGING LIGHTWEIGHT THINGS ON WALLS: To hang lightweight wall decorations, calendars, etc. without damaging walls, with pliers break the eye off a sewing needle, and use the needle as a nail.

When you need to remove it, just pull it straight out from the wall and close the tiny hole with your fingernail.

• **HEADBANDS,** *Recycling, Storing Neatly:* Empty three-liter soft-drink bottles, washed and dried, will hold headbands neatly and the ones with bows or ruffles won't get crushed.

• **HEATING,** *$aving, Energy-Saving:*
1. Practice "zone heating." Close the registers or heating vents in all unused rooms; heat only the rooms you actually live in.
2. Room heaters are not as efficient as furnaces, but will heat rooms or areas with less energy consumption. They generally plug into a 110-volt socket. Check the label for wattage, too. The rule of thumb is that you need one watt per cubic foot of air volume in the room. Also see ENERGY saving ideas.

• **HEIRLOOMS,** *Passing Them On:* Many people like to pass on family heirlooms before they pass on themselves because they enjoy seeing the heirs using them. For example, a silver service that is seldom used by parents who don't entertain much anymore is a treasure to a daughter who is just beginning to entertain more formally. The trick is to give possessions when the time is right, to the child or children who will really love, use, and appreciate them. A good time is on happy occasions when all the people involved are present so they all share lifetime memories. My father and I "share" certain special family treasures that we trade back and forth.

• **HELPING PEOPLE,** *Checklist, How to Offer Help So That It Can Be Received:*
1. Be specific about what you can do. Say: "I'm going to the dry cleaners on Wednesday. I can stop by and get your cleaning, too." Or: "I'm grocery shopping on Friday. If you make me a list, I'll shop for you." Or, "I'm getting my hair done (or going to the movies, taking a class) Thursday, would you like to go with me?"
2. If you take over a casserole, and this is a wonderful help, especially when there's a new baby in the house or the family cook is sick, take it in a disposable container, and maybe include paper plates, napkins, and cups so there's no clean up or returns.
3. Offer to mail items or buy stamps for shut-ins or to take a shut-in's pet to the vet or groomer.

4. If you have a friend who is disabled, or a friend with a periodically disabling disease like arthritis, offer to change beds, dust, wash windows, clean blinds, rake leaves, sweep sidewalks, do minor repairs, or other everyday chores which are difficult for someone who isn't agile.

5. Offer to host a birthday party for a disabled friend's child or to take the child somewhere where the friend can't go, such as trail hiking or roller-skating. If your friend is having a party, offer to come over an hour early to help in preparations.

6. People who have disabling or chronic illness say they would rather answer questions about their problems than have people wonder about or assume certain things about the illness. And then, after the questions are answered, they would like to move on to lighter conversation and not dwell on illness. Also, a hug is always welcome even if it's awkward to hug someone in bed or in a wheelchair and, if your friend has arthritis, a hug is better than a handshake which can be painful to arthritic fingers.

• **HEMMING,** *Time-Saver:* Instead of threading just one needle, thread two or three before you start to hem a garment. Then when you run out of thread, you can pick up another threaded needle without stopping and breaking your work rhythm.

• **HEMMING-TAPE MISTAKE:** If you put iron-on hemming tape on the wrong side of the fabric, try this:
Place a damp cloth over the tape, hold a warm iron on it for at least ten seconds, then pull off the tape while it's still warm. It may take several tries. If residue remains, hold a steam iron above the area and the residue should disappear into the fabric. Wash as the care label directs.

• **HEMS,** *Repairing Suede or Leather:* These garments are hemmed with acrylic latex glue (water-based and clear-drying) made especially for leather and suede and sold at leather-craft stores.

• **HERBS,** *Growing Your Own Herbal Teas:* There are many herbs which grow indoors as well as outdoors. Grown indoors, herbs can be decorative houseplants as well as tea leaves. **Caution:** Do not experiment with unfamiliar herbs when making homemade tea blends. Some herbs are actually poisonous (like some ferns) and others, like some mints, have medicinal properties that could be harmful to people with certain health conditions. Get information from your county agent or local botanical center. (See GARDENING, Herbs.)

• **HERBS,** *Preserving for Tea* (See **Caution** above):
1. For herbs that don't dry well, brew a concentrate and freeze it in cubes so that you can thaw one cube for a cup of hot tea or add melted cubes to lemonade. To steep: mash leaves, cover with hot water, allow to steep for a day or so, strain liquid, and freeze in cubes.
2. To make tea "infusion," strip leaves from stems and chop; measure twice as much water as you have chopped leaves; add leaves to water when it boils; boil for 5 minutes; let cool; strain into a jar for storage in the fridge. For a cup of tea, add twice as much boiling water as infusion, sweeten to taste with honey; lemon, optional.
3. To dry herb leaves for tea: Cut branches just as they mature or flower, hang for about a week in an airy, shady place, then crumble dried leaves into airtight jars. To make tea from dried leaves, steep in boiling water. To make one cup of tea, place a few leaves in a cup; pour boiling water over them; add honey and lemon juice to taste.
4. Mint is a common tea herb. To make tea from fresh mint, choose larger leaves or pinch off leaf clusters at the stem end (instant pruning); drop a handful or so into a quart of boiling water; steep 10 minutes; strain and serve. To dry mint leaves for tea, cut branches before blooming, hang in a shady place until dry, then gather dried leaves and store in an airtight jar.

To make frozen concentrate, add about 2 cups coarsely chopped mint leaves and stems to a pint of boiling water; allow water to boil, remove from heat, cover, let cool about 1 hour; strain; freeze in ice-cube trays. For tea, heat a cube with enough water to make 1 cup or add cubes to other teas, punches, or soups. For a special treat, freeze a block of mint concentrate (with a nice sprig or two in the middle for decoration) and let it float in the punch bowl.

• **HERBS,** *Making Your Own Herbal Vinegars:* Heat vinegar in an enamel pan and pour it into a vinegar bottle; add one or several culinary herbs to taste. Do not let vinegar boil. Let the mixture steep for two weeks before using. Any type of vinegar can be used; it depends upon your preference.

• **HERBS,** *Making Herbal Butters:* To one stick of unsalted butter, add 1 to 3 tablespoons dried herbs or 2 to 6 tablespoons fresh herbs, ½ teaspoon lemon juice, and white pepper to taste. Combine ingredients and mix until fluffy. Pack in covered container and let set at least one hour. Any culinary herbs and spices may be used. (See Herbal Combinations below.)

• **HERBS,** *Making Your Own Herbal Combinations for Cooking:*
1. Fine herbs: Includes parsley, chervil, chives, French tarragon (and sometimes you can add a small amount of basil, fennel, oregano, sage, or saffron).
2. Bouquet garni mixtures: Bay leaf, parsley (two parts), thyme. The herbs may be wrapped in cheesecloth or the parsley can be wrapped around the thyme and bay leaf.
Note: When you cook herbs, bay leaf, whole peppers, etc. in soup or stew, put them in a mesh or perforated metal tea ball so that they are easily removed and nobody bites into a pepper ball or risks choking on a piece of bay leaf.
3. Barbecue blend: Cumin, garlic, hot pepper, oregano
4. Italian blend: Basil, marjoram, oregano, rosemary, sage, savory, thyme
5. Vegetable herbs: Basil, parsley, savory
6. Tomato sauce herbs: Basil (two parts), bay leaf, marjoram, oregano, parsley (optional additions could be celery leaves, cloves)
7. Salad herbs: Basil, lovage, parsley, French tarragon
8. Poultry herbs: Lovage, marjoram (two parts), sage (three parts).
9. Fish herbs: Basil, bay leaf (crumbled), French tarragon, lemon thyme, parsley (options include fennel, sage, savory)
10. Egg herbs: Basil, dill weed (leaves), garlic, parsley

• **HINT, POSTING FOR PROMPT USE:** When you cut out diet or food hints, put them on the fridge door; if you cut out makeup or bathing hints, tape them inside the medicine cabinet. When hints are stored where they'll be used, you're more likely to remember to try them.

• **HOLIDAY DECORATIONS SWITCH:** When holiday decorations replace knickknacks in certain places, solve the problem of where to safely put the knickknacks by storing them in the containers that normally hold the holiday decorations.

• **HOLIDAY DECORATOR LINENS:** Wait for after-holiday sales to buy Christmas Santa, Easter Bunny, Valentine Heart and other fabrics and then make special holiday pillowcases for cheery decorations in children's or adults' rooms.

• **HOLIDAY DESSERT TOPPING:** Add a few drops of food coloring to dessert topping to make it festive. Try orange-colored topping on a Thanksgiving pumpkin pie, red and green for Christmas, red for Valentine's day, green for St. Patrick's day, or a favorite color of the birthday person.

• **HOME BUILDING,** *Photos:* Photograph everything that goes underground like pipes, wires, septic tank, gas lines and then it will be easy to find them when you need repairs—hopefully, with a new home, you won't need repairs too soon!

• **HOME BUYING,** *Checklist:*
1. The general cost formula is that the home price should not exceed two to two and a half times your annual family income or the monthly mortgage, electric, water, and maintenance bills should not exceed 25 percent of your total monthly income.
2. Get a house inspector or construction expert to look for flaws, damage, and possible repair problems in the future before you buy, unless the price is such a bargain that the repair costs are not a factor.
3. To make sure you've chosen the right house, consider distance to schools, availability of bus service, how long it takes family members to get to work or school.
   Are there shopping malls, grocery stores, post office and hospital nearby? How high are area taxes? Are ambulance and fire service available?
   Are any unusual restrictions enforced? Ask area neighbors if they have encountered any unique problems.

• **HOME PERMANENT,** *Catching Drips:* Put on a terry-cloth sport/exercise headband and tuck cotton inside. It will catch drips better than cotton stuck to your skin with petroleum jelly, the usual drip solution.

• **HOME PERMANENT,** *Sectioning Off Hair:* If you don't have hair-pins or clips to hold sections in place, try twist-ties. Just make sure no metal wire touches the permanent solution because it might discolor.

• **HOME PERMANENT PAPERS,** *When You Have Leftovers:* Carry in your purse to absorb oil on your face without disturbing your makeup and to blot lipstick. They work so well, you may want to buy the papers for that purpose from a beauty supply house.

• **HOME PERMANENT PAPERS,** *Substitute If You Run Out:* Coffee filters cut to the proper size.

• **HOME SECURITY:** One reader puts a large (size 14), dirty pair of men's work boots outside her front door to dissuade would-be intruders. She occasionally runs a little water over them to make them appear as if they had recently been worn. This may be false security, but if I were an intruder, I'd think twice before risking confrontation with a guy who wears size-14 boots!

• **HONEY,** *Reclaiming Sugared:* If honey gets sugared in storage, place the jar into the microwave for a couple of minutes and it will return to a pourable state. **Caution:** Microwave time will vary according to amount; better to zap it less time than too much. Also, do not place metal containers in the microwave and for extra caution, place the honey jar in a dish you know is microwave safe.

• **HONEY SUBSTITUTE:** Generally corn syrup can substitute for honey in most recipes but since it's not as sweet as honey, the dessert won't be as sweet. As with all substitutions, the texture and flavor can be slightly altered.

• **HORSE BLANKETS,** *Recycling:* Instead of putting saddle pads right on the horse, first put down an old baby blanket. It's soft on the horse's back, keeps the pads clean and is easier to launder in the machine than bulky pads are.

• **HORSES' FEEDING CAUTION: Note:** I'm not sure how many hints books have "horse hints" but I live in Texas where horses are working animals as well as "pets." However, horses graze in fields all over the country where dangers lurk. This warning information was sent to me from the Illinois Animal Poison Information Center. 1. Partial List of Plants Poisonous to Horses—Alsike clover, bladder pod, black locust (strip bark), black walnut, bluebonnet (lupines), buckeye, castor bean, chokecherry (wilted leaves), cocklebur, coffeebean, corn cockle, death camas, ivy bush, Jerusalem cherry, jimsonweed, Klamath weed, lantana, larkspur, laurel, laurel cherry, locoweed, milkweed, oleander, pigweed, red maple, rhododendron, tobacco, wild jasmine, yellow star thistle, yew, and rayless goldenrod.

2. Ingestion of fresh summer annual forages of Johnson grass, Sudan grass, and common sorghum causes a condition in the southwestern U.S. called enzootic equine cystitis and ataxia. This condition is only from eating FRESH Sudan or grazing on the plant in pasture. Clinical signs are straining to urinate, dribbling urine, lack of coordination, and mares who appear to be in constant heat.

3. Fescue grass is a commonly fed pasture forage. There is a caution against allowing brood mares to graze fescue during the last three months of gestation. If mares cannot be removed from fescue pastures, they should be feed good quality alfalfa hay.

4. Check areas near fence rows, ditches, and springs where poisonous plants flourish. If some plants are seasonal or hard to control, horses may have to be removed from some pastures at certain times of the year.

5. Horse owners can get help from local veterinarians, extension advisers, or local plant stores.

• **HOSE $AVER:** My readers say that if you put new panty hose into the freezer for twenty-four to forty-eight hours, then allow them to thaw, they don't run nearly as often.

• **HOTEL RATES AND VACANCIES:** While major hotel/motel chains have 800 numbers to call for reservations, calling the individual hotel, even if it costs a dollar or two, may help you get a discount and, when a special event has filled your destination city's hotels, you may be more likely to get a room since the national reservation office may not be aware of recent cancellations at individual sites. **Note:** Since larger cities often have several locations of national chain hotels/motels it's best to make sure you're staying on the most convenient side of town. Also, you'll need to tell the airport taxi driver which one to take you to.

• **HOT TUB,** *Recommended Temperatures:* My sources say the maximum temperature should be 100°F; heat stroke can occur in some people at temperatures above 104°F. Many people find that 95°F is comfortable. **Caution:** People with certain health problems, such as high blood pressure, diabetes, or epilepsy, shouldn't soak when home alone.

• **HOUSE,** *Checklist for Making Your House Appeal to Buyers:*
1. Get rid of outside clutter; trim bushes, weed flower beds, and mow grass to give a good first impression. Also repair or remove fences if they are unsightly.
2. Clean doors and windows and sweep the sidewalks and driveway. Remove stains from sidewalks, driveways, and patios.
3. Clean the entire house inside, paying special attention to the kitchen, bathroom, and master bedroom. Make the stove, oven, sinks, and floor shine and fix any drippy faucets.
4. Clean, orderly closets and cabinets appear larger and make the whole house appear less cluttered.

• **HOUSE,** *Selling Trick:* As close to showing time as possible to allow for cleanup time, bake a batch of cookies to entice buyers with a homey, friendly aroma. (Refrigerator cookies will do, there's less cleanup, too!) Or, simmer a potpourri in your microwave!

• **HOUSE,** *Selling Yours:* Ask your friendly real-estate broker the following questions before you allow it to be listed.
1. Will you work up a fact sheet and brochure on my house?
2. Where will the sale be advertised and how often?
3. Will my house be placed in the multiple-listing service?
4. Will other brokers be invited to an open-house showing?
5. How will you publicize open houses and who will attend?
Interview at least three brokers and pick the one who best answers your questions. Don't be surprised if the broker says your asking price is too high, most people overevaluate their houses. The broker has to find someone who loves your home as much as you did and is willing to pay the asking or negotiated price for it.

• **HOUSEHOLD INFORMATION NOTEBOOK,** *Time-Saver:* Record all floor and window dimensions to make buying new curtains and flooring a snap. Record the different paint colors and brands and glue the paint-store samples of paint colors of the different rooms on the page with the description of that room; the same for swatches of wallpaper.

• **HOUSEKEEPING CREED,** *Letter of Laughter:* A reader sent in this Housekeeping Creed which she thought was a good New Year's Resolution.

> *I get into an awful state, just 'cause I procrastinate.*
> *And jobs that I abominate, pile up and accumulate.*
> *This new year I plan to liquidate,*
> *each lousy task immediate!*
> *That is, if doing what I hate,*
> *doesn't make some pleasure wait!*

• **HOUSEPLANT HELPER,** *Letter of Laughter:* My stepson Russell, trying to be helpful, volunteered to mist some avocado plants. He got so enthused that he misted all the plants—then found out that one big green plant was actually artificial!

• **HOUSEPLANTS,** *Safety:* If ingested, many common plants can be harmful to children and pets—philodendron, dieffenbachia, rhododendron, and various anemone species, to name just a few. Even the medicinal aloe vera plant, popularly used for skin irritations, can be harmful if eaten.
1. Keep the name tags on your plants and record their botanical names so that if a curious child or pet tastes any part of it, you can give an accurate description and proper name to your Poison Control Center. Call information to get the number and then keep it by the phone or program it into a programmable phone BEFORE you have an emergency.
2. If you have to rush a child or pet to an emergency facility, take the plant along with you to confirm its identity. If the plant's too large, cut off a twig; if it has flowers, seeds, fruits or exposed bulbs, take them, too.

• **HOUSEPLANTS,** *Watering While on Vacation:* Water plants thoroughly, then set on a small rock- or pebble-filled tray. Fill the tray with water, but don't overfill so that plants are soaked. Place tray with plants in indirect sunlight (direct may be too hot), and they will wait happily for you to return from a short vacation.

• **HOUSEPLANTS,** *Watering Without Mess:* Place a few ice cubes here and there; they'll melt slowly and you'll have no spillovers.

• **HUMIDIFIER,** *Removing Mineral Deposits:* Always check the manufacturer's instructions for details on cleaning your particular room humidifier. If you don't have instructions, the following method works for most humidifiers.

1. Fill the humidifier bowl with white vinegar and soak it for a couple of hours, or overnight for heavy buildup. Pour out the vinegar and rinse with fresh water. If deposits remain, repeat the procedure.

2. To soak an impeller (the little rod that actually sticks down into the water), fill a tall glass or jar with vinegar and immerse the impeller in it. Be careful not to bend the impeller or to get vinegar or water into the motor.

3. Regular soaking will cut down on the amount of buildup and soaking time. Using distilled or mineral-free water will also help prevent buildup. **Note:** Keeping the humidifier clean and deposit-free helps it work better and last longer.

• **HUMIDIFIER ALGAE,** *Avoiding It:* When small humidifiers get algae buildup in the water, frequent thorough cleaning is needed to remove the yucky slime. Add about one tablespoon of household bleach each time you fill the reservoir and the water will stay nice and clean. This small amount of bleach won't give off an unpleasant odor.

I

- **ICE CHESTS,** *Storage, Preventing Odors:* See COOLERS, Storage and COOLERS, Preventing Odors.

- **ICE CREAM,** *Healthy-Planet Freezing Individual Portions:* Save on the cost of individual ice cream portions (vs. quart or gallon sizes) and recycle clean one-cup lidded yogurt containers at the same time. Buy large containers of ice cream and put individual portions in the yogurt cups—there's no mess when children serve themselves and dieters aren't tempted to take larger portions than allowed.

- **ICE CREAM,** *Making Ice for Homemade Ice Cream:* Freeze water in empty quart-sized milk cartons overnight. Then, take a hammer and strike all four sides of the frozen carton a couple of times. Open the top and the crushed ice drops neatly into the ice-cream maker. Five quarts of ice with a layer of rock salt after each one is enough for the average ice-cream machine processing.

- **ICE CREAM,** *Snow-made:*
1. You must have fresh, clean snow. Collect it in a large plastic container as it falls.

2. Season heavy cream with a couple of drops of essence of lemon or maple syrup and powdered sugar.

3. Stir in snow until it's stiff like ice cream. Enjoy!

• **ICE CREAM,** *When It's Hard as a Brick:* Zap a half-gallon of ice cream in the microwave on "Low" for about 30 to 45 seconds depending on the wattage of your microwave—experiment to find the right amount of time. It will be easier to scoop.

• **ICE-CREAM CONE,** *Preventing Drippy Messes:* Place a small marshmallow in the bottom of the cone before you put the ice cream in. Then, if the ice cream melts, the marshmallow keeps it from dripping out of the bottom.

• **ICE-CREAM CONE,** *Quick-Fix, No Mess Serving Cup:* Put children's healthy snacks, such as dry cereal, small crackers, raisins, etc., in an ice-cream cone—no dishes to wash or clean up when the container is edible!

• **ICE-CREAM CRYSTALS,** *Prevention:* Ice cream should be kept at 20 degrees below zero. Crystals form when temperatures fluctuate and can indicate that the freezer is opened and closed too often or that there is a problem with the freezer itself. Keep track of your family's freezer use and if fewer open/close times don't help, the freezer may need servicing.

• **ICE-CREAM STICKS,** *Healthy-Planet Recycling:* Wash and save for stirring coffee; scraping mud or other goo from shoe bottoms; keeping in canisters to level off measuring cups; marking with depth measurements to help you plant seeds, bulbs, etc. and you can write on them for plant markers.

Also, they can spread condiments at picnics; glue, paste, grout or anything else that requires a disposable spreader. They can also stir paint in small containers. Check out craft books and shops for children's "keep-busy" ice-cream stick projects.

• **ICE CUBES GRANDE:** When the weather is hot and you need serious-size ice cubes to keep drinks cool, freeze them in muffin tins. Please see ICE CUBE SURPRISE below.

• **ICE-CUBE SURPRISE:** Freeze a maraschino cherry or a couple of mint leaves in each cube for pretty drink decorations.

- **ICE-CUBE TRAYS,** *Stuck Cubes:* Most ice-cube trays are coated and putting hot water into them melts off that coating; so does washing in hot, soapy dishwater or in the dishwasher. If cubes stick in your ice-cube trays, try spraying the trays with non-stick vegetable spray every now and then.

- **ICED TEA AND COFFEE:** Freeze leftover tea and coffee in ice cube trays to avoid dilution by regular cubes in your iced tea or coffee.

- **ICE PACK,** *Emergency for a Child's Lip Injury:* A frozen juice treat stops the tears and swelling when a child falls, hurts a lip, and needs a distraction as well as an ice pack.

- **ICE PACK,** *Homemade:* Mix one part rubbing alcohol with two parts water and freeze in a zipper plastic bag. It will be pliable enough to conform to a knee or elbow and can be refrozen after each use. Be sure to place a damp cloth between the skin and the ice pack to prevent frostbite.

- **INFLATABLE POOL RAFTS,** *Recycling:* If the raft has two valves—one for the pillow and the other for the body—and the body section is too leaky to patch, cut off the pillow section and save it for car trips, slumber parties, or for a bathtub pillow.

- **INFORMATION,** *Free:* More than 200 booklets with information on just about any subject you can think of are offered free or for reasonable prices by the Consumer Information Center. To get the catalog, send your name and address, requesting a current Consumer Information Catalog, to: R. Woods, Consumer Information Center, Pueblo, CO 81009.

- **INFORMATION,** *Source:* Your local County Extension or Cooperative Agent is an excellent source of free information on just about anything connected to family, home, and garden. This branch of the Department of Agriculture offers advice, booklets, information over the phone, and sometimes tele-information services (you dial to hear information tapes on specific subjects). Look in the government section of your phone book, under United States Government, Agriculture Department of, Extension Service County & Home Economics Agents.

• **INGREDIENTS,** *Keeping Safe from Foragers for Recipes:* If you don't want a family member with a case of the munchies to eat certain ingredients bought especially for a recipe or meal, have a code worked out with your family such as placing a red dot sticker on the container or just stick a warning note on the item. You'll save quick trips to the store and avoid those moments when you've got ingredients all mixed up, and you reach for the last one, and . . . need I say more?

• **INHERITANCE,** *Marking Household Possessions for Heirs, Letter of Laughter:* A reader wrote that she, her children, and grandchildren had a week-long party while she was marking household possessions with the names of the people who would inherit them and attaching notes saying where she got the item, how old it is, etc. She noticed that nobody ever found anything that wasn't wanted by somebody except the tax bill!.

• **INSURANCE,** *Trip Cancellation Insurance Checklist:* Basic travel insurance policies cover such elements as trip cancellation or interruption, baggage loss, emergency evacuation, worldwide telephone assistance, accidents, sickness, or accidental death or dismemberment. Most travel insurance is bought through a travel agent.
1. If you are traveling to just one destination or to just one country, the Insurance Information Institute says extra insurance may not be necessary, but a long trip to many places or special medical conditions could warrant it.
2. Before buying, check your homeowner's and health policies to find out what's already covered while you travel (theft, baggage loss, health problems).
3. Trip cancellation insurance may reimburse you for first-class tickets if you cancel just because you change your mind, but there's no reimbursement on non-refundable discount tickets for that reason. Basic costs are based on number of days away from home and the coverage.

• **INVENTORY:** If you keep a small notebook and write in it the names and locations of seldom used items, you don't have to play the "Lost and Found" game with yourself.

- **INVENTORY,** *For Insurance Purposes:* Whether or not you are moving, having photos of your possessions is proof of ownership, their description, and condition. If you have a lot of jewelry or other valuables, you may want to use an instant camera; then you can immediately write on the back (or on a label to put on the back) the original cost and any other information that will help you make a claim if the item is lost through theft or fire. The photos should be in a safe or safe-deposit box so that they don't get damaged with your possessions in fire or flood.

- **INVITATIONS,** *Checklist:* When sending invitations to weddings or other similar events, include an emergency phone number for out-of-town guests. For example, wedding invitations tell the location of the church and reception, but parents of small children hiring a sitter for the event would want to also provide the phone numbers, just in case of emergency.

- **IRON,** *Starch Buildup:* If the sole plate is stainless steel, remove the brown, gummy film by wiping with a cloth dampened with rubbing alcohol; then buff with extra-fine steel wool, and wipe off any residue. Follow manufacturer's directions for other sole plate finishes. If you've lost the directions, call 1-800-555-1212 to find out if the manufacturer has an 800 customer service/consumer information number.

- **IRONING BOARD,** *Other Uses:* Cover the cloth top with a plastic sheet or old flannel-backed plastic tablecloth and you have an adjustable worktable for crafts, wrapping gifts, etc. that's kind to your back because you can adjust the height.

- **"IRONING" IN A HOTEL:** Tried and true is to hang a garment in the bathroom while you shower to let the steam "iron" it. If the fabric is not very frail, you can "iron" some creases out over a hot light bulb. Remember to put the shade back on the lamp.

- **IRON SKILLET,** *Storing:* Place a paper towel on the inside of the skillet when you put it away to absorb moisture and prevent rust.

J

• **JACKET, IDENTIFYING YOURS IN A CROWD:** If you have a popular-style jacket that looks like everyone else's jacket when hung on a rack at a restaurant, turn one of the sleeves inside out before hanging it up so you can see at a glance which is yours. No more walking out wearing one that's not yours! **Note:** If it will stick to the lining, a self-sticking address label on the inside-out sleeve will help prevent someone from accidentally walking off with your jacket. I stick one in the pocket of my black raincoat because there are so many black raincoats.

• **JAMS/JELLIES/FRUIT SPREADS,** *Definitions:*
1. Jam is fruit (or vegetables like chutney) which has been cooked and pureed into a soft and thick consistency.
2. Jelly is made from fruit juice or clear liquid and syrup or sugar. It's called jelly because the cooked mixture gels.
3. Fruit spreads are usually smooth and thick and made from fruit pulp and spices. Some of the newer ones are sugar-free or have greatly reduced sugar content. You have to read those labels!

• **JAMS/JELLIES FOR GIFTS:** Instead of putting the jelly in jars, divide it into coffee mugs, seal with paraffin, and then add a bow and ribbon when you give it as a gift.

• **JAR LABELS,** *Removing for Special Offers:* Moisten a couple of paper towels or a cloth with hot water and wrap it around the label on the jar. Leave it on for a few minutes and remove. The label should peel off. If not, remoisten the cloth and try again. Or, soak the whole jar in warm water until the label comes off. **Note:** labels tear easily when damp; handle gently.

• **JAR LIDS,** *Tightening Hot Jelly Jar Lids:* Put on a clean pair of gardening gloves when you make jelly to prevent hot hands while stirring and to tighten lids after processing. No more juggling hot wet jars with pot-holder mitts or dish towels.

• **JEANS,** *Prevent Fading:* Before the first washing, help set the color by soaking them in a few gallons of water containing either one box of salt or one gallon vinegar—not both!

• **JELLY,** *$aver, Using It All:* When there's just a bit of jelly or jam left in the jar, add milk and shake vigorously and you'll have a delicious fruity shake.

• **JET LAG,** *Checklist for Prevention:*
1. Give your body time to adjust to changing patterns of sunlight and darkness as you travel by car, train or ship through different time zones.
2. Drink plenty of water, at least one glass per hour. Dry atmosphere in airplanes can cause dehydration. I like to mist my face and put lotion on my hands periodically.
3. Eat lightly. Most airlines offer special menus but you must call ahead. When I reserve my plane space, I always ask for a fruit or vegetarian plate.
4. Wear comfortable shoes and clothes, nothing tight. Stretch periodically and put your feet on a tote bag so your knees are higher than your hips. Try to move about the cabin every now and then and find an out-of-the way place to stretch and keep your circulation moving.

• **JEWELRY,** *Homestyle Cleaner:* Mix sudsy ammonia with an equal amount of water. Soak jewelry for a few minutes, then carefully clean around stones and designs with a soft toothbrush. Rinse well, dry and buff with soft cloth. **Caution:** Don't use this solution on gold electroplate or on jewelry with soft stones such as pearls, opals, or jade.

• **JEWELRY,** *Precautions:* Remove rings and other jewelry before doing housework.
1. Silver jewelry tarnishes when exposed to rubber gloves and ordinary household compounds like mayonnaise, salt, vinegar, eggs, and some cleaners.
2. Gold is damaged by exposure to mercury and some chemicals. Alloys in gold and soldered areas are weakened by chlorine and so it's best to remove jewelry when swimming in a pool or cleaning with bleach solutions.
3. Various precious and semi-precious stones can get scratched by housework or have their surfaces dulled by household compounds. Pearls, opals, and jade are especially at risk.

• **JEWELRY,** *Preventing Green Marks on Skin:* Paint the part that touches your skin (like the inside of a bracelet) with clear fingernail polish or have it coated by a jeweler.

• **JEWELRY,** *Quick-Fix Cleaning:* Rub a bit of toothpaste on the jewelry with your finger, rinse well, and polish with a soft cloth. **Caution:** Don't use this method too often, it could be too abrasive for some jewelry. Also don't use it for soft gems such as pearls, opals, or jade because they could be damaged.

• **JEWELRY,** *Quick-Fix, Safeguarding at the Gym:*
1. Keep a stray athletic sock in your gym bag to hold jewelry that you take off while working out. Stick the sock into your shoe and you won't waste time digging in a gym bag looking for it.
2. Put small earrings, rings, and other valuables in a 35mm film case and then into your shoe or gym bag pocket.
3. Poke hook earrings into a cork or foam packing chip for safe keeping.

• **JEWELRY,** *Recycling Old Costume Jewelry:* Instead of just throwing it away, give it to children to use as prizes when they play games.

• **JEWELRY,** *Rinsing After Cleaning:* Put jewelry in a tea strainer; there's no risk of its going down the drain when you rinse it after cleaning.

• **JOGGING,** *Safety at Night for Joggers or Bikers:* Sew silver reflective tape from major fabric stores around each leg or wrist of your jogging suit and sew ½-inch stripes across the back of a jacket. The tape makes you visible 1,000 feet away!

• **JUMPER CABLES,** *Recycling:* Cut off the alligator clips from a non-working set of battery jumper cables and save them for workshop projects.

• **JUMP STARTING YOUR CAR,** *Checklist for How-To:* Put a copy of these directions in your student driver's glove compartment and maybe in your own, too.

1. Position both cars so they face each other. If your car is against the curb, park the other car next to yours on the battery side. Put both vehicles in "Park;" apply the emergency brake, and turn ignitions off.

2. Important SAFETY measure—remove the cap from the top of each battery.

3. Locate the positive cable (red clips) and the negative cable (black clips) on the jumper cables. Locate the positive and negative terminals on the batteries. (You may need to clean the battery surface around the terminals to find the markings—there should be a " + " or "pos" to denote positive and a " − " or "neg" to denote negative.)

4. Attach one of the red clips to the positive terminal of the dead battery. Attach the other red clip to the positive terminal of the good battery.

5. Then, connect the negative cable to the negative terminal of the good battery and to the engine block of the stalled car, away from the battery, carburetor, fuel line, and any tubing or moving parts. (NOT to the negative terminal of the dead battery.)

6. When the jumper cables are properly hooked up, start the car with the good battery. Then try to start the car with the dead battery; when it begins to run, let it idle with the motor on for a minute or two.

7. To disconnect the cables, remove the black (negative) clip from the engine block first, then the red (positive) clips. To avoid electrical sparks, don't let the positive and negative cables touch each other.

Note: Most newer batteries have vented caps. With these, you must check to make sure they are tight and level before hooking up the battery to be jump-started. If a damp cloth is available, place it over the vent caps to decrease the chance of a spark igniting fumes that might be released from the battery. **Caution:** Serious eye injuries can result from batteries exploding. Exercise caution and wear safety eyewear to protect yourself and NEVER stand over a battery looking down at it when jump-starting it.

• **JUNK-MAIL ENVELOPES,** *Recycling:*
1. Large (9 × 12-inch) envelopes: Cut the envelopes at the edge instead of the top and slip in newspaper articles you want to save. Then turn the envelope over so that the address is facing the back; put a title at the top and file it in a shoebox. This system allows you to file newspaper or magazine recipes with their pictures!
2. Business-size envelopes: Write shopping lists on the backside and put your coupons inside. While shopping, paper clip the used coupons to the outside of the envelope and take the unused ones home in the envelope.

• **JUNK MAIL "GRANNY" TOY,** *Recycling:* Grandma can save all the junk mail and then when grandchildren visit, they can open their personal "mailbox" and play with "important papers" while adults chat. Many mailouts have nice stickers to stick and colored pictures to cut out, too!

K

- **KEY,** *Safekeeping:* It may be a sign of the times, but readers have begun sending me safety hints in case of mugging or theft. Attach your housekey to the band of your skirt or pants with a large safety pin; then if you are mugged, you can get into your house, and it prevents giving a thief your key along with the address found in your wallet. It's a good idea also to carry concealed change for phone calls or taxi money so that you can get home if you lose your wallet or purse. My mother used to pin my key inside my coat pocket when I was a child.

- **KEYS,** *Avoiding "Mystery Keys":* When you get new keys, trace them on a sheet of paper and keep it in your household files or trace on a sheet of paper in a household information notebook. Then you have a pattern to match when you are trying to solve key "mysteries."

- **KEYS,** *Car Key Reminders:* Put your car keys on anything you need to remember to take or to check; you can't leave home without them. Some examples are listed below.
1. Hang them near the kitchen stove and/or coffee pot and you'll check that the kitchen appliances are off before leaving the house.

2. If you tend to forget if you've unplugged your curling iron or hot rollers, hang car keys there so that you have to check these appliances before you leave.

3. Put them on your "doggy bag" in the refrigerator and when you leave "Mom's" (or some other generous nice person's home) you won't forget the goodies.

• **KEYS,** *Recycling Old Ones:* Attach keys with fishing line to a clothes hanger, piece of tree branch, wooden embroidery hoop, or other hanging device and you'll create a novel wind chime. Old keys can also substitute for missing parts of an existing wind chime.

• **KEYS,** *Safekeeping Spares in Yard:* One reader attaches the spare housekeys to her dogs' collars along with the rest of their ID tags. She says neither dog "takes kindly" to having a stranger mess with its collar but relatives and friends who need the key can easily get it from one of the dogs.

• **KEY-TABS, KEY RINGS,** *Recycling Extras:* Plastic fluorescent key-tabs, often given away as promotional items, make great glow-in-the-dark light pulls in a closet or basement. Others may be attractive enough for ceiling fan pulls.

• **KITCHEN,** *Cleaning Ranges, etc. Letter of Laughter:* One reader sent me a surefire method for keeping a stove clean—Don't use it! This reminded me of an old joke in which a husband says that for their wedding anniversary, he's going to take his wife on a trip to somewhere she's never been—their kitchen! In these days of working couples sharing kitchen chores, a wife might tell the same joke about her husband!

• **KITCHEN TIMER FAMILY PEACEMAKER:**
1. For a very young child who dislikes naps, set the timer and leave it in the child's room to show when nap time is over. **Note:** The ticking lulls some children to sleep!
2. Set a kitchen timer to limit teen phone conversations.
3. Set the timer to limit your own conversations; it'll make the process seem fairer to the teen.

• **KITE FLYING SAFETY,** *Checklist:*

1. Never use any metal in making a kite, including wire or string containing metal fibers.

2. Never fly your kite on rainy or stormy days, and always make sure your kite string is perfectly dry. Wet string conducts electricity.

3. Fly your kite in an open field, away from overhead, electric lines, and public roadways. Never take a chance!

4. If a kite becomes tangled in an electric power line or catches on a utility pole, leave it. It is simply too dangerous to try and retrieve it.

5. Never climb on utility poles, towers, or other utility equipment. Aside from the danger of being electrocuted, you could fall and injure yourself.

• **KITTENS,** *Feeding Abandoned Newborns:* If a mama kitty abandons a litter, you need to keep the kittens warm—a box lined with shredded paper and a soft cloth will do.

1. They need to be kept at about 88 to 92°F when they are a week old; about 80 to 85°F when they get to fourteen days old; about 80°F when they are about a month old. It helps if you have a thermostatically controlled overhead infrared lamp.

2. Keep a pan of water near the box to add humidity since dehydration can be a problem.

3. If you can't get to a vet to buy the proper formula, this emergency formula can substitute. Mix 2 cups of milk, 1 teaspoon corn syrup, the yolk of an egg, and a pinch of salt. Keep the formula in the refrigerator and take out what's needed for each feeding. Feeding should be room temperature and feed only eight to ten drops per tiny kitten.

• **KNICKKNACKS,** *Remembering Arrangements:* When you are dusting shelves that hold figurines, framed photos, or other collection arrangements, snap a picture of the display with an instant camera so that you can put them back as they were when you are finished. This is especially helpful if you're dusting at a relative's or friend's house. Keep the photos for insurance records.

• **KNIFE CASE,** *Carrying a Knife Safely in a Picnic Basket:* Put a paring knife in a toothbrush holder or flatten an empty paper-towel roll and tape the end shut to hold a larger knife.

• **KNIT GARMENT,** *Care Label for Hand-knit Gift:* Enclose a label from a yarn skein so that the person receiving the gift will know what kind of yarn was used and how to care for it.

• **KNITTING NEEDLES:** Knit with two different-colored, same-size needles and you will always know which row you are on—even or odd.

L

- **LABELS,** *Quick-Fix, Removing Gummy Glue:* To soften gummy glue on a glass or plastic jar, put it in the microwave with a damp towel over it; set on Low and check it every 30 seconds or so. The heat softens the glue and you can usually pull the label off easily.

- **LABELS,** *Removing Sticky Residue:* See STICKERS, Removal.

- **LADDER TOOL HOLDER:** Instead of climbing up and down the ladder to get this tool or that, hammer some nails along the right edge of a wooden ladder so that before you start a job, you can assemble all the tools you need and hang them at the height at which you will work. If you hang your tools at your usual work bench with self-gripping fabric tape you can stick self-gripping tape to a metal ladder. Either way, you'll save ladder climbing.

- **LAKES,** *Remembering the Great Lakes Hint:* Think the word "HOMES"—Huron, Ontario, Michigan, Erie, Superior.

- **LAMPSHADE,** *Quick-Fix Dusting:* Blow dust away with a hand-held hair dryer set on cool.

- **LANDSCAPING,** *Hanging Plants:* Make a plain fence or apartment balcony rail into a garden focal point by hanging potted plants from it with S-hooks or, if you are handy, attach shelves for plants to a wood fence.

• **LANDSCAPING,** *Fish Ponds:* If you are installing a fountain out-doors and plan to have fish in it, it should be at least 10 inches deep. If you install the pool at ground level, you can insert into the hole you've dug a fiberglass pool like those used for children's swimming pools or a heavy-duty rubber or plastic liner. Pools made specifi-cally for fountains (fiberglass or copper) can be above ground, but they're more expensive than make-it-yourself models.

• **LANDSCAPING,** *Fountains:* A water fountain in a garden room or outdoors in the yard makes a soothing, therapeutic sound and adds a luxurious touch to the decor. Many need no plumbing at all because they operate with water-recirculating pumps. (Basic pumps cost about $40; good professionally-made fountains cost $300 to $1000 and up.) If you buy the complete fountain "works" from a specialty shop, all you do is fill it with water and plug in the pump; no skills required! **Caution:** Make sure all electrical outlets are grounded.

• **LAUNDRY,** *Bleaching:* Always follow care labels on garments and never allow undiluted chlorine bleach to contact clothing; it can damage color and fabric. If your washer doesn't have a bleach dispenser, dilute bleach with one quart of water and add the solu-tion to the washer after it has filled with water.

• **LAUNDRY,** *Dryer Filter Safety:* Dust and lint buildup in dryer filters and exhaust ducts is a major cause of home fires (about 14,000 a year). Clean the filter after each load and check the exhaust duct regularly. Also check the outside vent tube to make sure excess lint isn't plugging the air exit; this also can be a fire hazard.

• **LAUNDRY,** *Dryer Safety:* We know it's best to remove clothing from the dryer as soon as the cycle is finished to prevent crushing, but did you know that some materials, when left in the heated dryer drum, can spontaneously heat up enough to catch fire?

• **LAUNDRY,** *Getting Dryer-made Wrinkles Out:* Add a large damp bath towel to a load of dryer-crinkled clothing and run the dryer for about 15 minutes. Be sure to remove garments as soon as they are dry!

• **LAUNDRY,** *Getting Help from Children:*

1. Give each child a personal laundry basket. The basket of dirty clothing is to be brought to the laundry room each morning before breakfast. Children then take their clean laundry back to their rooms in the same basket at the end of the day.

2. Teach children to sort laundry when they bring it down. Have a framed cloth hamper for each load—each of a different fabric according to how you sort your laundry. For example, a denim hamper is for jeans, pants and heavy clothes; a sheet fabric hamper holds sheets, towels and whites; a print fabric hamper is for light-weight colored clothing. Even the youngest child or adult with "selective incompetency" can sort laundry when it's coded this way, and it trains children to do their own laundry when they leave home.

• **LAUNDRY,** *Healthy-Planet Energy Saving Checklist:*

1. Match water level to the load size—set lower water levels for smaller loads or delay washing until you have a full (but not over-loaded) large load.

2. Pretreat spots and stains and then set the cycle and wash time to the type of load to avoid rewashing.

3. If your washer has a water return system, when you reuse water you need to start with lightly soiled items first; you may need to add more detergent for additional loads.

4. Wash in hot water only when necessary for heavy or greasy soils, whites, etc. and wash with cold for light soils. Rinse all loads in cold water.

5. Reduce dryer time by using a high spin speed in the washer for highly absorbent fabrics.

6. Dry full (but not overloaded) loads and separate lightweight and heavy weight items for faster, uniform drying.

7. Don't overdry. In addition to wasting energy, it can give a harsh feeling to some fabrics and shrink others. Allowing garments to stay in the dryer after it's shut off causes wrinkles.

8. Use residual heat—reload the dryer while it's still warm from a previous load.

9. Keep lint screens clean—buildup increases drying time and can be a fire hazard.

10. Do laundry during off-peak hours, usually early morning and late evening. Check with your local utility company to find out about off-peak hours.

• **LAUNDRY,** *Ironing:* Dry place mats draped over the side of the bathtub; some may not need ironing if they are "handpressed" against the sides of the tub while they are still wet.

• **LAUNDRY,** *Lint on Clothes:* Today's dryers catch most lint in their filters but some people still have problems with it. Most of the time, poor sorting before washing, overdrying and static electricity cling cause lint to cling to clothing.
1. Sort properly. Don't wash and dry lint-makers like bath towels with lint-collectors like synthetics or permanent press.
2. Remove all papers and tissues from pockets before washing and drying clothes. Tissues seem to expand when laundered.
3. Use fabric softeners to reduce static electricity.
4. Don't overload washers and dryers; they won't work as well as they can.
5. Try to remove clothing when it's still slightly damp. Static electricity builds up in overdried clothing so that lint clings more easily.
6. Clean the dryer lint screen after each load so that it can catch more lint; you'll be saving energy, too, because the machine is working more efficiently.

• **LAUNDRY,** *Soaking Bleachable Stained Items:* Mix ¼ cup chlorine bleach with one gallon of water in a sink or pail and soak for five minutes. **Note:** Chlorine bleach doesn't remove protein-type stains such as egg, grass, or blood; these are best removed with a pre-soak product. Please see SPOTS AND STAINS on page 398.

• **LAUNDRY,** *Sorting, Letter of Laughter:* One mother solved the problem of putting away her teen's laundry. She just put underwear, etc. in the wrong drawers for several weeks and finally, her teens said they preferred to put their own away!

• **LAUNDRY,** *Sweaters:* To handwash, use cool or lukewarm water. With the sweater inside out, immerse it for 5 to 10 minutes turning it over once or twice and squeezing suds through the fabric—gently.

Rinse the same way in basins of water until the water is clear. Air dry flat so you can block the sweater back into shape.

To machine wash (if care label says so), turn sweater inside out (place delicate sweaters in a mesh bag or pillowcase) and use cool or lukewarm water; remove before the spin cycle. Some machine-washable sweaters can be put into the dryer for a short time and then removed while damp so that they can be dried flat and blocked. But some synthetics require tumble drying for the full cycle to be re-blocked into shape; check care labels.

• LAUNDRY, *Test for Colorfastness of Fabric:* Make a solution of 1 tablespoon of bleach and ¼ cup of water. Put a drop or two of this solution on in inconspicuous spot such as an inside seam and check for color loss.

• LAUNDRY, *Turning Socks and Underwear Right-side Out, Letter of Laughter:* After many years of marriage and four children, and many many hours turning socks right side out after they came out of the laundry, one reader decided to tell her family that anyone who had to turn socks inside out when removing them could just turn them for himself before wearing them again. She discovered that she was the only person in the family who cared if socks were right-side out. Everyone just wore them as is. And, one of my staff read this and agreed; she doesn't turn underwear right side out either, she said, "It's not my problem."

Seems to me that a lot of us allow ourselves to get aggravated about chores which are really just unnecessary "busy work" because we're the only ones who care. Anyhow, consider that these families wear their socks and underwear the "right" way 50 percent of the time! Not a bad percentage for anything!

• LAUNDRY, *When Suds Overflow:* Please see SUDS OVERFLOW.

• LAUNDRY, *When Washer and Dryer Are in a Garage or Basement:* If you can't hear the cycle change buzzers, you'll get to the washer and dryer before the wrinkles do if you set a kitchen timer to go off approximately when a cycle will finish and keep it where you are in the house.

• LAUNDRY APPLIANCE SURPRISE: When an appliance service person asked, "Did you check for valuables?" before hauling away her old washer and dryer, a reader opened the fronts of her appliances at his suggestion and found her wedding band, earrings, $7.42, and other odds and ends in the accumulated lint! Check it out before it goes out!

• **LAUNDRY BAG,** *For Travel:* Put a drawstring in the open end of an old pillowcase. It will fit to any shape in your suitcase if traveling by plane; it protects souvenirs on the way home, too. When traveling by car you can toss the laundry bag into the trunk fender well so it's out of the way.

• **LAUNDRY BASKET,** *Safe Carrying:* If you have to carry your laundry down steep steps to a cellar, it may be unsafe to carry a basket which limits your vision and puts you off balance. Instead you can put your laundry in a plastic bag or in pillow cases and just toss it down the steps ahead of you! If it won't hit anything, you could also just let a plastic basket of laundry slide down the steps.
P.S. However you do it, considering how most of us feel about doing laundry, tossing it down the steps any way at all could be a happy, frustration releasing experience!

• **LAUNDRY DETERGENT BOX,** *Quick-Fix:* Open pour-type boxes with a beer can opener to save fingernails and temper.

• **LAUNDRY DETERGENT, LIQUID:** After measuring liquid laundry detergent and pouring the liquid into the washer, toss in the measuring cup so it gets rinsed off automatically.

• **LAUNDRY AND LAUNDROMAT LESSONS,** *For the Novice:*
1. Sort clothing into whites that can be bleached, whites that can't be bleached, light colors, dark colors, heavily soiled items and lint-giving articles. These should be separate loads but most college students dump all together to save a few coins and end up ruining garments that cost dollars. Compromise by making one light/non-fade load and one load of dark jeans and other dark colors.
(You can always tell a freshman college student—pink socks from mixing white and colored loads are a dead giveaway; upper-class students have only grey shirts, gym socks, and underwear from years of washing light-colored clothing with jeans.)
2. Buy large, light-colored duffel bags and a couple of indelible pens. Write washing instructions on hot-, warm- and cold-water washing on the face of each laundry bag with the pen.

3. Cut a pocket from an old shirt and sew it into the inside of the duffel bag with a little snap for closure. This is a convenient place to put laundry money for the machines. Or toss in a plastic yogurt cup with a lid to hold change.

4. Premeasuring detergent and fabric softener into small margarine tubs, yogurt cups or self-sealing plastic bags is a big help—you don't have to lug around the whole box or bottle.

5. After placing clothes in the washer and shutting the lid, place a large colorful magnet or a stick-on paper dot on the machines you are using so you can find your clothes at a glance.

6. Take hangers with you so that you can hang up clothes from the dryer and avoid ironing them.

• **LAUNDRY POWDER,** *Preventing Lumps In Damp Climates:* Store in a clean plastic gallon milk jug with a tight-fitting lid. It will be easier to handle, too.

• **LAUNDRY PROBLEMS,** *Checklist for Avoiding Them:*

1. Keep jeans and other cotton pants from fading by turning them inside out before washing and drying.

2. Prevent pilling on sweaters and printed T-shirts by laundering them wrongside out.

3. Make it a family rule for each member to spot-treat clothing or at least to warn whomever does the laundry about spots and stains.

4. Do not use chlorine and non-chlorine bleaches together.

5. Check pockets—then you won't wash pens, crayons, tissues or other things that stain or leave lint behind.

6. Close all zippers and fasteners to prevent their snagging other garments.

7. Mend rips and tears; sew on loose buttons—a stitch in time really does save nine or more!

8. Don't add wet garments to a partially dried load in the dryer.

9. Clean lint filters before every load.

10. Select the proper cycle, water temperature, time, and load level recommended by your laundry equipment books. Manufacturers spend a lot of money developing these booklets and since you've paid for the information, you may as well use it!

• **LAUNDRY, TANGLED,** *Sanity-Saving Checklist:*
1. To avoid washing machine cruelty to you and your clothes, make sure all hooks are fastened (especially bras and other undergarments), close all zippers.
2. If shirt or blouse sleeves seem to be the cause, button each sleeve to a buttonhole on the front.
3. Place clothing into the machine piece by piece laying each garment in a circle around the agitator. Make sure you set the appropriate water level and washing time. If you have mostly bras, long-sleeved, soft/silky fabric blouses or shirts, nylon slips, etc. in a load, wash on "Delicate" or "Knit" and set a higher water level than when you had the tangles; more water and less agitation time in the washer-machine may prevent agitation of the washer-person.

• **LAWN FURNITURE,** *Painting:* Get a large cardboard box from a local furniture store; cut out one side. Place lawn furniture into the box and spray paint for no mess or painted grass.

• **LAWN MOWING,** *Safety Checklist:*
1. Wear proper protective clothing—long pants, sturdy shoes, and protective eye wear.
2. First walk the area to be mowed to find and pick up objects that could be thrown by the mower or could damage the mower.
3. Never disconnect safety controls; they are there to protect you.
4. Never refuel the machine while it is running or the engine is still hot—gas fumes are flammable.
5. Don't mow wet grass; it clogs the mower and may damage it.
6. Store the mower in a ventilated area, especially in hot weather, to prevent combustion of the gas remaining in it after you finish.

• **LEFTOVERS,** *Bread:*
1. Stale bread makes good bread pudding. Dried bread can be cubed and oven toasted for croutons or if dry enough, made into bread crumbs. (Take dried bread, put it into a sturdy plastic bag, place it on the floor, and step on it until the bread is crumbs. You can also place it on the counter and use a rolling pin but it won't be as much fun.)
2. Stale, but still soft, sliced bread can be pushed into greased muffin cups, baked until toasty, then used as an egg cup.

3. Use old bread for French toast or cut bread in cubes and mix with egg or egg substitute for "egg cubes."

4. Dip days-old bread slices in sweetened condensed milk, then in flaked coconut and then place on a baking sheet and toast in hot oven until bread is hot and coconut is brown for quickie cookies.

• **LEFTOVERS,** *Cake:*
Recipe 1. Break in pieces and layer with slightly softened ice cream, freeze and slice for a new dessert. (You can drizzle an appropriate liqueur over each serving, such as coffee-flavored liqueur over chocolate ice cream and angel food cake.)

Recipe 2. Prepare one package of cooked chocolate pudding mix as directed, cool. Whip one cup whipping cream with ⅓ cup confectioners' sugar and fold into cooled pudding. Cut up one layer of cake (white, yellow, or chocolate) and place in bottom of an 8-inch-square baking dish. Pour pudding over cake and sprinkle with ½ cup chopped nuts (optional). Chill several hours in fridge before serving. Serves 4 to 6.

• **LEFTOVERS,** *Cheese:* Bits of leftover cheese can be melted with canned skim milk and turned into cheese sauce for veggies or noodles or for cheese dip. The more different kinds of cheese, the better the flavor.

• **LEFTOVERS,** *Disguising for Fun:* When you have accumulated several meals of leftovers, have a family "Buffet Day" to eat them up. One reader makes a joke of her leftover day by posting a menu on the fridge that has the name of a leading restaurant of her city printed on top and a list of the "Choices du Jour."

• **LEFTOVERS,** *Egg Whites or Yolks:* Save egg whites for meringues or fruit whips. Save yolks for custards, sauces or to add to scrambled eggs.

• **LEFTOVERS,** *Fruits:*
1. Too many grapes? Freeze them for snacking later.
2. Too many bananas? Freeze them and use them (sliced in hunks) instead of ice cubes and malt to froth up blender milk shakes.
3. Slightly bruised fruits? Cut off bad parts and make a fruit salad, pie, or add fruit to tuna salad—apples and grapes are delicious!

• **LEFTOVERS,** *General Use:* I like to think of leftovers as pre-cooked convenience foods. To make any leftover taste new, add a fresh ingredient such as browned onions, garlic, vegetables, bouillon or new spices or herbs, or all of the above.

• **LEFTOVERS,** *$aver, Getting Every Smidgen Out of a Container:* When you get to the bottom of the dishwashing liquid, shampoos, conditioner, ketchup, salad oil, salad dressing, hand/body lotion or baby lotion, prop the container upside down for a day or so and you get at least one more "dose" out of it.

Also, add water to a ketchup bottle and flavor noodle, rice or meat dishes with the "puree." Add water to dishwashing detergent and you can squirt a sponge with the mixture to wash odds and ends at the sink. The diluted detergent rinses out faster and is kinder to detergent-sensitive skins.

• **LEFTOVERS,** *Meats:*
1. Any leftover meat can be used as slices in a sandwich or ground up to make sandwich spread (add commercial sandwich spread or mayo and chopped carrots, celery, mushrooms for filler).
2. Heat meat slices in leftover sauce for hot open-faced sandwiches or to serve over leftover rice or noodles.
3. Cubed meats can be mixed with noodles or rice and salad dressings for a luncheon salad.

• **LEFTOVERS,** *Vegetables:*
1. Keep a tightly covered container in your freezer and add all bits of leftover veggies and their cooking water, then, when you have enough, make vegetable soup by adding browned onions, bouillon or stock, and your favorite herbs/spices to the mix. Simmer at least 20 to 30 minutes to blend flavors.
2. Add leftover cooked veggies to any salad—mixed combination salads, sandwich spread, or just on top of your lettuce.
3. Cut up leftover potatoes and add them to scrambled eggs or scrambled egg substitute. Brown the potatoes and add some onion, if you wish, before adding the eggs.
4. Mash leftover starchy vegetables, add egg, leftover egg yolk or egg substitute, crumbs to thicken, and deep fry like hushpuppies for "veggie puppies."

5. Make vegetable hash by cutting up leftover mixed vegetables such as corn, peppers, potatoes, peas and beans, then fry in skillet with onion, garlic and other seasonings of choice.

• **LEMON,** *Aids:*
1. Add a few slices to drinking water to perk it up or to bathwater to perk you up with the fresh scent.
2. Rub your hands with pieces of lemon to remove odors like onions and garlic.
3. Add lemon juice to rinse water for your hair.
4. Put rinds down the garbage disposal to freshen it.
5. Cut in half, remove insides and fill with gelatin.

• **LEMON/LIME JUICE PLASTIC BOTTLES,** *Recycling:* When empty, rinse well and fill with water so that children can carry them for a handy squirt of drinking water.

• **LEMONS,** *Freezing:* Seal them in a sturdy plastic bag and freeze. When you need one, take it out of the bag and microwave it for a few minutes; let stand on counter for 10 more minutes before using.

• **LEMON SQUEEZER,** *Substitute for a Strong Grip:* Place a lemon half in a nutcracker and squeeze away.

• **LETTER WRITING,** *Time-Saver:* Buy carbonless paper which comes in pre-collated two- to six-sheet sets. For example, if you have four people to whom you write regularly, buy four-part carbonless. Then instead of writing four separate total letters you can type or hand write your main body of news only once, add personalized notes, questions and comments and mail the letters off. You'll enjoy writing more often to friends, kids at college, and so forth. Of course if you have a computer or word processor, you can do the same without the carbonless paper, just print out different letters with different headers and personalized notes.

• **LEVEL,** *Substitute:* If you are hanging a shelf and have no level, try filling a tall straight-sided plastic bottle three-quarters full of water. Tightly close the lid so that you can lay the bottle on the shelf on its side. Adjust the shelf until the water is level. Then screw the shelf to the wall.

• **LIBRARY LIST:** Keep a log of books checked out from the library and then you'll not only see how many books your family has read in a month, but you'll have a checklist to help you gather all of the books when it's time to return them. No more forgetting and paying overdue fees!

• **LICKING LABELS AND STAMPS:** Fill a shallow dish with water and place a burned-out light bulb in it. The bulb turns with a touch in the water and you can glide stamps, etc. over it without ever licking yucky stamps, labels or envelopes again.

• **LIGHT BULB,** *Changing Without Burning Fingers:* Take the new bulb out of the corrugated cardboard "box" and place the "box" over the old light bulb to unscrew it. You don't get burned fingers and the bulb ends up inside the "box" ready for disposal!

• **LIGHT BULB,** *Removing a Broken One:* **Caution:** First make sure the switch is turned off. Then insert an old-fashioned clothespin, not spring-type, so that the two prongs are inside the broken socket and carefully unscrew it.

• **LIGHTING,** *Brighten Without Using More Energy:* Lighting accounts for more than 16 percent of our electric bills and most of us overlight our homes. You can brighten and still save.
1. Use 25-watt reflector flood bulbs in high-intensity portable lamps. They'll give about the same light but use less energy than the 40-watt bulbs that usually come with these lamps.
2. If you have "pole" or "spot" directional lamps, try using 50-watt reflector floodlights which give about the same light as standard 100-watt bulbs but with half the wattage.
3. When using night-light bulbs, get 4-watt bulbs with a clear finish instead of the usual 7-watt ones; they'll be almost as bright with half the energy use.
4. Put photocell sensor units or timers on outdoor lights so that they will turn themselves off in daylight.
5. Install dimmer switches or high-low switches when replacing light switches to reduce light intensity and save energy.
6. When buying new lamps, get those with three-way switches so you can use high for reading and low when you don't need bright light.

7. Fluorescent lights give out more lumens (light measurements) so use them whenever you can. New 20-watt deluxe warm white fluorescent can be used in makeup and grooming areas for a warmer light.

8. Keep all lamps and lighting fixtures clean; dirt absorbs light.

9. When decorating, save lighting energy by choosing light-colored walls, rugs, draperies and upholstery which reflects light and so reduces the amount of artificial light needed.

• **LINEN CLOSET,** *Organizing for No Mess Time-Saving:* Linen closets can become a jumbled mess, especially when children make their own beds. Organize bed linens into sets: Fold one flat sheet in the middle, fold it in half and then in half again (both folds the long way). Then fold a fitted sheet the same way, and lay it on top of the folded flat sheet. Add one or two pillowcases, each folded in half the long way also. Then roll them all together into one neat roll. Whoever is making a bed can grab only a roll instead of rummaging around and making a mess.

• **LINT,** *Removing It from Self-Grip Closures on Children's Shoes:* Accumulated lint affects the "grip" in addition to looking unsightly. Remove it with a small crochet hook. Avoid lint accumulation problems by closing the self-grip tapes when children take their shoes off.

• **LINT ON LAUNDRY,** *Avoiding It:* Turn inside-out before washing garments made from fabrics that attract lint, such as corduroy, dark cotton socks, etc.

• **LINT PICKING:** A clean mascara brush will get lint out of hard-to-reach places on clothing like shirt-front plackets, shirt pockets and hems.

• **LIPSTICK,** *Preventing Loss in a Purse:* Put lipstick, a few tissues and other cosmetics in a self-sealing plastic bag. You can move the bag from purse to purse and never have to dig around in the bottom for a lipstick tube. No more rumpled new tissue clutter either!

• **LIPSTICK,** *Using It All Up:* Use up the last smidgeons of lipstick in the tube with a lipstick brush. Or, do as I do: Scoop out those smidgeons with a toothpick or clean frozen treat stick and put several different colors of lipstick in a small compact (one left over from other lipstick, rouge or powder) and then you'll have a color-choice lipstick compact in your travel makeup kit or purse. Be sure to include a lipstick brush for application.

• **LITTER BAGS,** *For the Car:* Save the small plastic bags from frozen foods, card shops and drug stores and keep them in a larger bag in the car so they'll always be handy.

• **LOLLIPOP TREE,** *Gift for Hospitalized Child:* Into a potted plant, stick drinking straws and then poke lollipop sticks into the straws for a "lolli-flower" arrangement. **Caution:** Check first to find out if the child can have regular candy or if the child can have sugar-free lollipops before you tantalize with forbidden foods!

• **LOW-FAT COOKERY:** Frying meat adds fat. When you want to reduce the fat in your diet, try other methods.
1. Roasting—Roast leaner beef and lamb on a rack in a roasting pan. When you cook in the oven by dry heat, the temperature of the meat should be between 135° to 140°F. Cook pork to 160°F; veal to 170°F; a whole chicken to 180°F.
2. Broiling/Barbecuing—Cook quickly and by direct heat in your range broiler or on a barbecue grill. Marinades add flavor and soaking meat in an acid solution tenderizes it. Make a marinade with a base of vinegar, wine or lime juice and your favorite herbs and spices.
3. Poach/no-fat Braise—In a non-stick pan, add a little oil and brown the meat. A regular pan, sprayed very lightly with non-stick vegetable spray can also be used. Cover the meat and let it finish cooking in the simmering liquid until tender. This can be done on top of the range or in a medium oven.
4. Stir-fry—Fry meat, which has been sliced thinly across the grain, uncovered in very little oil (or in a very small amount of bouillon if you want to avoid fat altogether).

• **LUGGAGE,** *Identifying Lost Bags:* Clip a picture of your suitcase, hanging bag, etc. from a catalog or ad and tuck it into your wallet so that if it's lost in transit, you can show exactly what it looks like. ALWAYS keep receipts for luggage and possessions you travel with so that you can establish insurance claims if the luggage is never found.

• **LUGGAGE,** *Preventing Lost Luggage:*
1. Take off old flight tags to avoid confusion about your destination, and check to make sure the correct tag is put on to the exact destination.
2. Place an identification tag on the inside and outside of each piece of luggage. Don't put your home address on the outside; it alerts people in the airport that you are away.
3. Avoid traveling with obviously expensive luggage; it attracts thieves.
4. Claim baggage as soon as possible; the longer it waits, the longer it tempts thieves.
5. Never leave luggage unattended, even for a minute—it can disappear that fast. Also, most airport security now collects unattended bags and the announcements on PA systems in some airports say that security requires destruction of picked-up unattended baggage, so a word to the wise should be sufficient!

• **LUGGAGE,** *Quick-Fix to Identify Yours on a Conveyor:* If your suitcase looks like everyone else's, tie on a piece of colored yarn or ribbon, add a yarn pompon to the handle, or stick on a bumper sticker, bathtub applique, or just a design with colored plastic tape.

• **LUGGAGE,** *Sizes for Carryons:* See TRAVEL, Luggage Sizes for Carryons.

• **LUGGAGE TAG:** One reader's luggage was returned safely to her home when it was lost by the airline; unfortunately, the mishap occurred at the beginning of her trip so all she had was her overnight case. Now she puts the address of her DESTINATION instead of her home base on her luggage tags.

• **LUNCH, BROWN BAGGING IT,** *Fruit:*
1. Juice—Freeze individual containers of juice; they will thaw by lunchtime and keep the other lunch foods cool.
2. Whole fruits—Place softer fruits (like peaches, plums, grapes) in clean yogurt cups or other containers to keep them from getting squashed.

• **LUNCH, BROWN BAGGING IT,** *General Protective Packing:*
1. Place foam meat trays in the bottoms of paper lunch sacks to keep them from getting wet and having their bottoms fall out.
2. Keeping cold foods in clean used food containers prevents them from sweating so much that the bag tears and best of all, follows my Heloise philosophy of trying to reduce garbage output by re-using packaging as often as possible.
3. If you need to send lunch or milk money along with a very young child, poke a hole into the lid of a 35mm film canister, then poke both ends of a cord (that's long enough to go around your child's neck) through the hole. Knot the ends several times so that the cord won't come out of the hole. Put the money in the canister, attach it to the lid and your child will have a safe lunch money "necklace."

• **LUNCH, BROWN BAGGING IT,** *Salad lunch:* Pack a green or chef's salad in a clean 16-ounce yogurt or 12-ounce cottage cheese carton and add a 35mm film canister containing salad dressing. Just before you eat, pour the dressing over salad, replace lid so that you can toss the salad neatly, and enjoy.

• **LUNCH, BROWN BAGGING IT,** *Sandwiches:* Make sandwiches on grocery-buying day, assembly-line style, and freeze them: Each sandwich has two slices of bread lightly spread with margarine—no mayonnaise or mayonnaise-type salad dressing, since it doesn't freeze—two slices of two different lunch meats (usually turkey types to reduce fat) and one slice of cheese. Breads are sliced white, grain, whole wheat or rye. Each sandwich is placed in a plastic sandwich bag and then returned to the original bread bag so that all know what kind of bread was used. Lunchmeats and cheeses are a surprise. Frozen sandwiches will thaw by lunch time and taste fresher than those made daily and they help keep the other foods in the lunchbox cool.

• **LUNCH, BROWN BAGGING IT,** *Veggies:* Toss an ice cube or piece of wet paper towel into the zipper bag (or clean yogurt/margarine container) containing carrot and celery sticks to keep them fresh and moist.

• **LUNCH LEFTOVERS AT THE OFFICE:** One group of men wrote that they all keep lunch leftovers in the office refrigerator and color-code them with a different color of plastic wrap for each day. Then they know which day the food came in and when it should be thrown away. I presume they write the day of the week on the box of wrap so that everyone knows the code!

• **LUNCH MONEY,** *Time-Saver, Keeping It Handy:* See "Workday Survival Hints."

M

• **MAGAZINE RECYCLING:** One Middle West library grossed $4,800 in one year by offering donated used magazines for sale at 10 cents each. Volunteers sort and group magazines by type and stand them in boxes on a table with a locked coin box nearby. Payment is on the honor system; buyers drop a dime into the box.

• **MAGAZINES,** *Organizing Clippings:* As you read a magazine, tear out the pages you want to keep, then store them in file folder or punch holes and store the pages in a ring-binder. The information you want will be where you can find it and you can pitch the magazine to get rid of clutter.

• **MAGAZINES,** *Renewing or Canceling Subscriptions:* Cut the address label from the last issue of the magazine and paste or tape it to the space for name and address; there won't be any mistakes when you renew or cancel because your subscriber number and other identifying codes will be on that label.

• **MAGAZINE SYSTEM,** *To Avoid Getting Overwhelmed by Saved Stacks:* As soon as a magazine arrives, scan the articles and cut out everything of interest; cut out and file coupons. Save the articles in a "to read" file and discard the rest of the magazine.

• **MAGNET:** Keep one in your sewing kit to help you find and pick up pins and needles quickly. **Note:** The other way to find and pick up dropped pins is to walk around barefooted—you'll never miss one but it sure is the hard way!

• **MAGNIFYING GLASS:** Keep a small magnifying glass in the car to help you read maps. One of my readers wears one of those large magnifying glasses you hang around your neck to do needlework when she travels. She can see a larger area of the map and doesn't get lost on vacation trips anymore.

• **MAILING,** *Checklist:* The U.S. Postal Service handles more than a half billion pieces of mail daily and says properly addressing letters speeds up delivery.
1. Print or type addresses clearly.
2. "Attention" lines should be put above the address not in the lower left corner as is often done.
3. Street address lines should always include directions such as North or South, whether it's an Avenue or Street, and a room or apartment number if applicable.
4. ZIP code is a must and should be next to the city and state; include the extra four numbers if you know them.
5. Always include a return address.
6. When envelopes are included in a bill or correspondence, use them—they are coded to facilitate mail routing.

• **MAIL ORDER:** Write on your check the phone number of the company from which you order. Then, when you have a canceled check but no merchandise, the number to call will be handy.

• **MAIL ORDER,** *Keeping Track of Orders:*
1. Make a note on the calendar of the approximate merchandise arrival date. If delivery is promised in six to eight weeks, make a note to check on the order in week nine.
2. Make copies of the order and keep an "in progress file" for reference if there is a problem.
3. If your checkbook is the kind with stubs, write the name and address of the company and numbers of items ordered on the back of the stub, then, if you have a canceled check but no merchandise, you can write to the company to inquire.

• **MAIL ORDER PROBLEMS:** ALWAYS save copies of your order so that you have dates, check numbers and address of the company so that you have proof in case there is a problem. Sending a complaint that includes all the above information by certified or registered mail will get more attention, too. But if your complaint is ignored, there is help.

1. If your local newspaper has one, contact the consumer-action reporter, they usually get timely responses.
2. Look in your phone book for your state and local consumer protection agencies and contact them.
3. File a complaint with the Better Business Bureau.
4. You can also file a complaint with The Direct Marketing Association (DMA), 6 East 43rd St., New York, NY 10017.

• **MAIL ORDERS,** *Checklist:*
1. Write name and address neatly or attach an address label. Illegible writing makes filling orders properly difficult.
2. Include ALL digits of your credit card number and the expiration date if it's requested. Orders with incomplete credit card numbers must be returned to customers; a delay!
3. Address must include all numbers, street name, apartment number or lot number for mobile-home parks, and zip code or the post office and / or parcel delivery service will not deliver.

Mail order houses receive thousands of orders daily and can only process them promptly if all information is complete.

• **MAKEUP,** *Checklist for Buying Foundation:* When choosing a makeup base, you need to consider skin-type as well as color and manufacturers use various terms to help you.
1. Hypoallergenic—less likely to irritate sensitive skin.
2. Non-comedogenic—helps prevent pores from clogging which results in blackheads; for women with large pores.
3. Hydrophilic—contains hydrophilic ointment; this makeup is combined with water which is recommended by dermatologists.
Caution: Always consult a family physician or dermatologist if skin problems persist; skin or nail conditions can signal certain health problems.

• **MAKEUP,** *Keeping It Off Clothing:*

1. Before slipping a dress or sweater over your head, place a shower cap under your chin and up over your face, then pull the garment on. Carry one in your purse when you go shopping so that you don't leave makeup on garments you try on. Disposable shower caps found in hotels and motels are good for this hint.

2. Instead of a shower cap, drape a large, square, silky scarf over the top of your head and you won't mess your hair or makeup. If you're traveling and don't have a scarf, a slip or nylon panties can substitute.

• **MAKEUP,** *Making It Last Longer:* Cosmetologists say most makeup probably won't last more than six hours, no matter what type or application method.

1. Powder sets makeup and helps it last longer. Apply loose or pressed powder then dab a lightly dampened sponge over it to give your skin a glow. You can also dampen a sponge or cotton ball in astringent lotion instead of water to set the makeup. Hint—the area around your eyes will have a moister look if you don't powder it.

2. Store powder so it keeps dry. Loose powder is easier to shake out from a salt or pepper shaker. Shake it into the palm of your hand, then dip a powder puff or makeup brush into it. Brushes can be old blush brushes or a clean dry shaving brush.

• **MAP,** *Marking:* When you move to a new city or in a city you visit often, mark with red or other color places you've gone. It will jar your memory and help you orient yourself to your new surroundings. If there is a space, you can put a red "X" or dot on 1234 Maple Street and then draw a fine line to the margin (or into a river or lake if there is one on the map) and note "Acme Book Store," or "Smiths."

• **MARBLE,** *Water Stain:* If a water ring is only on the surface, try rubbing with a good marble-polishing powder, usually tin oxide, from a hardware store or marble manufacturing company or funeral monument manufacturer. These companies are a good source for advice on polishing marble. Avoid trouble in the future by trying to convince your family and friends that marble is porous and absorbs moisture. Also, wipe up spills, even plain water, ASAP.

• **MARGARINE SQUEEZE-CONTAINERS,** *Recycling:* Since these containers fit so well in refrigerator door space, wash them well so that they can hold syrups, ketchup, mustard, salad dressings, steak sauces and anything else you want to squirt on your food. Less clutter in the fridge and fewer search missions into the back to find things. Don't forget to write on the outside what's stored on the inside!

• **MATCH HOLDER,** *Safety Idea:* Hold the match with a spring-type wooden clothespin when you light candles, barbecue or fireplace starters. No more singed finger tips!

• **MATERNITY SLACKS,** *Creeping and Slipping Down When You Sit:* Wear suspenders under your blouse or sweater to keep them in place.

• **MATTRESS,** *Anchoring Slippery Ones:* Mattresses quilted with shiny, satiny fabrics often slip off the box springs and can make it difficult to keep sheets neat. Place a thin sheet of foam rubber between the mattress and the box spring, then another thin sheet of foam rubber on top of the mattress before you add pad and sheets. Sometimes, just placing foam on the corners of a mattress will hold the pad and sheets on. (Foam corners are sold in catalogs and elsewhere and some catalogs sell special non-skid sheets to place between mattress and box spring.)

• **MATTRESS,** *Turning Cues:* Turning a mattress every few months makes it last longer and prevents "dips" in the springs. But who can remember which way to flip the thing?
Method 1: Write the date you turn the mattress on some masking tape and tape it to a top corner of the box spring so you'll know at a glance when you should turn it again.
Method 2: Write a code on the corners of the mattress with permanent marker. For example, on one side of the mattress, mark J-M for January-March and on the diagonal corner, mark A-J for April-June. On the other side of the mattress, mark two diagonal corners again with J-S for July and September and O-D for October and December. Then you'll know which corner to turn when.

• **MEAT,** *No Mess Marinating:* Put all the ingredients in a plastic bag large enough to accommodate the meat and seal, forcing out as much air as you can. Then put the bag in the fridge (on a dish if you're afraid of leaks) and then when you need to turn the meat all you turn is the bag.

• **MEAT,** *Quick-Thawing a Solid Hunk of Ground Meat for Meatloaf or Meatballs:* Unwrap the meat; slice the frozen meat with a sharp knife; place the slivers in a bowl and they will thaw in about an hour. **Note:** Mix beef bouillon powder into ground turkey and you'll have a beefier flavor when you substitute it for beef in your favorite recipes.

• **MEATBALLS,** *Swedish & Italian, Time-Saver:* Place on shallow baking dish; bake at 374°F. for about 10 minutes (depending on size). You don't even have to turn them!

• **MEAT, FLOURING OR BREADING,** *Avoiding Mess:* Open the plastic wrap on the meat carefully and lay it on the counter, then you can put flour and/or bread crumbs on the plastic wrap and/or on the foam meat tray. After breading, toss the mess away. **Hint:** Don't forget to let the meat rest on the wrap or foam trays for 10 to 20 minutes after breading or flouring to let the surface dry (turn over once during drying); the coating will stick better during cooking.

• **MEATLOAF,** *Substitutes for Bread Crumbs:* Try crushed or blender-ground unsweetened dry cereal, dry oatmeal, instant mashed potatoes or crushed soda cracker crumbs when you have no bread or bread crumbs.

• **MEAT MARINADE,** *Quick-Fix:* Bottled Italian or other vinegar and oil-style salad dressing will give flavor and tenderize meats and chicken.

• **MEAT RE-WRAPPING FOR FREEZER:** When re-wrapping meats for the freezer, cut the label off the original grocery package and tape it to the newly wrapped one. The label has all the information— type of meat, date of purchase and weight. No more guessing at how much is in the package.

• **MEDICINE,** *Getting Small Children to Take Bad-tasting Liquid Medicine:* Mary Poppins used a spoonful of sugar to help the medicine go down but here's a non-sugar idea. Have the child suck on an ice cube or frozen fruit treat for a few minutes to numb the taste buds. To avoid choking in very small children, let the child suck on some crushed ice.

• **MEDICINE,** *Identifying Meds in the Cabinet:* Mark containers with the malady for which they were prescribed as soon as you bring them home. For example, for headache, for cough, for allergy, diuretic (water pills), high blood pressure, etc. While you should always take all of the medication as prescribed for an illness and should not have leftovers, some prescriptions are for ongoing problems (like allergy, diuretic, etc.) and you may forget what (tongue-twister chemical-name) is for. **Caution:** If you forget what a certain medicine is for, call your pharmacist who can look it up in computerized records for you and tell you what it's for and how it should be taken—with meals, not with dairy products, not with certain other medications, if the instructions are not printed on the container.

• **MEDICINE,** *Remembering to Take the Next Dose:* Buy a "will be back at" clock from an office supply store. Then when you take medicine, set it for the next time a dose is due. Hang it where you will surely see it and you won't miss a dose.

• **MEDICINE BOTTLE,** *Easier Opening Safety Lids:* When the cap's directions say "Squeeze at arrows while turning" and your fingers don't do that without complaining/paining, put a nutcracker to the cap. The extra pressure and "torque" makes opening safety caps a snap.

• **MEDICINE CABINET,** *Cleaning Checklist:* Make it a habit to clean out your medicine cabinet at least once a year—perhaps on your birthday, or during the Spring Forward or Fall Back switches between standard and daylight saving's time.
1. Check labels for expiration dates; if expired, discard as noted in Medicine, Prescriptions, below. If there is no date, discard any medicine that's two years old.
2. Discard cracked, smashed or discolored tablets or capsules which have become soft and/or stuck together.
3. Discard aspirin tablets that smell of vinegar.
4. Discard any liquid medicine that has separated.

5. If the prescription label has come off, you can't be sure about contents, dosage or age, so discard it.

6. Keep all medicines in a cool, dry place. The warm, steamy bathroom medicine chest is not good for storage and if kept in a closet, don't keep medicines near mothballs or insect repellent whose vapors can be absorbed by medicine.

• **MEDICINE CABINET SAFETY:** Dowel pins (round wooden sticks sold at hardware stores for less than $1) can be placed in the mirror track of sliding-door medicine chests to prevent young children from opening the doors.

• **MEDICINE, PRESCRIPTIONS,** *Using Leftovers:*
1. If the prescription is for a specific illness, such as antibiotics, you won't have leftovers if you take the medicine exactly as it was prescribed.
2. Medicines should not be taken if they are older than the use-by date on the label or older than one year. Old medications deteriorate and can become either ineffective or even dangerous. Call your doctor or pharmacist before taking any leftover medications regardless of age.
3. **Caution!** When you buy Over-the-Counter (OTC) medicines, ask the pharmacist if they are compatible with your prescription medicines; OTCs are real drugs and can react with your prescriptions.
4. **Caution!** Protect curious children and pets. Flush old medications down the toilet, rinse out containers, and replace caps tightly before discarding.

• **MELON,** *Quick Fix, Removing Seeds:* Try an ice cream scoop!

• **MEMORY ALBUM:** When couples celebrate 25th or 50th wedding anniversaries and don't want gifts, friends can write a personal letter to the couple relating a fond memory that they shared, their first meeting or the like. Put all the letters in a scrap book for many happy hours of reminiscing.

• **MENU PLANNING,** *Quick-Fix:* When you just can't decide what to serve, look at frozen dinners to see combinations of meats, starch and vegetables that you can duplicate with your own home-cooking.

- **MERINGUE,** *Checklist for Success:*

1. Beaters and bowls must be sparkling clean and free from all grease and oil. Use only metal or glass bowls. Plastic bowls, even clean ones, may have a greasy film that prevents foaming.

2. Separate eggs carefully. Fat in the egg yolk is the culprit; even a bit of yolk prevents the whites from foaming properly. **Hint:** Separate eggs while they are cold.

3. After separating, let egg whites set for about one-half hour so that they come to room temperature. They will produce greater volume than if beaten when cold. **Note:** Add ⅛ teaspoon cream of tartar for each egg white before beating.

4. Procedure: Beat with rotary beater, whisk or electric mixer at high speed just until foamy. Gradually begin adding sugar, about one tablespoon at a time, beating as you slowly sprinkle the sugar in. **Hints:** Powdered sugar dissolves more easily than granulated. Always move the beaters or the bowl so that all of the egg-sugar mixture reaches the beaters.

Continue to beat at high speed until the sugar is dissolved. **Hint:** Rub a little of the mixture between your fingers to test if all the sugar is dissolved. If you feel grittiness, beat some more. Whites should stand in soft or stiff peaks, depending on the recipe directions.

- **METAL,** *Polishing:* Please see individual metal's listing.

- **MICROWAVE,** *Container Size for Boiling:* Milk or creamy mixtures and some cereals boil up quickly and tend to overflow; allow plenty of headroom. Containers should be two to three times the volume of the ingredients to avoid messy boil-overs.

- **MICROWAVE,** *Cooking Bags:* Twist-ties contain metal and can cause "arcing" sparks that can damage your oven. Tie microwave cooking bags closed with dental floss and ALWAYS open bags AWAY from you to prevent steam burns.

- **MICROWAVE,** *Cooking in Ring Pan:* Because microwaves cook from the outside in, veggies and some other foods are best made in a ring mold or bundt pan. To make one, place a glass ovenware custard cup, microwave-safe water glass or preserving jar in the center of a microwave-safe round casserole which has the proper diameter.

• **MICROWAVE,** *Covering Food While Cooking:* Waxed paper used to cover food containers won't blow off if you crumple the paper slightly.

• **MICROWAVE,** *Identifying Cookware:* Identify your microwave-safe cookware with an indelible mark (use pens for marking glassware, etc.) so that everyone in the family knows which containers are safe. Then, when you place the container in the microwave oven, make it a habit to center the mark at "12 o'clock" so that if you have to give it one-quarter or one-half turns during cooking, you'll know how much of a turn you've made.

• **MICROWAVE,** *Reheating Chicken and Keeping It Crisp:* Pop chicken in the microwave for one minute on "High," then finish in conventional oven at 400°F for 5 minutes. The chicken will be warmed to the bone and be crispy without burning the coating or making the insides rubbery.

• **MICROWAVE,** *Reheating Rolls and Pastries:* Heating too long makes bread products tough and dry; a few seconds—about 15—is usually enough. To prevent soggy bottoms on sweet rolls or pastries place them on a paper towel or paper plate (real paper, not foam); you can use the plate several times.

• **MICROWAVE,** *Reminder to Rotate Foods:* Put a wooden toothpick under the front of the dish, then move it with the dish as you rotate it. For example, start at 6 o'clock; move to 9; then 12, and so on. You can tell at a glance how often the dish was turned.

• **MICROWAVE COOKING,** *Dont's:*
1. Never warm baby bottles; bottles can feel cool to the touch on the outside but the milk or other fluid inside can be hot enough to scald a baby's throat.
2. Stuffing in stuffed birds (turkey, chicken) may not cook completely and could cause food poisoning.
3. Eggs in the shell can explode due to steam buildup and damage the oven.
4. Popcorn should be cooked only in microwave-safe containers or pre-packaged microwave bags. Kernels can scorch and cause a fire inside the oven if improper containers are used. Reheating popcorn in the microwave also is a fire hazard.

5. Canning in the microwave is dangerous because there is no way to tell if harmful organisms are killed.

6. Deep-fat frying in the microwave is a fire hazard.

7. Let steam out of baked potatoes by piercing them with a fork; otherwise they can explode and possibly cause eye injury or burns if they pop when you are opening the door.

8. Never operate a microwave oven when it's empty. To avoid doing this accidentally, leave a water-filled microwave-safe coffee cup in the oven.

• MICROWAVE COOKING, *Packaging:* When you use foods with heat susceptor packaging experts recommend:

1. Don't microwave products any longer than instructed on the package; it increases chances of the temperature going too high.

2. Don't eat foods, such as popcorn, if the package has become very browned or charred—signs that the food may have been over-heated.

3. Don't re-use container with heat susceptors or remove the susceptors for use with other foods.

• MICROWAVE COOKING, *Foil-covered Frozen Foods:* Although many new products packaged in foil are safe for some microwave ovens under certain conditions, you still need to check the cookbook that came with your oven to make sure it is safe for your oven to avoid serious damage. If your care manual doesn't give you the information you need, call the manufacturer's consumer line which should be given in the manual.

• MICROWAVE COOKING, *Seasonings:* Add most seasonings as usual to microwave recipes. However, don't sprinkle salt on food; the crystals reflect the microwaves and cause uneven cooking. Dissolve salt in liquid, mix it into the food or better—add it just before serving. Pepper becomes more intense when microwaved, so use it sparingly and add more after cooking if you wish.

• MICROWAVE DISPOSABLE TRAYS, *Recycling for Workday Lunches When Your Workplace Has a Microwave:* Wash trays and plates well after home use so that you can put leftovers in them to reheat at work on your lunch break. There's no clean-up or toting dirty dishes home.

• **MICROWAVE DISHES,** *Which Are Best:*

1. Check if the material is safe for microwave cooking and if the size and shape are suitable for that particular food or recipe. Don't cook with any dishes trimmed with gold or silver or any made of metal. Microwave safe materials include glass, ceramic, pottery, special microwaveable plastics and paper. Most sold today will indicate suitability for microwaving. Test older dishes as described below.

Test for Microwave Cooking Safety: Place the dish in the microwave and next to it place a glass measuring cup with one cup of water. Heat on full power for one minute, then check the temperature of the dish. If the dish is cool and the water is very warm, the dish is safe. If the dish is slightly warm, it can still be used, but only for very short-term warming. If the dish is hot, it's not for microwave cooking.

2. Food in deep containers cooks more slowly than food in shallow ones and will require more stirring. Shallow containers expose more food surface to microwaves so more food cooks at the same time.

3. Round and oval casseroles give more even results than square or rectangular ones. More energy penetrates the corners so food there is apt to overcook, giving you dried-out corners and underdone centers.

4. Straight-sided dishes and pans are better than slanted-side ones. Straight sides keep food at a more uniform depth and so it cooks more evenly. Sloped dishes let food on the edges get more energy because it's not as deep; it cooks faster and can overcook before the center is done.

5. Ring-shaped pans are best for foods like cakes and muffins that can't be stirred during cooking. The open center allows microwaves to contact the food from all sides as well as top and bottom for more uniform cooking.

• **MICROWAVE POTPOURRI:** To get your house smelling like baking pies, add 2 teaspoons of pumpkin pie spice to 1 cup of water in a microwave-safe dish. Microwave on "High" until it boils, then cook for 3 more minutes. For delicious roast turkey, cook 2 teaspoons of thyme or sage in water the same way. You can use your imagination to create a tempting aroma any time with any spice you like.

• **MILDEW,** *Prevention in Basements, Closets, and Bathrooms:* Air conditioners and dehumidifiers are the best solutions in damp climates. Leaving a light on in the bathroom or closet helps. Commercial products such as silica gel or activated alumina, found in hardware stores, work well in enclosed spaces like closets. These chemicals absorb moisture from the air. Follow package directions exactly and keep away from small children and pets.

• **MILDEW,** *Removing from Plastic-Mesh Outdoor Furniture:*
Method 1: Mix 1 cup of bleach to 1 gallon of water and test solution on an inconspicuous area to make sure there will be no fabric color changes. If it is safe, apply solution to the fabric and scrub with a soft brush or rag. Be sure to rinse well.
Method 2: If the bleach solution is not safe, vinegar may remove the mildew. Wash the furniture with white vinegar and rinse well.
Hint: Always dry furniture completely to help prevent more mildew growth.

• **MILK SUBSTITUTE FOR COOKING:** Mix non-dairy creamer with a little water to complete a recipe in a hurry, when you're out of milk and can't even borrow some from a friendly neighbor.

• **MINI-BLIND DUSTER:** Try a new and clean two-inch paintbrush.

• **MIRROR,** *Removing Hair Spray:* Clean with rubbing alcohol on a soft cloth. Please see GLASS CLEANER, Homemade.

• **MIRRORS,** *Cleaning:* Mix 2 ounces of non-sudsing ammonia, 2 ounces of rubbing alcohol, a couple of drops of blue food coloring (optional) with 12 ounces of water in a spray bottle which has been clearly labeled. The food coloring helps you quickly distinguish window cleaner from other cleaning liquids but you should label the container anyway.

• **MITTENS,** *Decorating for Identification:* Stitch or embroider the owner's initials on them or "R" and "L" for right and left; add favorite-color buttons or bows.

• **MITTENS,** *Recycling an Old Sweater to Make Mittens:* See SWEATER, Recycling.

• **MITTENS,** *Storing:* Hang a sixteen-pocket shoe bag on the closet rod to hold mittens. No matter what height the child and others in the family are, some pocket will be reachable.

• **MITTS,** *Kitchen/Oven:* When the non-stick surface of your iron-ing board cover wears out, the less-worn parts can be lined with washable fabric padding and sewn into hot mitts and pot holders. Cover one side with the ironing board cover fabric and the other with a print that coordinates with your kitchen. Bind the edges with bias tape.

• **MIX 'N' MASH,** *Quick-Fix:* A pastry blender is a super masher for avocados, bananas or any other slightly soft food. It quick mixes dips, cream cheese or anything too stiff to mix with a blender. It also substitutes for a wire whisk when you beat eggs.

• **MONEY MATTERS,** *Letter of Laughter:* One reader asks, "Have you noticed that with the economy the way it is that life's little pleasures are now considered luxuries?"

• **MOSS,** *Removing from Patio/Walkway Bricks:* Sprinkle a solu-tion of half water and half bleach onto the moss. **Caution:** This should remove moss without discoloring brick but it's always best to test in an inconspicuous place.

• **MOTHERHOOD,** *Letter of Laughter:* When a four-year-old attend-ing a meeting with his mother heard the word "motherhood" men-tioned, he turned to his mom and whispered, "She must be Robin Hood's Mother."

• **MOTHER SCRAPBOOK,** *The Way We Were:* Write down young children's cute sayings and add their "quotables" as they get older and you'll end up with a wonderful and funny record of the joys and sorrows of childhood and teens. Keep the original and make a copy for your children as they leave home.

• **MOUSEPROOFING,** *Healthy Planet:* Instead of dangerous poisons, stuff all the cracks around gas and water pipes with steel wool to keep the varmints out.

• **MOVING,** *Getting Information About the New City:* Subscribe to the Sunday or daily newspaper to find out about the area and write to the Chamber of Commerce to find out about special events and happenings. Some chambers of commerce offer newcomer welcome packets or visitor information packets that are useful to "perma-nent visitors," too.

• **MOVING,** *Healthy-Planet Packing Materials:* Wrap dishes and breakables one at a time in clean towels, washcloths, sheets, pillow-cases and clothing. They arrive clean and you've nothing to throw away.

• **MOVING,** *Making It Easier for Children:*
1. Type your new address and phone number in columns with two-inch margins and fold on lines above and below each address segment so that you and the children can tear off new-address segments for friends. Then, at the new location, make stationery, envelopes and stamps available for children to write to their friends. Allow one five-minute long-distance call per month per child (depending on your finances). Each child keeps track of the date and length of call on a calendar placed near the phone and pays for the call with allowance money when the phone bill arrives. Long distance calls will be kept to the minimum and children will be encouraged to write letters to their friends instead and they will also be encouraged to develop a rewarding life-long habit of writing.
2. Christen your new home by tying a big bow on the front door—one for each child. While each child cuts a bow, take a picture to put into your moving-day scrapbook. Later in the evening, have a family party with cookies, punch and talk. Remember that the talk may be more a "refreshment" than the cookies and punch! Moving can be hard for kids.
Also, please see VIDEO MEMORIES.

• **MOVING COSTS:** When contracting with a moving company find out if charges are different for weekday and weekend; if they charge overtime rates and at what hour does overtime begin. It may be better to schedule two days instead of one with overtime.

• **MOVING FURNITURE THAT WILL BE REASSEMBLED,** *Avoiding Loss or Confusion Over Which Hardware Belongs to Which Furniture.*
Instead of putting all of your nuts and bolts in one basket, box or jar, when furniture is disassembled, gather all screws, bolts and brackets in a sturdy envelope or bag and tape it securely to the underside of a part of that bookcase, desk, etc. Or, securely tape the hardware to the undersides of furniture with duct tape so that it's ready when you reassemble the furniture at your destination.

• **MOVING IN:** Protect carpets from dirt with plastic drop cloths which you can save for later use in the garden or for painting; protect varnished or new flooring from scratches with old flannel-backed plastic tablecloths, bedspreads, and rugs but **Caution:** be sure that the floor "protection" is non-skid people-protection too.

• **MOVING INFORMATION:** Contact the phone company in the city to which you are moving to get a phone book. Then, you can call utility and cable companies to find out what information and fees are necessary to get "hooked-up" in your new location and to set the wheels rolling for faster service. You can look up service people to install appliances and find the name of the local newspaper and order a subscription to the Sunday paper that lets you get acquainted with stores, politics, and other facts before you get to the new city. You can check out the chain department stores and know which credit cards will be useful and which to cancel.

And, take your old phone book with you when you move, just in case you leave a few "loose ends to tie up." And, you'll have your neighbors' street address numbers, too, when you want to send them a Christmas card!

• **MOVING OUT:** Be kind to the next tenant. Leave an envelope with helpful information such as utility companies, cable TV, garbage pickup days, the local pizza or other food delivery number, a roll of toilet tissue, paper towels and soap, and any appliance booklets for the ones you leave behind.

• **MUFFIN,** *Quick-Fix Removal from Tin:* A shoe horn lifts muffins out of the tin without tearing and can go right into the dishwasher. Of course, the shoehorn is for kitchen use only!

• **MUFFIN TIN GREASING,** *No-mess When You're Out of Non-stick Spray:* Pour about a fourth cup of oil in one of the muffin cups, then dip a waded-up paper towel into the oil. Rub the other cups with the towel, re-oiling it as you go.

• **MUSHROOMS,** *Non-slimy Storage:* Don't wash mushrooms before you put them into the fridge, instead, make sure they're dry and then put them into a paper, not plastic, bag. Paper bags let them "breathe" so that they stay fresh longer; plastic bags or wrap makes mushrooms slimy.

• **MUSHROOMS,** *Quick-Slice:* After washing, cut off stems level with the mushroom cap and then place each mushroom in the egg slicer stem side up—all will have equal thickness.

• **MUSTARD SQUIRT BOTTLE,** *Healthy-Planet Recycling:* Wash thoroughly so that it can be a cooking oil dispenser—a help if you buy the large economy size oil and find it awkward to pour.

• **MUTUAL HELP TRADE-OFFS TO SAVE MONEY:**
1. Set up a babysitting co-op in your neighborhood. Each family gets a beginning bonus of hours (2 or so) and then must "sit" for others to put "hours in the bank" which they can withdraw when they need sitters. Different people can be the "banker" for each month so the responsibilities are divided or you can elect a "banker" for a period of time. Naturally you have to set a limit to "credit" hours so that no parent ends up not paying back hours used.

Also, with so many women (some statistics show it's 20 to 30 percent) caring for sick and elderly parents, trading elder-sitting is an idea whose time has come. One could even trade elder-sitting for baby-sitting to get an exchange of viewpoints—younger vs older.
2. If all you need is a perm in your bangs, and that's all your friend needs, too, you can share one boxed home permanent and roll each other's hair. You'll both get curls for less than the cost of one person's perm. (Some shops charge $5 per curl when you just have bangs done!) While you're at it, make it a beauty day and give each other facials and manicures, too.
3. If you can't afford a maid, share housework chores with a friend. If you like to wax furniture and your friend likes to shine bathrooms, trade your waxing for her shining. Or, work together on each other's houses; four hands work more pleasantly than two and you can treat yourselves to a nice luncheon out after you finish.
4. Trade talents and interests. For example, if your friend likes to hang wallpaper and paint woodwork but doesn't garden, and you are a gardener, trade off wallpapering a room for planting your friend's flower beds planted with annuals.
5. Trade off house chores for free or reduced rent. Many elderly people who live alone need help with minor chores and yard work as well as companionship so that they can maintain their independent lifestyles. Check out classified ads in the newspaper or place an

ad yourself that says, "Will do work around the house in exchange for free rent . . ." Be sure to spell out in writing exactly what chores you will do for what household benefits and rental charge (if any) so that there is no confusion. Many large cities have programs to match renters with people who need such help. There is also a national agency, Shared Housing Resource Center, which will help you find a local agency on aging that has a house-sharing/room-mates for the elderly program; call 215-848-1220.

6. Trade off homes with couples or families you know in other cities or trade with families in other countries through an exchange program to have a vacation without hotel/motel fees. Some church groups have such exchange programs with overseas churches in which couples trade houses for a period of time.

N

- **NAILS,** *Quick Pickup:* Please see SPEAKERS, Recycling.

- **NAMES CONFUSION,** *Ending Check Payment Confusion:* When Mom remarries and children's names differ from hers, payments to school, Scouts, and other activities may not be recognized as for that child when the mother's new name is printed on the checks. One mother solves the problem by having her children's names printed on the checks beneath her and her husband's names. The bonus is that the children feel as important as the parents in the family and the name association is more recognizable by activity directors.

- **NAPKINS,** *Healthy-Planet Quick-Fix, $aver:* Instead of paper table napkins or cloth ones that need ironing or show food stains, substitute small, cheap washcloths or finger-tip towels for family dining.

- **NAPKIN RINGS:** See COOKIE CUTTERS, Seasonal Plastic Ones.

- **NECKLACE,** *Lengthening:* If clasps are compatible, add a thin metal bracelet to the necklace. The bracelet will be concealed under the collar so your extension won't show.

• **NECKLACES,** *Avoiding Tangles:* Hang necklaces to a mirror with clear suction-cup hooks; to a wall or in the closet on an expanding peg coatrack; from clothes screwed into a closet door or wall; layer them in a drawer on shoebox lids (line lids with a piece of soft scrap fabric to keep them from slipping too much); place lengthwise on felt and roll necklace "sausages" to be placed in a drawer.

• **NECKTIE PROTECTION:** Many men tuck their neckties into their shirts when they eat—especially on airplanes when a bump could ruin a favorite tie.

• **NECKTIES,** *Care:*
1. Undo the tie before removing it; sliding the knot or leaving it ties causes it to lose shape.
2. Take care when using cologne or after-shave; they can fade colors.
3. Hanging keeps ties from wrinkling; try draping them over a dry cleaner's pants hanger—the kind with a paper tube.
4. If you must press a tie, do it on the backside to avoid shine on the fabric.
5. If you get a spot or stain, just blot it off and take the tie to a dry cleaner. Club soda or water can leave water spots, especially on silk ties. Tell the dry cleaner what the stain is so that there's a better chance of getting it removed.

• **NEEDLEWORK,** *Framing:* Larger cities have do-it-yourself (with help) framing shops to help you save money framing needlework and craft art.

• **NEEDLEWORK,** *Framing:* Use an embroidery hoop, painted or unfinished, to frame and hang a needlework project.

• **NEEDLEWORK,** Hint: Tie your needle threader and embroidery scissors on a string, yarn, or old shoelace and you won't lose the threader. (If you haven't done needlework for a long time, new threader designs make using thread or yarn easier than you could ever imagine.)

• **NEEDLEWORK,** *Hoops:* Tack, staple, or tape (masking) smaller embroidery work to an old sturdy picture frame if you don't have a hoop or embroidery frame to work on.

• **NEEDLEWORK,** *From Kits:* Read packets before you buy them to find out what's included. Most needlework pattern designs (needlepoint, embroidery, cross stitch, long stitch) have instructions for the types of stitches used so you don't have to know how; you can learn from the pictures. Full kits usually include the needles as well as yarn or thread.

• **NEEDLEWORK,** *Learning How:* Most needlework and craft stores offer free advice and demonstrations to help you get started in such hobbies. Ask about classes for adults and children.

• **NEEDLEWORK TRAVEL:** Replace scissors in your needlework travel kit with a pair of fingernail clippers. They'll snip the threads but are smaller and won't poke holes in anything, including you!

• **NEIGHBORHOOD SWAP MEET,** *Recycling, $aver:* Lots of neighbors join for a garage sale, but how about a swap meet for books, records, tapes, even children's clothing if it doesn't disturb the children. Aside from saving money, it's a friendly, get-acquainted thing to do!

• **NEWSPAPER BAGS,** *Recycling:*
1. Store sewing patterns.
2. Store celery, green onions, and other "long" veggies.
3. Wrap several around a wire hanger to pad it.
4. Place on ceiling-fan blades when you paint to keep spatters off.

• **NEWSPAPER BILLS,** *Keeping Track of Paid Weeks:* If you pay in advance, as many people do, highlight the paid-for weeks on your calendar so you can tell when the next bill will be due. A good calendar for this is the bookmark-style ones we get from various businesses at Christmas time.

• **NEWSPAPERS,** *Recycling:*
1. Wet the edge and use as a dustpan, especially for sweeping up glass or messy things. (Used paper plates from dry foods like sandwiches can be cut in half for the same purpose.)
2. Comics can be gift wrap.
3. Children can make paper airplanes and hats from them.
4. Roll and stuff inside wet boots and shoes to shape them as they dry.

5. Place inside a plastic bag to pad your knees in the garden or your "sitter" at a picnic.

6. Shred for hamster/guinea pig cages or for the garden compost pile.

7. Place under and inside refrigerators/freezers to absorb water during defrosting.

8. Place under pet feeding dishes for absorbent, disposable place mats.

9. Spread over plastic drop cloths while you paint. They absorb spills and prevent tearing the drop cloth which may let paint get on the floor.

• **NEW YEAR'S RESOLUTIONS,** *Making and Keeping Them:* One reader sent in her system which is similar to business goal-setting. Instead of making resolutions and then forgetting about them, she decides what her resolutions are, plans a definite date on which to start them and a definite time in which to accomplish them. For example, what date will she start her diet? If she will plant a garden, what date will she buy seedlings, when might she put them outside, and so on. Then, the most important step is to mark all the dates on the next year's calendar so that she's reminded of what she wants to do and when.

• **NIGHT-LIGHT:** Plug a night-light in at the bathroom vanity level and you won't have to startle your eyes switching on the regular light if you get up at night. Get an automatic, light-sensor type; it remembers to turn itself on!

• **NON-STICK SPRAY CAUTION:** A reader who frequently sprayed pots and pans with non-stick spray wrote that, apparently, the spray built up on her floor so much that one day she slipped and fell. Now instead of holding a dish "in the air" to spray, she places it in the sink.

• **NUTS,** *Easy Cracking:* Freeze Brazil nuts before cracking. If freezing doesn't work for pecans, try placing them in a microwave-safe bowl, add enough water to cover and heat on "High" in the microwave for about three minutes. Take the pecans out of the water and let them cool. The shells should crack easily.

O

- **OATMEAL,** *Flavoring:* Perk up oatmeal by adding chopped fruit (fresh or dried); nuts; chocolate or butterscotch chips; crumbs from the bottom of a dry cereal to make it crunchy, and then the old favorites—brown sugar and cinnamon, raisins or applesauce, honey or molasses.

- **OATMEAL,** *Homestyle "Granola" in Yogurt:* Add dry oatmeal to your fruited yogurt for extra fiber and a fuller feeling. It won't look particularly pretty, but it tastes good, expecially if you add a few chopped nuts.

- **OATMEAL MASK,** *Homestyle Beauty Aid:* Mix a little water with some oatmeal until it's a smooth paste. Spread mixture on your face, keeping it away from the delicate skin around the eyes. Allow it to dry and rinse off with warm water. Your face will be clean, refreshed, and smooth.

- **ODORS,** Please see the special section on odors on page 420.

- **OFFICE DUSTING:** Dust the copy-machine glass with a coffee filter instead of a paper towel or cloth. It leaves no lint and you'll get clearer, neater copies.

• **OIL BOTTLE,** *Avoiding Mess:* Slip a plastic sandwich bag over the bottom of the bottle, leaving the sides open around the bottle to catch drips that run down the sides. You'll have a clean shelf!

• **OIL PAINTING,** *Faking It:* Put a piece of cheesecloth or swatch of nylon net over a picture, taping around the edges to keep it flat and taut. Then brush on a very thin coat of shellac and gently remove the net or cloth and allow the picture to dry completely. When dry, the picture will have a texture similar to an oil on canvas painting.

• **OINTMENT,** *Applying Smelling One Without Smelly Hands:* Keep a supply of plastic disposable gloves in the medicine chest to keep your hands away from ointments. It's more sanitary anyway.

• **OLIVE OIL,** *Storage:* Olive oil keeps longer than other edible oils. Store in a cool, dark place, protected from light. While it doesn't need refrigeration, you can store it there. Refrigeration makes olive oil thick and cloudy, but bringing it back to room temperature will lighten it again.

• **OLIVES,** *Perking Up for Parties:* Drop a clove of garlic into a jar of olives and add a drop or two of olive oil. Let set for a couple of days and the olives will be tasty and shiny.

• **ONION,** *Quick-Fix:* When you want only one slice of onion for a burger or other sandwich, there's no need to peel the whole onion. Slice through the middle of the onion, cut off one slice, put the two parts back together, then wrap or seal in a plastic bag and refrigerate.

• **ONIONS,** *Peeling Without Tears:* Chopping or slicing onions releases a gas that reacts chemically with the water in your eyes to form sulfuric acid. (Saying the name of the gas almost makes you cry, too—propanethiol S-oxide.) Tears are your defense against the acid irritant and some people are innately more irritated by onion gas than others. The good news is that the more onions you cut the greater your tolerance. If you seldom cut onions, you're likely to cry more. Here are some ways to help you avoid crying while dealing with onions.

1. Place in freezer 30 to 45 minutes before slicing. **Caution:** Don't leave them in the freezer too long or they will get mushy; however,

if you should forget and freeze them, you can still cook with them later.

2. If you only cook with onions occasionally, try dried onions found in the spice department of most supermarkets. You can even brown them for casseroles and other recipes that require it, just watch them carefully because once they start to brown, they can burn to black in a few seconds. *Letter of Laughter:* One reader, whose chile sauce recipe requires lots of chopped onion, wrote that since she began wearing her son's scuba mask while chopping them she hasn't shed a tear.

- **ORANGE PEEL,** *Homemade Drying:*
1. Scrape as much of the white off the peel as possible.
2. Cut into small pieces and place on paper towels.
3. Cover with a paper towel to protect from dust.
4. Let sit for four to five days. The top of your refrigerator is a good place to dry things—flower petals, peels, etc.—because it's usually warmer there (unless it's under an AC vent), and the stuff is less likely to be disturbed.
5. Store in fridge or freezer in self-sealing plastic bags. Grate as needed.

- **ORGANIZING,** *Time-saver Filing New Recipes, Cleaning Hints:* Tape that special tuna casserole recipe to the tuna can or that special cleaning hint to the thing that needs cleaning, and they will be handy when and where you need them.

- **OVEN-CLEANING SQUEEGEE:** Scrape oven-cleaner goop from the oven walls with a short-handled window squeegee. When all the goop is on the center bottom of the oven, scoop it onto a piece of newspaper or brown paper bag and then discard in the garbage. Next, wipe down the inside of the oven with a wet rag and you're done. Also, see OVEN CLEANER in the ODORS section on page 420.

- **OVEN-DOOR LOCK:** If you have a self-cleaning oven, you can keep a toddler from opening the oven door while something is baking by locking the door with the lock lever as you would when cleaning the oven.

- **OVEN-DOOR WINDOW,** *Cleaning:* Wipe the glass window with ammonia and let it set for a few minutes. Then, scrape away goop with a plastic ice scraper like those for removing ice from auto windshields.

- **PACKING FOAM "PEANUTS,"** *Healthy-Planet Recycling:*
1. Sprinkle with a favorite perfume and place in potpourri jars to deodorize a room.
2. Stuff into plastic newspaper bags and you have tubes to stuff into clothing for mailing or travel (for arms, put the bag into the suit coat arm and fill with "peanuts").
3. Toss into the bottom of a pot for drainage beneath your plants.

- **PACKING LIST FOR TRAVEL,** *Computerized Checklist:* Compile a packing list to keep from forgetting anything on your trip and save it in the computer. Then you can print it out when you need it. Make two copies—one for your purse and one in the suitcase to be used as a checklist for remembering to take it all home again. Having the list in your purse is very valuable if your luggage is lost or stolen—so would a magazine picture or instant photo of your suitcase; it's sometimes difficult to compare your luggage with the claim-form line-drawings the airline provides to help you identify the type of luggage.

- **PACKING PEANUTS:** Pad "care packages" and other gifts with real peanuts in the shell instead of foam ones; they are edible!

• **PADDING,** *For Pots, Pans, China, etc:* Please see BLANKETS, Recycling.

• **PADDING FOR WORK SPACE:** Buy carpet samples and place them upside down on work surfaces to protect them from damage; this is especially good on a washer or dryer which is a good back-saver height for many chores, including grooming a small pet.

• **PAINT,** *Artist's Oils:* Oil paints on sale may not be a good buy; make sure they aren't so old that they are hard!

• **PAINT,** *Artist's Oils:* Don't throw away expensive oil paints at the end of the day; cover your palette with plastic wrap and aluminum and store it in the freezer overnight for the next day.

• **PAINT,** *Artist's Oils, Tube Cap:* When the caps get lost or don't fit anymore, insert a roofing nail; it's easy to remove and replace.

• **PAINT,** *Color Selection:* Before you paint the whole room, test the color choice by buying a small can of the paint, painting a poster-board, and then holding it up in various places around the room to see how you like it. Also, you can tell how it looks day or night by sun or lamplight.

• **PAINT,** *Homemade, Healthy-Planet Artist's Paint:* Add just enough hot water to instant non-fat dry milk to reconstitute it into a smooth syrup. Add powdered pigment (from art-supply shops) in small amounts until desired shade is reached. Apply to raw wood with a brush or rag while still warm. This homemade paint will dry to a flat finish.

• **PAINT,** *Removing Enamel Paint Drips/Spills:* Instead of turpentine, wipe up spills and drips with a soft wet towel lathered with pumice soap. Remember, the sooner you remove such paint, the better!

• **PAINT,** *Removing from Skin:* Rub with mineral oil; then wash with soap and water.

• **PAINT,** *Storage to Prevent Drying:* Thoroughly clean a plastic container with a tight-fitting screw-on cap. Pour in leftover paint; apply petroleum jelly around the treads; squeeze container until the paint reaches the top and hold it steady until the cap is screwed on tightly. Identify the container by taking the label from the paint can and writing the needed information on the back and then attaching it to the new container with a rubber band. No more "skin" on top of paint to deal with.

• **PAINT,** *Storing to Prevent Discoloration by Rust from Cans:* Pour leftover paint in empty mayo jars, cover the top with plastic wrap and screw on the lid. You can see the color through the jar and the plastic wrap protects the paint from a rusty lid. Be sure to mark the jar with type of paint, cleanup instructions, and any other important information.

• **PAINT,** *Touch-Up:* A cotton swab easily touches up chipped paint on woodwork or small scrapes on walls, and the bonus is no brush to clean!

• **PAINTBRUSHES:** Keep your good paintbrush bristles from getting bent while soaking in thinner: Cut an X for each brush in a plastic lid and then suspend the brushes in the solvent by poking their ends into the Xs.

• **PAINTBRUSHES,** *Easy Cleaning:* Pour a little solvent into a self-sealing heavy-duty clear plastic bag—enough to cover the bristles. Put the brushes in and squeeze the solvent through the bristles, getting all the paint out. When you are finished, pour the solvent into a container with tight lid. You can reuse it.

• **PAINTING,** *Easel:* Make an artist's easel for a child with an old chair. Pound in a couple of nails at the front of the chair to keep the art work from sliding off when you prop it against the chair back. An old bar stool with back could make a taller easel.

• **PAINTING,** *Hand-painting Small Objects:* Keep them in place on cardboard with double-stick carpet tape; you'll keep your fingers clean.

• **PAINTING,** *Inaccessible Corners:* Places like abutted door frames often can't be reached with a paintbrush. Try a wedge-shaped makeup sponge. Dampen it slightly, dip in paint and poke into hard-to-get-at spots.

• **PAINTING,** *Spraying Small Objects:* Place the objects (craft items, hardware) inside a carton to confine the spray "spritzing" and ALWAYS spray in a well-ventilated area.

• **PAINTING A CHAIN-LINK FENCE:** Pour paint into a paint tray and dip a roller or sponge into it to paint. Wear rubber gloves if you paint with a sponge and speed up the job by having another person sponge painting the other side of the fence. This really gets the job done in a hurry, and the bonus is that you can visit while you work and make time pass even faster!

• **PAINTING CAUTION:** When you paint around a phone jack, do not get paint inside the jack box; it could block a proper phone connection and make a repair by the phone company necessary. Instead, place masking tape around the wall jack before painting to protect it.

• **PAINTING FLOOR MOLDINGS,** *Knees-Ease:* Instead of sitting and sliding across the floor as you paint, sit cross-legged on a skateboard and wheel yourself around the room.

• **PAINTINGS,** *Cleaning:* Valuable oil paintings should be cleaned by professionals. Have your painting appraised if you aren't sure about its value. Remove accumulated dust with a soft, clean paintbrush. Commercial cleaners from art-supply stores will remove residues from grease or smoke. **Caution:** Don't dust paintings with a vacuum, it can pull chips off and rags can catch on raised peaks in the paint and remove paint sections.

• **PAINT SPATTERS,** *Keeping Them Off Yourself:* Everyone spreads drop cloths to keep paint spatters off furniture and floors while painting. Here's how to keep paint off the painter: Cut a hole in the bottom of a large plastic leaf bag that's large enough for your head and cut one hole on each side for your arms. Put the bag on to protect clothing, then put a disposable shower cap on your head to protect your hair. You'll emerge from your painting unspattered!

• **PAJAMA/PANTS,** *Helping a Child Find the Front of Elastic-Waist Garments:* Sew a button on the front so that the child need only look for the "belly button" to know front from back.

• **PALETTE PAPER,** *Substitute:* Tape a piece of waxed paper about 12 inches long to a piece of cardboard. Some people also use aluminum foil over a wood palette or piece of sturdy cardboard.

• **PAN,** *Removing Burned-on Gunk:* When a pot or pan is black from frying, sprinkle a small amount (1 or 2 teaspoons) of automatic dishwasher detergent in the pot with a little water and the put the pot on the stove, let it come to boil, turn the burner off. After it's cool enough to handle, wash and rinse well. Avoid scrubbing frying pans; make it a habit that when you take the food out, you pour in enough warm water (and a few drops of liquid dishwashing detergent, if there's lots of grease) to cover the bottom about an inch. Then, allow the water to boil while the burner cools down on electric stoves or allow to boil a minute or so before you turn off a gas stove. The pan cleans itself and cools while you eat. Wash as usual.

• **PANCAKE FUN:** When you are making pancakes, take a cake-decorating tube (or pour with a spoon if you are handy) and make faces or names on pancakes, then flip them over. Or, instead of pouring one large round pancake, make squiggles, critters (one larger plus one smaller circle, two "ear" dots and a tail), or large initials of the pancake lovers.

• **PANCAKE OR FRENCH TOAST TOPPING:** Heat up some chunky-style applesauce with a teaspoon or two of cinnamon and spoon it on— Yum! And it adds the nutrition of fruit instead of just sugar from syrup!

• **PANCAKES,** *Keeping Warm:* Keep them in a bun warmer until the whole batch is cooked, then you can serve all at once and the pancake-cooker won't end up eating alone!

• **PANCAKES,** *Serving to Small Children:* Avoid sticky messes—cut up the pancakes and add the syrup before serving them and serve in soup bowls instead of plates.

• **PANCAKES, WAFFLES,** *Freezing Leftovers:*
1. Make bigger-than-needed batches and prepare as usual, but cook the extras until almost done; they will finish cooking later.

2. Cool on racks, separate them with waxed paper or cut up cereal-box liner, put in freezer-safe bag or container and pop in freezer.
3. To serve, heat in microwave oven for about a minute and a half. Some folks like to toast leftover waffles. Enjoy!

• **PANCAKE SYRUP,** *Homemade Substitute When You Run Out:* Mix 1 cup of brown sugar and ¾ cup of water in a saucepan. Bring mixture to boil, let simmer for about 15 minutes. (Don't let it boil again or overcook.) Add a teaspoon or so of maple flavoring to suit your taste.

• **PANTS ELASTIC,** *Replacing:* If the waistband elastic of stitched waistband pants gets stretched out before the pants are worn, you can replace it easily.
1. Remove the four lines of stitching through the waistband, cut a small slit at one of the side seams and then pull out the old elastic.
2. Measure your waist and cut a piece of the new non-roll elastic about 2 inches smaller than your waist measurement. Do not pull the elastic tightly while measuring it.
3. Attach a small safety pin to the end of the elastic to feed it through, and insert the new elastic all the way through the waist casing. Then stitch the two ends of elastic together; sew the opening shut. You may want to add a lengthwise stitch to both side seams to keep the elastic in place.

• **PANTS PATCHES:** Save the bottoms cut off when you hem children's pants, and then you can fuse the fabric to wherever you need a patch.

• **PANTY HOSE,** *Recycling:*
Hairbands, Ponytail Holders—Cut across the leg to make rings, roll the rings up, and you have a ponytail holder that won't break and damage your hair like rubber bands will. Cut off the panty and the foot, tie the ends together, and you have a stretchy headband or hairband. Colored panty hose can be coordinated with your clothing.

• **PANTY HOSE SYSTEM:** Before putting the panty hose of the day into the laundry, mark the waistband tag with a check if they have no runs, an X if they have a run but still can be worn under slacks, and turn inside out the ones that can no longer be worn. Old panty hose can be recycled for many uses. I have at least one hundred uses in my files. They can also be donated to a local school or group that does crafts with panty hose.

• **PAPER-TOWEL CORES,** *Recycling:*
1. They will hold extension/appliance cords (write on the outside to identify the cord size or type), Christmas lights, small plastic grocery bags.
2. Flatten, and insert sharp knives to protect points of knives and your fingers.
3. Wrap ribbon around the outside to keep it untangled and neat.
4. Tape two or three together for a boot tree.

• **PAPER-TOWEL PACKING,** *Recycling:* When moving, pack your glassware and other breakables with paper towels. They are clean, won't leave newsprint marks like some newspapers and best of all, can be used again when you clean up the new home.

• **PAPERWORK AT WORK:** Wear plastic or rubber gloves when preparing and/or collating many sheets of paper for mass mailing. You don't have to lick your fingers or use sticky stuff to get a good grip on the paper and you won't get paper cuts!

• **PARAKEET CATCHER:** Here's a *Letter of Laughter* that might also help you catch a fly-away parakeet. A reader, whose parakeet loved to play with a bell in its cage, got outdoors and she thought she'd lost him. She took the bell from his cage, stood outside ringing it, and sure enough, the parakeet flew down from a tree to perch on her shoulder and play with his toy. She quickly walked back into the house and returned him to his cage . . . with bell, of course!

• **PARROT FEEDING:** Instead of leaving dishes of your parrot's favorite foods in the cage, feed twice daily and remove the dish after each feeding. Then, the bird will be hungrier at feeding time and therefore more receptive to the wider variety of foods needed for proper nutrition.

• **PARTY BEVERAGE COOLER:** Please see COOLER, For Party.

• **PARTY CAKE,** *Special Occasion Friendship Cake:* When you send out invitations for a special event such as a Golden Anniversary, ask each guest to bake and frost a small square cake using their favorite recipe. Then as the guests arrive, piece the cakes together to make a large patchwork cake. Don't forget to take pictures!

• **PARTY FAVOR,** *Recycling Rolls from Paper Towels, Toilet Paper:* Cut paper-towel rolls in half for this idea. Cut colored tissue paper 6 inches longer than the tube; wrap paper around the tube with 3 inches on each end. Gather one end and tie with ribbon. Fill the tube with candy or small trinkets, then gather and close the other end with ribbon. One reader made these favors with her children and took them to nursing homes at Christmas time. (If you do this, fill some of the favors with sugar-free candy and mark them, then those who can't have regular sugar will get a treat, too.) The favors are fun for birthday and school parties, too.

• **PASTA FOR CHILDREN:** Spiral macaroni is easier for children to self-feed neatly than long spaghetti.

• **PASTA COOKING,** *Ending Boil-overs and Pasta Stuck to the Bottom:* Grease the pot (or spray with non-stick spray) before putting the water in to boil. **Note:** Also spray the colander so that draining pasta won't stick to it.

• **PASTA COOKING,** *Energy-Saver:* Add a pinch of salt and a bit of olive oil when you first boil the water, then add the pasta. When the water begins to boil again, cover the pot with its lid and turn off the burner, leaving the pan on the same burner for the recommended cooking time without the heat. After the cooking time has passed, remove the lid and drain the pasta. You'll save energy and keep from heating up the kitchen at the same time!

• **PASTRY BRUSH,** *Getting All the Oil Out:* Most of my readers write that they don't wash pastry brushes. After using a brush, they wrap it in foil or put it in a resealable plastic bag and keep it in the freezer. It only takes a few minutes to thaw when you need it again. However, if you want to wash the brush, soak it in hot water and dishwashing soap immediately after it's used, rinse well and dry before storing it. Some brushes can be run through the dishwasher cycle.

• **PATCHES, MILITARY, SCOUT,** *Easy Sewing on Straight:* Instead of pinning them before sewing, keep them in place with cellophane tape. Tape three sides of the patch to the fabric and start sewing on the remaining fourth side, untaping one side at a time as you go.

• **PATCHING,** *With Labels:* Cut the designer/manufacturer's tag from the neck of a garment and sew it over small tears or holes on that garment or any other. You mend and designer-decorate clothing at the same time!

• **PEACH SAUCE, JELLED,** *Substitute for Holiday Cranberry Sauce:*
    1 large can of peaches
    ½ cup of sugar
    ½ teaspoon of nutmeg
    1 box lemon gelatin
    Drain canned peaches saving the syrup. Puree the peaches in the blender. To the drained peach syrup, add enough water to make one cup of liquid. Pour into a saucepan and add sugar and nutmeg. Bring mixture to boil and let boil for about one minute.
    Empty the box of gelatin into a bowl and stir in the hot liquid mixture until the gelatin is dissolved. Add pureed peaches and pour into a mold. Chill until set.
Note: If you are limiting your sugar intake, substitute diet gelatin and peaches in light syrup or omit the sugar.

• **PEANUT BUTTER,** *Softening Natural-style Types:* When you buy natural peanut butter, the oil is usually separated and floating. Place the jar on its side for a day or so; it will be easier and less messy to mix in the oil if it's not all on top. (If you remove the oil to save fat or calories, you'll end up with very hard and dry, nearly inedible peanut butter so it's better to leave the oil in and count the calories into your daily total. Peanut oil is one of the "good" oils anyway!) Store this peanut butter in the fridge to keep the oil mixed in. If the peanut butter should become hard, put the portion you'll use in a microwave-safe dish and zap it for a few seconds to make it spreadable again.

• **PEANUT BUTTER/JELLY SANDWICH,** *Preventing Soggy Bread:* Spread the peanut butter on both pieces of bread and put the jelly in the middle so that it can't soak through and mess up a lunch sandwich. Substitute a banana or raisins for the jelly to get a change in flavor.

• **PENCIL ERASER,** *Quick-Fix, When It Smudges:* Rub the eraser with a few strokes of an emery board or fingernail file and it won't smudge your paper anymore.

• **PENCIL HOLDER,** *Recycling:* Magnetic plastic flashlight cases will stick to the inside of a school locker door and hold pencils and pens so there's no more hunting for them in the bottom of the locker. The cases can also hold pencils in truck cabs.

• **PENCILS,** *Healthy-Planet, Recycling Short "Leftovers":* Donate them to your church or any other organization; then it's no loss when they "walk away" after people fill out forms.

• **PEN HOLDER,** *For People with Arthritis or Other Finger Problems:* To get a better grip, poke the pen through a tubed foam hair curler or through a small rubber ball.

• **PERFUME,** *Shelf Life:* It's only about twelve to fourteen months. Heat makes a fragrance evaporate and the more alcohol in the product the shorter its shelf life. Storing perfume and cologne in the fridge will give you a refreshing cool splash in the summer or anytime and helps it last longer, too.

• **PERFUME BOTTLE,** *Removing Scent to Recycle the Bottle:* If baking soda or vinegar don't work, try washing the bottle with soap and water, then fill it with rubbing alcohol. Let stand overnight or longer if needed. Rinse again with clear water.

• **PERSONAL AFFAIRS,** *Checklists for Updating:*
1. For tax filing:
   All 1099 forms (dividends and interest income) and W-2 forms; cancelled checks and checkbook registers; receipts for charitable contributions; deductible expenses receipts; property-tax receipts; and records of mortgage interest paid, brokerage confirmations and statements.
   If you're self-employed, you need a bookkeeping system that records your expenses and stores your receipts according to the various tax-deduction categories (income, repairs, travel, dues and

publications, meals and entertainment, etc.) as listed on the tax form to save time in tax preparation.

2. Here's a list that should be kept up-to-date for emergencies: Copy of will and trust agreements; doctor and hospital information; family records (births, marriage, divorce, social security, military service, citizenship); insurance-policy information (numbers, agent, beneficiaries); funeral information (preferences, location of cemetery plots, deeds, etc.); safe-deposit box (key and location, person authorized to open it); bank account (number, locations); debts (your own and owed to you); all pension/retirement plans; financial/legal advisors' names and phone numbers; brokerage accounts (with brokers' name and phone number); all business records; and all charge accounts.

3. Keep irreplaceable documents in a safe-deposit box but keep copies for your home records. Remember that a safe-deposit box can be sealed when a person dies so that important information may not be available when it's most needed, such as funeral preferences, wills, etc.

• **PERSONAL FILES,** *How Long to Keep Them:*
1. Most canceled checks over six years old can be tossed. Statements and canceled checks from utility, telephone, and water companies should be saved for at least six months unless you need them for a specific reason or just want to keep them to compare costs from year to year. Save checks for home improvements and other deductible costs.

2. Bank statements should be kept for at least a year. (I pare them down to checks I might need for the Internal Revenue Service (IRS) or other reasons and bunch all statements together and keep them for three years, just in case the IRS calls.)

3. Keep all paperwork on major purchases and any investments.

4. The IRS usually has three years to audit tax returns, but in some circumstances can go back further. Be sure to keep copies of the tax returns as well as all receipts, canceled checks, and other necessary tax records.

• **PET,** *Finding Lost Ones, Checklist:*
1. Contact local veterinarians and animal organizations, especially shelters, and give them flyers describing your pet. It helps to have

photos of the pet and to be able to show its distinguishing scars or marks.

2. Tell your neighbors about the loss and post signs in the neighborhood describing your pet and giving a phone number to call.

3. Put signs on both sides of your car describing your pet and giving your phone number.

• **PET,** *Shipping by Air Checklist:* Airlines have specific requirements and some states have immunizations requirements, so check this out long before you have to ship your pet.

1. Generally, the cage should be large enough for the pet to stand, sit, and turn around and should have a water dish attached to the inside to prevent spills during flight.

2. Be absolutely sure that both the pet and the cage have clear identification.

3. Check with your vet to determine if your pet is fit to travel by air and if prescription tranquilizers are appropriate. A week or so before the flight have the vet give your pet a checkup and make sure all immunization shots are up-to-date. You need to have a record of shots with you and if the animal is being shipped by someone else to you at a later time, a copy of shot records may be needed to attach to the cage so that the animal can enter the new state. Also, your vet knows your pet and can advise you about any precautions to take about pre-travel feeding or including pet toys in the cage.

4. Try to book a non-stop or direct flight so there is less chance of anything going amiss and for the quickest trip with least trauma for your pet.

5. Some dogs are comforted (when being boarded) by familiar owner's scents like an old towel or sock that you slept on the night before the trip; ask your vet if this is a good idea for a travel "security blanket" for your pet.

• **PET FEEDING,** *Recycling, No-mess:* Shallow carton-bottoms from canned goods serve as tray place mats for pet-food dishes. Cat-food can "trays," for example, can be renewed each week as you buy your supply. If you don't want to toss out the "tray" each week, you can cover it with adhesive plastic; it is easily wiped and looks nice.

• **PET FIRST AID:**

1. NEVER give a pet medicines of any kind unless prescribed by a vet. "People" medicines can be poisonous to animals.

2. Keep your vet's or your local animal emergency-facility's number handy at the phone and know the emergency-facility location so you can easily find it even when you may be unnerved by the animal's distress.

3. Heatstroke is the greatest danger in summer. If your pet is staggering, vomiting, panting loudly, and looking bleary-eyed, put it in a shady place, sponge him with cool water or even submerse him and cool him down as quickly as possible, especially his head. Then call the vet for further instructions. NEVER leave a pet in a car; it can become an oven in just a few minutes.

4. Minor cuts and scratches (that don't bleed a lot and don't need stitches) need cleaning with soap and water or hydrogen peroxide, followed by mild antiseptic and a bandage. If the wound swells or shows other signs of infection, call your vet; antibiotics may be needed. **Note:** Some pets won't leave a bandage alone and may need a special collar to prevent their reaching a bandage with their mouths. Consult your vet.

5. Cuts that bleed a lot may need vet care. Press a clean rag or gauze over the wound, hold it firmly to slow the bleeding until you can get to the vet. Tourniquets can cause damage to tissues; don't attempt to use one.

6. If you suspect a broken bone, you may be able to put a splint on a limb. A small animal can be placed on a board or large, firm section of cardboard carton. Or, you can wrap a pet in a blanket or large towel.

Caution: Even the gentlest pet may snap at anyone when it is in pain. You may want to make a muzzle by lightly tying the pet's jaws closed with a soft rag or old panty-hose leg.

• **PET-FOOD DISHES:** If your cat or dog leaves a few morsels of moist food in the dish and you find them "cemented" to the bottom of the bowl at the end of the day, try spraying food dishes with vegetable oil spray. The food washes off easily and the pets get some extra oil for their coats. They may even lick off the food bits if they like the spray taste, like butter-flavored spray!

• **PET HAIR,** *Quick-Fix Removal:* Try a damp sponge, a damp hand, transparent tape wrapped around your hand with sticky side out on clothing, rugs, or furniture.

1. Keep a child's broom and mop handy for gathering tuffts of pet hair between vacuuming.
2. Keep tape or a clothes brush in your car so you can do a last minute de-fuzz before going to a party.
3. Check air conditioner/furnace filters frequently during shedding season; hair blocks them and can also go through to the mechanism causing damage.
4. Comb and brush a shedding pet often to remove loose hair.
5. Love your shedding pet anyway! It doesn't really mean to drive you batty!

• **PET HAIR,** *Removal from Furniture:* Rub "hairy" area with a clean sneaker that has a ribbed bottom.

• **PET HAIR,** *Removing from Bedding:* If you have trouble getting all the pet hair off in the laundry, try spinning bedding in the dryer on the fluff (no heat) cycle to remove the pet hair before you launder it. Sometimes, you may not even need to launder it after the hair is off!

• **PET HAIR,** *Shedding Problems:* In addition to regular seasonal shedding, some pets have "stress shedding" and it can result from changes in routine, visits to the vet or boarding kennel, new visitors in the house, etc. If the condition persists for a long time after the stressful situation has gone, have the pet examined by a vet to make sure it's just stress, not disease.

• **PET HELPER,** *Letter of Laughter:* A beauty operator and owner of a "weenie dog" attached a magnet to the low-slung dog's collar, so that as the dog walked around the shop hairpins were neatly collected. She said the dog was down on the floor anyway so it could earn its keep and save its owner the chore of bending down and crawling around to pick up hairpins. What a great and hilarious idea! Most of us have dogs that just go around gathering dust in the house and twigs in their hair when they roam the outdoors!

• **PET IDENTIFICATION:** If your pet has no identifying marks (all black or all white cats, for example), dab on some colored paint or nail polish or snip out a patch of fur on its back or leg so that your pet won't get mixed up with a "twin" when left at the vet or boarding kennel. Collars can slip off and mix-ups can occur even when people are careful. Be sure to point out to the vet or kennel person that you have marked your pet. Some cities have facilities to tattoo an owner's social security number on a pet. Inquire at your vet.

• **PET PEN,** *Puppy Housebreaking with Indoor Pen:* If you have an old playpen or can get one at a garage sale, put an old plastic shower curtain or drop cloth on the floor of the pen; cover it with lots of newspaper. You can put paper on one side and a small blanket on the other. When you start taking the puppy outside, take some soiled paper and put it in the area you'd like your puppy to use and he'll get the hint from the scent. It takes a while but time and patience is rewarded.

• **PET PILLOW/BEAN-BAG CHAIR,** *Stuffing Recycling:* As the plastic pellet stuffing gets mashed and you receive mail with plastic foam "peanut" fillers, just add the "peanuts" to the pet pillow or bean-bag chair.

• **PET PING-PONG,** *Letter of Laughter:* One cat owner wrote that his twelve-year-old Ping-Pong–playing cat always jumps into the game to swat the ball when anyone plays. Everytime they have company, he's the hit of the party!

• **PETS,** *Checklist for Boarding:*
1. If you plan to board the pet, costs usually relate to the pet's size and type of facility. Don't shop by phone and don't use a facility that discourages you from visiting it.
2. When you visit a boarding facility, boarding areas should be clean, well-lit, and free from strong odors. The facility should require current booster immunizations and have policies for emergencies. Observe the people who care for the pets—do they seem friendly and comfortable with animals?
3. Some pets are happier left in their own homes even if they are alone part of the time. If you can't get a friend or relative to pet-sit, a bonded-pet sitting service may be the answer. They will charge by the day or by the visit (three or four per day for a dog; one or two for a cat). Leave the pet-sitter the same information you would

leave a baby-sitter: emergency vet number; information on how to reach you or a local person in case of emergency; written advice on your pet's medications, eating and living habits.

• **PETS,** *Ticks on Dogs or Cats:* It's especially important to protect your animals from ticks in areas of the country where Lyme disease (spread by ticks) is prevalent.
1. For short-haired dogs and cats, try using a lint removal roller, the kind made from sticky masking tape. It will pick up nymphal ticks that are no larger than a tiny speck.
2. If you find a tick on your pet, remove it with tweezers as soon as possible and then flush it down the toilet without touching it.

• **PETS,** *Water:* Drop a few ice cubes in your pet's water dish on hot days to keep it fresh and cool.

• **PETS,** *When They Are Sick and Vomiting:* Vomiting may or may not be a danger signal. When you have two dogs or two cats the dominant one may eat so fast that it may vomit. Especially if the animal exercises a lot after eating. Cats frequently vomit due to hair balls. Get a laxative from the vet to alleviate this problem.

If there are no other signs of illness, home treatment for vomiting includes stopping all food and water until the vomiting stops. However, a small amount of chicken or beef broth given every few hours can help prevent dehydration. Strained meat baby food can be added. Also, a bland diet of boiled rice and well-cooked drained hamburger meat may be good. If the pet does well, it can go back to its regular diet after a few days. **Caution:** If the illness persists, take the pet to the veterinarian. Vomiting can be a symptom of such diseases as kidney failure in dogs and feline distemper in cats. Very young pets that don't respond within a day or two should be taken to the vet.

• **PET SAFETY,** *Puppies, Cats, Ferrets, Gerbils, Hamsters, etc.:* Many kinds of pets like to burrow and so you must always be cautious around folding/recliner chairs, clothes dryers and washers, and any other place they might wander into. Cats and puppies have been killed in recliner chairs when their owners didn't check before operating them. On the lighter side, burrowing animals can surprise you!

I used to have a very curious ferret named Freddie, whom I'd let loose in my office every now and then, and who will never be forgotten by my secretary, Joyce. Freddie ran up her slacks' leg and, for a moment, she didn't know if she should just scream or scream while pulling her slacks off. The happy ending is that Joyce, an animal lover and cat owner, was able to coax Freddie out of her slacks in a few minutes without any harm to either one of them.

• **PET VACCINATION TAGS,** *Dealing with S-clips:* S-clips on vaccination tags are hard to pry open when you want to replace old tags with new ones. Instead, bend the S-clips and slip them onto round metal key rings, then put the key rings on the collar and next year's change will be easier. Use the smallest possible key ring to prevent it from getting caught on fences if your dog is a jumper or if it's on a cat. **Note:** Be careful not to lose the tags if you remove the collar to bathe or flea-spray the pet.

• **PHONE,** *Hearing It Ring While Outdoors:* If you have one, place a child's amplifier near the phone when you go outdoors for an "intercom-outercom."

• **PHONE,** *Ringing, Letter of Laughter:* Have you noticed that the phone is always ringing as you are fumbling with the door keys and that it stops just as you fall over the cat and pick up the receiver!

• **PHONE BOOK,** *Healthy-Planet Recycling:*
1. Recycle old phone books by using pages to hold potato peels and other vegetable scraps for discarding or tossing into your garden compost pile. (Paper is compost, too.)
2. Also, layer seven or eight pages in the bottom of the bird cage so that you can just remove them one at a time as they get soiled.
3. Stack two or three old phone books and join them with duct tape or a fabric cover to make a child's booster seat. If you need to use the books again, join them with lots of rubber bands.
4. Keep the current phone book(s) under your desk for a footrest.
5. Use pages for packing material.
6. Give to relatives and friends who live near but not in your city so that they can refer to businesses they need.
7. Keep one in the car trunk to check addresses or phone numbers.

• **PHONE BOOK,** *Storing Out-of-the-way:* If you have a closet near the phone, slip a couple of wire coat hangers into the middle of the book(s) and hang in the closet.

• **PHONE CORD,** *Quick Fix No-mess Cleaning:* Put a coiled telephone cord on a long wooden spoon handle, pushing the coils close together; wash them with household cleaner on a cloth or sponge and rinse with a clean sponge.

• **PHONE NUMBERS,** *Emergency and Others for Children Who Can't Yet Read:* On a piece of posterboard placed near the phone, put a picture of people to be called with the phone number and address next to it. Pictures of police or firefighters can be placed by the 911 or other community emergency number. To practice dialing, unplug the phone. **Caution:** Teach children the importance of not playing with the phone and that emergency calls are serious business.

• **PHONE NUMBERS:** Write the out-of-town numbers you call on the phone book page where you would normally find them if they were local numbers; they'll be easy to find.

• **PHONE NUMBERS:** Either highlight or make a red check mark by the phone numbers you have used so that it's easier to find them the next time you look.

• **PHOTOS,** *Proper Care:*
1. Don't write on the face; to identify them, write either on the page of the album or on the back with a soft-lead pencil or felt-tip pen—lightly. Ballpoint pens can leave indentations.
2. Handle photos and negatives by the edges to avoid fingerprints.
3. Store negatives in a dark, dry place separately from the pictures in case of accidents. Special storage envelopes that help keep out humidity are available.
4. I always mark the envelopes (Christmas '90, Summer '89, etc.) so that I can easily find the ones I need.
5. Photos are best mounted in a photo album with acid-free archival paper, held in place with triangle photo corners, not tape, glue, or rubber cement. Magnetic or self-adhesive page albums are not considered good storage for photos.

• **PHOTOS,** *Copying:* I get lots of questions about restoring old photographs. To get copies of one-of-a-kind photos, especially very old ones that you're afraid to let anyone work on, take them to a professional photo shop that makes copies with a color-laser copier. The results are great!

• **PHOTOS,** *Mailing:* To safeguard against loss in case the envelope opens or tears, stick mailing-address labels on the backs of precious family photos before mailing them.

• **PHOTOS, NEGATIVES, STORAGE:** To organize negatives, starting with each roll of film you have developed, write a number (for example, 1) on the back of each of the photographs. Put all the negatives from the film role in an envelope and number it "1" as well. The next roll of film developed would be number 2; repeat the same steps. Be sure to add the date of the photos and names of the people in them.

• **PIANO KEYS,** *Yellowed Ivory:* Clean ivory with a mixture of mild soap and water, wiping the keys with a slightly damp cloth—take care not to soak them, just wipe. Rinse well with a damp, clean cloth and dry thoroughly. Never use wax or abrasive cleaners on ivory. **Hint:** Ivory yellows naturally over time but some say leaving the lid open so that the keys get daylight will slow down the process. It is possible to replace the keyboard with new plastic keys without affecting the quality of the sound but if your piano is an antique, plastic keys will devalue it for some collectors. It may be a better idea to sell an antique piano with yellow keys to someone who loves it "as is" and use the money to get a new one with white keys if that's important to you.

• **PICKLES,** *Leftover:* When life gives you too many leftover jars of pickles, make pickle relish. Take the one or two pickles left in each jar and put them through a food processor, and you'll have relish for hot dogs and hamburgers. Add some of the flavored vinegar to salad dressing for a zingy new taste.

• **PICNIC COOLER,** *Child's Camp Trunk:* Pack a child's clothing in a large picnic cooler. The shelf holds small articles, the handles make carrying it easy, and it's waterproof storage at camp as well as a cabin "bench."

• **PICNIC TRAYS,** *Healthy-Planet Recycling:* Cut cardboard box bottoms about 2 inches deep. A cardboard tray holds your drink and plate, keeps plates from sliding, and keeps bread, chips, and other food from falling to the ground, especially for children.

• **PICTURES,** *Displaying Family Photos:* Make a memory wall of family happenings and milestones (first day of school, weddings, etc.). When there are several children, make composite "collages" for each one in a larger frame instead of a frame for each.

• **PIECES,** *Picking Up Small Ones:* Wrap small pieces of double-stick transparent tape around one or two fingers and dab away at bobby pins, paper clips, jigsaw puzzle pieces, stuck pages of a book, and more. This is an especially good hint if your fingers are a bit fumbly due to a physical handicap of some sort.

• **PIE COVER,** *Recycling, Quick-Fix:* Don't throw away the plastic cover from store-bought pie crusts; instead save it to cover the pie!

• **PIE-CRUST EDGE,** *When It's Browning Too Fast:* Cover the edge of the crust with an aluminum foil strip while it bakes. Or make a reusable crust cover by cutting out the center of a foil pie pan to within an inch or so of the edge, leaving the rim of the pan; this is a time- and aluminum-foil saver and a recycling idea especially if you bake a lot of pies.

• **PILL,** *Easy Swallowing:* While most pills and capsules have slick coatings that help you swallow them, some are uncoated. If you have trouble swallowing such a pill, roll it in a bit of butter or margarine; just enough to help it slip down when you swallow. **Caution:** Check with your doctor or pharmacist to make sure the butter/margarine won't interfere with your body's absorption of that medicine. Also, do not cut pills or capsules to make them smaller unless your pharmacist or doctor approves; some are made for "time-release" and you could be changing the way they work.

• **PILL BOX:** Small plastic containers that breath mints come in can hold aspirin (or other pills) for a purse or briefcase. **Caution:** Always label containers when you switch contents and keep these away from children who might mistake the pills for candy.

• **PILLOWS,** *Freshen, Fluff:* Place bed pillows in the dryer with a fabric-softener sheet and tumble on the air cycle for 20 minutes to fluff them up and give them a fresh, clean smell.

- **PILLOW SHAM,** *Stuffing Decorative Ones:* Use the shams to store extra bed pillows or rolled-up blankets/quilts. Or stuff them with saved-up foam dryer softener sheets, leftover foam rug backing, pillow stuffing, shredded old panty hose, and other soft materials, then stitch them shut.

- **PINECONES,** *Burning in Fireplaces:* You can burn pinecones in the fireplace; but **Caution,** they pop and send out sprays of sparks, so keep the fireplace screen in place and never leave the fire unattended while pinecones are burning in it.

- **PINS,** *Storage:* Place a magnetic strip in the bottom of your pin box and even if you drop it, you won't be stepping on pins and needles.

- **PIZZA CUTTER,** *Other Than Pizza Uses:* Cuts brownies or pan cookies, slices dough for noodles, cookies, pastry.

- **PIZZA DOUGH,** *Prevent Sticking to Pan:* After spraying the pan with non-stick spray, sprinkle a tablespoon of cornmeal on the pan before placing dough on it.

- **PLACE MATS,** *Removing Spaghetti Stains from Vinyl:* Soak place mats in an enzyme stain-remover bleach mixed with a little detergent and warm water. Follow the box directions for amounts. After soaking, scrub the spots with a brush and rinse thoroughly. If stains still remain, put the place mats outside on a hot, sunny day and let the sun bleach them out.

- **PLACE MATS,** *Renewing Limp Straw Ones:* Wet placemats, lay them on a flat surface. Push down and flatten all edges, then liberally spray them with spray starch. When they dry, they should look good as new.

- **PLANT POTS,** *Reusing:* Always clean before reuse to avoid spread of plant diseases. Wash pots in hot water with a squirt or two of regular dishwashing detergent, let them soak for several hours in a solution of one part chlorine bleach to eight parts water. Rinse well and dry, then reuse.

- **PLANTS,** *Maintenance:* Sometimes, people who don't have a green thumb find it easier to maintain big plants than small ones because they don't need as frequent watering or repotting.

• **PLANTS,** *Propping, Healthy-Planet Recycling:* Prop drooping plants with balloon sticks, plastic forks, the name-card holders from florist's arrangements, or "trellises" made by bending wire coat hangers into a round loop and burying the hook-end.

• **PLANTS, WATERING:** Wick Method for Vacation Watering: Plants will draw their own water from buckets with this method.
1. Place a couple of bath towels in the bottom of the bathtub. Place the plant pots and one large or several small buckets of water on the towels. Be sure the water buckets sit higher than the plant pots.
2. Snip cotton string lengths to reach from the inside bottom of the water bucket to the top of the plant pot soil. Gently push one string end into the soil to hold it in place and put the other end at the bottom of the water bucket. Fill the buckets with water. And that's all that's to it.

• **PLANT TERRARIUM,** *When You Go Away:* Water the plants well, then cover the entire pot with a plastic bag, tucking it around the bottom. It should stay moist for at least a week. Very delicate plants may need TLC from a neighbor or friend while you are gone, but most plants will last a week or two without their owners.

• **PLASTIC,** *Remove Melted Plastic from Pots and Pans:* Try heating the pan in a warm oven, then scraping the plastic off before washing in hot soapy water. Is there anyone with an old-style toaster who hasn't melted a plastic bread bag onto the toaster? Love the new, cool-sided appliances!

• **PLASTIC BAG STORAGE:**
1. Hold empty plastic bags together with a terry-cloth elastic wristband, the kind tennis players wear.
2. Bend the ends of a hanger all the way up and hang it on a hook, then slip the handles of plastic bags on the hanger ends for neat and orderly storage.
3. Separate different types of plastic bags to save time digging through a pile—put grocery bags in a grocery bag; newspaper bags in a newspaper bag, and so on.

• **PLASTIC CAPS,** *Recycling Those from Fabric Softener or Liquid Detergent:*

1. Keep at kitchen sink to hold soap scraps and a small sponge ready to scrub anything.

2. On the dresser, one lid holds five tubes of lipstick, also makeup brushes, and other small items.

3. At the workbench they help sort screws and nuts; are handy for mixing small amounts of paint for crafts.

• **PLASTIC "FLATS" FROM NURSERY PLANTS,** *Recycling:* Wash, rinse, dry, and they are "IN/OUT" baskets for your home office.

• **PLASTIC FOOD CONTAINERS,** *Cleaning Them When Greasy:* Leftovers can make plastic ware greasy, sticky and just plain yucky. Spray them with laundry pre-wash spray, let stand awhile, scrub with a brush and full-strength dishwashing liquid. Rinse thoroughly and enjoy using again.

• **PLASTIC-LID COASTERS,** *Recycling:* Any size lid that fits under a glass makes a good coaster and my readers have decorated them in many creative ways.

1. Punch holes around the perimeter with a paper hole-punch and then crochet a "frame" linking the "frame" to the holes; or instead of crochet, just make a yarn overcast stitch border in colors that match the room.

2. Cut out colorful pictures and cover the paper with clear adhesive-backed plastic, then push the picture into the lid.

3. Cut plastic needlepoint mesh or buy mesh rounds, then needlepoint designs or solid colors and push the rounds into plastic lids for really absorbent coasters.

4. Cut rounds of leftover fabric, carpet, felt, and push them into the lids.

• **PLASTIC MESH BAGS,** *Recycling:* Tie in a ball and use to scrub pots, pans, car windshields, bathtubs, etc. Or, use them to dry and store plant bulbs, pool and tub toys, picnic supplies such as plastic ware.

• **PLASTIC PICNIC WARE,** *Recycling:* Instead of throwing away plastic "silverware," put it in a mesh bag and secure it to the top rack of the dishwasher. It will come out clean and ready to use again.

• **PLASTIC SIX-PACK RINGS,** *Healthy-Planet Recycling:*
Caution: These rings can become nooses around the necks of large and small birds, squirrels, turtles, and other small animals who then strangle as they try to escape. Cut the circles and loops apart before discarding even if they are going into a trash bag. Many birds and small animals feed at landfills! Instead, recycle.
1. Fold in half to make three "holes," then hook one over a sturdy hanger in your closet. Then hang four or more clothes hangers in each hole to make more closet space.
2. If you crochet, cut them into separate rings, then crochet around them with cotton yarn to make coasters from individual rings or hot mats by combining several rings.
3. Dip in bubble solution to make giant soap bubbles.
4. Cut into individual circles and make hangers for tools such as hammers.
5. Join a couple of them with twist-ties or heavy yarn to make a beach bag.

• **PLASTIC STRAWBERRY BASKETS,** *Healthy-Planet Recycling:*
1. Playpen for small dolls.
2. Candy baskets for holidays. Weave ribbon through the holes, and attach other decorations with appropriate glue.
3. Hold soap and scouring pads in the kitchen.
4. Store perfume, nail-polish bottles, sample cosmetics, small medicine containers.
5. Place over damp area in carpet so it can dry without being stepped on.
6. Hold packets of sauce mix, spices, etc. in cupboard. (Double them to make them stronger.)

• **PLASTIC STRAWS,** *Recycling:* Put several together and secure them to a dinner knife with a rubber band, then wash in the dishwasher. They'll come out clean and can be reused many times. Soaking straws used for milk in cold water helps get them clean.

• **PLASTIC WARE,** *Keeping It Stain-free:* Spaghetti sauce or chili stains plastic containers. To prevent this, line them with plastic wrap before pouring in the food after it has cooled.

• **PLASTIC WRAP,** *Keep It from Tangling:* Store in freezer or fridge.

• **PLASTIC WRAP,** *Prying Film from a Roll:* Wrap stuck to the roll? Apply a piece of transparent tape vertically at the edge of the wrap; lift. You'll pull the wrap free.

• **PLAYPEN MESH,** *Remove Mildew:* Place playpen outside and protect the bottom (if it's cardboard,) with a plastic shower curtain or other waterproof cover. Mix half water and half chlorine bleach in a spray bottle and spray it on the mesh from both sides. To rinse, spray with clear water from a spray bottle. To remove lingering bleach smell, mix 2 capfuls of fabric softener and 2 cups of water in a spray bottle and spray on mesh. Rinse very well and let sit in sunshine for a day or two.

• **POCKETS,** *Making Them Secure:* Sew strips or dots of self-gripping fabric tape on the inside edges of pants or jacket pockets so that wallets or checkbooks won't fall out.

• **POISON IVY:** A tall climbing vine clinging to trees and fences, it's leaves are composed of three leaflets which vary in shape. Leaves are red in the spring but turn to shiny green later.
1. To Get Rid of It—WEARING RUBBER GLOVES, pull up small vines; seal in plastic bags and discard. Wash gloves in soap and water afterward. Kill larger vines with herbicide on foliage and by cutting plants at ground level. **Caution:** Protect "good guys" foliage with a sheet of plastic when you spray. **Hint:** Don't cover good foliage in the hottest part of the day; heat buildup under plastic sheets could burn the good plants.
2. First Aid—You have about 10 minutes after exposure to avoid a skin reaction. Wash affected area thoroughly under running water. Some sources say wash WITHOUT SOAP; that soap removes the natural protective oils of your skin and can increase the penetration of the irritant. Other sources say with soap. They do agree on washing thoroughly and quickly.

• **POOL COVER,** *Healthy-Planet Recycling:* If you cover your pool for the winter, hold the cover in place with large plastic jugs filled with water. **Caution:** Children and pets may mistake a pool cover for a walking surface and can drown if they slip under the cover and get trapped. If you have children and pets, it may be safer not to cover the pool.

- **POOL COVER:** Keep leaves from falling into a small plastic child's pool by covering it with a large piece of nylon net when it's not being used. Either secure the net to the pool's side with clothes pins or weigh down the edges of the cover with gallon jugs filled with sand or water.

- **POPCORN,** *Extra Flavoring:* Try sprinkling with seasoned salts; salt-free herb blends; dry salad-dressing mixes; taco or chili seasoning mixes; grated hard cheeses like Parmesan or Romano or the powdered cheese from macaroni-and-cheese dinners.

- **POPCORN,** *Popping in the Microwave:* Regular paper bags can catch fire at the temperature needed to pop corn and regular bowls and casseroles aren't shaped properly to concentrate the heat needed for kernels to pop. Microwave corn poppers are cone-shaped to concentrate the heat and will give you best results. You can also buy corn in microwave-safe bags if the directions for your microwave say it's okay, however these "kits" usually have added salt and fat.

- **POPCORN BALLS,** *No-mess Serving at Children's Parties:* Form the popcorn balls around lollipops. No more sticky-fingered party guests! Be sure to tell the children there's a surprise in the center so that they don't bite too enthusiastically on the hard core and chip a tooth!

- **POPCORN CUPS:** For edible party munchy holders, shape popcorn-ball mix over the bottoms and side of glasses well-greased with margarine. After mixture hardens, remove "cups" and fill with nuts or other treats. Please see CAKE, POPCORN.

- **POPCORN TOOTH-SAVER,** *Removing Unpopped Kernels:* Popcorn is a good low-cal snack. When you make a batch at night, save some for workday or school lunches. Put the cooled popcorn in a large resealable plastic bag and cut a small hole in the corner of the bag. Give the bag a good shake and all the unpopped kernels will fall out of the hole. Then, when you or a child grabs a handful of popcorn, you're not likely to break a tooth on an unpopped kernel.

- **POSTCARDS,** *For the Letter-phobic:* If you never get around to writing letters, remember that it's the thought that counts and friends would enjoy knowing you think of them even if you don't have time to write the "minutes" of your life since your last meeting with them. Keep postcards on hand so you can send off quick notes, comments to politicians, and even "hints" to Heloise. P.S. You can also FAX hints to me: 1-512-HELOISE.

• **POSTCARDS,** *Making Your Own:* Cut them to size from poster-board or shirt cardboards. You can place colorful stickers on the shiny side of the paper and write on the dull side just as if it's a regular postcard. Draw a line down the middle with address on the right and message on the left. Just remember that a postcard should not exceed 4¼" by 6" to be sent by the lower postcard postage rate.

• **POSTCARDS, GREETING CARDS,** *Recycling Pretty Pictures and Pleasant Memories:* Old greeting cards, postcards and even photos can be page markers in recipe books. Each time you open the book you'll get pleasant thoughts!

• **POSTAGE STAMP ROLL,** *Unsticking:* If dampness sticks the whole role of postage stamps together, try placing the stamps in the freezer for about an hour. When you remove them, they should separate. If not, you can return the stamps to the post office for replacement.

• **POSTAGE STAMPS,** *Easy Licking If You Hate the Taste of the Glue:*
1. Lick the envelope's corner instead of the stamp.
2. Put an ice cube in a small bowl or on a dry washcloth and pass the glue side of the stamps over the ice cube.
3. Put water into a clean roll-on deodorant applicator and roll moisture over the stamps.
4. And, tried and true, run stamps over a wet sponge set in a saucer.
5. Avoid moisture altogether—buy a glue stick and just glue stamps and envelope flaps in place.
6. *Letter of Laughter:* Or, train your dog like the Heloise fan whose Rottweiler sits, eyes above table level, nose handy to moisten stamps. After each stamp, he licks his nose so it's ready for the next—he likes the glue!

• **POSTERS,** *Hanging Without Damaging Walls:* Apply pieces of double-stick tape to the backs of posters, pull away the liners and attach the posters to the walls. If there is any residue left on the wall when the posters are removed, you can wipe it away with your finger.

• **POTATO,** *Baking in Microwave:*
1. Check your microwave manual for suggested time; it varies according to wattage and other factors.
2. Poke several holes in the potato with a fork or ice pick to let moisture out.
3. To cook one, place it in the center of the oven in a double-layer of paper towels. To cook more than one, place them in a circle with the smaller ends of the potatoes toward the center.
4. Halfway through the baking time, turn the potato over to help it cook more evenly.
5. Wait about 5 minutes before testing for doneness; potatoes continue to cook after removal from the oven.
6. Top with your favorite topping. I like low-fat yogurt and some parsley.

Or you could make a spread with ½ cup butter or margarine, 2 teaspoons salt, ¼ teaspoon black pepper, and 2 teaspoons finely chopped fresh chives.

Or, when you tire of sour cream, chives, bacon bits, or yogurt, try spaghetti sauce, a sprinkle of oregano, grated mozzarella cheese or Parmesan for a potato-meal.

• **POTATO,** *Baking in Microwave, Techniques:* To avoid rubbery, hockey puck potatoes when baking in the microwave try the following:
1. Place potatoes on a large microwave-safe dinner plate (the plate you'll eat from if it's dinner for one) and slice each twice to allow moisture to escape. Put a little water on the plate, cover with microwave-safe bowl; microwave on "High" for about 4 to 7 minutes per potato (depends on size and your oven wattage) or as directed by your oven's directions.
2. Wrap potatoes in cereal-box liner; bake in microwave about 4 minutes or as directed by your oven's directions.

• **POTATO BUYING AND COOKING,** *Which to Buy for What Purpose:* Pick potatoes that aren't soft, bruised, cracked, wrinkled, sprouting "eyes," or greenish-looking. Potatoes retain more vitamins if cooked whole with skins on. They are high in vitamin C and potassium, low in sodium, and a good source of fiber and complex carbohydrates. A medium-sized potato has only about 100 calories. It's the stuff you pile on top that breaks the diet.

1. Russet Burbank potatoes are large, oblong, with dark, rough skin. They cook up fluffy and make great mashed potatoes and french fries. Idaho Russets are baking favorites.

2. California and White Rose are all-purpose long, oblong potatoes, with thin, smooth skin. They're best for roasting, boiling, steaming, and pan frying.

3. Round reds or whites are sold immediately after harvesting and without being stored. They are called "new potatoes."

- **POTATO-CHIP CAN,** *Recycling:*
1. Make a Cover-up: Cover with adhesive paper or paint to match your bathroom or bedroom decor and then slip them over hair spray, room deodorizer, and other un-aesthetics on the vanity.
2. Mail cookies or other fragile things in them.
3. Store fireplace matches, craft pieces, knitting/crochet needles, spaghetti, etc. in them.

- **POTATO PEELER,** *Other Uses:* Pit cherries and still leave them whole; hull strawberries; grate cheese.

- **POTATO SCRUBBER:** Instead of wasting the vitamins in potato skins by peeling them, scrub with a plastic pot scrubber.

- **POTATO STORAGE:** Keep in a dark, dry place that's relatively cool, about 40 to 50 degrees. Don't put them in the fridge; the cold makes the starch change to sugar and changes the taste and texture. Also, don't store potatoes with onions; moisture from potatoes can cause onions to sprout.

- **POTATOES,** *Leftover Mashed:* Add grated cheese to leftover mashed potatoes and then fry them in margarine for breakfast or other meals.

- **POTATOES,** *Quick-Fix When You Over-cooked:* Wash three or four potatoes, poke with holes and pop into the microwave. Then, peel them; add to the "mushed potatoes," and whip up briefly to make "mashed potatoes." The alternative is to turn the mush into potato soup (add a bit of canned skim milk or dry powder skim milk—only the powder, not mixed with water, and your favorite flavorings like a dash of Worcestershire). Sprinkle a few croutons on top and pretend it's what you planned to serve in the first place!

• **POT HOLDERS,** *Healthy-Planet Recycling:* Cut circles or squares from old towels and blue jean legs (leftover when you turn jeans into shorts) and sew them together for sturdy, heat-protecting pot holders.

• **POT PLANTS,** *Preventing Wind from Blowing Them Off a Balcony Rail:* This works best for clay pots with a large single drain hole. Hammer a large (three-inch) nail into the railing where each pot belongs. Then place each pot over a nail so that it fits through the drain hole. This idea might also work on a wood deck to prevent pots from being nudged over by passing pets.

• **POTS/PANS,** *Cleaning Aluminum:* Put about 3 tablespoons of cream of tartar and about 1 quart of water in the gunky pot. Bring the mixture to a boil and let it continue to boil for about 10 minutes. Wash and rinse the pot well.

• **POTS & PANS,** *Cleaning Burned Gunk Off Stainless Steel:* **Caution:** This method is only for stainless-steel pots and pans, NOT for aluminum pots or pans.
1. Place the pot in the oven to slightly warm it.
2. Spread a plastic trash bag over some newspaper on the counter and place the pot in it.
3. Generously spray the pot or pan with oven cleaner and allow to set for 5 to 10 minutes.
4. Rinse off oven cleaner; wash in hot, soapy water; rinse well.
5. Very stubborn gunk may take more than one application.

• **POUND-CAKE TOPPING,** *Quick-Fix:* Heat about ¼ cup of preserves and 1 tablespoon of flavored liqueur in a small saucepan and dribble it over a slice of pound cake for a yummy dessert.

• **PRESCRIPTIONS,** *Recycling Containers:* If your pharmacist allows, take your prescription bottles for refills instead of getting a new bottle each time. Less plastic in landfills!

• **PRE-WASH SPRAY,** *Homemade:* **Caution:** When you apply this solution, wash the clothing immediately. Allowing it to set for any period of time may create a difficult stain to remove. Mix equal parts of water, ammonia, and dishwashing (not dishwasher) liquid (read the label to be sure it doesn't contain bleach). Put it into a clean spray bottle and label it as pre-wash spray. Please see SPOTS & STAINS on page 398.

- **PRICE STICKERS, LABEL RESIDUE:**
Method 1, Household Items: Apply pre-wash spray or liquid, scrub with nylon scrubber.
Method 2, Household Items: Saturate with vegetable, baby, or mineral oil before removing with nylon scrubber.
Please see STICKY RESIDUE.

- **PRINT WHITE ON DARK PAPER:** For special effects on notes, letters, or invitations, print with typewriter correction tape (the kind that prints, not the one that lifts print off) on dark paper.

- **PROOF-OF-PURCHASE LABELS,** *Removing for Mail-ins:*
1. Soak the container in water until the edge of the label starts to peel. Remove it from the water and blot with a paper towel.
2. Put a strip of transparent tape over the label, covering it completely and rub over it. Cut around the taped area with a single-edge razor; gently raise the lengthwise edge of the tape and pull it off.

A very thin layer will come off in one piece. To recycle the container, remove residue with a plastic scrubber and either a paste of baking soda and water or pre-wash spray.

- **PUMP-SPRAY BOTTLES,** *Recycling:* Wash thoroughly, allow to dry and ALWAYS label with contents.
1. Put pre-electric shave liquid in it. This is especially helpful for someone whose hands or fingers are disabled so that pouring liquids is difficult.
2. Store homemade cleaning solutions, such as vinegar and water, ammonia and water.
3. If the pump spray is from an edible or is a new bottle and so is safe for food, you can put oil in it to spray on pots and pans and also on your breaded chops before turning them over (they don't stick as easily). Or spray oil on a salad for diet portions. You can also spray flavored vinegars on salads to avoid dribbling too much.
4. Take a spray bottle of plain water with you to the zoo or other hot place and spritz yourself and companions when needed. If

you're on a picnic and have a cooler, keep the spritzing bottle in the cooler and really get refreshed!

• **PUNCH,** *Ice:* When you're using punch or store-bought eggnog, pour half into ice-cube trays and freeze so that you can cool the rest of it at serving time without watering it down.

• **PUPPY,** *Checklist for Selecting One:*
1. Shyness usually occurs when pups live with their litter for more than twelve weeks, or when a timid pup gets trampled into a subordinate position. Shy dogs hold back while the others bark and run around, and may be afraid of noise or people. Such a dog may become frightened and attack a person. Also, some owners cause shyness in an otherwise lovable pup by excessively authoritative training or abuse.
2. Look for a curious and somewhat assertive puppy who is not afraid of strangers. Pups need to be handled properly at an early age by humans so that they won't be frightened.
3. If you have a shy adult dog, try giving it loving gentle care; talk to it in a soothing way. In time it may grow out of its fear and be as good a pet as any other.

• **PUPPY,** *Protecting Carpets:* Until a puppy is well housebroken, keep it in an old baby playpen with newspapers layered over an old shower curtain or other waterproof mat. Then puppy can stay in the room with you without causing "accidents" on the carpet.
    Letter of Laughter: One reader tried this hint and wrote that it was not for Springer Spaniels. As soon as he learned to "spring" he would spring up and down like a yo-yo, landing with a reverberating crash on the playpen floor. It was hilarious to watch but definitely wearing on the nerves after a while!

• **PURSES,** *Changing Without Forgetting Essentials:*
1. Keep a drawer or box just for your purse items and dump them in when you come home. Then you won't have to search through several purses looking for scattered bits and pieces when you're in the A.M. rush.
2. Keep all of your bits and pieces (cosmetics, pen, pins, sewing kit, medications, etc.) in a plastic zipper pencil case (the kind you can put into ring binders) or just a plastic zipper bag. They'll be in one place when you switch purses.

- **QUICHE,** *Variations:*
1. Add grated cheese, chopped almonds, or ground pecans to the crust recipe.
2. If you aren't eating bacon, substitute imitation bacon bits for flavor.

- **QUILT,** *Recycling:* Worn parts of quilts can be cut off and the remaining good parts can be finished with a new border to make lap robes, child-size bedcovers, hot-dish holders, or, if the design is suitable, even a vest or skirt.

- **QUILT,** *Repair:* Repair old quilts with fabric from old clothing so that the patch won't be so obvious, as it can be if you make the repair with fabric that's not faded like the rest of the quilt.

- **QUILT MAKING,** *Recycling:* Traditionally quilts have been made from scraps of fabric left over from sewing projects and from the unworn parts of old clothing in addition to making them from new fabric. You can back a quilt with a sheet that matches the decor of your home and pad the inside with a blanket that is too washed-out to look nice on the bed.

• **QUILTS,** *American Art on the Wall:* To make a colorful wall hanging, attach wooden rings to a quilt or attach matching cloth "tabs" and hang it from a wide wooden rod. Or just drape the quilt over a bracketed wall-hung rod.

• **QUILT SHOWER:** Revive the "quilting bee" (the tradition of relatives of the bride getting together to make quilts for her "hope chest"). If the bride and groom's friends and relatives sew, ask each to make a square (perhaps with a special appliqué or embroidered design that recalls special times of their lives) and join the squares for a keepsake wedding present.

• **QUINCE,** *Uses:* When cooked, it's a dessert. It can also be a fruit jelly. But in Victorian times, before chemical air fresheners were invented, quince—like lavender—used to be placed in clothes closets and dresser drawers to prevent musty odors.

R

- **RABBITS,** *As Pets:* Rabbits are cute, trainable pets, but should never be given to very young children as an "Easter Surprise" to be discarded when children tire of them or when injured. Remember, they are domestic animals, unable to fend for themselves; they won't live if they are just dropped off in the wild. If you buy a rabbit from a reliable pet shop, get books on its care.

1. Rabbits can be trained to use a litter box and so are good, quiet apartment pets.
2. They need a cage large enough to be comfortable and they need to be played with to get enough exercise. They are affectionate; stroke them on the head and back like you do a cat.
3. NEVER pick a rabbit up by the ears or scruff of the neck; don't pull its tail. When carrying a rabbit, support its back by holding it by the hind legs; rabbits have been known to injure their spinal cords or even break legs when kicking and squirming.
4. As with all animals, do not allow small children to handle them without supervision and consult a veterinarian if you think the animal has been injured or is ill.

- **RAIN GAUGE,** *Marking for Easy Reading:* Mark with red nail polish or red tape the one-, two-, three-inch levels on your garden rain gauge so that you can see them more easily and possibly check how much you have watered from a hose or how much nature has watered from the sky by looking out of your window. Put a drop of red food coloring into the gauge whenever it's emptied to help see the levels from your window without going outside. *Note of Laughter:* In one family I know, the children were assigned chores to help their mother when their father went out of town. When the children heard that Dad was coming home that night, the youngest one looked out of the window at the garden and said, "Oh boy, somebody is going to be in big trouble. Somebody forgot to fill Dad's rain gauge."

• **RAINY-DAY GAME FOR CHILDREN,** *Go Fishing:*
1. Cut various shapes from cardboard and write different numbers on each one. Then put a metal paper clip on the edge of each shape and put all into an empty bucket.
2. Attach a large magnet to a broom handle or fish pole and let children "fish" for shapes. Different numbers represent point values for "catching" each shape.

• **RAISINS,** *Preventing Them from Sinking in Baked Goods:*
1. Mix the raisins with the dry ingredients before both are added to the wet ingredients mixture. The flour will help suspend them.
2. Or, cut each raisin in half with a pair of kitchen shears so that they are lighter in weight and won't sink. The bonus here is that the flavor is spread better throughout the batter.

• **REBATES,** *Recycling:* Recycle manufacturer's coupon rebates to help others and feel good yourself. Save all your rebate money and donate it to charity at the end of the year.

• **RECIPE CARDS,** *Holding Them at Eye Level While You Cook:* Tape or tack photo pages with clear plastic pockets to the inside of your kitchen cabinet doors. When you plan a guest menu, insert the cards into the pockets and they'll be easy to see.

• **RECIPE FOR FAMILY LIFE:** I've had to reprint this popular recipe which was sent to me by Francesca Ugolini, a young girl from Corpus Christi.

   LOVING FAMILY LIFE RECIPE
      2 or more people
      2½ cups of love

¼ cup of peace
9 tablespoons of faith
6 tablespoons of trust
1¼ cup of caring
7 tablespoons of forgiveness
5 teaspoons of sharing

Mix all ingredients together gently. The result is a happy family full of love, peace, faith, trust, caring, forgiveness, and sharing. **Note:** My editor says there's a part of the directions missing. It's "Don't ever put any of these ingredients in hot water!"

• **RECIPE INGREDIENTS:** To make sure roommates or family don't eat specially bought ingredients before you get a chance to prepare the recipe, have a code such as marking the package with a red X or writing a note on it. Then everyone knows which foods are off limits.

• **RECIPES,** *Family Favorites:* Either clearly write favorite family recipes in notebooks (or type them and make duplicates to be pasted in notebooks) and then give the collection of old favorites to children and grandchildren. P.S. If giving them to grandchildren, you could leave enough space so that both parents' childhood favorites could be placed in the notebook.

• **RECIPES,** *Finding Favorites in Cookbooks:* Note on an index card the name and page of the cookbook in which you can find favorite recipes then file in the recipe box under the appropriate category. You'll save time paging through a whole cookbook collection to find the recipe you want.

• **RECIPES,** *Interpretation, Letter of Laughter:* Told to "add a small glug of butter flavor and a larger glug of vanilla," by his mom when he was making cookies, a teen paused for a while and said, "Mom, I always goof up on the glugs . . . can I just use a spoon instead?" And then, Mom had to try to figure out just exactly how much a glug was when you used a measuring spoon. I also cook with a pinch of this, a smidgen of that, and dollop of this and a blob of that. Now let's see, is a "glug" a pinch or a smidgen? I'll bet it's less than a dollop or a blob . . .

• **RECIPES,** *Recording Those Given on TV:* It's easy to miss some of the ingredients or instructions for recipes given on TV even when you're not interrupted by a phone call. Keep a tape in the VCR and tape the recipe presentation; you can copy it at your leisure and make notes on "how-to."

• **RECIPES,** *Storage:*
1. Instead of piles of clippings, buy an inexpensive binder and polypropylene "sheet protectors" (from office supply stores) or a binder-style photo album with magnetic pages and tabbed dividers to separate recipe categories (breads, meats, leftover uses, low-cal foods, sugarless desserts, vegetarian dishes, Italian, etc.). They'll even hold the pictures with newspaper/magazine recipes. As you collect more, add more refill pages. And, if you keep the binder near your reading chair, you can file each recipe as you clip it—no more messy piles of clippings! These books make nice gifts, too.
2. Tape recipes with non-yellowing transparent tape to index cards and file the cards in a loaf-size plastic bread container which holds more than ordinary file boxes.

• **RECLINER SAFETY WARNING: Caution:** If you have one of these chairs and a small cat or dog, be cautious when you change positions. I've received many letters from people who have crushed their kittens, puppies, or adult pets in recliners.

• **RECORDS,** *Cleaning:*
1. Removing Mildew from Old 45s, 78s, LPs—Hold the record by the edges, wet it well under cold running tap water. Then squirt a little mild liquid soap on your fingers and rub along the grooves in the record, not across them. Once both sides are thoroughly cleaned, rinse again under cold water. Dry placed on end in a safe location or dry with a cloth sold at record stores made especially for drying records.
2. Compact Discs: It's best to use commercial cleaning kits. You can dust them with a clean, lint-free, soft, dry cloth but instead of the circular motion used with analog records noted above, with CDs, you use straight strokes out from the center of the disc to the edge, like spokes of a wheel.

• **RECORDS,** *Recycling Old Ones:* Make flower pots from old 78 rpm records by melting them into shape over clay pots in the oven. To keep the melted shape symmetrical, make a plug out of aluminum foil and force it though the hole in the record and the hole in the clay pot below.

• **RECORDS,** *"Unwarping":* Sometimes, when old records get warped, you can place them on top of a television set where it's warm and dry, and then weight them down with several books. Leave them there for a few days. You may not be able to salvage all of them but this does work for some records and so it's worth a try.

• **RECYCLABLES & NONRECYCLABLES,** *Lists:* The following items are generally recycled.
1. Paper: Newsprint, corrugated cardboard, computer paper and office stationery.
2. Plastic: One and two-liter soda bottles, milk jugs, vinyl siding, antifreeze containers, motor oil and other auto fluids in hard plastic, hard plastic dish and laundry detergent bottles, ketchup and condiment bottles in hard plastic, shampoo bottles, baby wipes containers, Clorox and other bleach bottles, salad oil bottles, and most hard plastic containers.
3. Glass: Clear, brown or green glass bottles and containers. No need to remove labels.
4. Metals: Aluminum and tin cans, clean aluminum foil, clean aluminum food trays, aluminum siding.
   Non-recyclables at this time include:
1. Paper: Colored newspaper inserts, funny papers, cereal boxes, food boxes, detergent boxes, magazines, phone books, junk mail, wax and wax-coated cellophane.
2. Plastic: Cottage cheese and margarine tubs, plastic bags, foam plastic containers (some are beginning to be recycled but not everywhere in the U.S.).
3. Glass: Windows, plates, light bulbs, casserole dishes.
4. Metals: Bottle caps or metals mixed with paper or plastic such as frozen fruit juice containers.

• **RECYCLABLES,** *Magazines, Office Paper, Computer Sheets, Greeting Cards, Boxes, Jars, Paper Rolls, Sewing Scraps, etc.:* Call local pre-schools, day care centers, nursing homes, handicapped persons' craft centers to find out if they can use such things. I get letters from pre-school and other teachers telling me that with budget cutbacks, school art classes can use many items for their projects.

• **RECYCLING,** *Getting General Information:* The Plastics Industry introduced a coding system in 1988 in which a three-sided triangular arrow with a number from one to seven is stamped on the bottom of most plastic containers shows how to separate plastics for community recycling programs. Look under "solid waste" or "waste management" in the white or blue pages of the phone book for the phone number of your state, city, or county recycling agency then call to find out what kinds of plastics, etc. are recycled in your community.

If you want to do your part to keep beverage bottles and cans out of landfills but your city has no recycling program, call the Environmental Defense Fund's toll-free hotline to get information about recycling programs in your area. The number is 800-CALL-EDF.

• **REFRIGERATOR GASKET,** *Cleaning, Removing Mildew:* Wash with mild soap and hot water. Do not wash with bleach; it can cause the gasket to become brittle and crack. The trick is to keep it clean with frequent washing. Badly mildewed gaskets may have to be replaced.

• **REFRIGERATOR GASKET,** *When to Replace:* A brittle or torn gasket won't provide the seal needed for proper refrigerator temperature. Close a dollar bill in the door; if it slips out easily, you probably need a new refrigerator gasket.

• **REFRIGERATOR NOISE,** *Letter of Laughter:* A reader found that her refrigerator made loud vibrating noises because it was "hungry." She lives alone, therefore the fridge was mostly empty. She stopped the shelves from vibrating by "feeding them" several water-filled plastic jugs!

• **REFRIGERATOR TOP,** *Avoid Cleaning Greasy Residue:* Cover the top of the fridge with plastic wrap; clean by removing wrap and replacing it with clean wrap.

• **REMINDER,** *Answering Machine:* Please see ANSWERING MACHINE.

• **REMOTE CONTROLS,** *When They're So Remote You Can't Ever Find Them:* These days, some people have as many as three remote controls—stereo, VCR, TV. Find a suitably sized board, sand it smooth, and then put all your controls on one holder with strips of self-gripping fabric tape. Attach the fuzzy strips to the board and the hooked ones to the controls—then the controls will be unpleasant to carry around and will more likely be left on the board.

• **RHUBARB:** Eat only the stalk; the leaves are poisonous. Because rhubarb is bitter, it is cooked with sugar—either poached, stewed, or baked.
1. To stew: Cut up one pound of rhubarb into small pieces and place in a heavy pot with a couple of tablespoons of water and one-half to one cup of sugar. Simmer for about 20 minutes.
2. Adding strawberries in the last few minutes of cooking makes rhubarb delicious. Remove from heat; cool, then chill.
3. Serve it plain or with ice cream on it. *Note of Laughter:* Since rhubarb doesn't grow in Texas where I live, I got this recipe from our local County Extension Agent for a reader who found it growing in the yard of her new house and asked me what to do with it. When one of my editors saw the recipe in my column, she said in her family, rhubarb was usually liked by adults and hated by children, who were forced to eat it, and, when the reader asked what to do with the rhubarb, I should have responded, "Pour weed killer on it." I'd guess my editor hated it, wouldn't you?

• **RICE-CAKE TOPPINGS,** *When You Think They Are Too Bland:*
1. Spread on margarine and sprinkle with cinnamon and sugar; spread on peanut butter and jelly.
2. Make 'em Mexican—spread on refried beans, some sour cream, and top with grated cheese and then put it in the oven for a couple of minutes.

• **ROACHES,** *Heloise's Boric Acid Mixture:* No Heloise book is complete without the recipe that brings thousands of requests each year. Ingredients: Eight ounces of powdered boric acid, one-half cup flour, one-eighth cup sugar, one-half of a small onion (chopped), one-fourth cup shortening or bacon drippings and enough water to form a soft dough.
1. Mix boric acid, flour and onion. Next, cream shortening and sugar and add flour mixture to this. Blend well and then add enough water to form a soft dough.

2. Shape into small balls and put around the house in areas prone to roaches. If you place balls in open sandwich bags, they'll keep longer without drying out. When dough balls become hard, replace them with fresh ones.

Caution: Keep out of reach of children and pets; large amounts of boric acid can be toxic.

• **ROAMING ROCKING CHAIRS:** Glue velvet ribbon on the bottoms of the rockers along the entire length. Trim off excess. Allow glue to dry completely before turning the chair right side up. You can rock without roaming.

• **ROAST, GRINDING LEFTOVERS,** *Quick-Fix, Time-Saver;* To get the last bits of meat out of the grinder, grind a slice of bread last to push the meat out. You can wash away the remaining bread.

• **ROASTING RACK,** *Quick-Fix, Healthy Planet, Substitute an Edible Rack for a Metal One:* Place three or four whole stems of washed celery across the bottom of a roasting pan and place a roast or whole chicken on top. At serving time, garnish the meat with the celery.

• **RODENT PREVENTION:** These unwelcome guests are difficult to control. Rats and mice can live unseen for months, foraging through pantries, closets and cupboards for cereals, crackers and pet food. Mice can enter your home through a hole as small as one-half inch in diameter, climb almost any wall or pole and drop 50 feet to the ground and land on their feet. Rats can chew their way into your home, too.

1. Make sure all food is stored in covered containers, especially bulk pet food. Garbage should be kept in sturdy cans with tight-fitting lids.

2. To prevent mice and rats from squeezing their way in, be sure all possible entrances to your home are sealed with steel wool, which they can't chew through.

3. Cardboard boxes and cartons are favorite mouse nesting areas. Remove as many boxes as possible from closets and other storage areas.

4. Even with protective measures, you may still find signs of rodents in your home or hear them "go bump in the night." Rodenti-

cides are effective but some can cause the rodents to die slowly within your walls where they will decompose and smell until the remains mummify. If your problem is greater than just an occasional mouse passing through, you may need to call in a professional exterminator.

• **ROOF,** *Inspecting Yours, Checklist:* Early spring and late fall are the best times to inspect your roof so that all is ready for seasonal changes.
1. If you have a shingle roof, look for loose shingles or shakes for curling, fraying and tears at the edges.
2. With tile or slate roofs, look for missing or cracked pieces.
3. Check the flashings around chimneys, vents, skylights and other roof penetrations. They should be tight and in good condition. Call a professional contractor for a more thorough inspection if you have doubts.
4. Clean gutters and downspouts of leaves, sticks and other debris.
Caution: Stay off the roof; walking on its surface can do a lot of damage. If you must get up on the roof to inspect, climb only on a firmly braced or tied-off ladder with rubber safety feet.

• **ROOM DEODORIZER,** *Recycling:* If the container can be opened, place potpourri in it for permanent air freshener. You can add a few drops of your favorite perfume to renew scents.

• **ROSES,** *Defensive Cutting:* Hold stems with a spring clothespin to keep prickly thorns from sticking you.

• **ROSES AND ROSEBUSHES:** A reader, whose husband always brought her roses when they were dating, wrote that after they were married and had more responsibilities, they couldn't afford them anymore. But, still romantic, her husband planted a rosebush for her on each major holiday so that now she has a yard with many different shades of roses and a heart with lots of happy holiday memories.

• **RUBBER BANDS,** *Storage:* To keep rubber bands from being tangled in a drawer (if you don't use the time-honored method of looping them over a doorknob) loop them into a ball. The ball grows each day if your newspaper comes with a rubber band. The bonus for grandparents is that this ball can be a toy when the grandchildren come to visit.

• **RUBBER GLOVES,** *Healthy Planet, Recycling Old Ones:* Cut good finger tips off and put them into new gloves to reinforce fingertips; cut cuffs and parts of fingers in strips for rubber bands; cut ends of fingers and use them to protect opened spools of thread; use the palm/back for traction when opening jars.

• **RUBBER GLOVES TREATMENT:** Slather lotion or oil on your hands before putting them into rubber gloves for washing dishes or general cleaning. The gloves will slide on and off more easily and your hands will get a good moisturizing treatment, especially if they'll be in hot water.

• **RUGS,** *Making Them Non-Skid:* Either buy rubber-mesh pads for this purpose and place them under the rug, or tack a piece of old rubber-backed drapes (or other flat rubber sheet) to the backside.

• **RUGS,** *Stop Slipping Ones in the Bathroom:* Put a rubber tub mat under the rug.

• **RUGS AND CARPETS,** *Brightening:* Dull colors may not be faded, just dirty. One home remedy is to vacuum to remove dust, then, taking care not to saturate the backing, sponge the rug with a wet rag which has been dipped in a mixture of 1 quart white vinegar and 3 quarts boiling water. Allow to dry completely, then rub surface with warm bread crumbs and vacuum.

• **RUGS AND CARPETS,** *Buying New Carpets:* You can save on carpet if you get top quality thick padding but when considering the overall cost, remember that installation and padding may or may not be included in the price.

• **RUGS AND CARPETS,** *Checklist Care for Oriental Carpets:*
1. Don't use steam cleaners; they remove the wool's natural oils and prematurely age the rug.
2. Blot; don't rub spills. Get a professional cleaner for dried stains. You can dilute the spill with cool water, continuing to blot until the rug seems clean. Don't ever soak unstained parts and always dry the rug thoroughly using absorbent towels on top and underneath the stain.

3. Never put house plants on rugs; moisture will condense beneath the pot causing mildew damage to the rug.

4. Old-fashioned beating is mean; it breaks the foundation of the carpet.

5. Sweep fringes with a broom instead of vacuuming, which can tear them. Broom-sweeping brings out the wool's sheen as well as removing dirt.

6. Vacuum in the direction of the nap. Find the nap by running your hand over the surface.

7. Padding reduces wear and prevents slipping. You can get special pads to prevent slippage of Oriental rugs placed over carpeting.

8. Turn rugs annually to prevent wear paths and equalize light exposure.

• **RUGS AND CARPETS,** *Identifying Hand-Loomed Orientals:* When you see an Oriental rug that appears to fade gradually toward one end and both ends are not finished/fringed exactly the same way, it's likely to be hand-loomed the traditional way. Fringes/threads at the "top" of the loom are tied differently from those at the "bottom" and, because the yarn is dyed in hanks with natural dyes, the first yarn used (from the outside layers of the hank) will be darker hued than the inner layers; the "top" of the rug (woven first) will be darker than the "bottom" edge.

• **RUGS AND CARPETS,** *Repair:* For wear or burnholes, cut out burned section of fibers. I like to use cuticle scissors. Gather strands of fuzz or fiber from an out-of-the-way spot and glue them in the hole with fabric glue. Place a piece of waxed paper over the repair, weight it with a book, and allow it to dry for at least twenty-four hours. Large burns in rugs or upholstery may need professional repair.

• **RUGS AND CARPETS,** *Repairs:* To cover worn areas, buy water-proof colored markers to match the worn spots and just color the carpet backing that's showing through. This works especially well with dark-colored patterned carpets like Orientals.

• **RUG WASH,** *When Washable Rugs Don't Fit Into the Washer:* Take a washable area rug to a do-it-yourself car wash that has high-pressure hoses, dispenses soap in one wash and rinse water in the other. No scrubbing is necessary. After washing and rinsing, roll up wet rugs, place in a large plastic garbage bag and take them home to dry over a fence or a couple of sturdy clotheslines.

• **RUST RINGS FROM SHAVING CREAM, HAIR SPRAY, ETC. CANS:**
1. To prevent them on bathtub or shower surfaces, place shaving cream can in a 3 ½-inch round plastic beverage holder, the kind that holds soft drinks on car doors. You can hold the can in the ring to the hand-rail of a shower door.
2. To prevent rust rings from shaving cream, hair spray or other cans put them in styrofoam or foam rubber soft drink can insulators, fit plastic lids from containers like potato chip tubes to the bottoms, or just place on any plastic lid large enough to hold the can.

• **RUST SPOTS ON STAINLESS STEEL,** *Removing from Flatware and Pots:* Sorry, there's no permanent solution to this but you can remove little spots with a silver or stainless-steel cleaner. Corrosion occurs when acids, salt and even normal use removes the protective coating put on stainless steel items. Avoid rust spots by always rinsing all food residue from flatware so that it doesn't have time to corrode. If you aren't planning to run your dishwasher for a day or two, it's best to wash stainless flatware by hand. I rinse mine before putting into the dishwasher even if it will be run that day.

- **SACHETS,** *Free:* Take the perfumed sample paper inserts from magazines and tuck them into your lingerie drawers, clothing or linen closets, and with your stationery and greeting cards for free sachets.

- **SACHETS,** *Soap:* Store scented soaps (unwrapped or even wrapped, if the scent permeates the wrapper) tucked amid the towels in your linen closet. The towels will smell nice and after the scent becomes faint, use the soap for your bath where getting it wet will reactivate some of the scent. The bonus is that soap dries when stored unwrapped and then dissolves more slowly when wet so it lasts longer.

- **SAFETY PINS:** So useful to hold up a torn hem, close up a blouse with a popped button, hold the temple of your glasses to the frame when the screw falls out! My dry cleaner pins tags to the garments and so when I remove the tag, I pin the safety pin to the hem of that garment so that I always have a safety pin handy for emergencies.

- **ST. PATRICK'S DAY GREENS:** Start the day or end it with green food-colored pancakes! Surprise children by putting a few drops of green coloring in milk. Serve green gelatin, green mashed potatoes, green vegetables and salad, too. And don't forget to wear some green to avoid getting pinched!

• **SALAD,** *Preparing in Advance:* To prevent soggy salad, put the desired dressing in the bottom of the salad bowl, layer in tomatoes and vegetables. Last, add the lettuce or spinach leaves. Place the prepared salad in the refrigerator and toss just before serving.

• **SALAD BAR,** *To Encourage Family Salad-eating:* Since your objective is to get the family to enjoy eating healthy, nutritious fare, accept the reality that not everyone likes the same ingredients in a salad. Make salads more inviting by offering a family salad bar. Offer sliced mushrooms, carrots, beets, celery; chopped green onions, olives; garbanzo beans, kidney beans, sprouts, radishes, etc. in the cups of muffin tins, served beside a large bowl of greens and several salad dressings. Let family members customize their salads; you'll be surprised at how youngsters will try new things if other siblings seem to be enjoying them. Cover the muffin tins with plastic wrap after dinner to store leftovers in the refrigerator for the next day or two. Food like celery, radishes, carrot shreds will keep fresher for the next day if you put a wet, not drippy, paper towel on top before the wrap.

• **SALAD GREENS:** Many new greens are sold in grocery stores and you can combine them for delicious salads. Just remember that you don't usually wash and store lettuce in the refrigerator. Just rinse what you will use immediately.
1. Boston lettuce has green outer leaves with yellow-green inner leaves. Its buttery flavor is best enhanced by a mild salad dressing.
2. Bibb lettuce has soft, green broad leaves. Its delicate taste is also best enhanced by a mild dressing.
3. Red-leaf lettuce is usually a large head of frilly green leaves with reddish tips. It also has a delicate taste and is best with a subtle dressing.
4. Curly endive is a chicory and has a somewhat bitter flavor. Its leaves are large, lacy and fringed. The outer leaves are darker in color and have a stronger taste. Mix with some milder greens and a strong-flavored salad dressing.

5. Watercress leaves are small, dark green and have crisp stems. Its strong peppery taste is good when teamed with other pungent greens.

6. Belgian endive has a long, small, firm head. Its leaves are creamy white and have a hint of yellow at the tips. It's crisp, has a pleasantly bitter taste and is best mixed with stronger flavored greens.

- **SALAD-OIL STOPPER:** To prevent bottled salad oil from gushing out too fast, instead of removing the entire seal when you first remove the cap, cut a slit or punch a hole in the seal. It will be easier to measure or sprinkle. **Note:** When you tear up romaine lettuce for a large company salad, wash and put it in a large clean pillowcase and then spin it dry in the washer spin cycle. You won't bruise the romaine and it's fast and neat! Plus, it will entertain your friends, too!

- **SALAD TOSS,** *Quick-Fix:* Tear greens into a large plastic bowl with a tight-fitting lid; add dressing, give it a few shakes and no more tossing and "bruising" the lettuce.

- **SALAMANDERS,** *Feeding:* Salamanders will eat a diet of strained or pureed fruits and vegetables like baby food, insects and, only once or twice a week, canned cat or dog food.

- **SALT,** *Avoiding Lumps:* If you don't want to keep rice or crushed crackers inside the salt shaker to keep it free-flowing in humid weather, up-end a small clear jelly glass over the shaker. The jelly glass "dome" will keep the salt dry and ready to shake.

- **SALT,** *Removing Excess Salt from Soup or Other Heated Liquids:* Add sliced raw potato to absorb the salt. Remove slices when they begin to soften if you don't want to eat them.

- **SALT (SODIUM),** *Reducing in Canned Foods:* Discarding the liquid that vegetables are canned in will lower the sodium content by one-third; rinsing will decrease it even more. This hint is good also for canned tuna and shrimp (rinse shrimp very gently to prevent breakage).

- **SALT SUBSTITUTE,** *Homemade:* Mix 5 teaspoons onion powder; 1 tablespoon each of garlic powder, paprika, dry mustard; 1 teaspoon thyme; ½ teaspoon white pepper; ½ teaspoon celery seed. Combine, store in clean, empty spice jar in cool, dry place.

• **SANDBOX,** *Indoors for Child's Play:* Take a large plastic tray (like those used for busing dishes or mixing cement) and pour a five-pound bag of cornmeal into it. This "sand" is clean, light and safer than real sand if it accidentally gets into the mouth of a youngster. Clean-up is even easier if you place a plastic shower curtain or drop cloth under the play area!

• **SAP,** *Dripped from Trees:*
1. On a wooden patio, carefully scrape off as much sap as you can with a paint scraper and remove remaining residue with turpentine, which will also remove any paint or water sealer from the patio, too, so you'll have to redo the wood.
2. If the sap is on your car, you may be able to get it off chrome parts with turpentine but for painted surfaces, contact your car dealer's service department for advice. Service departments have specific products that work with different auto paint finishes.

• **SAVING MONEY,** *Getting Into the Habit:* One reader who found it hard to save any money at all decided that after she finished paying off a loan, she would put the amount of the loan payment into her savings account. She pretends that she is still paying on the loan and is building up a nice nest egg so that she can handle the next financial emergency without a loan. The big bonus is that she is receiving interest on her money instead of having the possibility of paying interest on an emergency loan!

• **SAW BLADE,** *Storage, Recycling Idea:* An old record rack will hold saw blades safely and protects the cutting edges from damage.

• **SCALE,** *Recovering a Worn One:* Replace dirty, curly-edged covering on a scale with adhesive-backed floor tile. You can trim the edges and cut out the area for the dial and then make an adjustment for the extra weight. If you have such tile in your bathroom, you can make your scale match the floor and be less conspicuous. **Note:** And we want scales to be inconspicuous, especially on those days when the munchies grab us!

• **SCARF HANGER,** *Keeping Scarfs Free of Fold Lines:*
1. Hang them over a pants hanger—the kind designed to hold several pairs on different rods.
2. Crafty Idea: Tack plastic rings about the size of a silver dollar from craft shops across the bottom of quilted or crochet-covered hangers (about three inches apart) and hang scarfs from the rings.

• **SCARF RINGS,** *Recycling Jewelry:* When rings don't fit or even if they still do, they can be scarf rings if you slip the ends of a scarf into the ring, pull up and secure.

• **SCHOOL BUS REMINDER:** Here's a solution from a part-time working mom to remind her young child of which days she will be picked up by her mom in the car and which days she should come home on the school bus. Buy two brightly colored plastic buttons. On one paint or draw a school bus and on the other a car. Attach a safety pin to the buttons with quick-drying glue and then pin the buttons to the child's clothing each day. It eases the child's apprehension and helps the teacher get the child to the proper waiting area after school.

• **SCHOOL-DAZE SURVIVAL (ALSO SEE WORK DAY SURVIVAL):** To avoid having children dart around gathering books, jackets, caps, backpacks and other things in the morning, place a bookcase near the door so that they can put all their school things on a single shelf ready for the next day. Each child gets a personal shelf. Or, keep small laundry baskets near the door for each child's possessions.

• **SCOOPS,** *Recycling Plastic Coffee Scoops:*
1. Put your daily vitamin dosage in them or use them to store small objects like tacks in a drawer.
2. Use to measure household cleaners.
3. Place one in each kitchen canister.
4. Make a stool for a doll house.

• **SCRAPBOOK,** *Quick-Fix for Newspaper Clippings:* Cut out columns, recipes, stories, and then tape or glue with rubber cement to pages of a school composition book. Highlight the line that tells you the subject of the clipping at a glance.

• **SCREEN,** *Repairing Wire Ones:* Cut a piece of wire mesh from an old screen and sew it over the hole with some fishing line or plastic thread. Also look for screen-repair kits in hardware stores. Small holes can sometimes be sealed with clear fingernail polish.

• **SCREENS,** *Cleaning Window and Door Aluminum Screens:* Remove screens from doors or windows; place up against a tree or fence. Scrub with a mixture of one cup ammonia to one gallon of water. After scrubbing, rinse well with water and dry in sunshine.

• **SCREENS,** *Removing Crayon "Kid-art" from a Window/Door Screen:* Put a couple of sheets of paper toweling behind the screen and spray the area with pre-wash stain remover. Scrub with a stiff brush and rinse well. If crayon remains, repeat the process.

• **SCREWDRIVER,** *Substitute for Phillips Screwdriver:* Try a metal potato peeler. *Letter of Laughter:* A friend, who likes to innovate, told me about her daughter pounding a nail into the wall with the handle of a screwdriver and having her husband, a fanatic about his tools, get horrified. "Where did you ever learn that," he gasped. "My mother taught me; she can do it with the side of pliers, too. Anybody can pound a nail in the wall with a hammer," the daughter replied. The next weekend, she was given a tool set of her own for the kitchen, which is a very good idea—include screwdrivers (Phillips and regular), pliers—and also a hammer, if you're conventional about nail pounding!

• **SEARCH FOR LOST FRIENDS OR RELATIVES:** Main public libraries and some universities have telephone directories from major cities; look in them for names of lost friends or relatives. Or, from the library's information service, get the telephone number and address of the county courthouse. Call or write to them for family records, like birth, death, or marriage certificates. Remember that whenever you send a request for information, include a stamped, self-addressed business-size envelope and it usually gets a faster response.

• **SEASHELLS,** *Don't Throw Away Beach Souvenirs:*
1. Put them into a large clear jar and use as a paperweight, door stop, or, if you are handy, make a large shell-filled vase into a lamp.
2. Cover soil of pot plants to hold in moisture and make it less attractive to digging pets.
3. Larger flat shells make good soap dishes.

4. Glue them on an old picture frame and then frame a picture or mirror with it. Boutiques at the seashore sell seashell-framed shiny mirrors! (Say that fast, ten times!)

• **SEAT CUSHIONS,** *Stop Them from Slipping:* Try putting a thin sheet of foam rubber, a rubber sink or bathtub mat, between the sofa or chair cushion and the springs.

• **SEEDLINGS,** *Growing Your Own, Recycling:* It's easy to get seedlings out of their containers whole and undamaged at planting time.
1. If you start your seedlings in paper cups, you can tear away the cup at planting time.
2. If you cut both ends out of juice cans, set them on a tray and plant seeds in them, at planting time, you just gently push all the dirt and roots out at the same time.
3. Start seedlings in egg cartons, but place a section of eggshell in the bottom of each cup so removal is a snap.

• **SEEDS, STORAGE:** If you buy tub margarine, the butter compartment of your refrigerator is unused and just right for storing seed packages. Seeds will keep and still germinate several years after the date shown on the package if they are kept in the refrigerator.

• **SEEDS,** *Testing for Germination:* If you find old seeds in packages, try sprinkling a few between two damp paper towels. If they're still fresh enough, they'll sprout in a couple of days and you can plant the sprouts as well as the seed. Some seeds, such as tomato, cabbage, cucumber, lettuce and squash, will stay fresh for several years and others should be bought each year. Many gardeners keep seeds, sealed in zipper bags, in the refrigerator for many seasons.

• **SENIOR CITIZEN,** *Definition, Letter of Laughter:* When a grandmother took her four-year-old granddaughter to a Senior Citizen meeting, the child leaned over and asked Grandma what the meeting was about. When Grandma explained that it was mostly for old people, the child whispered loudly, "Aren't there any new ones?" Grandma hugged her and told her grandchild that she was the only one there that was close to being new.

• **SEWING,** *For Toddlers:* If your child squirms so much that you're afraid you'll stick him with a pin, mark hems and buttonholes with masking tape.

• **SEWING,** *Hand-sewing Hints:*
1. Keeping your thread shorter than 20 inches avoids knots and tangles.
2. Use a larger-holed needle if your thread keeps fraying.
3. If fabric puckers or gets pulls, your needle might be bent, dull or point-damaged. Get a new needle.
4. If you cut thread on an angle instead of breaking it, needle-threading is easier.
5. You won't save time or money by using old thread from wooden spools because it's likely to break. Wooden spools haven't been used for years and have become collector's items.

• **SEWING,** *Mending:* Embroidery floss is a good substitute for regular thread when you are mending. You can more easily match colors with it and it's stronger, too.

• **SEWING,** *Using Fabric Glues:* **Caution!** If you use those wonderful timesavers like glue stick, liquid seam sealant and basting tape, be aware that they can damage your sewing machine and cause expensive repair bills if you don't follow directions exactly. One important rule is: Always let glues dry completely before stitching over them.

• **SEWING MACHINE,** *Maintenance, Letter of Laughter:* When the sewing machine clatters for six months begging for oil and you finally "feed" it, it's a good idea to sew on mending or other old stuff just in case some oil leaks out. But one reader wants to know why, after you finish with the old stuff, and then start on some pretty new material does the "blamed thing disgorge its last excess drips that you were sure weren't there?" Why? It's another of those "irony of life rules."

• **SEWING MACHINE,** *Quick-Fix Cleaning, Recycling:* A well-washed and dried mascara brush will clean bobbin and shuttle carriers in the sewing machine. It fits into those tight places and you can twist it around to pick up lint.

• **SEWING NEEDLES,** *Letter of Laughter:* A seamstress wrote that when the only needle in her pin cushion was too big for the job at hand, she began kneading the pin cushion because she thought she spied a tiny golden one peeping up. To her surprise, she found thirty-seven needles buried inside her pincushion. Her question was, "Do you think they might have been in there breeding?" I didn't know, but I sure advised her to keep an eye on the situation!

• **SEWING NEEDLES,** *Threading:* Can't thread the needle? Dab a tiny bit of clear nail polish on the tip of the thread, allow to dry, and it's no problem.

• **SEWING NEEDLES,** *Sticky:* Your needle will glide through fabric more easily if you stick it through a fabric-softener sheet a few times. Thread the needle and knot the thread BEFORE doing this.

• **SHAKERS,** *Flour and Sugar:* Keep large shakers of flour and sugar on the kitchen counter to avoid hauling out canisters when you need just a teaspoon or so of either one.

• **SHALLOTS,** *Substitutes in Recipes:* Shallots are members of the onion family but their flavor is somewhere between onion and garlic. Substituting regular onions for shallots won't give you the same flavor in a recipe and can change the taste. **Note:** Shallots become bitter when overcooked so they are usually minced and browned quickly.

• **SHEEPSKIN RUGS,** *Cleaning:* Since it's almost impossible to know what type of tanning process was used on these skins, it's best to take them to a reputable dry cleaner where special cleaning processes and chemicals can be used. **Note:** White sheepskins tend to yellow after they are cleaned.

• **SHELF,** *Level Installation:* Measuring from the floor up to the height for installation and marking both ends may not make the shelf level due to imperfections in construction. Instead, measure to the height on one end and then use the level to mark the shelf line on the wall, making sure that the bubble is in the center before you extend the line.

• **SHELF COVERING,** *Shelves with Pots and Pans:* Shelf paper usually tears in this situation but vinyl floor tiles are easy to install—cut to fit and peel off the backing—and easier yet to maintain by wiping clean.

• **SHELF PAPER,** *$aver:* Buy wallpaper remnants and cut to fit.

• **SHELF PAPER,** *When It's Too Wide:* Cut off the excess through the whole roll with a handsaw.

• **SHELVES,** *Better Storage Capacity:*
1. Rectangular plastic dish pans, new or clean used ones, can double your shelf storage capacity if you fill and stack them. Print contents on tape or labels instead of directly on the dish pans just in case you want to change the contents. They're easier to remove and replace than stacks of items.
2. Small plastic mesh baskets can serve the same purpose and a rectangular plastic laundry basket can hold shoes on the closet floor.

• **SHIRT COLLAR,** *Quick-Fix, Prevention of Frayed Ones:* Apply a commercial product sold in fabric stores to stop or prevent fraying to the collar points when the shirt is new. Reapply periodically.

• **SHIRTS,** *Ironing:*
1. Do cuffs, collar and sleeves first.
2. Using the rounded end of the ironing board, start with the back of the shirt, ironing on the inside instead of outside for a nicer finish, especially on dark fabrics.
3. Begin at the corner where shoulder and armhole meet and work your way down and to the middle. Do the front using the same method.
4. Turn shirt right-side-out and do any touching-up.

• **SHOE BAGS,** *Compartmentalized Hanging Ones:* Yes, they organize shoes when hanging on the closet door, wall or attached to a sturdy hanger, but they also hold socks and undies, school supplies, knitting/crocheting supplies; toys; rolled T-shirts and polo shirts, pantyhose and tights; and just about anything that takes up drawer space or makes it jumbled. You'll want more than one in a closet!

• **SHOEBOX,** *Recycling:* A child's shoebox makes a handy cupboard-file for sauce and gravy mixes.

• **SHOEHORN,** *Substitute:* The tongue end of a man's belt can be an emergency shoehorn.

• **SHOEHORN SUBSTITUTE:** Cut a plastic margarine tub lid to the right shape and it will bend around your heel better than a "real" shoe horn.

• **SHOELACES,** *Keeping Them in Children's Shoes:* Stop laces from pulling through the eyelets when children remove their shoes by tying a knot at each shoelace tip after the first lace-up—makes kid's shoes almost kid-proof.

• **SHOELACES,** *When Toddlers Pull Them Out and Lose Them:* When you lace a toddler's shoes for the first time, knot the laces after putting them through the first two holes. The toddler can still take the laces out of the first couple of holes but not all the way out. No more lost laces!

• **SHOES,** *Checklist for Leather-shoe Care:* The gloss sprayed on new shoes does not protect like polish so polish new shoes before wearing them.
1. Use a sponge and saddle soap at least once monthly to remove dust and grime. Follow with good quality paste or cream to moisturize the leather; never use liquid polish on leather.
2. Use a soft cloth to apply polish, allow to dry; buff with brush in long easy strokes; finish shine with buffing in circular motion with soft cloth to remove excess polish and deepen shine. Clean or get new brushes and shine cloths every six months.
3. Strip off polish build-up every eight shines with leather balm to prevent cracking.
4. Dress the heel edge with black dressing product to lock out moisture which leads to cracks.

• **SHOES,** *Cleaning Heel Marks Off White and Colored Ones:* If the shoes are just marked and the finish is not ruined, pre-wash spray will remove heel-kick marks. It may take a bit of scrubbing but it works.

• **SHOES,** *Coordinating with Wardrobe:* Replace plain white laces in white tennis shoes with colored ribbon or cord.

• **SHOES,** *Drying:*
1. Stuff wet shoes with old pantyhose to help keep their shape while they dry.

2. If you can't toss them into the clothes dryer, put them on the floor next to the hot-air exhaust of the refrigerator to hasten drying. **Hint,** Healthy-Planet Recycling: If children want to go back outdoors and their shoes are still wet, put their feet into bread bags and then into shoes and their feet will be dry even if their shoes are not.

• SHOES, *Fixing Driving-Damaged Heels:* A good cleaning and polishing may remove scuff marks. To remove scrapes, heat a curling iron to warm and gently press it against the scraped area. The "ironing" will remove wrinkles so that you can smooth the leather and glue it back into place. **Hint:** Avoid the problem by keeping a pair of slip-on shoes in the car to wear while driving.

• SHOES, *Quick-Fix Cover-up for Brightly Colored Shoes:* Fix up little scrapes and scratches on pink, purple, and non-neutral colored shoes with colored felt-tip markers. They come in many shades to match almost any color.

• SHOES, *Quick-Fix to Stop Squeaks, Preventing Squeaks:* Moisture in the soles is the usual cause of squeaky shoes.
1. Try shaking some talcum powder in the shoes before and after each wearing.
2. Turn each shoe over and nail a couple of short tacks in the bottom of the sole on either side of the metal arch support. Do not push the tacks all the way through the sole or they will stick your foot.
3. If the above fail, take the shoe to a shoe-repair shop for advice.

• SHOES, *Recycling Energy, Quiet-Drying Tennis Shoes:* If the clanging of your shoes drying in the dryer is annoying, place them under the dryer vent so that the warm air flows into them to dry them while you dry other loads.

• SHOES, *Suede-shoe Care:* Brush weekly with stiff-bristled brush to remove dirt. Gum eraser can remove light stains; heavier stains need cleaning professionally. Apply water and stain-preventing spray after cleaning and brushing.

• SHOES, *TLC Checklist to Make Them Last Longer:*
1. When putting them on, untie, unbuckle and use a shoehorn to avoid ruining the shoe's "mouth." Shoe trees help shoes keep their shape.

2. Let shoes rest in ventilated areas between wearings to dry out; don't store in their original boxes.

3. Clean and polish them regularly. Don't wait until they are scuffed and shabby. See Above.

• **SHOES, REPAIRS:** Replace heels when one-fourth of the heel is worn off. At winter's end, before I store my good leather boots, I like to have them professionally cleaned and shined at my shoe repair shop.

• **SHOES, SCUFF MARKS,** *Removing from White Shoes or Sneakers:* Spray with prewash spray, let set a few minutes and wipe off. Remove hard or stubborn stains by scrubbing with a brush. Washable sneakers can then go into the machine. **Caution:** Although this method has been used on rubber, plastic and cloth parts of sneakers and on other white shoes, it's still best to test all cleaning methods on an inconspicuous place to make sure no harm will be done.

• **SHOE STRAPS THAT SLIP:** Put a piece of moleskin on the inside of the heel strap where it hits your heel or try sticking a piece of thin foam rubber weather stripping. Either material can be trimmed to fit a heel strap and should help keep it in place.

• **SHOPPING,** *Credit Cards:* Compare grace periods, annual fees, and interest rates. If you have a lot of cards, protecting them by joining a credit card protection service may be a good idea, but if you have only one or two cards, you can easily report loss or theft yourself. **Caution:** Never sign up with a registry by phone; there are fraudulent protection services that ask for your card numbers but instead of protecting you they make unauthorized charges on your card.

• **SHOPPING,** *For a Fitness Center:*

1. Ask for a one-day pass so that you can sample the facility. Be sure to visit it during the hours you plan to use it so that, if you plan to go after work, you'll know if it's so busy then that you'll spend all your time waiting for equipment or have overcrowded classes. When you try out classes, make sure the instructors are encouraging and that they note the different ability levels of participants. Talk to members to find out if they are satisfied.

2. Does the facility offer what you want to do? Some high-tech facilities offer sophisticated weight machines and aerobics classes. Others offer ballroom dancing, karate, cardio-fitness classes and other programs.

3. What about the equipment? Is it up-to-date and well-maintained or are there several broken machines, as is common in many facilities? Studios and workout rooms should be spacious, clean, well lit, and ventilated, and have floors of appropriate materials to avoid injury. (Springy wood floors for dance/exercise, resilient surfaces for weight training areas.) Class sizes should allow for enough space for safe, comfortable movement and for individual attention from instructors. Staff should be supervising all areas at all times and there should be enough equipment so several people can work out simultaneously. Are showers, dressing rooms, saunas, pools and steam rooms clean? Are lockers secure?

4. Does the club require a stress test before you start a new program? If you are over forty-five, overweight, at risk for heart disease, disabled or have other health problems, you should have a doctor's exam before starting any new exercise program even if the club doesn't require it. (Be leery of clubs that claim their diet, exercise or fitness programs are better than those suggested by recognized medical sources.)

5. Ask about the qualifications of the staff. Certification is not the law but staff can be certified by the American College of Sports Medicine, International Dance Exercise Association, Aerobics and Fitness Association of America, and the Institute for Aerobics Research. Find out if the club requires its teachers to take in-house training. For example, the YMCA has its own instructor training program. It's best if instructors have degrees in exercise-related fields, such as exercise physiology, kinesiology, or physical education. Instructors and staff should be trained in first aid and CPR and the club also should offer CPR training to members.

6. If you decide to join: Avoid "today-only" sale prices; you should be able to take a couple of days to make your decision. (Most states mandate "cooling-off" periods of three days so that you can change your mind.) Read contracts very carefully. You should be able to take a short-term membership before committing to a year or more and you should be able to freeze your membership temporarily in case of illness, injury or travel.

• **SHOPPING,** *Forming Co-ops to Save Money:*
1. If your city has vegetable or farmer's markets where you can save money by buying produce in bulk, get together with five or six friends and buy bulk produce weekly, dividing purchases and their cost for substantial savings. You'll get a taste of veggies that you might not otherwise have tried, too. In some co-ops, each person takes a turn each week to shop and divide the produce; in others they make it a fun, get-together day for several of the co-op people to shop together.
2. Organize your neighbors, bridge club, etc. if several people are shopping for stereo equipment at the same time and try to buy as a group. Some group members research audio magazines in the library to find out which brands are best quality and how to combine the various components—speakers, CD player, receiver, etc., and others scout local stores to compare prices. Then, all go to a dealer together and try to negotiate a "group discount." Even if you don't get a discount, you'll surely get the best researched buy on your equipment.

• **SHOPPING,** *Gas for Your Car:* Contrary to popular belief, premium gas is not a must for all cars. More than 90 percent of cars run well on mid-level or regular octanes. Experts say that if your car's manual doesn't specify using high-octane, you may not need it. Lower octanes are a bonus for the environment because more expensive premium gas is a pollution source; it doesn't burn as cleanly as lower octanes. And, the engine cleaners advertised as "musts" aren't necessary either. So, you can save money and our air at the same time!

• **SHOPPING,** *Insurance:* Read all policies carefully to make sure you are not paying for duplicate coverage with several policies. (This is especially prevalent with Medicare supplements. Also, people often buy extra insurance on rental cars when their own auto insurance policies already provide the needed coverage.)

• **SHOPPING,** *Layaway Checklist:* Super prices on sale clothing, especially on last year's winter clothing, makes buying on layaway a tempting idea—you don't use credit or pay full price immediately, the store holds the garments and you'll probably be finished paying for the garments by the time you'll need to wear them. **Caution:** If you don't understand the store's layaway policy, you could have problems.

1. Terms: Know how much time you have to pay, when payments are due, what minimum payment is required, and what charges, if any, are added to the purchase price. Some sellers charge a service fee; some charge a penalty for late payments.

2. Refunds: If you decide you don't want the item, some stores may give all of your money back, some may give you credit to apply to other purchases. This information should be in writing.

3. Availability of Layaway Items: Some items are immediately available and others are on display to be ordered upon request. If you buy an item on layaway, find out if it will remain on display (the possibility of getting shopworn) or be stored in a separate area of the stockroom until you get it. If the item must be ordered, find out how far in advance you need to order it so you can get it when you finish paying. To make sure you are getting exactly what you placed on layaway, the receipt should say, for example: "One (1) red 2-piece dress, Size 12, (NAME) Manufacturer, Style No. 678."

4. Pitfalls: If the store goes bankrupt while you are still paying, you may lose your money and the merchandise. Consider the store's reputation before you buy; check with the local Better Business Bureau before buying an expensive item on layaway.

5. Records: ALWAYS keep good records of payments so that you have them in case of disputes.

• **SHOPPING,** *Long Distance Phone Service:* If you make only a few long distance calls each month costing less than $10, the major long distance phone services cost about the same. Compare the following before you decide on a long distance service: monthly service fee, minimum charges, if and how easily will you get credit if you get wrong numbers, bad connections or disconnected calls.

• **SHOPPING,** *Sales:* Learn to spot a real sale. Sale items are those which will return to their previous higher prices after the sale is over. "Clearance Sales" are on items substantially reduced. "Promotional Sales" usually are on items not always in the store's regular stock; they are specially priced but not necessarily great savings. "Going Out of Business Sales" can go on all year-round at some unscrupulous dealerships; this is especially prevalent in Oriental rug and furniture stores.

• **SHOPPING,** *Supermarkets:* Stores are designed to promote impulse buying. That's why the most expensive items are placed on shelves at eye level. To avoid impulse buying, don't shop hungry, shop from a list, make your list according to planned menus, and, if you can, leave the children at home. Otherwise, let each child pick one thing only. Coupons save money if you use them to buy things you actually use.

• **SHOPPING,** *Supermarkets, Ways to Cut Spending:*
1. Plan meals from your cupboard using ingredients you already have on hand so that you can use up these foods and free up money to spend on this month's sale items.
2. Before you decide on your menu, check grocery ads to see what's on sale.
3. Plan all three meals for the day, but don't feel bound by tradition—if you like pancakes for supper or lunch and soup or sandwiches for breakfast, it's okay.
4. Change your eating habits. The U.S. Government studies show that nutritious foods are less expensive than junk foods.
5. Experiment with substitutes in recipes: If green beans are on special and the recipe calls for peas, use the beans, both are green. Rice and noodles can be interchangeable and so on. Chicken or turkey can substitute for beef in some recipes; you can doctor them up with seasonings or beef bouillon or French onion soup mix.
6. Avoid convenience foods when you can. They cost more and many are over-packaged, adding to our over-trashed landfills. Also, many are high in fat and salt content.
7. Be creative with leftovers and plan them. For example, if you cook enough rice or noodles for two meals, you can use the leftovers in a casserole another day. Bake double the number of potatoes you need for one day and use the leftovers for stuffed baked potatoes another day, saving baking energy.
8. Be flexible—change your menu to accommodate specials and remember that sometimes buying after the promotion of specialty foods can be a good buy, especially in January when overstocked gourmet foods and condiments get marked down.

9. Avoid too many shopping trips where you "pop into the store to pick up a few things." This encourages impulse buying.
10. Make budget-stretching a game not a burdensome chore. See if you can shop more economically each week and make notes of your savings so that you can take pride in your efforts.

• **SHOPPING,** *Travel Clubs:* Travel clubs can make vacation trips fun and less expensive but beware if you are asked to prepay for a trip before your reservations are confirmed in writing, or if you are required to buy something as a condition of membership that has no relationship to the trip.

• **SHOPPING,** *Warranties and Service Contracts:* Always read the fine print and if you are trying to decide between two similar items, take the one with the most extensive warranty. If you decide to buy a service contract, find out how long the contract will be valid, will repairs be done in your home or a service center, who will do repairs (dealer or repair center), and, if repairs are done by a third party service center, will your contract be honored if the third party goes out of business. Also, will the contracts still be valid if you buy the item under your name and give it away as a gift?

• **SHOPPING WITH CHILDREN,** *Mother-Saver:* If your child gets cranky while you shop, promise that when you finish your shopping, you both will go to the child's favorite store or other place. There's a fine line between bribery and rewarding a child for good behavior but when you're shopping with a child, there's no point in even looking for that line! Whatever works is good!

• **SHOPPING FOR GROCERIES WITH SMALL CHILDREN,** *Keeping Them Busy, Recycling:* Cut out pictures of food and grocery items from magazines, food ads and newspapers. Glue several on a heavy piece of cardboard (like a cereal box side) to resemble a bingo card. When you leave for the store, give each child one of the cards and a crayon. As you shop, the children mark off the items they see. If you want to make it a competitive game, the first child to mark off all of the items gets to pick a special treat. If you don't want it to be competition, each child that marks off all items on the card gets a treat at the end.

- **SHOPPING LIST:** Avoid repeated shuffling through your coupons—note on the list which items have coupons and also the best-buy "amount off" with brand name.

- **SHOPPING LIST:** For short lists, write your needs on a self-stick note, attach it to the fridge. When you go shopping, you can stick it on your dashboard or a junkmail envelope holding your coupons and then, you can stick your list on the handlebar of the shopping cart so that your hands are free. *Letter of Laughter:* A funny thing happened to a Heloise fan on the way to the grocery store—she apparently sat on one of the many stick-on notes she writes to herself as reminders. While she was shopping, someone tapped her on the shoulder and said, "Something is on the seat of your slacks." Was she embarrassed! The note printed in large letters read, "LARD." Of all the notes to get stuck there! She's switched from stick-on lists to regular paper.

- **SHOPPING LIST,** *Computerized:* After you've listed every possible thing you could or would buy at the supermarket, save the list in your computer and make a printout when needed. You'll never have to waste time making up a new shopping list again. Keep the list on your fridge door and highlight items to be bought.

- **SHORTENING,** *Measuring and Substitution:* An easy way to measure solid shortening or lard is to use the displacement method. For instance, if you need ½ cup of shortening, fill a one-cup measuring cup with ½ cup of water, then add solid shortening until water level reaches one cup. Drain off water and shortening comes right out without scraping.

  When you substitute vegetable oil for butter or lard in recipes other than baking bread and desserts, you may need to experiment with your recipes—as a rule you use one-third less oil. For example, two teaspoons of vegetable oil replaces one tablespoon of solid shortening. Remember that while a good vegetable oil may be low in cholesterol, it's still fat.

- **SHOULDER PADS,** *Quick-Fix:* Tuck shoulder pads under bra straps when you don't have time to sew them in. If you have the "teeth" section of self-gripping fabric tape and the pads are of a soft fabric, you may be able to secure the pads in place by putting a strip of the tape over strap and shoulder pad.

- **SHOULDER PADS,** *Quick-Fix Placement:* If you don't like self-gripping fabric tape or pin-ons, try sticking the double-sided tape safe for walls on the pads and inserting them. The tape is good for emergency hem repair, too.

- **SHOULDER PADS,** *Recycling:* Stuff pillows or children's toy animals or soft-sculpture crafts; make knee pads for gardening or cleaning by holding them on your knees with the tops of old socks or, if you feel ambitious, sew them into work pants knees; insert in bras for "push-up pads" or "enhancers."

- **SHOWER CAPS,** *New Uses for Hotel "Freebies":*
1. Cover leftover food in bowls.
2. Cover round 35mm slide carousels to keep them dust free and to keep the slides in place. Place an identifying index card under the cap so you know what's inside.

- **SHOWER CURTAIN (PLASTIC),** *Laundering:*
1. To remove Water Spots—Spray full-strength vinegar to both sides of the curtain, leave on for at least 30 minutes. Scrub persistent spots with a brush.
2. To remove Mildew—Launder in machine with warm water and ½ to 1 cup liquid chlorine bleach, regular detergent and a couple of white bath towels. Run through a whole cycle. Toss in the dryer for a few minutes to remove wrinkles and re-hang immediately after removing from the dryer.

- **SHOWER CURTAIN,** *Quick-Fix Repair:*
1. When the hanging holes tear, take a hand-held hole puncher and punch a hole about a half-inch from the torn one.
2. For a more permanent mend—if you have clear plastic mending tape handy, it helps to reinforce the area with it before you punch the hole either in the same place or a half-inch from the torn place. Fold the tape over the top so it reinforces on both sides.

- **SHOWER CURTAINS,** *Clear Plastic with Water Spots:* Either get a second shower rod and curtain as a splash guard for a clear plastic one or put a thin film of lemon-oil furniture polish on to prevent the "gunk" from sticking.

- **SHOWER CURTAINS,** *Quick Cleaning:* Pour full-strength vinegar on the shower curtain to remove soap film and mildew.

- **SHOWER CURTAIN SLIDE,** *Quick-Fix:* If your family (Not you, of course, because you are more careful!) tears the shower curtain because it doesn't slide shut easily, it could be due to the rings sticking on the curtain rod. Grease them with petroleum jelly.

- **SHOWER CURTAIN TIE-BACK:** When the adhesive hook that comes with some shower curtains won't stick to the tile, substitute a rubber suction cup to hold the tie-back. It's easy to remove and replace when you clean the tiles.

- **SHOWER DOOR,** *Keeping It Clean:* Install an adjustable shower rod inside the shower next to the door and hang a neutral shower curtain on the rod. The doors stay dry and you can toss the curtain into the washer when it's spotted.

- **SHOWER DOORS AND TILES,** *Removing Water Spots:*
1. Shower doors—Rub with lemon-oil furniture polish to soften gunk. Leave on a few minutes and scrub with nylon net or scrubber. Remove stubborn lime deposits from glass with a single-edged razor taking care not to scratch the glass. **Caution!** Don't get oil on the shower floor; it could be dangerously slippery. After the shower door is clean, apply another coat of oil to prevent water spots.
2. Shower tiles—Remove soap and hard water buildup with tile cleaner. Then apply a good paste wax and buff with dry cloth to deter future water spots.
3. Leave a large sponge or a window squeegie in the shower so that walls can be wiped down after each use to save time for more pleasant things than cleaning showers!

- **SHOWER-DOOR TRACK,** *Cleaning:* Pour full-strength vinegar into the track, let soak for a few minutes, rinse the gunk and vinegar right off.

- **SHOWER SHOCK,** *Avoiding It:* Store your favorite body lotion within the tub or stall area, then after bathing, towel dry yourself lightly and apply the moisturizer before opening the shower curtain or doors. The oil will keep you warm when you do open the door and you'll benefit more because moisturizers capture and retain water for the skin.

- **SHOWER STALL,** *Easy Rinsing Walls:* After scrubbing, rinse with the flow from a long, skinny-nosed plant watering can.

• **SHOWER WALLS,** *Minimizing Cleaning and Children's "Shower Stalling" at the Same Time:* Make a rule that each day, the last person to take a shower wipes down the shower walls and door when they finish. Water spots will be minimal and children seldom ignore parents when they say, "Who's going to shower first?"

• **SICK-IN-BED:** When an elderly, incapacitated or young person is bed-ridden at home and has lost interest in daily life, place a bird bath near a large window where it can be watched from inside the home. Nature perks interest like few other happenings! **Note:** If the bird bath is plastic, fill the base with water, soil or stones for more stability.

• **SIDING,** *Cleaning Aluminum House Siding:* Mix ⅓ cup of ordinary, mild, non-abrasive laundry detergent to each gallon of water used. To clean, apply detergent solution with a soft bristle brush and rub gently. (Rubbing too hard will take the shine off.) Reduce streaking by washing the house from the bottom up and rinsing as you go. To remove stubborn stains, contact the siding manufacturer or a local siding installer for instructions. (To find out if the manufacturer has a toll-free number, dial 1-800-555-1212 and ask the operator.)

• **SILVER,** *Polish:* Rub with paste of baking soda and water.

• **SILVER,** *Storage Cautions:*
1. Never store silver in plastic wrap or thin plastic bags. Thin plastic can melt in the heat of an attic and adhere to the silver.
2. Also, instant silver polish and the instant cleaning method of detergent water in an aluminum foil-lined pan is not safe for antique silver; it can remove all the oxidation that fills darkened parts of the design and make the silver look too white to be old.

• **SILVERWARE,** *Quick-Fix, Cleanup:* Sometimes, if tarnish isn't too bad, you can wash enough of it off for respectability with regular liquid hand-dishwashing detergent squirted full-strength on a sponge. Rinse well and shine with a soft towel.

• **SINK,** *Mending Chipped Areas of a Colored One:* If you can't find the right color in touch-up enamel at paint or hardware stores, check out the automotive department for car touch-up paint. You might find a match, or at least a color close to matching.

• SINK, *Shining Dull or Scratched Stainless Steel:*
1. Replace the luster with stainless-steel polish, sold at most grocery stores.
2. Clean regularly with mild detergent, rinsing well and buffing dry with a clean, soft cloth. This avoids water-spot build-up.
3. Wipe with vinegar or a touch of oil on a cloth to make the sink sparkle.

• SINK DRAIN, *Avoiding Clogs:* Before draining foods in the sink, place a paper towel (preferably reuse one which has already dried your hands) over the drain; after the liquid drains through it, remove the towel and food bits and toss. No bits down the drain!

• SINK, PEDESTAL: When your bathroom has a pedestal sink there's no countertop to put cosmetics, hair curlers, etc. Place a clear acrylic cutting board or an appropriately sized tray of a coordinating bathroom color across the basin—you get a wide, sturdy temporary counter and you can lift away everything on it at once when you need to use the sink.

• SIX-PACK CARRIER, *Recycling:* Store and tote baby bottles to day care or cleaning supplies around the house in cardboard carriers.

• SIX-PACK RINGS, *Recycling:* Please see PLASTIC SIX-PACK RINGS.

• SKILLET, *Care of Iron Ones:*
1. To season cast iron, wash in hot, sudsy water, rinse, dry immediately. Then cover inside of the skillet with vegetable cooking oil and place in a 300°F oven for about two hours. **Caution:** Be careful when removing the skillet; it will be hot. Wipe out excess oil with paper towels. Re-season when necessary.
2. Never let cast iron pots and skillets soak in water or sit with food in them. Always scrub with hot water and a nylon scrubbie (never steel wool), and then rinse and dry quickly to prevent rust.

• SKIN FRESHENER/SOOTHER, *Healthy Planet:* Add pulp-free aloe vera juice to water in a spray bottle and spritz your arms, legs, back and face for a quick cool-off and moisturizer. This feels especially good at the beach!

• **SKIN,** *Freshener:* Witch hazel, the old-fashioned barbershop aftershave, is an inexpensive and effective skin freshener, and it's especially nice in the summer if it's been refrigerated. Apply with cotton ball and allow to dry before applying makeup.

• **SKIN,** *Healthy-Planet Cleansing:* Using a washcloth to wash off makeup and skin remedies instead of cotton balls or other throwaway pads is one way to decrease your trash output! Every little bit counts!

• **SKIN,** *Moisturizers, Makeup Remover:* Baby oil or just plain mineral oil cost less than expensive lotions and potions and can be applied harmlessly to soften skin or remove makeup. The oils are especially useful if you react to food dyes, lanolin, perfumes and other ingredients found in many commercial creams. These oils can also be put into your bath water when you soak, but **Caution:** They can make the tub slippery.

• **SKIN,** *Home Skin Test for Sensitivity:*
1. Apply a small dot of the test material, about the size of a match head, to a half-inch square or circle of unmedicated gauze adhesive bandage. Mix dry materials like herbs with a couple of drops of water or mineral oil. Mineral oil is good because it doesn't evaporate.
2. Place the patch on a hair-free area of the skin like the inside of your arm or elbow, or your back. Leave it there for forty-eight hours without getting it wet.
3. If the test area burns, itches, aches or feels even a little bit irritated, remove the patch immediately and flush the area with water. If the irritation continues, get a non-prescription cortisone ointment from your pharmacist or see your doctor. If you are sensitive to the material, you will probably have a reaction in two to forty-eight hours after putting the patch in place and if you have no reaction, such as redness, swelling, pimples, blisters or itching, the material is safe for you.

This test may seem like a lot of trouble, but think about how you'd feel if you soaked in an herbal bath and your whole body reacted to an allergen! I have an allergy-prone friend who spent three days itching from an expensive spa herbal bath. It was anything but a relaxing experience!

• **SKIN,** *"Kitchen" Remedies for Soaking in the Bath:*
1. Milk: Swirl a package of powdered nonfat dry milk or pour a quart of regular low-fat milk into a tubful of warm water and soak. (This also sooths sunburn.)
2. Sea Salt: Add a half pound of sea salt to warm water for a super skin-cleansing bath.
3. Scent-senses: Add leftover perfume, perfume samples or rinse out an "empty" perfume bottle in your bath water and add some coconut, almond, baby or other oil before soaking. **Caution:** Oil and water don't mix and can be slippery in the tub!
4. Cider Soother: Add about two cupfuls of apple cider vinegar to a tub of warm water to sooth sunburned, itchy skin. Some people prefer to splash the cider on their bodies before sitting down in the water; others just add it to the water before soaking.
5. Oatmeal Skin Soother: Dangle a cloth bag of oatmeal (two cups or so) on the faucet as the tub fills and then rub your skin with the bag after it's moistened by the water flow. Or, just add oatmeal to the water, then soak in it. This also is a sunburn or itchy skin soother.
6. Herbal Bath: Many herbs, alone or combined, can be put into a cloth or net bag, tossed into the tub or hung on the faucet as the tub fills so that you can have a soothing herbal bath, with herbs from your garden. They include: rosemary, chamomile, any mint variety, comfrey, rose petals, lavender, yarrow or camphor. About ½ cup of dry or fresh herbs is the usual amount, depending upon how much "flavoring" you want. **Caution:** If you have allergies to plants, do a skin test before soaking your whole body in herbs or herbal combinations.

• **SKIN,** *"Kitchen" Remedies for Sun/Heat Irritation:*
Remedy 1: Rub dry, irritated skin gently with juices from peach or cucumber at night.
Remedy 2: Apply mashed avocado to skin, leave on for a few minutes and rinse off gently to clean and condition it.
Remedy 3: Apply buttermilk as a soothing lotion to cleanse and soften.
Remedy 4: Add one-half cup baking soda to tepid water for a soothing soak for dry, irritated skin.
Remedy 5: Apply cornstarch to prickly heat rash.

Remedy 6: A paste of baking soda and water, vinegar or yogurt can sooth minor sunburn. **Caution:** If your skin is very red or blistered, see a doctor.

• SKIN MOISTURIZING: Heating systems dry out the air and can make our skins feel tight and dry even when we apply lotions and oils. You don't need to buy an expensive humidifier to put moisture into the air of your home.
1. Simmer an 8-quart pot of water on the stove for a few hours. Add some potpourri or spices and put a pleasant fragrance in the house, too. Place pretty containers of water around the house to evaporate moisture into the air, but remember to keep them filled!
2. Plants help rehydrate air. Ferns, bamboo, begonias, zebra plants and coleus are among those liking lots of moisture and they grow fast, too. Put the pots in a shallow tray filled with pebbles or moss and water to help keep moisture in the plants and in the air. Keep plants well watered and mist them frequently.
3. Mist your face with a spritz from a spray bottle several times a day. If you can't spritz, dab on water with a cotton ball or makeup square. It's refreshing as well as moisturizing for your face.
4. Let dishes air dry in the dishwasher to save energy and put moisture into the air. Stop the dishwasher after the final rinse and open the door. Hold your face where it will be moistened by escaping steam, but **caution:** not where the steam is hot; it can burn.
5. Avoid overheating; keeping the house a few degrees cooler saves on utility bills and energy use and also prevents the air from becoming too dry.
6. Moisturize skin from within. Drink five or six or more glasses of water daily. Keep a pretty glass on your desk, counter or wherever you'll most likely see it as a reminder to drink water.

• SLEEPING BAGS, *Cleaning:* ALWAYS check care labels for cleaning instructions. Most can be laundered or dry-cleaned and should be repaired before cleaning.
1. Home Laundering—Set the washer on slow speed and high water level. A suds cycle should remove heavy soil and a second rinse should thoroughly remove detergent from the filling. Tumble dry to fluff up batting. Fluff down-filled bags by throwing in a clean pair of sneakers or tennis balls.

2. Before dry cleaning repair tears, broken stitching and point out heavy stains or other problems to the cleaner.

• **SLEEPING BAGS,** *Arranging Them to Please All:* Often at slumber parties, cousin or grandma visits, when children bunk on the floor in sleeping bags, nobody wants to sleep on the "outside" and everyone wants to sleep in the middle or next to one child or other. The solution is simple—place the sleeping bags in a circle with all the pillows in the center so that the children and their sleeping bags are spokes on a wheel. Everyone is sleeping next to a "buddy" and can hear all conversations and all have plenty of foot room.

• **SLEEVE LENGTHS,** *For Men's Clothing:* Shirtsleeves should reach to the end of the wristbone. Jacket and coat sleeves should cover the tops of the wristbone.

• **SLIDES,** *Videotaping:* See VIDEOTAPING SLIDES.

• **SLIDING GLASS DOORS,** *Safety Marking:* If you are lucky enough to have a family that keeps these doors so clean people can't tell if they are open or closed, the Quick-Fix way to signal they're closed is to place a stick-on note at eye level. Permanent markers can be decals, stickers, auto window decals, or tub safety decals.

• **SLIP,** *Full-length Colored Slips $aver:* When you need a full-length slip to match a formal gown, buy a full-length nightie in the matching color, cut it off at the right length and hem. Nylon nighties are less costly than full-length colored slips.

• **SLIP,** *Storage:* If you hang slips on a skirt or trouser hanger, they won't be wrinkled and it's easier to tell the length when you have several of the same color.

• **SNAKE,** *Feeding:* If you can't stand to feed your pet snake live mice and other rodents, one reader says you can trick a snake into eating other meat if you get a little mouse, keep it in a separate cage, let it sniff and scramble all over the meat you'll feed the snake. The mouse scent gets on the meat and the snake will swallow it.

• **SNAPS,** *Repairing Those on Baby Clothes:* When they begin to pop open easily, hammer the point part of the snap once LIGHTLY. You'll flatten the snap enough to hold tightly to the other half.

• **SNEEZE STOPPER,** *Letter of Laughter:* A reader sent this rhyme she says helps her to stifle sneezes in crowded company:

> *When you feel that warning tickle,*
> *And your nose begins to prickle—*
> *Open your mouth and take*
> *Two or three quick breaths to make*
> *That sneezy feeling disappear.*
> *I hope it works for you, my dear.*
> *But if you find it's not your day,*
> *That sneeze will come out anyway!*

• **SOAP DISH:** Flat seashells make good soap dishes.

• **SOAP DISH,** *Avoiding Mess and Goo:* Put three rubber bands around the soap dish lengthwise. Rest the soap on the rubber bands and it will dry without the messy goo.

• **SOAPS,** *Decorative, Letters to Think About:* When a reader wrote for advice on preventing guests from using decorative soaps and towels, an overwhelming 94 percent of the responses from other readers agreed with my advice to just use them; they recalled cleaning out attic-fulls of new, "too good to use" things after loved ones had died. My mother also always advised using your decorative or "good" china, silver, linens (and fancy guest towels and soap), etc. She always said that if you don't use your "good" things, somebody else will after you're gone; you may as well enjoy them. One reader, who lost everything in a house fire now enjoys using everything and never cares if they get broken or "used up." Best Advice: "Carpe Diem" (Seize the Day)!

• **SOAP SLIVERS,** *$aver, Recycling to Make a Bar:* Tried and true is to moisten sliver and the new bar until they are sticky and press together, blending the edges. Let dry and you have a bigger new bar.

• **SOAP SLIVERS,** *Recycling to Make Liquid Soap:* Separate hand from deodorant soap; they don't mix well for this project.
1. Cut into slivers and soak overnight to soften (optional step).
2. Place all soap slivers into a blender with some hot water. Blend on "Grate" setting. Add more water to thin out the liquid to the consistency you prefer, and blend a bit more.

3. Pour the liquid into a pump-style soap bottle for bathroom or kitchen.

Note: The plus is that your blender gets a good washing, too!

• **SOCIAL SECURITY,** *Checking on Amounts Deposited:* Request a Statement of Earnings (Form SSA-7004) at any Social Security office or by calling 1-800-325-0778. Fill out the form, mail as directed, and in a few weeks you will receive a statement of the total wages or self-employment income credited to your earning record. If your records don't match theirs, contact your local Social Security office to get them corrected.

• **SOCKS,** *Making Non-skid Slipper Socks:* Draw stripes (or designs, or names of sock-owners) on the bottom of socks with a craft pen used to decorate T-shirts. The raised design will keep you off the skids. **Note,** Healthy Planet $aver: Don't waste paper. Buy red socks and substitute them for Christmas Wrap, then write gift recipient's name on the sock bottoms and insert the gift. (If there is just one gift, put the second sock inside with the gift.) Tie the sock shut with yarn or crinkle-tie.

• **SOCKS,** *Preventing Loss in Laundry:* Agitating socks sometimes flip over the edge of the basket and may be found between the drum and washer basket. Some find their way into the drain, believe it or not. Pin them together as they are removed so they will stay together through washer and dryer. *Letter of Laughter:* Here's an ode to socks you can give to family members as a reminder to pin 'em up or lose 'em.

> *Do your socks disappear when you wash 'em out clean?*
> *Does it seem that they're eaten by the washing machine?*
> *Then pin 'em together and this simple chore*
> *Will keep your socks mated forevermore.*
> *So from this day forth, no need to despair;*
> *Just reach in the drawer and pull out a pair.*

And, here's an odd socks story that's truly odd:

Annoyed at her youngest son's habit of tossing dirty socks under his bed and the number of odd socks in that day's wash, one mother marched angrily into her son's room, thrust her arm under his bed to feel around for the odd socks and . . . gasp! Her hand touched something definitely "odd." To her amazement and near heart failure, when her hand came out from under the bed it was holding the biggest black snake she'd ever seen! For a moment, her life passed before her eyes. Then, her eyes focused and she saw that the snake was plastic! Now when she has a load of odd socks, she just puts them into the drawer to wait for their mates.

• **SOCKS,** *Recycling Lonely Ones:*
1. Slip your glass of iced tea or canned beverage in a sock, roll the top down and you'll have dry hands and no puddles under the glass.
2. Keep an old sock in the car to wipe fog from your windshield, sticky fingers, an oily dip stick, and tie it to the steering wheel when fuel is low to remind you to get gas on the next trip.
3. Slip an old sock over a yardstick or ruler so that you can clean crevices such as beneath the fridge, washer or dryer.

• **SOCKS,** *Separating for Color-blind Men:* Men's navy blue, black, and dark brown socks tend to look all the same in a drawer even if you're not color-blind. It helps if you buy small plastic baskets and then put navy socks in a light blue basket, dark brown socks in a tan one, and black socks in a white one.

• **SOCK SORTING,** *Time-Saver:* Black and dark-navy sock colors and styles can look the same when you're matching them. Instead of pinning them in pairs or holding them together with a plastic hook, buy paint pens at a craft store. Match up the socks and label each pair of black socks with a letter and each pair of navy socks with a number. You'll find mates at a glance. If several family members have similar socks, write with different pen colors.

• **SOCK TOPS,** *Recycling:* Cut off the foot and use the cuffs.
1. To cover a crawling baby's knees. They add protection even when baby's wearing long pants.
2. To cover a gardener's knees, or to close up the opening at pants or sleeves cuffs so insects don't get in as easily.
3. Wear for leg or knee warmers.
4. Slip on cool drinks to keep your hands dry.
5. Sew on to child's jacket sleeve to lengthen it.
6. Put on over mitten tops and jacket sleeve bottoms to keep snow out of children's jacket sleeves.

- **SODA-POP FIZZ**, *Maintaining It in Two-Liter Bottles:* Put the cap on loosely, then squeeze the plastic bottle until the remaining liquid comes right up to the neck or as close as possible. Then, while holding it there, tighten the cap. With almost no air in the bottle the contents keep more of their fizz. This works except for the last few ounces.

- **SODA WATER**, *When Two- or Three-liter Bottles Go Flat, $aver:* Instead of discarding flat soda, pour it into ice cube trays and you'll have flavored cubes for your drinks that don't dilute!

- **SOFA**, *Shopping:* Measure the space for the sofa to make sure it will fit AND measure doorways that the sofa will go through. One couple had to return a sofa that just wouldn't fit through the doorway!

- **SOFA**, *Straying Sectionals:*
1. Hook sections together by attaching screen-door hooks to the underside frames. Attach the eye of the hook on the outside frame of one section and the hook on the outside frame of the adjoining section and then hook 'em up so you won't lose friends in the cracks.
2. Keep your sectional sofa from coming apart by using large metal hose clamps around the sections' legs.

- **SOFT-DRINK RATIONING FOR CHILDREN:** When children like bubbly soft drinks, provide nutrition by mixing fruit juice with club soda.

- **SOUP**, *Getting the Fat Out:* Instead of just storing the soup in the fridge so that the fat rises to the top and hardens so it's easier to lift off, put the soup in a container with a tight lid and turn it upside down when you put it in the fridge, then you can just pour the broth off the top.

- **SOUP**, *Quick-Fix When It's Too Hot (Especially for Children):* Put an ice cube in each bowl of soup and tell children to stir until it melts. The soup will cool and they will have something to do while they are waiting. (Children often lack patience when you interrupt their play for something so "irrelevant" as eating lunch!)

• **SOUP,** *Thickening:* Add instant mashed potatoes. Potatoes tend to take salt from dishes so check to see if more is needed after they are added.

• **SOUP CRACKERS (OYSTER CRACKERS):** Pour the tiny crackers into a well-washed and dried plastic quart- or gallon-size jug and put the lid on. You'll have airtight storage for retaining freshness and a handy pouring container, too.

• **SOUP STOCK SEASONING:** Make your own soup stock from left-over necks and backs of poultry (or bones cut off steaks and chops) and lots of herbs and seasonings. Then freeze the stock in cubes, store the cubes in a sealed bag, and you can toss a cube of stock into dishes you want to season. The bonus is that you can make it salt-free, low-fat if you have special diet needs.

• **SPACE-AGE SCHOOL DAZE,** *Letter of Laughter:* When a mother of a young son was explaining that he would ride the big kids' school bus when he went to his new school, the youngster said, "Mommy, I'll have to get up at six o'clock!"
  "Why so early?" Mom asked.
  "Because it takes a long time to get into those space suits!"

• **SPILLS,** *Quick-Fix Wipe-up, Healthy-Planet Recycling:* Place newspapers over spills and let them absorb the mess in a few minutes.

• **SPILLED MILK,** *Letter of Laughter:* A reader reminded me that when people used to say, "Don't cry over spilled milk," it didn't cost $2 a gallon.

• **SPAGHETTI STRAPS,** *Keeping Them on Hangers:* Cut foam padding which has adhesive on one side into narrow strips about two inches long. Stick the strips on the ends of the hanger where the straps would normally be placed. No more dresses on the closet floor!

• **SPEAKERS,** *Recycling:* Old stereo speakers are great magnets. When you finish a task that involves nails, you can drag them around and they will pick up what you've dropped. This is especially good when you've been nailing outdoors where nails in the grass could ruin a lawn mower blade.

• **SPECIAL OFFER PROOF OF PURCHASE:** Cut out the "proof of purchase" (UPC symbol, bar code) from empty food packages before throwing them out. Then write the name of the product on the back and save them in an envelope so you'll have them when special offers are made.

• **SPICE BOTTLES,** *Recycling Empty Ones:*
1. Fill with cinnamon sugar for toast.
2. Fill with dusting powder for a shaker.
3. Use as a toothpick holder.
4. Store glitter for crafts in it.
5. Put embroidery thread in it and feed through holes to prevent tangling.
6. Keep embroidery/needlepoint needles in it.
7. Fill with flour to sprinkle on meats before frying.

• **SPICES,** *Storage & Determining Age/Usefulness:* Spices don't spoil but they do lose potency over time. If they don't have full aroma, toss them out.
1. Store in cupboard or rack away from stove, oven, and sunny windows.
2. When adding to food, avoid allowing the upside down spice container to absorb heat and moisture from cooking food—measure into a spoon or your hand. Spice cans won't get messy, hard-to-close powder-caked tops with this method.

• **SPLINTER REMOVAL,** *Quick-Fix:* Apply a thin layer of white glue over the splinter, spread it around the area and let it dry. Then peel off the glue and out comes the splinter.

• **SPOON REST NEAR A RANGE,** *Recycling:* I get lots of hints for spoon rests but since you can put a spoon on anything, why not avoid counter clutter and rest a stirring spoon on the dishwashing sponge or cloth, or a paper towel that's only wiped one pair of clean hands?

• **SPOTS AND STAINS,** Please see the special section on page 398.

• **SPRAY CLEANERS,** *Using It All:* Get out the last two inches in the spray bottle by dropping in some marbles to raise the liquid level back to where the spray pump works.

• **SPRAY NOZZLES,** *Preventing Clogs:* After using hair spray, spray starch, or other aerosol cans or pump-spray containers, remove the sprayer and run clear water through it so that it's clog-free and ready when you need it the next time.

• **SPRAY SCENTS,** *Letter of Laughter:* A young reader wrote that her grandmother came home from the hairdresser with a new permanent and then went into the bathroom to spray her hair to keep it neat. Then she noticed a funny smell in the bathroom. As she reached to pick up the hair spray to return it to the cupboard she noticed it was pine air freshener. She smelled like piney woods all day!

• **SQUASH, SUMMER,** *Selection and Storage:* Summer squash is harvested before full maturity and while the rind and seeds are still tender and edible and its flesh is tender and string-free. Select smaller and firm squashes; if either end is soft or if the squash is rubbery, it's old; don't buy it. The most popular summer squashes are green zucchini, straight- and crook-neck yellows and flat, discus-shaped white squash. Store in the refrigerator.

• **SQUASH, WINTER,** *Selection and Storage:* Most winter squash have hard rinds (avoid those with soft spots on the rind) and may be kept for three to six months in a cool dry place, but not in the refrigerator unless cut. The most common winter squashes are: acorn (dark green or orange and green and shaped like an acorn—what else?); buttercup (oval and dark green with whitish stripes); turban (brightly colored with rounded lumps on one end); butternut (long, tubular and creamy brown in color); hubbard, one of the largest squashes, (bumpy all over and in various colors); spaghetti (smooth yellow outside and stringy spaghetti-textured inside).

• **SQUEAKS,** *Stopping:* Petroleum jelly applied to moving parts may help. It's safe around pets so you can use it on that squeaky exercise wheel in your hamster or gerbil cage.

• **STAINLESS STEEL,** *Removing Water Spots:* Rub area with clean, soft cloth dampened with white vinegar. Wipe dry to avoid spots.

• **STARCH,** *Homestyle Sugar Starch:* When regular spray starch won't hold up frail fabrics, try the old-fashioned method great-grandma used for her lacy doilies.

1. Mix ¼ cup water and ¾ cup sugar in a small pan. Stir the mixture over low heat (don't boil) until clear, not sugary. Shut off and let cool.

2. Wet the collar and cuffs of a blouse (or lacy doily); roll in a towel to remove excess moisture and dip it into the mixture. Squeeze out excess starch, then shape the collar and cuffs. (People used to dry small round crocheted lace doilies over a bowl after starching this way; you get a lace-bowl.)

3. Allow to dry and iron on a warm setting. (Lace doilies don't need ironing when you use this starch, just smooth out and shape while wet on a clean flat surface.)

• **STARCHING IN A WASHER:** Although this sounds like a good idea, my sources tell me that few people have enough items to warrant filling a machine to starch them and it's no longer advised. The main problem is that you can't mix colors or colors with whites in a machine starch load because even garments with colorfast labels tend to "bleed" in a starch load. Most people use spray starch these days.

• **STATIC CLING,** *Quick-Fix:* When your slip and skirt have a life of their own and it's embarrassing you, rub a little hand lotion on your hands and then rub your hands over your slip.

• **STEAM IRON CLOGS,** *Homestyle Remedy:* Commercial cleaners are available but you can try white vinegar. Fill the iron with white vinegar, let it steam about five minutes, then disconnect the iron and let it sit for a while. Empty the vinegar and rinse the iron well several times. You may need to poke a toothpick in the steam holes to get gunk out of a badly clogged iron. **Hint:** To avoid the problem, clean your iron regularly and always pour out non-purified water when you finish ironing.

• **STICKER FUN FOR CHILDREN:** Have children put stickers on waxed paper then they can be repositioned many times before the child decides how to stick them permanently in a scrap book.

• **STICKERS,** *Removal:*
1. Remove stickers and sticky residue from wood paneling by rubbing with mineral oil on a cloth or paper towel. Let oil set a while and repeat if necessary.

2. Remove sticky residue from labels with pre-wash spray. Apply, let set, rub off with nylon scrubber.

3. Remove bumper stickers with spray lubricant, following the instructions in Method 2.

• **STICKY RESIDUE,** *General Hints for Removal:* Gummed labels or price tags, children's stickers, bathtub appliques, and similar things often leave a stubborn residue. The remedy is to remove what you can and spray with petroleum-based pre-wash spray or you can spray some labels with the spray without removing any pieces. Allow spray to remain for a while to soften and then scrub off with a plastic scrubber. You can use this on most surfaces, including appliances. **Note:** Acetone (or acetone-based fingernail polish) will remove sticky residue from glass and some surfaces but may also damage some other surfaces and fabrics—it'll also take your nail polish off!

• **STORAGE,** *Finding Space in a Small Apartment:*
1. Store seldom used items in empty suitcases.
2. Stash boxes under the bed.
3. Fold winter blankets and store them between the mattress and box spring.
4. Buy a large plastic garbage can, fill it with stored items, invert the lid and top it off with a round piece of plywood. Cover with a tablecloth and you have a lamp table/storage unit for any room.
5. Put shoes in shoe bags to free the closet floor for other things.
6. Stack storage boxes or add shelves to closet shelves.
7. Have a system of making a proper place for everything and to put everything back in its place; clutter takes up space.

• **STORAGE,** *Organizing:* If you just can't throw it out, store it so that you can get at it when you will use it—whatever it is! Check out closet/storage shops, hardware and discount stores, department store home furnishing sections; you'll find an infinite number of easy-to-install shelves, rods, etc. that will make storage more convenient without major expensive building-in. Many install without tools; others need only a screwdriver, pliers and minimum skill.

• **STORAGE,** *Time-Saver:* Color-code books, records, video tapes with colored stick-on dots according to categories so that you don't have to shuffle through them each time you search for something.

Books can be coded according to fiction, biography, etc.; records according to jazz, country and western, etc.; video tapes according to comedy, drama, homemade family films, home-taped favorite shows or movies.

• **STORYTIME,** *When Mom and Dad Have No Time:* Record children's favorite stories on cassette tapes, using a cooking-timer bell as the chime telling them to turn to the next page. They may not have Mom's or Dad's lap, but they will have the familiar voice reading to them.

• **STOVE,** *Keeping Kitchen Stoves Clean, Letter of Laughter:* A Heloise fan sent this hint for keeping a stove clean: Just don't use it! I like that!

• **STOVE STORY,** *Letter of Laughter:* A reader who always removed all stove knobs when her young grandchild came to visit as a safety measure wrote that one day, when she forgot to do it her grandson went straight to the stove, pulled all the knobs off and brought them to her, saying "Memaw, you forgot to take the knobs off."

• **STRAWBERRIES,** *Quick-Fix Slicing:* After pinching off the green "hat" of the strawberry with a metal gadget made for this purpose, slice it with an egg slicer. No stains on your fingers and uniform slices, too!

• **STREET-MAP DIRECTIONS,** *For Out-of-Town or Other Guests:* Copy your neighborhood's section of your city map or the page of a street map book that has your area. (These books can often be found in the public library.) Then highlight the best routes to your house. If the map print is very small, you can enlarge the section around your house with some copy machines to make it easier to see.

• **STUFFED ANIMALS,** *Washing:* First of all, keep labels and tags so you'll have complete care instructions.
1. If the animal is washable but the stuffing is not, make a small opening in a seam and remove filler before washing by hand if the animal is irreplaceable or by machine if you can risk it. Dry on regular cycle or fluff in dryer before air-drying. Then restuff and sew up the seam.

2. If the animal is not washable, sprinkle liberally with cornstarch; brush with good stiff brush to remove dirt.

• **STUFFED PEPPERS,** *Keeping the Stuffing in While They Cook:* Bake them in a well-greased muffin tin; the peppers stay upright and look more appetizing when served.

• **STUFFING,** *Removing from Turkey, Chicken; Time-saver:* Before stuffing the bird, line the cavity (also the breast cavity of a turkey) with cheesecloth, being careful to leave a generous amount outside to be tucked in after the dressing is inside. Pack dressing loosely; it swells during cooking. You can then remove a sack of stuffing, with none left behind and the flavor remains the same.

• **SUDS OVERFLOW IN LAUNDRY:** Sprinkle salt on soap suds so suds swells subside. (Then say that sentence fast five times before you scold the person who put too much detergent in the machine . . . even if the culprit is you.)

• **SUGAR,** *Coloring:* Add a few drops of food coloring to a cup of granulated sugar in a glass bowl. Mix well until the coloring is distributed evenly. Darken color by adding a drop or two more of the food coloring. Let dry and store in a sprinkle-top bottle for decorating cookies and cakes.

• **SUGAR,** *Softening Brown Sugar:*
1. In a microwave safe container, microwave for a minute or so to soften.
2. Place a slice of fresh bread or piece of fresh apple into the sugar canister or box, seal, and it will soften after a while. *Letter of Laughter:* A reader wrote that when she told a young bride to "put the sugar in a container with a tight-fitting lid and put a slice of bread on top," the bride said it didn't work. When the reader visited the bride, she saw why. The sugar was in the canister and a piece of bread was lying on top of the tightly closed jar.
It's not only what you say, it's how you say it!

• **SUGAR,** *Storage, Recycling:* An empty, clean, plastic milk jug keeps sugar from attracting bugs, from getting hard and lumpy, is easier to handle than a bag, lets you see how much is left, and, best of all, is free for the recycling!

• **SUN-BLOCK FORMULA:** For best protection, you need a good sun block with a sun-protection factor (SPF) suitable for your skin. SPF numbers are based on the time it takes unprotected skin to turn pink. The highest number is the greatest protection. Read labels for your type of skin.

• **SUN-BLOCK LOTION,** *Applying When Nobody Nice Can Help You:* Apply to your back or other unreachable spots with a sponge-type dishwashing mop having a long handle.

• **SUPERMARKET,** *Product-Dating Terms:* Check dates on all items to get the most for your money.
1. Expiration Date—The last day the item should be used or eaten.
2. Freshness Date—Stamped on the item by the manufacturer to tell how long freshness is guaranteed; if the item is stale before that date, manufacturers usually refund your money.
3. Pack Date—Date the product was packaged or processed by the manufacturer. It does not tell how long the food will stay good, but only when it was processed.
4. Sell or Pull Date—The last day an item should be sold; after this date it should be removed from the grocery shelf.

• **SUPERMARKET PRICE MARKING,** *When Your Market Has Scanners:* Who can remember the price of each item? As you put away groceries at home, find each item's price on the register tape and mark it on the container. Then you'll have some way to compare regular prices to weekly specials advertised in the newspaper. It may be too much trouble to do this with everything but would help on frequently purchased foods.

• **SUPERMARKET SHOPPING,** *Healthy-Planet Style:*
1. Avoid products with excess packaging and look for those in recyclable packaging.
2. Take a few minutes to mail wasteful packages back to the manufacturer with a note explaining that as much as you like the product, you will quit buying it if it continues to be over-packaged. Manufacturers listen when money talks.
3. Do recycle all packaging materials that you can. Many supermarkets collect plastic and paper bags, bottles, etc. and many cities

have recycling programs but nobody can come into a consumer's home to get recyclables! You have to sort and deliver!

4. If you don't know what's being recycled in your area, look under "recycling" in the Yellow Pages or call your state's recycling coordinator or the Environmental Defense Fund, 800-225-5333.

5. Take your own bag to the supermarket to reduce the number of bags you take home. Or, collect supermarket bags and take them to the store for reuse with your food.

6. Recycle grocery bags you do take home so that you don't have to actually buy bags. Plastic bags are good for garbage, storage, and all sorts of uses. Paper bags hold newspapers for recycling, absorb grease from fried foods, can be "racks" for cooling cookies, and on and on.

7. As this book is being written, the new "degradable" plastics are considered a waste of money and the Center for Science in the Public Interest is calling for a boycott. Degradable plastic usually ends up in landfills anyway where the landfill's design minimizes the rate at which they degrade. Also, degradable plastics have hindered plastic recycling because some recyclers have quit recycling bags; they say degradable bags get mixed in with the others and cause problems.

8. Wrap your lunch in a reusable container with a lid to avoid disposable products altogether. Reuse yogurt and margarine containers for soft foods. Margarine tubs, which are made from high-density polyethylene, are being recycled in some parts of the country but nobody recycles yogurt containers which are polystyrene or polypropylene.

9. Although aluminum foil is the only sandwich wrap that's recyclable, if you are just going to use the foil once and throw it out, it's better to use something else. The process by which we make aluminum is harmful to the environment.

10. Use a thermos for lunch juices instead of aseptic containers which are made from multi-layers of paper and other products and can't be recycled.

11. Buy canned juice concentrate instead of juice in polyethylene jugs which just use a lot of packaging for extra water that you can add to concentrate at home in a pitcher.

12. If you recycle the jugs, it's better to buy milk in polyethylene jugs than in cartons which are made of paperboard coated with

polyethylene; it's too costly to separate the coating from the carton paper and so these are not recycled.

13. When buying vegetables, look for the most food in the least packaging: A pound of peas in a plastic bag generates less waste than two 8-oz. boxes of peas that have paper wrappers since both types of packaging will end up in a landfill. Buy canned vegetables if you can recycle the cans and don't mind the extra sodium and fewer vitamins in canned veggies.

14. Avoid packaged microwaveable foods in which special bags or separate trays or dishes are used for cooking; these are just marketing gimmicks. If you use these quickie products, look for those where you can serve right out of the package.

15. When you buy eggs, instead of polystyrene cartons, look for molded pulp cartons which are usually made from 100-percent recycled paper.

16. Recycled paper cereal and other boxes are usually grey or tan inside and some have the "Recycled" logo on the outside; non-recycled boxes are white inside.

• **SWEATERS,** *"Pills":* Gently and carefully remove "pills" with a tiny scissors or a commercial sweater shaver. Always brush or shave gently to avoid damaging the area around the "pill."

• **SWEATERS,** *Recycling:*
1. Make mittens by tracing an old one on paper or putting it on the bottom of an old sweater. The bottom is a ready-made cuff. Cut and sew around the "hand" shape, double-stitching for extra security.
2. Make leg warmers from sweater sleeves.
3. Save buttons from cardigan sweaters for recycling.

• **SWEATERS,** *Shrinkage:* Before buying a sweater, check the label for shrinkage potential and if there is no such information, assume the sweater will shrink at least one size. Threads get stretched during the knitting process and that's why knit clothes shrink more than woven ones. Even some synthetics shrink one size like cotton, wool and rayon do.

• **SWEATERS,** *Snags:* Never cut or tug snags. Try to pull the snag to the underside with a large sewing needle or crochet hook working from the inside of the garment. If the yarn is broken, try to fasten the broken ends on the inside of the sweater with a needle and transparent thread, which you can also use to close up a hole from the inside.

• **SWEATERS,** *Storage:* Most knits are best folded for flat storage because hanging on hangers stretches them out of shape. If you wish to hang them, drape them over a cardboard tube-type hanger, like those cleaners use for pants, or slit a tube from gift wrap to cover the hanger; you'll avoid creases. (If the cardboard tube is slippery, you can wrap it with old panty hose to provide some friction.)

• **SWEET SUBSTITUTES:**
1. You can't substitute corn syrup or honey for baking because sugar is a dry ingredient—it adds bulk as well as sweetness.
2. If you substitute corn syrup for honey, you'll need to add a bit more because it isn't as sweet as honey.
3. If you have to limit your sugar intake, try to substitute other flavorings instead of adding sugar. For example, add cinnamon, vanilla, or other extracts to your coffee; add vanilla or fruit (dried or fresh) to plain non-fat yogurt; sprinkle cinnamon on baked apple or in applesauce; sprinkle pumpkin pie spice mixture on sweet potatoes with a sprinkle of butter substitute; add chopped dried fruit to your cereal.

• **SWIMMER'S EAR:** Getting too much water in the ear canal can make ears susceptible to infection. To avoid spoiling summer fun and vacations with ear infection pain, never swim in polluted lakes or rivers and, if you swim frequently, very gently dry the outer areas of the ear. Use one or two drops of rubbing alcohol and vinegar mixed together in the ear to help dry the canal. **Caution:** Don't scratch inside the ear and, if you should get an infection, ask your doctor for advice on how to protect your ear while bathing or showering until the infection is cleared up.

T

• **TABLECLOTH,** *Keeping It on Outdoor Tables by Weighting Corners:* Sew pockets on the corners to hold small rocks or just knot a rock into each corner.

• **TABLECLOTH,** *Padding Beneath:* The good section of an old mattress pad makes good padding and protection but you'll still need to put a hot mat beneath oven dishes.

• **TABLECLOTH,** *Preventing Stains:* When the cloth is clean or brand new, spray it several times with soil-repellent spray—tough stains won't set in.

• **TABLECLOTH,** *Removing Wrinkles from a Flannel-Backed Vinyl:*
1. Put the tablecloth in the dryer with a couple of damp towels, set dryer on the lowest setting. Then check the tablecloth frequently until all wrinkles are removed. Allow to lay flat for cooling to avoid more wrinkles.
2. You can remove wrinkles by ironing at a warm setting with a steam iron on the flannel side—never the vinyl side.

• **TABLECLOTH,** *Securing When a Toddler Is in the House:*
1. Even a flannel-backed tablecloth will slip when a toddler pulls on it. Crisscross a pair of suspenders under the table and secure

them to the underside edges of the tablecloth. Make the tablecloth fit snugly by adjusting the tabs on the suspenders.

2. If the table separates to allow leaf insertion, pull apart, tuck the tablecloth into the crevice, close and the cloth is secure. Anyone who understands life with a toddler will excuse the crease across the tablecloth!

• **TABLECLOTH,** *Warning About Plastic or Foam-Backed Plastic:* Laying plain plastic or foam-backed plastic tablecloths directly on a wood-finish table can result in the plastic or foam sticking to the finish and the only solution may be to refinish the furniture. You can try removing stuck-on foam with a plastic scrubbie or nylon net and vegetable oil. Picking up plastic sheeting that has been on the table for a while can just pull up sections of varnish on some pieces.

• **TABLECLOTH STORAGE,** *Time-Saver:* Whether you hang your tablecloths on a hanger or fold them and store in a linen closet, save yourself aggravation—safety-pin a small piece of paper to each cloth giving its dimensions and the size of table it fits (one or two leaves or none).

• **TABLE EXTENSION,** *When You Need More Space:* Place a thick pad on the table and then on top, place a piece of plywood, four feet by eight feet long; pad again and cover with a tablecloth. You will be able to seat 10 or more people. Store the plywood under the bed in between dinner parties.

• **TAXES,** *Checklist of Six Common Mistakes to Avoid:*
1. Overwitholding: If you claim fewer exemptions on your Form W-4 than you're entitled to, you'll get a tax refund but, according to the experts, you will have been giving the IRS an interest-free loan of money that could have been in YOUR account earning YOU interest.
2. Underwitholding: If you claim too many exemptions on your Form W-4 or fail to pay estimated taxes, the IRS will impose a penalty. If you think you'll have income increases in 1991, recalculate your W-4 or estimated tax payments.
3. Not Keeping an Eye on Your Tax Bracket: There's a big gap between the rates of 15 and 28 percent so you must be alert when dealing with your investments. For example, if your joint taxable income in 1991 will be $32,450, the tax rate is 15 percent, but if you

sell investments which have increased in value by $5,000, that amount of gain will be taxed at 28 percent or $1,400. If the gain is taxed only at 15 percent, the amount would be only $750.

4. Not timing capital losses/gains. If you think you will take a capital gain, then you need to consider selling a losing investment to offset the gain. You can use as much as $3,000 in capital losses to offset ordinary income and if the loss is greater than $3,000, the excess can be carried forward to future years.

5. Incorrectly calculating mutual funds gains: Keep all customer confirmation and account records because when you sell shares, part of the profit may include dividends and distributions you have already paid taxes on.

6. Mixing deductible and non-deductible IRAs: To avoid paying taxes on the same money twice, you must keep careful records of deductible and non-deductible IRA contributions. Then, when you begin to withdraw the money, you can prove to the IRS what percentage of your savings comes from non-deductible contributions.

• **TAX FILING,** *Checklist:* Brokerage confirmations and statements, cancelled checks and checkbook registers, receipts for charitable contributions and deductible expenses receipt, property-tax receipts and records of interest paid on your mortgage, 1099 forms (dividends and interest income) and W-2 forms.

• **TEA,** *Brewing in Coffee Maker:*
1. For a Mug: Drop a tea bag into the basket and add 2 cups of water, then brew like coffee.
2. For a Pot: Measure the amount of water needed into the coffee-maker tank, put the appropriate number of tea bags in the carafe, turn it on, and presto—hot tea. You can make iced tea with the leftovers. **Note:** Let the bags steep for at least 3 to 5 minutes for fullest flavor.
3. For a Pot: If you prefer loose tea, sprinkle tea leaves into a coffee filter in the brewing basket as you would ground coffee. Try the same amount of cut tea leaves that you would brew in a tea pot or experiment to get the perfect amount for strength and flavor.

• **TEA,** *Spicing-up Iced Tea:* Mix one-half teaspoon ground cinnamon and one cup of orange juice. Pour the liquid into an ice cube tray and freeze. Add a cube to your glass of iced tea. Delicious!

• **TEA,** *Zinger:* Stir your tea, herbal or other, with a cinnamon stick. It can be reused for numerous cups of yummy lightly spiced tea.

• **TEA BAG,** *Avoid "Fishing" in Hot Tea:*
1. Wrap the tag around the pot or cup handle.
2. Cut an L-shaped slit in the tag, starting at the bottom edge and then when you make a cup of tea, open the slit and hook the tag on the cup lip.

• **TEA BALL:** Put peppercorns, bay leaf and other whole spices in a tea ball so that you don't have to fish them out of soup or stew to avoid biting into them. **Caution:** Bay leaf (whole or in pieces) is a special hazard because it can cause choking if it gets stuck in the throat.

• **TEACHER'S AIDE:** One teacher/reader carries her own supplies, such as pens, pencils and scissors, from one class room to another in a spoon caddy instead of relying on each room's desk to be fully equipped with whatever she needs.

• **TEAPOT,** *Healthy Planet, Removing Mineral Deposits:* Fill the teapot with full-strength vinegar, let it boil a few minutes and let the pot sit overnight. If the mineral deposit film is very thick, you may need to soak it for a couple of nights. In the morning, wash and rinse the pot. Avoid excess hard-water buildup with regular cleanings.

• **TELEPHONE, CELLULAR,** *Checklist for Safety Features to Look for When You Buy and Safe Use:* The safest phone is one with the fewest distractions when dialing, talking or answering. Buy one that lets you keep both hands on the wheel and your eyes on the road without having to hold on to a receiver or tuck it between your head and shoulder.
1. A speakerphone with voice command that can be programmed to recognize two voices and up to ten commands per voice is a best choice. A push of a button and a simple voice command will have the phone automatically access the cellular network and dial the correct phone number.

2. Speed dialing means only having to push a one- or two-digit code to have the cellular phone automatically dial a complete, pre-entered phone number.

3. Get a demonstration from the sales representative and become familiar with all the phone's features before you buy.

4. The safest time to dial a phone number on your car phone is when you are completely stopped at a red light or stop sign.

5. If you don't have a speakerphone and you must talk and drive at the same time, move into the far right-hand lane so that you can pull off the road if need be to complete a call.

• **TELEPHONE DIRECTORY,** *Lighten It Up:* Sometimes people with arthritis or hand disabilities have problems handling big thick phone books when their cities don't separate white and yellow pages into two books.

1. Carefully cut apart the white and yellow pages with a sharp knife. Reinforce the spines of both sections with heavy duty plastic tape like that used to seal cartons.

2. Either tape the back and front pages from last year's directory to the coverless sides of the new half-books or make covers from halves of a manila folder.

• **TELEPHONE DIRECTORY,** *Time-Saver:* When you find the number you've searched for in the phone book, highlight it so that it's easier to spot the next time you need it.

• **TELEPHONE MOUTHPIECE,** *Yuck Removal:* A moist towelette will wipe an earpiece and mouthpiece clean with a whisk.

• **TELEPHONE NUMBERS,** *Directory for People with Limited Vision:* Big push button phones help elderly or visually impaired people dial phones, but phone books are a challenge. Make a phone book with a looseleaf notebook filled with unlined note paper. Turn the pages sideways and, with a broad, black (or red for some people) marker pen, print names in large block letters with numbers beneath.

• **TELEPHONE PAD AND PENCIL,** *Time-Saver:* Stick a pen or pencil to the side of your telephone with self-gripping "dots"; remove several stick-on notes from the pad and stick them on the front of the phone (just a few, too many will be too heavy to stick). You'll always have paper and pencil ready for messages and recording information.

• **TELEVISION,** *Before You Call for Service:* Some newer sets have a "reset button" which should be checked if the TV has gone out due to a circuit breaker being tripped by a current surge. If pressing the button twice doesn't get the set on, then call for service. As with all appliances, always refer to the troubleshooting section of your manual before calling for service.

• **TELEVISION CHANNEL SELECTION:** When cable brings you forty or so selections and it's a bother to remember all the numbers, clip the list of stations and channels from your cable guide and tape it to the back of the remote control. You'll always have the right numbers in hand!

• **TELEVISION REMOTE CONTROL:** Prevent it from getting gooey or spilled on by keeping it sealed in a plastic zipper bag.

• **TELEVISION VIEWING CONTROL,** *Letter of Laughter:* A reader of my "Just For Kids" Sunday hints columns found a way to get her thirteen-year-old brother out of the TV room so that she could get to watch shows she wanted. Her hint: Get something good to eat and tell him he will have to get his own. As soon as he leaves, switch on your show. All I can say is "Out of the mouths of babes . . ."

• **TERMITES,** *Prevention:* Termites build little dirt tunnels to travel from one place to another and are always looking for water. If you find termites or their tunnels, destroy the tunnels.
1. Shrubs, fences, trellises, stacked firewood, wooden decks that touch the house and the ground at the same time all provide traveling routes for termites from the ground to your house.
2. Because termites seek water, keep water away from the house. Make sure all gutters drain away from the foundation and repair all plumbing leaks right away. Don't place wooden planters against the house. They are a double invitation to the termites—wood and water!
3. If you see any evidence of termites such as their tunnels, damaged wood steps, porches or decks (Other insects eat wood, too!), or fine powder beneath wood furniture, holes along stud lines of

your walls, or the termites themselves, call a professional exterminator. You won't save money ignoring them and their damage can be very serious, especially if they eat their way into the supporting structure of your house.

• **TERRARIUM,** *Watering:* An ordinary basting bulb syringe will help you get the right amount of water into a terrarium, especially a bottle-necked one, without disturbing plants or messing up the sides.

• **TERRY-CLOTH TOWELS,** *Recycling:*
1. When the middles are worn and the ends still thick, make potholders from the ends either by cutting circles and sewing them together or making long rectangular "casserole" potholders.
2. Make baby bibs from the good parts.
3. Roll lengthwise and place on windowsills, door thresholds to block drafts and blot condensed moisture.
4. Old terry cloth is great for polishing engraved or patterned silver or brass. Put the polish on with an old sock and buff with an old towel, then pitch it all if you don't want to wash rags.

• **TISSUE BOXES,** *Recycling for One More Time:*
1. Place an empty tissue box near the dryer to hold used dryer sheets and then toss box and all away when it's full. (But don't throw away used foam dryer sheets; they can stuff pillows, children's plush toys and cloth dolls, craft soft sculptures, etc.)
2. Square designer tissue boxes make good holders for cotton balls near your makeup area.
3. Store knee-hi stockings in a square designer tissue box—just put singles of the same color together and you have a dispenser!

• **TISSUES,** *Keeping Facial Tissues Dry on Bathroom Vanity Counters:* When you buy a new box, turn it upside down and stick a bulletin-board push pin in each bottom corner so that it has "feet" to keep it above water spills.

• **TISSUE-TOWELS,** *Healthy-Planet $aver:* Attach a toilet-paper holder to the inside of a kitchen cabinet under the sink and buy the least expensive tissue to hang there. Then you can save your paper towels for major wipe-ups and blot up most spills with less expensive, more environmentally kind paper. It's handy for nose-wiping, too—why waste a whole tissue for each sniffle?

• **THANKSGIVING TREE:** If your family can get together at Thanksgiving but not for Christmas, have a Thanksgiving tree. "Plant" a medium size tree branch in a coffee can weighted with rocks and sand and then put the can into a nice basket. Decorate the tree with bows, fall leaves and other Thanksgiving motif ornaments. Put presents under the tree and have Christmas in November!

• **THANK-YOU NOTES:** Include a picture of the item in use, or the clothing being worn, for a personal touch when you send thank-you notes. I like to send pictures of flowers sent to me by friends so that they can see how they look.

• **THERMOMETER,** *Letter of Laughter:* Families that laugh together make life fun. Young children like silly talk and it helps them develop a sense of humor as they grow up.
Child (who has just come home from school): The nurse took my temperature.
Mom: Did you tell the principal and get it back?

• **THIMBLE,** *Substitute:* Cut a finger off a rubber glove the length of your finger; the end of your finger won't get sore when you do needlework or hand-sewing and you'll have a better grip on the needle if it gets stuck in thick fabric.

• **THREAD SPOOLS,** *Recycling:*
1. String them on a cord for a young child's "necklace" toy.
2. Press cookie-dough balls with the ends of clean, empty spools to imprint a nice pattern.

• **THROW,** *Quick-Fix Comfy:* When you need a throw to keep cozy while napping, try snuggling under your robe if it's full length—but switch ends so that the "shoulders" are covering your feet and the lower robe portion is over your upper body where you need more "snuggle."

• **THUNDER,** *Fear of:* Help a fearful child or pet get used to the sound of thunder: Get a recording of thunder sounds from a record store and play it every other day or so, starting first with very low volume and gradually increasing the volume a little at a time. With a very small child, explain that the noise won't hurt and is far, far away and explain thunder to older children at their learning level. Books about thunder will help.

• **TIRES,** *Recycling Old Ones:* You can paint them or not.

1. Fill with sand to make a small child's sandbox or, if you can get a tractor tire, a larger sandbox.

2. Fill with potting soil for a planter. If you have four, build a pyramid planter with three on the bottom and one top and center. (Place pegboard piece inside the top tire to keep soil in.)

3. Stand at the back of the garage to be a "bumper" for your car.

4. Fill with cement and insert a pipe in the center to hold a pole for tether ball, basket ball, a mailbox stand, temporary small flag pole, etc.

5. Collect them from friends and neighbors and they can be steps on a sloping hillside. Dig into the hillside far enough to lay the tires flat, slightly overlapping each one. Fill them with sand and soil and plant native plants in them. Not only will the hillside look pretty, you'll keep the soil from running off in the rain.

• **TODDLER,** *Recognizing Sounds, Letter of Laughter:* A young mother wrote to say, "Did you know that to a mommy of a one-year-old, dry cat food being poured all over the floor sounds just like a play necklace being shaken in a play coffeepot?"

• **TODDLER TUNNEL,** *Homemade, Recycling:* Tear off the flaps of four large cardboard boxes and duct tape the boxes together to form a tunnel. Let the children decorate the outside with brightly colored paints and designs and use their imaginations playing games in their tunnel.

• **TOILET, LIME DEPOSITS,** *Healthy-Planet Removing:* Pour full-strength white vinegar in the bowl, let sit for several hours and brush away. If that doesn't work, pour a bucket of water quickly into the bowl to empty it, then cover the lime marks with paper towels soaked in vinegar. Let stand for several hours and scrub with sturdy brush or plastic scrubbie. **Caution:** Don't flush the paper towels down the toilet; toss them in the trash. Towel-strength paper can clog sewer or septic tank lines.

• **TOILET TANK,** *Healthy-Planet Water Conservation:* Raise the water level in the tank to use less water per flush with a quart-jar or plastic bag filled with water. Be sure that the water-savers are placed so that they don't interfere with the flush mechanism. **Note:**

People used to recommend a brick for this hint but bricks tend to crumble and damage the toilet's working mechanism.

• **TOILET TANK,** *Test for Leaks:* My husband, who is a plumber, recommends this test: Add some food coloring to the commode tank—green or blue is best. Do not flush the commode for an hour, then check to see if any coloring has seeped into the toilet bowl. If so, you need to replace the tank ball.

• **TOILET TISSUE,** *Tricking an Enthused Toddler:* Sometimes a newly pottie-trained toddler will unfurl most of a roll just for fun. One mom found the solution—after placing the roll on the roller, squeeze it until the inner cardboard roll is bent. This prevents a child from unrolling the whole roll at once.

• **TOMATO SAUCE,** *Substitute:* Add your favorite spices to undiluted canned tomato soup and go on with the recipe.

• **TOOLS,** *Recycling, Rust-proof Storage:* Mix some used motor oil with sand in a pail and then poke garden tools into the pail when they aren't being used. The bonus is that the sand automatically cleans them while the oil protects against rust, and you'll have all your tools in one bucket.

• **TOOTHBRUSH HOLDERS,** *for Travel:* Keep lipstick, eye shadow and eye- or lip-liner pencils in plastic travel toothbrush holders and you won't loose them when you travel or keep them in your purse for repairs. Get different colored holders for eye pencils and lip pencils so you don't have to open them each time.

• **TOOTHBRUSHES,** *Identifying Your Own in a Large Family:* A mother of seven children wrote that she solved the confusion by giving each of the boys different colored brushes (always the same color); all of the girls get the same color brush but personalize their brushes with leftover-lonely pierced earrings attached at the end hole.

• **TOOTHBRUSHES,** *Recycling Old Ones:* Bacteria can multiply in old toothbrushes and if bristles are bent or scraggly they don't clean properly and may cut your gums. Change toothbrushes about every three to six months. After a good rinse, old toothbrushes will clean nooks and crevices in furniture and appliances; apply shoe polish;

scrub stains on laundry before washing; clean a garlic press, graters, and other kitchen utensils; clean jewelry.

• **TOOTHBRUSHING SERENADE,** *When Children Rush and Brush:* One parent made a game of toothbrushing by putting a music box on the bathroom counter and having her child brush until the music stopped. Instead of rushing, the child enjoyed brushing.

• **TOOTH FAIRY TALES,** *Letter of Laughter:* When his six-year-old son lost his tooth while brushing and it went down the drain, dad consoled him and assured him that the Tooth Fairy was "magic," would find the tooth, and would still leave him something even if he didn't put the tooth under his pillow that night. The next morning, the boy came down to breakfast downcast and said, "Well, the tooth fairy did find the tooth but I told you she was going to be mad because she had to hunt for it. The last time I lost a tooth, she left me a dollar bill. Last night she only left fifty cents!"

• **TOOTH FAIRY MAGIC COIN:** Make a magic quarter for the tooth fairy to leave for a child who's lost a tooth. Spray the coin with hair spray and sprinkle it with gold glitter.

• **TOOTHPASTE TUBES,** *Keeping Plastic Ones Rolled-up:* Try holding the roll with a snack bag clip, a clothespin or clothespin-type hair barrette.

• **TOWELS,** *Identifying Houseguest's Towels:* When you have a hideaway cabin, your friends and relatives usually end up hiding away with you. Keeping track of whose towel is whose gets to be a problem, especially if swimming is involved. Write the names of guests on wooden spring clothespins with a pencil and ask them to clip the pins to their washcloths and towels. They can hang their towels outdoors to dry between swims with the same ID clothespins. You can erase the names after they leave so that there's space for the next arrivals' names. If you feel "crafty" you can decorate the clothespins with flowers and bows, too.

• **TOWELS,** *Removing Stiffness:* Usually it's due to detergent buildup or overloading the washer. Avoid the problem by using less detergent, hotter water and fewer towels per wash load. Remove detergent buildup by washing towels in very hot water with baking soda, borax or washing soda, then add a cup or so of vinegar to the rinse water. Repeat the "treatment" periodically to keep towels soft and fluffy.

• TOYS, *Games to Make:* Some families make up games with rules so silly that nobody can win, but that's the fun of it! For the following games, you can make gameboards or recycle old ones that no longer have their accessories.
1. Make an "opoly" game using streets in your neighborhood and city.
2. Make a war game pitting the football teams of two local high schools against each other.
3. Make up a Family History "pursuit" game listing relatives names, family happenings, etc. on the question cards.
4. Design a whole new game mixing up rules from previous "bought game" or card game favorites. It's your game, your rules! The sillier the better for more fun!
5. Make outdoor games like croquette or horseshoes more complicated by adding "Captain May I" to get permission to take one's turn.

• TOYS, *Storage:*
1. After birthday or Christmas, divide very young children's toys into groups (perhaps a bag for each day of the week) and then bring out and put away a "set" each day; young children will feel as if they have "new" toys daily.
2. Keep toys in an old toddler swimming pool; you can slide the whole mess under the bed at night.
3. Keep older children's stuffed animals off the floor hanging in a hammock made from decorator fish net from specialty stores or from Heloise's nylon net. **Caution:** Don't hang mesh net in a baby or toddler's reach.
4. Buy a new brightly colored plastic trash can or clean up an old one. Decorate by painting the child's name on the lid and side or with stickers or decals so that the child can tell the toy box from the real trash can.

• TOYS, *Pickup:*
1. Make "pickup" a game: Red things first, then blue; or soft things then hard things; toss unbreakables into a suitable container; play

who's the fastest picker-upper—Mom/Dad or child; choo-choo toy boxes or bags into the closet; whatever works, including, "We'll have more time to read (child's favorite book) if we get the toys picked up faster."

2. If everyone is tired, don't bother to pick-up. Even little children need a day off, just like Mom and Dad.

• TOY "SANDBOX": To confine children's building blocks and other small toys so they aren't stepped on or vacuumed up, either use a small plastic wading pool or build an indoor sandbox with four 3-foot or longer 1′ × 6′ boards. Nail or screw them together to form a square with the floor as the bottom. Children can build cities and cabins but all of the pieces stay in the toy "sandbox."

• TRASH BAG STORAGE: Toss the whole roll of plastic bags into the bottom of your trash can after it's been cleaned. Draw up the first bag, leaving it attached to the roll, open it and drape it around the top rim. Hold it in place with the elastic from pantyhose or men's shorts. When the bag is full, tie it shut, lift it up and tear the plastic bag off the roll as you grab the next bag. Then drape the new bag over the rim as before.

• TRASH CAN GARTER, *Recycling:* Cut off the elastic from men's shorts or old panty hose and use it to hold plastic garbage bags in place in trash cans. Just put the bag in so that several inches go over the lip of the trash can and put the elastic over the bag like a garter. You can also tie together pieces of elastic from your sewing supplies.

• TRASH CONTAINER, *Recycling, Mini-trash Can:* When there's no space for a small waste basket, like near a dressing table, vanity or clothes dryer, substitute a designer square tissue box. You can pitch the box out when it's full of used tissues, makeup pads, dryer lint, or any other small trash. And, it's free! Plastic-lined woven-tray baskets that come on florist-delivered plant or floral arrangements make good small bathroom or bedroom wastebaskets; line with small plastic bags from the stores.

• TRAVEL, *Checklist, Dealing with Fear of Flying:* Some people feel safer if they take a few special precautions.

1. Pay attention to the flight attendant's emergency instructions and read the safety materials provided.

2. Make note of all exits and how the doors operate. If you are seated at an emergency exit and think you couldn't open the door, ask to be relocated.

3. When you board the plane, notice which other passengers might become obstacles if you have to get out quickly.

4. Avoid alcoholic beverages so that you will be alert in case of an emergency. You'll feel better anyway; alcohol and caffeine can make you feel uncomfortable even when there is no emergency.

5. Don't sleep during takeoffs and landings.

6. Keep your seatbelt fastened even when the light is off.

7. When traveling, dress comfortably with natural fabrics (less of a fire hazard). Don't wear spiked heels that prevent you from walking steadily and quickly. Carry a handkerchief or cotton scarf to cover your nose and mouth in case of choking fumes.

8. If there should be an accident, unfasten your seatbelt immediately and go to the nearest exit. If the fuselage is damaged, go toward the nearest source of light and, like exiting in case of fire anywhere, try to stay low so you avoid inhaling smoke and noxious fumes.

• TRAVEL, *Cruises:* Some cruise lines will put families in larger quarters at no extra cost if they book a certain number of months in advance. Some lines will let people who can travel on short notice fill empty rooms at lower costs. Check with your travel agent or individual cruise lines.

• TRAVEL, *Free Admission and Shopping Discounts:* If you belong to a local museum, zoo or arboretum "friends" association, your group may be offering tours at reasonable prices. Sometimes, these memberships are tax deductible and having a membership card in one association gives you free admission and/or discount shopping opportunities in other cities' facilities. For example, members of the World-Wide Reciprocal Admission Program for Arboretums can get free general admission to eighty-one arboretums and public gardens in the U.S. and abroad. For information on this program, contact the Dallas Arboretum & Botanical Garden, Dept. NC, 8525 Garland Road, Dallas, TX 75218; 214-327-8263.

• **TRAVEL,** *Handling Your Money Checklist:*
1. Find out if your bank is tied to an Automatic Teller Network (ATM) and where the outlets are in your destination city. You may be able to use your ATM credit line and/or get cash amounts from $100 to $500 a day.
2. Don't leave your personal checks at home; many tourist places accept them.
3. Don't put all of your traveler's checks and receipts in the same place; you could lose both at the same time.
4. Traveling couples shouldn't carry duplicate credit cards. Divide them up so you'll still have some to use if one person has a wallet lost or stolen.

• **TRAVEL,** *Home Swaps:* Home Swapping with a family or couple is a relatively inexpensive way to see life as a neighbor instead of just as a tourist. Among the organizations that specialize in matches between house-swappers are: INTERVAC U.S. in San Francisco (415-435-3497); Better Homes and Travel in New York (212-689-6608); Vacation Exchange Club, Youngstown, Arizona (602-972-2186).

• **TRAVEL,** *Hotel-Motel Information:* Most hotels and motels have 800-numbers to call for reservations and information on whether or not pets are accepted or facilities for pets are available nearby. But you can also ask if the facility offers pool and spa services, hairdryers, ironing equipment, or anything else that will make your stay more pleasant and let you travel lighter without your own "electronics." Also, you'll know if you need to pack spa clothing/robes, etc. And, don't forget to ask if you can get room discounts for membership in fraternal, business, insurance or other organizations at some national chain hotels.

• **TRAVEL,** *Luggage Sizes for Carryons:* Airlines differ on the sizes, weight and number of pieces you can carry on but here are general guidelines from the Air Transport Association to help you buy the right size:
1. Underseat bags: Should be $9 \times 14 \times 22$ inches, with total dimensions of 45 inches.

2. Garment bags: 4 × 23 × 45 inches, total of 72 inches.
3. Overhead bags: 10 × 14 × 36 inches, total of 60 inches.

• TRAVEL, *With Pets:* It may be better to leave your pet at home if it is old, in poor health or is just not a good traveler. See PETS, Checklist for Boarding.

• TRAVEL, *Protecting Your Home While You're Away Checklist:* It's most important to make sure that your home doesn't look empty.
1. Set a timer that automatically turns lights on and off in several rooms at various hours. A timer can also turn a radio off and on.
2. Park your car halfway up the driveway to prevent thieves from parking vans or trucks near the house.
3. Be sure to have a neighbor pick up your newspaper, mail and other deliveries. (It's safer to have these things picked up than canceled, I'm told by the police. Canceling tells a lot of strangers that you'll be gone and for how long.)
4. Have someone take your trash out on pick-up day and have your lawn mowed or snow shoveled to maintain an "occupied look." (Check out bonded and insured house-sitting services in your city. Some of these services are nationally franchised and provide people to water plants, care for pets in addition to keeping your home looking occupied. The cost varies but is certainly worth it to keep you from worrying during your fun-time vacation.)

• TRAVEL, *Quick-Fixes for Clothing Problems (Also See Spots and Stains Chart):*
1. Wine or Coffee Spills: Blot the fresh spill with a cloth soaked with tried and true club soda.
2. Oil (Like Salad Dressing) Stain: Rub white chalk into the stain before laundering. Chalk's easy to carry in a purse or bag.
3. Laundering in Hotels & Restaurants: Rub stain with bar soap and wash/rinse. Or, use hotel shampoo on the stain and for washing garments.
4. Some liquid handsoaps in restaurants can be used to quick-clean a spill. (If you want to conceal the wet spot, you can always hold your purse or a stole over it until it dries.)
5. Mud: Allow to dry, then brush off excess dirt and spot clean with detergent or shampoo.

6. Ballpoint Ink: Usually hair spray or rubbing alcohol will remove ballpoint ink from washable fabrics. Don't spray directly on the stain; lightly spot clean it with a cloth dampened with either solution; launder as usual.

7. "Ironing" in a hotel: Tried and true is to hang a garment in the bathroom while you shower to let the steam "iron" it. If the fabric is not very frail, you can "iron" some creases out over a hot lightbulb. Remember to put the shade back on the lamp!

• **TRAVEL**, *Rental Car Insurance:* Check with your insurance adjuster; your rental car may be covered by your policy and you don't need to pay for more. Also, some credit card users have coverage on rental cars if the fees are paid with that card.

• **TRAVEL:** *Renting an RV (recreational vehicle) Checklist:* If you are planning to rent a recreational vehicle (RV) it's more complicated than just renting a car.

1. Get information from local and national rental companies to compare seasonal rates and determine which model best suits your needs. Usually, the longer the time rented, the greater the discount offered.

2. Mileage is often packaged to include a maximum number of miles and the price is usually quoted as a combined total with the RV rental. Ask for the cost of additional miles beyond the package limit. The price quoted may not include prep charges, insurance, mileage, generator fees, linens or kitchenware and may not be in effect indefinitely. Since you pay for the gas, ask about average fuel consumption.

3. Most companies offer basic comprehensive insurance coverage for damage to the RV but check to see if your auto insurance policy provides coverage. If you use your own policy, the RV lessor may ask for a substantial deposit, refundable within thirty days if you return the RV undamaged.

4. Some people like to have trip interruption coverage. These policies vary greatly; read all the fine print carefully!

• **TRAVEL**, *Safeguarding Documents:* Make copies of such things as airline tickets, hotel reservations, rail passes and vouchers, credit card and passport numbers, and keep them in a place other than the originals so that if you lose your documents, you have proof for claims.

• **TRAVEL,** *Speaking "Travelese" When Booking a Tour:* You may need a second language even if you aren't leaving the United States. Here are some of the most frequently used package-tour terms to help you budget for your trip:
1. Add-on Fare: Cost of air travel to the city from which the tour originates.
2. All-Inclusive: The tour package price includes all land arrangements as well as round-trip air fare.
3. Force Majeure: Anything that happens that cannot be reasonably controlled or anticipated by the tour operator.
4. Fly-Drive Holiday: Independent tour that includes a rental car in its package fee.

• **TRAVEL,** *Staying Well Checklist:*
1. Rock and Roll: Don't spoil your cruise with motion sickness. See your doctor for a prescribed adhesive patch worn behind the ear, which will time-release the anti-motion-sickness drug scopolamine; or, buy over-the-counter preparations.
2. High Altitudes: Going to the mountains? Your body needs time to adapt to low oxygen pressure at high altitudes. Give it a chance to adjust for a few days before doing strenuous activities and avoid alcoholic beverages during the adaptation time.
3. Sun Protection: Ultra-violet light is more intense in the tropics than in temperate zones and it also increases by 4 percent for every 1,000 feet above sea level. Cover your skin with appropriate clothing and use maximum sunscreen protection and re-apply protection after swimming or perspiring. If you snorkle, protect your back with sunscreen and an opaque T-shirt.
   When boating, especially protect your eyes and lips from water-reflected sun. (Sunglass labels should say they meet or exceed "ANSI Z80.3" which is the newest American National Standards Institute rating adopted by the Sunglass Association of America in cooperation with the FDA.
4. Walking on the Beach: Invest in protective beach shoes for walking on the sand. Avoid insect bites by lying on a blanket or beach chair instead of directly on the sand; use insect repellent and

avoid highly scented colognes or after-shave. Highly colored clothing also attracts insects.

5. Seeing the Sights: Losing your glasses or a contact lens sure can spoil your vacation. Take along extras and a copy of your prescription to make sure you can see the sights you paid to see.

6. Medications: Take all medicines you usually need, copies of essential prescriptions and your personal doctors' phone numbers, just in case of emergency.

• TRAVEL, *Tickets:* Help speed up the boarding process. Have your boarding pass out and I try to fold it where it's supposed to be torn so that the ticket taker can tear it more easily.

• TRAVEL, *Tourist Information Sources:* If you are traveling out of state or even within your own state, call 1-800-555-1212 to find out if your destination state has an 800-number for its tourist bureau or traveler's and visitor's information department. Most states offer free brochures on what to see and do and often you'll find lists of free tours of special factories or museums, etc. to help your budget as well as how to contact visitor information sources in specific cities that you plan to visit. **Note:** Also, check out travel books, guidebooks and video tapes from your library for travel information. If you are driving, buying a road atlas will give you a lot of good travel information.

• TRAVEL, *Travel-agent Services Checklist:* Travel agents are paid by the tourist industry, but you may be charged for some long-distance phone calls, international telexes, visa and tourist card fees and extensive tailor-made itineraries. The following is a checklist of what a travel agent needs to know to give you the best service.

1. Your total travel budget;

2. If you have flexible travel times so that you can use special promotions;

3. What you've liked or not liked on past vacations;

4. Special diet or medical requirements, if any;

5. Your preferred travel companies and arrangements like non-smoking accommodations;

6. Names of frequent flier/frequent traveler programs to which your miles can be credited.

• **TRAVEL,** *Trip Cancellation Insurance:* Before deciding on trip cancellation or any extra health insurance when you travel, check your homeowner's and health policies to find out what's covered while you are traveling—theft, baggage loss, health problems. You may not need any extra and can save that money to spend on your trip.
1. Trip cancellation insurance can reimburse you for first class tickets if you cancel just because you change your mind, but there's not reimbursement on non-refundable discount tickets for that reason.
2. Costs for basic travel insurance policies are based on the number of days away from home and cover such factors as trip cancellation or interruption, baggage loss, emergency evacuation, world-wide telephone assistance, accidents, sickness, accidental death or dismemberment.
3. Typical costs are $20 per person to get reimbursed for 50 percent of the trip cost up to $200 if you cancel for any reason. At least two companies offer trip cancellation or interruption insurance separately from basic travel insurance policies for $5.50 per $100 with reimbursement up to $5,000.
4. Most of this type of insurance is bought from travel agents (who can then compute the cost since they know your trip cost).

• **TRAVEL ASSISTANCE SERVICES:** You can buy services that refer you to reliable medical care, replace medication and conduct medical consultations with attending physicians if you become ill when traveling out of the country. Some services arrange transportation back to the U.S. and others offer pre-trip information on destination cities, can relay urgent messages to and from friends and family and advance cash in emergencies.

• **TRAVEL CRAFT-SNACK,** *To Keep Children Occupied on Long Car Trips:* Place colored cereal rings and licorice stings into separate self-sealing plastic bags. When it's craft time (translation—when children get bored), tie a piece of cereal to the end of a licorice string and give the children more cereal to string on the licorice. After they tire of the necklaces and bracelets, they can eat their creations.

• **TRAVEL GAME,** *Car Trip Word Game:* Most states have three letters plus three digits on their car license plates. Score this game by adding the letter values according to the popular commercial word game plus the numbers of licenses sighted on the road. But please! No accidents by drivers getting too involved in the game!

• **TRAVEL GIFT,** *When a Child Leaves Home on a Cross-country Car Trip to College or a Job, Checklist:*
1. TLC Kit: Road atlas; state road map; change for toll roads; small container of snacks, hard candy and gum; small box of tissues; cassette tapes of music or favorite books; two index cards for the glove compartment—one with parents' name, address and phone number so that they can be contacted in an emergency and the second with the child's destination and name of the contact person there.
2. Road Kit: Can of propellant tire sealer; flashlight; couple of flares; extra set of car keys; jumper cables; book with step-by-step instructions for changing a flat tire and jump-starting a car.

• **TRUCK,** *Driving for the First Time:* If you've rented a truck to save money on a cross-country move, you'll need to adjust some of your driving habits, especially if it's your first time driving a loaded truck.
1. Remember that you're driving a vehicle that's taller and wider than what you're used to; be careful to clear overhead and roadside signs.
2. Trucks need greater stopping distance and a loaded truck doesn't accelerate as rapidly as a car so be especially cautious when following other cars and passing.
3. As always, map out your route before you start so that you don't drive beyond your energy level, especially since you'll be "working" harder driving an unfamiliar vehicle.

• **TUBES,** *Getting All the Toothpaste or Salve:* When no more will come out of the top, cut off the bottom to get every smidgeon out.

• **TUB TOYS:** Put a child's bathtub toys in a tiered plastic hanging basket. You can pull the drip tray off the bottom for drainage and hang the pot from the shower head.

• **TURKEY,** *Avoiding Leftovers:* During the holidays when turkeys are cheapest, have your butcher cut them in half from neck to feet, then freeze them. You can serve half a turkey with dressing, all the trimmings and give thanks all year round for having saved money on main dish meat.

• **TURKEY FOR CASSEROLES:** Divide leftover cut-up meat into two-cup portions (or other frequently needed amount) and freeze in separate freezer-safe bags so that you can just grab a bag of ready-to-use turkey (or chicken, beef) when you're cooking. If you have leftover gravy, freeze it in one- or two-cup portions to go with the meat.

• **TURNING OVER FRYING FOODS,** *Safety Hint:* Place one pancake turner on top and another on the bottom when you flip over fried patties, etc. and you won't spatter grease by plopping the patty into the pan.

• **TURTLES,** *Feeding:* Turtles are very messy eaters. One reader keeps the tank clean by feeding them in another tank. The turtles live in a beautiful tank, designed with rocks and plants, then are picked up and placed in their feeding tank at mealtime.

• **TV-TRAY LEGS,** *Recycling:* Make holders for plastic trash bags for collecting leaves/trash in the yard, storing cans for recycling and for any other time you need to have a bag held open. Fold the top of a plastic trash bag over the top of the tray legs and fasten with spring clothespins.

• **TWINS,** *Telling Them Apart, Letter of Laughter:* When her granddaughter told her about the twin girls in her class, Grandma asked how she could tell them apart. "Well, one wears blue sneakers and the other wears red," the child replied. When asked if that was the only way, the child added, "Well, if I call Elizabeth and she comes, that's Elizabeth." Surely another "out of the mouths of babes" story. Aren't children smart?

• **TWIST-TIES,** *Recycling Leftovers:* Temporarily mend eyeglasses, tie plants to stakes, make hooks for Christmas ornaments, organize loose keys, hold stitches when knitting, tie up stored extension cords.

U

- **UMBRELLA,** *Cleaning Mildewed Plastic Patio Umbrella:* A reader wrote that she just put hers into the swimming pool, left it there a day or two and all the mildew disappeared. **Caution:** This "swim" treatment is not for canvas umbrellas; canvas shouldn't be bleached. Also, be sure the pool has plenty of chlorine or you could cause an algae buildup in it.

- **UMBRELLA,** *What to Do with a Wet One When Shopping:* This is one of those "Why didn't I think of this before" hints: Tuck a plastic grocery bag in your purse or briefcase before leaving home so that you can put your drippy umbrella into the bag, slip the handles over your arm and proceed to wherever you are going without messing up your clothing or leaving your umbrella someplace where it will "walk off."

- **UMBRELLA REPAIR:** When material comes loose from an umbrella spoke, reattach it with dental floss—it's stronger than thread and waterproof.

- **UPHOLSTERY CAUTIONS:** Always keep cleaning instructions in a safe place so that you can clean upholstery properly.

1. If there is no care label on your upholstered furniture, you may have to rely on professional advice when it gets soiled or stained. Care depends on the type of fabric and if the fabric has coating materials on its reverse side.

2. Don't assume that when an upholstered item has zippered cushion covers that the covers can be removed for cleaning. For example, Haitian cotton is a common upholstery material; but while other fabrics can be hand washed, wrung out and air dried, Haitian cotton is uncleanable. If soiled the fabric does not respond well to water, leaving yellow rings that can't be removed. A good rule of thumb is never remove cushion covers for separate cleaning.

3. Any tumble cleaning method can destroy the backing, shrink or otherwise damage upholstery fabric. If no care instructions are attached to the furniture when you buy it, ask for some. If you have doubts about care and can't get advice it may be a good idea to choose furniture brands that offer care advice—unless the price is so low that the furniture is "disposable" if soiled which is very rare these days!

• **UPHOLSTERY FABRIC,** *Cleaning:* Vacuum pieces regularly to keep dirt and dust from getting ground in. Clean washable fabrics after first testing for color fastness.

1. Mix ¼ cup high-suds laundry detergent with one quart of warm water in a blender.

2. Apply just the suds with a medium-bristled brush. Work lather in small circles, overlapping as you go.

3. Wring out a towel in clean water and go over the entire upholstered surface.

4. When dry, vacuum the furniture to remove any remaining residue.

• **UPHOLSTERY,** LEATHER, *Cleaning and Care:* Always keep the instruction tags that come with leather upholstery; different finishes require different care methods. Generally, you need to dust and vacuum often and clean spots or surface soil with a weak solution of only a few drops of mild dishwashing liquid and water in a gallon of water. **Caution:** Never soak leather! After cleaning, rinse and dry well. Apply saddle soap or an oil made especially for leather if the manufacturer advises it to protect the leather from scratches or getting brittle.

• **UTENSIL BOARD,** *Organizing Kitchen Clutter:* Install on the wall a pegboard painted to match your kitchen and then you can hang on its pegs slotted spoons, skimmers, whisks, strainers and other utensils too large or bulky for kitchen drawers. It makes the kitchen look like it's inhabited by a professional chef, too!

V

- **VACUUM MIT:** If your upright vacuum cleaner gives you a blister on the palm of your hand when you push and pull it, wear an oven mitt—the padding keeps your hand safe.

- **VALANCE, POOF-STYLE,** *Recycling, Stuffing:* While the directions tell you to stuff the "poof" of valances or Austrian-style shades with tissue paper, when the sun shines through some fabrics, the tissue shows up as a shadow. Try stuffing the valances with clear plastic dry-cleaning bags to get fullness without shadows.

- **VALENTINE CAKE,** *When You Don't Have a Heart-shaped Pan:*
Step 1. Bake two layers—one in a round pan and one in a square cake pan with the same diameter (length across the middle) of the round one.
Step 2. Pour half of the cake batter into each pan, bake as directed.
Step 3. When layers are cool, place the square layer on a large serving platter in a "diamond" position. Cut the round layer in half to make two half-circles, and place the cut sides of each half against the top sides of the diamond. There's the heart.
Step 4. Frost with your favorite frosting, building up the joint where cake pieces meet to smooth the top. Decorate with red candy hearts or cinnamon candies or decorative frosting.

• **VALENTINE MAIL,** *Have a LOVEly Valentine:* To get your Valentine cards postmarked "Valentines," bundle up all of the cards, making sure they are properly addressed and each has the correct postage, and put them in a large envelope along with a note to the postmaster requesting the special postmark. Mail to Postmaster of Valentines, Valentines, VA 23887-9998. Don't forget to include a Valentine addressed to yourself so that you'll know what the postmark looks like.

• **VAPORIZER/HUMIDIFIER/DEODORIZER:** Fill a vaporizer-humidifier to the full line with water, add a little potpourri and as you mist the air, you'll also put a fragrance in it.

• **VASE,** *Cleaning:*
1. Remove lime deposits by filling vase with hot water and then drop in a couple of denture tablets. Let soak a few hours and then scrub with bottle brush, rinse well and let dry.
2. Remove lime deposits by allowing to soak with vinegar for several hours; rinse and dry. **Note:** Save vinegar for other cleaning; it's still good.

• **VASES,** *Avoiding Accumulation of Cloudy Residue:* Use only distilled water for floral arrangements; then washing them is easy. By the way, if you use distilled water to make coffee, it will taste better and cleaning hard water deposits from the pot is a chore of the past.

• **VCRS,** *Cleaning Heads:* Always check directions to find out what type of commercial cleaner kit should be used—wet method or dry method. An alternate method for cleaning a VCR if you have no cleaning kit handy is to record on a new tape for about 30 minutes, then play the recorded part of the tape back several times to let the heads rub against it so that they clean themselves. The next time you clean the heads repeat the process starting at the point where the tape is new and unused. After you have used all parts of this tape for cleaning, throw the tape away.

• **VEGETABLE CRISPER:** A dry sponge placed in the refrigerator vegetable crisper will absorb excess moisture and help keep veggies fresh.

• **VEGETABLES,** *Storage:* Don't wash until they will be used; the extra moisture causes spoilage. Use a container with a lid or a self-seal plastic bag; add a couple of sheets of paper toweling to absorb moisture and keep veggies from getting soggy and then replace the towels as they get damp. This method is especially good for lettuce, cucumbers and mushrooms.

• **VEGETABLE SPRAY:** To keep sticky ingredients like honey, corn syrup or molasses from making a mess in a measuring utensil, spray it before measuring to make clean up easy.

• **VEGETABLES, WASHING,** *Healthy-Planet Recycling:* Save the water for plants indoors or out, especially if you live in a drought area.

• **VIDEO CASSETTES,** *Care:* Videotapes are very fragile, thin plastic film which tends to stretch, wrinkle and break when improperly handled. Video rental stores ask you to rewind the tapes because inserting a cassette that has tape on BOTH reels can cause the tape to misfeed and get mangled. (Some stores charge an extra fee to your account if you don't rewind!)

This applies to your home recording tapes, too. Rewind them and then fast-forward when you add to the tape. Storing tapes without rewinding them allows the tapes to stretch and sag, then misfeed when played.

• **VIDEO MEMORIES:** One family wrote to say that when they moved, they felt sad about leaving their home and neighbors. So they decided to take their fond memories with them by making a film of their home, inside and out, and of their neighbors talking to their children. It made the move easier for the children, too.

• **VIDEO MESSAGES:** When one reader's mother was in the hospital for several weeks, and children weren't allowed in to visit, she made a videotape of her children for their grandmother—they talked to granny, told her stories, sang songs, drew pictures and cards for her and held them up to the camera. Granny was gratefully teary-eyed and the children were happy to do something nice for their grandmother. The bonus is that the tape is a treasured family keepsake.

• **VIDEO-MOVIE LOG FOR RENTAL TAPES:** By the time movies are available in video rental stores, you've usually forgotten what they were about. So, when the movie ads and reviews first appear in newspapers, cut them out, and file the clippings in a file box or envelope. (You can paste them to an index card if you feel ambitious.) Then you can take your file to the rental store to jog your memory when you make your rental selections.

• **VIDEOTAPE LOG:** Keep a small notebook near the VCR. When you tape a show, write the name of the show in the notebook, one per page, as well as on the jacket. After the previous week's TV guide has expired, cut out the description of the show and tape it in the notebook. Then, you have all the information about the show where it won't get lost. If you decide to erase the tape, just tear out the page from the notebook—it's easier than tearing taped information off the jacket.

• **VIDEOTAPES,** *Identification:* When you tape shows to be "keepers," cut out from your newspaper TV guide the tiny paragraph describing the show and use transparent tape to stick it to the "outer" edge of the tape (not the edge that goes into the machine). Each tape edge will hold three or four of these descriptions.

• **VIDEOTAPES,** *Identification:* When you've taped a show that several family members want to view, place a stick-on note on the outside of the jacket with each viewer's name on it so that as the tape is viewed, people can check off their names and nobody can complain about missing the show.

• **VIDEOTAPES,** *Keepers:* You won't accidentally tape over or erase a favorite VCR tape if you remember to remove the tab found on the left side of the tape cartridge edge. (The manufacturer puts it there for you!) If you change your mind and want to record over the tape, just place a piece of masking tape or several layers of transparent tape over the recessed area. You can also buy a small plastic gadget to put over the recessed area when you want to tape over.

• **VIDEOTAPES,** *Re-taping:* Since the recommended life of a tape is about 100 hours, you could get the most out of each tape if you tape daily programs on a tape for several viewings and then tape a movie or documentary "keeper" on that tape which won't be viewed frequently. **Hint:** VCR tapes don't last forever. If you have a favorite tape that is several years old, you should copy it to a new tape before it deteriorates too badly.

• **VIODETAPES,** *When to Discard:* Discard tapes used for daily recording after about 100 hours of playing and recording to prevent clogging of your VCR by oxide particles. (Oxide particles flake off tapes as they play. Using good quality tapes—"high grade" or "super high grade"—helps but you still need to clean your VCR periodically.)

- **VIDEOTAPING SLIDES:** You can have slides, photos, 8mm or 15mm film put on videotape for easy viewing. The process is called video or tape transfer and you can find stores that do it under Photo Finishing or Video Transfer in the phone book. **Hint:** Use good-quality slides; copying causes some quality deterioration; put the slides in order and number them; and be prepared to wait about a week or so. This would be an nice gift for a friend or relative.

- **VIDEOTAPING SLIDES YOURSELF:**
Step 1. Set the video camera on a tripod and project the slides onto a good screen. (Experiment until you get the distance just right.)
Step 2. Working with another person, have one show and focus the slides while the other operates the video camera and says when it's okay. The video operator turns on the camera and counts to four, then turns the camera off while the slides are being changed. One of them can even explain the photo.
Note: This takes a little practice and it helps if your video camera has a freeze-frame feature. There are machines that transfer photos or slides onto videotape, too. Check out photo-equipment stores.

- **VINEGAR,** *Cleaning with:* Keep vinegar in a clean squirt bottle so it's handy for pre-treating stains before laundering, cleaning bathrooms, etc.

- **VINEGAR,** *Homemade Fruit:* Combine a bottle of white wine vinegar with ½ cup fresh, washed and stemmed strawberries. Cover the mixture and let it sit at room temperature for one week. You can remove the fruit or leave it in, but if you leave it, the vinegar will continue to mellow and become stronger. Use in recipes calling for fruit vinegars.

- **VISITORS,** *Letter of Laughter:* A reader reminded us about one of life's ironic rules—that nobody every drops in to visit you when you've just cleaned up your home or apartment and someone always drops by when the place is a wreck!

• **VITAMINS & OTHER SUPPLEMENTS:** The Center for Science in the Public Interest has reported on research that shows more than half of the calcium supplements we buy in the marketplace don't disintegrate soon enough to get into our bloodstreams, which means we are wasting money on supplements if they just pass through our bodies undissolved. This is true of many other supplements, such as the large doses of niacin many people take to lower their cholesterol. Although you can't have yourself X-rayed regularly to find out if your tablets are dissolving in your body, you have some recourse.

1. Ask the manufacturer for laboratory results that show if the supplement you want to take has been tested for potency, stability, and ability to dissolve. (Get the phone number from the package or ask your pharmacist.)

2. If you take niacin to lower your cholesterol, take several smaller doses instead of a sustained-release preparation.

3. Check calcium labels (or call companies) to see if they meet USP (US Pharmacopeial Convention) dissolving tests.

4. Buy only supplements that have expiration dates. This is no guarantee, but it's better than nothing. (Time causes some supplements to decompose or become too hard to dissolve.)

5. You are more likely to get a poorer quality supplement when you buy less-expensive versions of name brands.

• **VOTING TOOL:** The little tool provided for punching out your choices on an absentee ballot need not be returned with the ballot and that's good. It's perfect for setting most digital watches.

W

- **WAITING GAME WITH CHILDREN:** In places like physician or dentist offices, send them on a scavenger hunt. Give them a list of items and a magazine and ask them to find pictures of the items. When they do, they should write the page number by each item. Such games make a wait more pleasant for parent and child.

- **WAFFLE IRON,** *Stop Sticking:* To temper a waffle iron, clean the surface well. Then take a slice of bread and grease both sides with unsalted fat (never salted fat). Lay the bread in the waffle iron and close the lid. As the bread browns, it greases all the small square surfaces. For a double waffle iron, temper with two pieces of bread. After removing the bread, crumple it and feed it to the birds.

- **WAKE-UP BELL:** When small children get up before their parents to start "exploring" the house, parents need a warning signal—put inexpensive or Christmas jingle bells on the tops of children's bedroom doors. Then, as soon as they touch their doors, the jingling will alert you!

- **WALKER BASKET,** *Handicapped Person Help:* Hang a child's bike basket on the front of a hand walker to carry light items. **Caution:** Carry only lightweight things to avoid getting off balance.

• **WALKING DIARY:** Keep a walking record of hours or miles as an incentive to get your exercise. You can tally up the totals at the end of the month or year to see how far you've gone on the road to good health. For fun, compare mileage totals to distances between cities on a map.

• **WALL DECORATING,** *Hanging Collections Without Damage:* When you are grouping wall decorations with different shapes and sizes, trace an outline of the objects (pictures, mirrors, etc.) on newspapers and cut them out. Tape them on the wall in arrangements until you get one you like, then, place the nails in the wall through the paper; remove paper and hang the real thing. This is a good hint even for one painting or mirror; you can tape the paper to the wall and step back to see if you have it at the right level and place.

• **WALLPAPER,** *Cleaning:*
1. Most washable wall coverings can be cleaned with mild liquid soap and cool water. Work from the bottom up, using as little water as possible. Work on small areas and overlap as you wash. Rinse with clear water and blot dry.
2. Non-washable wall coverings can sometimes be cleaned by rubbing gently with kneaded eraser, fresh white bread, or doughy wallpaper cleaners from hardware stores. If you use the commercial doughy cleaner, be sure to knead and turn it often so you use clean surfaces on the wall.
3. Spot-clean wallpaper before spots set by blotting grease spots with paper towels or facial tissue while you press lightly with a warm iron over the towels or tissue. **Caution:** If possible, always get manufacturer's directions for cleaning your particular kind of wallpaper. And, always test cleaning methods on an inconspicuous place before doing a whole wall or conspicuous place like the areas around light switches.

• **WALLPAPER,** *Leftover Uses:* Cover books or shelves, wrap gifts, make decals for sliding glass doors, cut and laminate for placemats, cut pictures out and frame them.

• **WALLPAPER,** *Saver for Making Borders:* Buy a double roll of striped wallpaper that matches your wall colors and then cut the stripes individually into border strips. You can make wider borders by combining strips. You'll save even more if you catch a wallpaper remnant sale. Whenever you buy wallpaper, remember to consider that you have to match patterns and to get all you need because remnants can be of discontinued patterns and different batches of wallpaper can have slight color variances.

• **WALLPAPER,** *Painting Over:* Before attempting to paint over wall paper, you need to apply a product that primes the paper before painting. It's sold at most paint stores. Painting over paper is easier than removing existing paper and repairing the walls. Also, painting over heavily textured paper is very attractive since the texture shows through the paper.

• **WALLPAPER,** *Removing Grease Spots:* **Caution:** This method is only for washable wallpaper.
1. Make a paste of baking soda and water. Apply the thick paste to the grease stain and let it dry.
2. Brush the residue off with a soft brush or cloth.
Hint: Avoid grease on special places such as behind the stove or beside the trash can, by putting clear adhesive plastic over the "grease magnet" area.

• **WALLPAPER,** *Replacing:* Cost may determine your selection so here's a quick way to estimate it.
1. Multiply Wall Width × Wall Height = Square Feet. Then add the total square feet for all four walls.
2. A single roll of American wallpaper usually covers 30 square feet depending upon the pattern. (You need to allow extra for pattern matching.) A single roll of European wallpaper usually covers 23 square feet.
3. If you are doing only one wall of a room, you may be able to take advantage of remnant sales, but be aware that sale wallpaper may be a closeout and if you underestimate your needs, you may not be able to buy more.

• **WALLPAPER,** *Selection:* Wallpaper is expensive to replace but may last longer than paint in some rooms, but may last too long if the pattern is too busy; less-busy designs stay pleasing longer.

• **WALLPAPER BORDER,** *Substitute:* When you can't find just the right wallpaper border or the right color, try buying heavy ribbon at a fabric store and putting it up with tacky glue.

• **WALLPAPER BORDERS,** *Easy Stick-up:* When putting a wallpaper border around a room at the ceiling, you can save climbing up and down a ladder and constant repositioning of the ladder if you line up all your chairs along the wall and cover them well with old sheets or drop cloths. Then you can step from one chair to the next as you work. If two people work on this project, one can walk in front of the other holding the wet strip of border while the second person applies the other end.

• **WALLPAPER MISTAKE,** *Quick-Fix, Cover-up:* When her dark blue print wallpaper dried, a reader was dismayed to see a strip of white in between each sheet where the paper strips had pulled away from each other. She solved the problem by painting right down the seam with a small brush and some stencil paint that matched the wallpaper. She did about five inches at a time and wiped excess paint from the wallpaper with a damp cloth as she worked. Stencil paint comes in many different shades so you can match just about any color when you need to make a quick repair.

• **WALLS,** *Painting:* When selecting paint colors, remember that blue, green and violet have a tranquilizing effect; use the cool colors in rooms where you want to relax. Warm colors like yellow, orange and red will energize.

• **WALLS,** *Painting Technique:* Sponging one paint color over a neutral color is a popular decorating scheme. Water-based paints dry faster, you won't have to wait as long to dab on the second layer of paint. Oil-based paints dry more slowly; you won't have to work as fast and you'll have time to correct mistakes.

• **WALLS,** *Quick-Fixes:* Quick patching is essential when you move or change wall art arrangements.
1. Patch nail holes in white walls with white toothpaste or moistened crushed aspirin pushed into the hole.
2. On colored walls, dab matching watercolor paints over the mend if you don't have leftover paint. Colored typewriter correction fluid also covers small patches.
3. Fill tack or pin holes with white or appropriately colored soap or toothpaste.

• **WASHCLOTHS,** *For Traveling:* Disposable cleaning cloths cut in half are just the right size for travel washcloths, especially in Europe where washcloths aren't usually provided in smaller hotels. They dry quickly and, if left behind, are no loss. Put a wet one in a zipper bag when traveling with children.

• **WASHER SUDS OVERFLOW:** Please see SUDS OVERFLOW.

• **WATCH,** *Checklist for Buying One:*
1. Whether it's a designer watch or a $15 special, consider it's guarantee of accuracy and the cost of upkeep, such as batteries, and not the price tag alone.
2. The two types are battery-powered by a mainspring. Battery-powered watches usually need a new battery, costing $5 to $10 about once a year. Before you buy, find out what type of battery is needed and how easily it's replaced and if stores in your area carry the batteries and if you can replace them yourself. Some mainspring watches need cleaning and oiling annually.
3. Check the range of overall costs of possible repairs and if they can be done locally. Watches powered by a mainspring and some battery-powered watches can be repaired by local watch-repair shops; but some battery-powered watches must be returned to the manufacturer.
4. Water-resistant means that the watch can be submerged in fresh water to 80 feet and in salt water to 75 feet without leakage or loss of accuracy. Some watches are no longer water-resistant after cases are opened for battery replacement.
5. "Shock resistant" means that a watch can be dropped from three feet onto a hard wood surface without being damaged.
6. "Anti-magnetic" means that the inside working parts of the watch are made from metals that will not magnetically attract each other and therefore work independently.
7. "Jewels" refers to the usually synthetic gemstones that serve as bearings inside a mechanical watch.
8. Watches need to be cleaned regularly to maintain accuracy and many antique watches need regular oiling to keep parts from wearing out or breaking. It can be very expensive to have special parts made for antique watches. A friend paid over $200 to have a mainspring made for a family heirloom watch.

• **WATCH,** *When You Are Allergic to the Metal:* Either paint the back side of the watch with clear nail polish or cut corn pads to fit the back side and stick them on to protect your skin.

• **WATER BED SPREAD,** *$aver:* A twin-size bedspread costs less than king-size and fits most king-size water beds if you tuck it in all around the edges.

• **WATER,** *Buying Bottled Water Checklist:*
1. Natural Sparkling and Sparkling Waters—water that is bubbly because carbon dioxide (but no other chemicals) has been added to it. The word "natural," according to the FDA, has not been defined, so products labeled "natural" may not be different from other brands.
2. Spring Water—comes from a spring and has no minerals added or removed.
3. Drinking Water—comes from a water well and has no minerals added or removed.
4. Purified Water—has all minerals and chemicals removed. Generally not consumed as drinking water unless ordered by a doctor.
5. Distilled Water—recommended to prevent mineral build-up in some appliances such as steam irons. It still contains a minute amount of minerals.

• **WATER,** *Recycling:*
1. When basement de-humidifiers collect water, save it in old plastic jugs and use it to water plants and in your simmering potpourri pots.
2. Place 30-gallon plastic garbage cans at the end of rain gutters so they collect water for watering house and garden plants.
3. Have the water drainpipe from your air conditioner drain water into a flower bed. (You may need to check periodically to make sure the end of the pipe doesn't get clogged with mud or vines; if clogged, the water will back up to its source!)

• **WATER,** *Reminder to Drink Eight to Ten Glasses Daily:* Put eight to ten pennies on the kitchen counter and remove one each time you drink a glass of water.

- **WATER,** *When Pipes Are Frozen in the Morning:* Melt ice cubes in the microwave to get enough water to brush your teeth and for a cup of tea or coffee.

- **WATER CONSERVATION,** *Healthy-Planet $aver:*
1. Shower instead of taking a tub bath.
2. Wash hands, clothing, anything else, with cold water whenever you can to conserve energy.
3. When brushing your teeth, turn the water off until it's time to rinse instead of letting it just run away down the drain.
4. Keep a container of cold water in the fridge to avoid wasting tap water by running it until it feels cool.
5. Wash only full dishwasher loads.
6. Either wait until you have a full load to run the washer or adjust the water level to avoid waste.

- **WATER PURIFICATION SYSTEMS:** As this book is being written, many of these systems are scams and don't do what they claim. Before buying any system, have your water tested by a laboratory to determine if you actually need one. You can get current information about water testing and purification systems from your Cooperative Extension Agent. Look in the government section of your phone book, under "United States Government, Agriculture Department Of, Extension Service County & Home Economics Agents."

- **WATER STAINS,** *Covering Up:* Water stains on ceilings will come back through paint. You need to seal the area first with a special sealant sold in paint stores for that purpose or with clear varnish. Make sure varnish dries before painting over it.

- **WATERING SYSTEM FOR PLANTS,** *Recycling Healthy-Planet Homemade Drip Irrigation:*
1. Pierce a tiny hole in the bottom of a gallon plastic milk jug and put it next to a young tree or shrub and fill it with water. The water will drip out slowly and seep down to the roots. Fill the jugs early in the morning and at night, during dry spells, and you won't waste water through evaporation.
2. A smaller plastic bottle could help you drip-irrigate houseplants without spilling over.

3. For slow drip watering/feeding of houseplants, mix plant food and water in a plastic jug; freeze it; then poke three or four holes in the bottom of the bottle and set it on the pot's soil.

• **WAX,** *Dripped on a Wooden Dining Table:* First scrape off as much of the wax as possible with a plastic credit card or the dull side of a knife. Clean with a good quality wood cleaner. If the stain doesn't go away, it has probably penetrated the wood and the entire table will need refinishing.

• **WAX BUILDUP ON FLOORS,** *Removal:* If you don't own one, rent a floor scrubber.
1. Boost the power of heavy-duty general-purpose household cleaner with 1 cup of non-sudsing ammonia.
2. Working a small area at a time, pour a small amount of the cleaning solution on the floor, let it set for a few minutes and go over it with the floor scrubber. After the entire floor has been scrubbed, go back over it with a damp mop.
3. After the floor is dry, apply a fresh coat of wax.
Caution: If you have no-wax flooring, you absolutely need to follow the manufacturer's guidelines for cleaning. It's not the same as traditional flooring. If you have lost the directions, either call a flooring company (which might sell the products you need) or call the manufacturer's consumer or customer service/information line. Most manufacturers have 800 numbers for this; get the number by dialing 800 information: 1-800-555-1212.

• **WAXED PAPER,** *Liners from Cereal Boxes, Healthy-Planet Recycling:* Cut in squares for dividing hamburger patties prepared for freezing. Store in a cut bottom of a cereal box.

• **WEATHERIZING YOUR HOME, INDOOR AIR POLUTION:** When you install storm windows, weather stripping, caulking, wall insulation, indoor pollutants (household and personal products, formaldehyde or asbestos in building materials, lead, pesticides, tobacco smoke, radon, molds, gasses from heaters) can become concentrated because less outdoor air is entering your home. Some weatherizers such as caulk can emit some pollutants, too.
Therefore, before you weatherize, you should also take steps to minimize pollution from sources inside your home due to inade-

quate air flow, stuffy air, moisture condensation on cold surfaces, mold and mildew growth. The good news is that sometimes, when you seal up your home to prevent heat loss, you can also reduce indoor pollutant levels. For example, sealing foundation cracks can prevent radon gas from getting into your home.

• **WEDDING ANNIVERSARY REMINDER:** When you buy a wedding gift, also buy a first-anniversary card. Then, when you get home make it ready to mail at the appropriate time. Write the name on the envelope and pencil the date it should be mailed on the corner where the stamp will go. **Note:** It's better not to write the address on the envelope because the couple might move.

• **WEDDING SHOWER GIFT,** *For the Couple Who Has Everything:* A fire extinguisher!

• **WEDDING SHOWER IDEA,** *For Couples Who Have Everything:* One reader had each of twelve guests draw slips of paper printed with the months of the year. Guests would bring gifts useful during certain months and marked the gift for that month. For example, March gifts were spring-cleaning needs; April included Easter goodies; May was vegetable seeds and gardening tools; October included Halloween goodies and a leaf rake. Another reader included a sample list of the couple's likes and dislikes in hobbies and home-entertainment choices when she sent the invitations. Guests had fun picking out such shower gifts as adult board games, craft and hobby kits, and gave gift certificates for videotape rentals, local home delivery restaurants, videotaping of the wedding ceremony, and other "couple" instead of "bridal" shower gifts.

• **WEDDING VIDEO:** Make a copy of the wedding ceremony's video-tape and send it via "chain letter" to all those who couldn't come to the wedding in person. Include a list of names and addresses to send with the tape that begins with the first person who received it and ends with the bridal couple; also include instructions to send the tape to the next person on the list. When the tape returns to the bridal couple, they'll know everyone has seen it.

• **WEDDING OR WEDDING SHOWER GIFTS,** *For Couples Who Already Have Furnishings:* Buy decorated recipe cards and send them to all of the couple's friends asking for their favorite recipes. Then assemble the cards in a file and add a gift certificate to their favorite grocery store or to a gourmet store.

• **WEED-CUTTER SPRINGS,** *Quick-Fix Finding:* One reader solved a problem he had with lost springs from his string weed edger. When the cotter pin dislodged, the cover would come off and the spring inside would fly into the grass. He'd have to stop work until he got another spring. Now he buys spares and paints them bright colors so they can be more easily seen in the grass.

• **WEEVILS,** *Keeping Them Out of Cupboards:* To eliminate weevils from grain products, place all grain products in a zero-degree freezer for seven days when you bring them home from the store; or place the product in the oven at 130°F for 30 minutes. In addition, many people keep grain products in recycled glass jars with tight lids after "treatment." They cut off labels and directions and put them into the jar, too.

• **WEIGHT-LOSS EASES HUNGER:** For each pound that you lose on your diet, buy a pound of dried beans or other non-perishable staple food. When you have lost all the weight you needed to, give the food to your local food charity pantry. Helping the truly hungry will be an added incentive for you to stay on your diet plan. Just lifting the weight will help you remember how cumbersome it was carrying all those extra pounds around, too, so you'll try harder not to gain it all back!

• **WHIPPED CREAM/TOPPING:** Add a sprinkle of allspice, cinnamon, or nutmeg and a drop of vanilla extract to whipped cream or topping to make it extra special. Also: Please see HOLIDAY DESSERT TOPPING.

• **WHIPPED TOPPING,** *Low-calorie, No-cholesterol Substitute:* Whip a couple of egg whites until stiff, add a drop of vanilla and sugar to taste, and whip until foamy and then dollop onto desserts.

• **WHIPPING CREAM/TOPPINGS:** The mixing bowl won't slip and slide across the counter if you place a damp washcloth under it before turning on the mixer.

• **WICKER,** *Washing:*
1. Brush dust out of all cracks with an old toothbrush or scrub brush, or vacuum with brush attachment.

2. With a soft brush, scrub wicker with a solution of 2 pints cool water and 1 tablespoon of salt. Rinse with damp sponge. After furniture dries, rub with furniture polish and soft cloth. **Caution:** Wipe excess polish off chairs with a second cloth to prevent damage to clothing of "sitters."

• **WINDOW,** *Framing:* Instead of curtains or to accent curtains, frame a window with fabric.
1. Buy wood molding which is 4 or 5 inches wide and ½-inch thick and cut it to fit the length and width of your window.
2. Cover the frame with foam padding and then tack a fabric to the back of it and attach to the wall.

• **WINDOW DECALS/STICKERS,** *Removing:* Some will come off if you paint a few coats of vinegar on, let soak for a few minutes, and wash right off. Others come off after applying petroleum-based pre-wash spray as you would the vinegar. Still others, like bumper stickers, come off if you heat them with a hair dryer before peeling them off.

• **WINDOWPANES,** *No-mess Painting:* Dip an old rag (old socks are nice) in petroleum jelly and smear it around the edge of the glass closest to the window frame. After you finish painting, paint smears wipe right off. After the paint is completely dry, you can easily remove the remaining petroleum jelly film with a glass cleaner containing ammonia.

• **WINDOWS,** *Homestyle Quick-Fix for Wet, Drippy Condensation in the Winter:* Wipe the moisture off the windows and be sure they are dry. With a couple of tissues, apply undiluted hair shampoo to the windowpanes. They may look cloudy at first but should clear up. **Hint:** The best solution is to try to vent extra moisture from your home with kitchen and bath exhaust fans. Too much moisture for too long can cause wood framing to rot or warp and can make paint peel.

• **WINDOWS,** *Quick-Fix If Stuck:* Try to wedge a putty knife around all sides of the window so that you can spray furniture polish into the space. "Shake" the window to get as much furniture polish as possible down the sides. When it gives a bit, move the window up and down until you can open it all the way. Spray more furniture polish on the inside of the frame to get it lubricated well.

• **WINDOWS,** *Securing Wooden Frames:* Drill a hole about four to six inches above each bottom window section in the inside framework. Insert a bolt into each hole. The windows can be opened only four to six inches, not enough space for a burglar, and you can remove the bolts when you want to fully open the windows.

• **WINDOW SCREENS,** *Cleaning:* See SCREENS, Cleaning.

• **WINDOW SHADES,** *Cleaning:*
1. If the shades are washable, take them down, unroll and lay them on a flat surface. Dust with a clean cloth, wash with mild detergent suds and warm water. Rinse well, wipe dry and hang immediately.
2. If the shades are not washable, they should be cleaned by a professional cleaner; a clothing dry cleaner can recommend someone for you. Or, you can buy a dough-type wall cleaner at paint or wall-covering stores and follow the directions carefully. Always test cleaners on an inconspicuous place before doing a whole project.

• **WINDOW SHADES,** *Healthy-Planet Recycling:* Cut up old window shades for shelf and drawer liners; they are sturdy and free!

• **WINDOW WASHING,** *Homestyle Cleaner:* Add one-fourth cup non-sudsing ammonia to a gallon of water and wash away grime. **Hint:** Minimize streaking by waiting until the time of day when the sun isn't shining directly on the windows; heat causes windows to dry too quickly, leaving streaks behind. Also, you'll get less streaking if you wipe off surface dirt and dust with a damp cloth before washing.

• **WINDOW WASHING,** *Removing Water Spots:* To dissolve hardwater deposits on windows, spray full-strength white vinegar on the window, let it set, then wipe. Heavy deposits may require two or three applications and scrubbing with a stiff brush.

• **WINDSHIELD,** *Cleaning:* Fill a spray bottle with equal parts of rubbing alcohol and water; spritz, and wipe clean with soft cloth or paper towels.

• **WINE,** *Miscellaneous Information:* When you see tiny crystal-looking particles on the bottom of a wine cork, don't panic and think it's broken glass. Usually, these bits are malic acid crystals which have solidified and are evidence of an inferior, but not unwholesome, wine-making process.

• **WINE,** *Selection:* The rule of white wine with white meat and red wine with red meat may help you select wines for food but this rule isn't the final word because the characteristics of both recipes and wines differ greatly. For example, the heartier flavor in a poultry roast might be better enhanced by a dry, light-bodied red wine instead of the traditional white. Vinegar, citrus juice, and egg yolks (sulfur) can give wine an off-taste. Artichokes, asparagus, onions, pineapples, also can have an unpleasant effect on certain wine flavors.

• **WINE,** *Storage:* Wine that doesn't require aging or that will be consumed soon can be stored standing up for a short time, but wine to be aged should be stored lying down to keep the cork damp and prevent air from reaching the wine. If you buy a case of wine for a party, just place the case on its side in a cool basement or other cool dark place. (Wine rests better in the dark.)

• **WINE,** *Storage, General Hints:* Wine can "breathe" through the cork, so it can absorb cellar odors. Also, keep stored wine away from laundry or other vibrating equipment; aged wines especially don't like vibrations.

• **WINE,** *Storage, Humidity:* The best humidity level for wine storage is 75 percent. (Humidity keeps the corks from drying out and allowing wine to evaporate and spoil.)

• **WINE,** *Storage of Open Bottles:* Don't just cork a half-empty bottle of wine leftover from a meal and put it into the fridge. Pour it into a clean, empty half-sized bottle that you keep for this purpose, then cork and store. Leaving air space between the cork and the wine speeds up deterioration of the wine. (This air space is called "ullage" if you're a Scrabble player or just like to astound your guests!)

• **WINE,** *Storage, Temperatures:* Most wine experts say the ideal temperature for a wine cellar should be 55° to 60°F, with 45 to 70 degrees as the outer limits. Keeping the temperature constant is even more important than the exact temperature.

• **WINE BOX PLASTIC BAGS,** *Recycling:* Remove the plastic bag from the wine box, fill half to three-quarters full of water and freeze so that you have a non-drippy, square ice block for your picnic cooler. You can drink the water as it melts. Then, after it's empty, inflate the bag with air and you have a pillow to make snoozing in the car on the way home more comfortable. But not if you're the driver, of course!

• **WINDSHIELD,** *Quick-Fix Cleaning the Inside of It on the Road:* Squirt washer fluid from the automatic windshield washer on a paper towel or disposable towel and then wipe the inside of the windshield. If you can't reach the window cleaning mechanism while holding the paper towel, just lay the towel on the windshield before operating the cleaner; it should get enough of a squirt to do the job. **Note:** The car should be stopped to do this, but then you knew that.

• **WINDSHIELD FILM,** *Removing with Homestyle Cleaner:* Mix one part vinegar or one part non-sudsy ammonia (not both) to three parts water and clean the windshield with it.

• **WINDSHIELD WASHER FLUID,** *When It Gets Too Frozen to Flow in Winter Weather:* Carry a small spray bottle filled with windshield-washer fluid. Then you can spray the windshield while the wipers are running to clean it off before you drive.

• **WINDSHIELD WIPER BLADES,** *Stopping "Fingernail-on-the-blackboard" Squeaks:* If blades are worn down they will squeak and even scratch the windshield; replace them. If blades are in good condition, tree sap or road tar can cause squeaks and washing with a good commercial cleaner should solve the problem.

• **WIPES,** *Homemade $aver for Baby or Cosmetics:* Fill an old baby wipes container (or other container with a tight lid) with paper napkins to the top. In a separate bowl, mix thoroughly ½ cup of water, 1 tablespoon of baby oil, and 1 tablespoon of baby lotion. Pour the mixture over the napkins and cover tightly. You'll have fresh-scented wipes for baby or makeup removing.

• **WIRE HANGERS,** *Recycling:* Do they really breed in dark closets as one of my readers suggested? If you don't like wire hangers because you think they are too flimsy, tape several together with masking tape for sturdier hangers; add plastic clothespins to some for skirt and pants hangers.

• **WISHBONE, TURKEY OR CHICKEN,** *Quick-Fix Drying:* Microwave a roast turkey or chicken wishbone for a few seconds to dry it immediately for those whose wishes can't wait.

• **WOODEN BREAD BOXES,** *Odors and Recycling:* I've had many letters about "woody" odors in these boxes that even get into the bread stored in them. We've tried every conceivable method to remove the wood-smell without any luck at all. We use our box to store letters and I'm sure there are other uses. The alternative is to return it to the store for refund.

• **WOODEN SPOONS,** *Reseasoning:* After washing spoons in hot sudsy water, scrub if needed and rinse well. Wipe dry and allow to air-dry completely. Then heat some mineral oil (not vegetable oil which can get rancid in wood) over medium heat and dip the spoons in it until they are completely coated. Drain on paper towels (save towels, place one layer of towels over newspapers) until they are cool enough to handle. Wipe them off and they are ready to use.

• **WOOD FLOORS,** *Homestyle Cleaning:* It's always a good idea to check with a flooring specialist for information on cleaning wood floors because certain treated flooring requires specific cleaning methods. But one general wood-floor cleaner is a solution of ½ cup of apple-cider vinegar in 1 gallon of warm water. With a soft cloth or sponge mop with most of the moisture squeezed out, wipe the floor without getting it really wet. Then buff after cleaning to bring out the luster.

• **WOOD STOVE,** *Maintenance Checklist:* If you have a wood stove in your vacation cabin or home, it needs an annual tune-up that includes the following:
1. Chimney cleaning.
2. Thorough cleaning of the stove, including cleaning the secondary air chamber.
3. Install new door gaskets to keep the stove airtight.
4. Adjust the door latch, the thermostat and polish the griddle.

Hint: This chore can be done by a certified wood stove professional or with a tune-up kit sold by stove manufacturers.

• **WOOD STOVE WINDOWS**, *Removing Creosote from Glass:*
1. In an old bowl, put some wood ashes and add enough vinegar to get the consistency of a light paste. Apply it to the window and allow to soak.
2. With a wet cloth, remove the paste and the creosote should be gone.

• **WORKDAY**, *Letter of Laughter:* A dress department store clerk says her job is like working in a comedy club. One day as identical twins tried on dresses, one said to the other, "That looks terrific on you. I wish I could wear it, but the color looks awful on me." Proof that we all see ourselves differently than others do.

• **WORKDAY SURVIVAL HINTS:** Readers with jobs, children, gardens, and who also participate in community activities, offered their hints for organizing their lives.
1. Put in a laundry load before leaving for work and put it in the dryer when you return, or have a rule that the first person home loads the dryer.
2. Put children's jobs on a list with space at the bottom for "add-on" jobs. The list eliminates the need to nag, and children check off jobs as they are completed, thus getting the satisfaction of seeing what they've accomplished.
3. Teach children to make their own lunches and breakfasts. On weekends, make meals so that there are leftovers for Monday and Tuesday and nobody has to cook. Have each family member list their favorite foods and make each person's favorite at least once every other week or so to keep everyone happy and cooperative.
4. After dinner dishes are done, set the breakfast table and include any foods that don't require refrigeration (like cereals) to get a few steps ahead in the morning.
5. To keep lunch, bus, or milk money handy and to save time and tempers on hectic mornings, many families keep a change bowl by the door. They drop all change into the bowl each night and take what's needed in the morning.
6. Realize that few people can really "do it all." Hire someone such as a teenager to vacuum and dust once a week or hire a profes-

sional cleaning service to do the whole house thoroughly every few weeks.

• **WORKING,** *Hints for Success:*
1. Make decisions between 7 and 11 A.M.; depression and anxiety are lowest at this time. Worst time is between 2 and 8 P.M. when depression and anxiety are highest.
2. Do complex tasks midday or late afternoon when body temperature reaches its normal high point.
3. Ask for a raise over lunch when people are most agreeable. A three-year study by Johns Hopkins researchers found that more business contracts are signed over "power" lunches than at any other time.

• **WORKSHOP ORGANIZER,** *Recycling:* Cut about one-third off an aluminum pie plate and tack it to the wall with the bottom side out and you have a handy holder for sandpaper sheets, especially disks for your sander.

• **WORMS,** *For Fishing:* Keep them in a plastic hanging basket filled with good soil. The planter can hang outside, has good drainage, and the worms can't escape but stay buried until you can go fishing.

• **WRAPPING PAPER,** *Recycling Storage:* Roll on paper-towel tubes and put two or so rolls in a newspaper bag.

• **WREATHS,** *Hanging When You Can't Make Holes with Nails:* When metal doors and some landlords don't let you hang holiday wreaths and other door decorations, try a clear suction-cup hook. It will work better than you think, unless the wreath is very heavy.

• **WRINKLE-REMOVING FROM POLYESTER CLOTHING:** Try this. Dampen the garments, put them in a plastic bag and place them in the freezer for a few hours. Then, press with a steam iron while they're still frozen. Use a pressing cloth to avoid making the fabric shiny.

• **WRIST WARMERS,** *Children or Adults:* Exercise wristbands put over jacket sleeve and mitten/glove tops will keep sleeves and mittens together so that your arms and hands stay warm and dry for winter play or sports.

X

• **XYLOPHONE,** *Child's Toy:* When a child's xylophone makes a tinny noise that keeps your eardrums vibrating, replace the wooden sticks. Instead make new sticks by attaching a small rubber ball, like the kind on paddle-ball sets or from jacks, to a pencil or piece of doweling. You won't have a musical treat but the sound will still be muted enough to avoid a really bad headache. **Note:** This reminds me of a joking "curse" a friend of mine used to place on people who annoyed her. It's "May all your children get drums for Christmas (or Chanukah)."

Y

• **YARN HOLDER:** Plastic six-pack rings will hold looped yarn strands or partial skeins of yarn so that they can be stored or carried neatly.

• **YARN SCRAPS,** *Recycling:* Save small lengths of yarn from needlework and craft projects so that you can loop the yarn on gift tags and tie them on package ribbons. Don't forget to make the gift tags from the fronts of old greeting cards for total recycling!

• **YOGURT,** *Flavoring Plain/Low-fat:* Add fruit, jam, vanilla, or other flavoring (about a ½ teaspoon per cup according to your taste). Vanilla yogurt is a delicious low-cal and nutritious dressing for sliced fruit. I have a dieting friend who adds plain cocoa, vanilla, and sweetener to non-fat yogurt when she has an attack of the munchies and finds that she's consumed all but her allocated calories of milk for that day. It's not ice cream or pudding, but it stops the cravings!

• **YOGURT "CREAM CHEESE,"** *Easy-Fix:* Place a coffee filter in a strainer and empty a container of low-fat or non-fat yogurt into the filter. Place the strainer over a bowl and refrigerate overnight. By morning the liquid will have separated from the solids. Mix with fruit, honey, wheat germ, vanilla, or a bit of sugar for flavoring; then, spread on whole-grain toast or bagel for a nutritious and tasty, low-cholesterol breakfast.

• **YOGURT CUPS,** *Recycling:*
1. Store small bits and pieces like paper clips, thumbtacks, rubber bands, nails, screws, and pins.
2. Save lids and cups, wash well and use for children's or dieter's individual ice-cream portions to avoid mess from large cartons and tempting the dieter to take more than allowed.
3. They are free drinking cups for kids at picnics and in bathrooms (personalize cups for reuse by family members until the cup gets yucky; then dispose of it).
4. Small yogurt cups can be ½- or 1-cup measuring cups; quart-size could be a measure for a dog's daily "dose" of dry food.
5. When packing lunches, they will hold chips, small cookies, grapes, and other fruits (no more squashed plums) and goodies that get crushed in a lunch bag.

Z

• **ZIPPER,** *Quick-Fix, Freeing One Stuck in a Boot Flap:* When this happened to me, I cut a small slit in the leather just above the zipper, then slid the zipper to the top to free it and back to the bottom.

• **ZIPPER,** *Quick-Fix for Stuck One:* Rub the teeth with dry bar soap or candle and zip!

• **ZIPPER PULL,** *Quick-Fixes Emergency Replacement:* If the movable zipper part has a hole on either side, a small paper clip or safety pin can replace the pull tab.

• **ZIPPER PULLS,** *Recycling:* When luggage, handbag, or other zippers are hard to grasp, attach a key chain (especially those brightly colored promotional key chains that accumulate in desk drawers); the remaining "dangles" of unmated earrings; other pieces of costume jewelry; charms; or even a loop made from a piece of leather thong or shoelace.

• **ZUCCHINI,** *Freezing the Inevitable Surplus:* Grate zucchini in a food processor and pack the pulp in freezer bags in portions for making zucchini bread or other recipes later in the year.

• **ZZZZ,** *Seven Things to Do When You Can't Sleep:*

1. Keep regular hours and bedtime routines.

2. Avoid caffeinated beverages for six to eight hours before bedtime. If you smoke, be aware that nicotine is an even stronger stimulant than caffeine. Alcoholic beverages can hamper your falling asleep easily and sleeping soundly, once you doze off.

3. Afternoon naps and sleeping too many hours at night can interfere with falling asleep.

4. If worries and distractions keep you awake, make "to-do" lists for the next day so that you don't worry about forgetting something as you try to nod off.

5. Keep a note pad and pen next to the bed so that you can jot down last minute thoughts on paper instead of keeping them inside your head where they keep you awake.

6. Starving or stuffing yourself can keep you awake. You can't settle down if a too empty digestive system is rumbling and a too full one is stressed.

7. Mother was right! A glass of warm milk at bedtime really does help—unless, of course, you are lactose-intolerant and can't drink it because it won't digest! Then, a nice hot cup of herbal or spiced tea—a tea without caffeine, of course—can sooth some people as much as the traditional warm milk.

SPOTS AND STAINS

Since spots and stains have a way of showing up when we don't always have exactly the right stuff needed to deal with them, I'm including as many ways to remove each type of spot or stain as I have in my files; some are Quick-Fix and some methods take several steps. Some methods allow full-strength applications of alcohol, vinegar, ammonia, non-iodized salt, etc., and others require diluting them. Let the fabric's sturdiness or delicacy be your guide.

Caution: With all spot removal techniques, ALWAYS test on an inconspicuous place to make sure the method won't harm fabric or fade colors. Of course, if a garment is useless unless a stubborn spot is removed, it won't hurt to try a variety of homemade remedies. However, when in doubt with your better garments, take them to a professional laundry/dry cleaner for advice and help.

• PROBLEMS A DRY CLEANER CAN'T SOLVE:
1. Some stains can't be removed without ruining the garment.
2. Some colors bleed even in dry cleaning. "Bleeding" occurs when manufacturers don't thoroughly test dyes.
3. Some fabrics may shrink during dry cleaning because some manufacturers don't pre-shrink materials used in making the garment.

4. Holes or tears can appear after the dry-cleaning process if the fabric has been damaged by insects or acid spills. While they don't show up prior to cleaning, weakened fibers fray or come apart during the cleaning process.

5. Excess shine caused by home ironing can't be removed by dry cleaning. Place a cloth over such fabrics or iron on the wrong side, which is a good idea for all dark colors no matter what the fabric type.

6. When working on spots, blot instead of rubbing which spreads the stain and may damage the fabric, especially silk.

- **GENERAL STAIN REMOVAL RULES:**

1. Fresh stains are easier to remove; old and set stains may not come out at all.

2. Before treating a stain, find out what kind of stain it is, the type of fabric and if it is colorfast (see label), and how old the stain is. Ordinary machine washing and drying will set some stains permanently.

3. Generally, you start with cold or warm water; hot water sets some stains.

4. When bleach is recommended, use a bleach appropriate to that fabric. Chlorine bleaches must be diluted for stain treatment.

5. Test stain removers on an inside seam or hidden area to make sure the fabric won't be damaged or the color won't fade.

6. Putting the stained area facedown on a paper towel or white cloth and then applying the stain remover to the BACK of the stain can force the stain off the fabric instead of into it.

7. Protein stains are easier to remove if you break them down with meat tenderizer or enzyme pre-soaks.

8. Always use dry-cleaning solvents in well-ventilated rooms.

- **ACNE MEDICATIONS WITH BENZOYL PEROXIDE:** Benzoyl peroxide can destroy fabric dyes permanently. To avoid damage to T-shirts, towels, and other garments (even wall paint when you grope for a towel!): after applying the medication, rinse off carefully and wash hands thoroughly to remove any residue before you handle or touch fabrics. **Hint:** Dry face and hands with white towels and switch to white bedding during application periods so that colored towels and sheets don't get ruined. It only takes a bit of this medication to bleach fabrics.

• **ALCOHOLIC BEVERAGES:**
Method 1, Washable Fabrics: Soak or sponge stain promptly with cool water; sponge with white household vinegar and rinse. If stain remains, rub in liquid laundry detergent, rinse, and launder as usual. See BEER, and WINE, SOFT DRINKS.

• **ANTIPERSPIRANT/DEODORANT:** Ironing may set these stains.
Method 1, Light Stains: Rub in undiluted liquid detergent and then launder with hottest water safe for fabric.
Method 2, Heavy Stains: Place stain facedown on a paper towel and sponge the back of the stain (on outside of garment) with dry-cleaning solvent, let dry, rinse. Rub in undiluted liquid detergent and launder with hottest water safe for fabric.
Method 3, Fresh Perspiration Stains: Apply diluted ammonia to the stains and rinse with water. For old stains, try applying white vinegar and rinse with water or launder.
Method 4: Before washing the garment, rinse the area with plain water, then wash with the rest of your laundry in either warm or hot water with good suds.
Method 5: Soak in warm water with enzyme pre-soak product. Wash in hottest water safe for fabric. If stain remains, dampen and sprinkle stain with meat tenderizer. Let stand 30 minutes to an hour. Launder again.
Method 6: If stain remains after Method 5, treat with non-flammable dry-cleaning solvent, then rub detergent into the stain, and launder.
Hint 1: Avoid buildup by washing garments in hottest water safe for fabric every third or fourth time.
Hint 2: If you allow your deodorant to dry completely before you dress, it may help to prevent stains from some brands.
Hint 3: If you want to use a non-staining natural deodorant, try dabbing/dusting your underarm area with plain baking soda.
Note: Also, please see PERSPIRATION in this section.

• **ARTIST'S OILS ON CLOTHING:** Turpentine removes oil paint but can discolor some fabrics. Try removing artist's oil paint with bar face soap. **Note:** You can even clean your brushes with bar soap. Put the soap and brush under warm running water and rub the brush into the soap from side to side, making sure the soap goes all the way up the bristles. Gently rub the soap through the bristles with your fingers until all the paint is removed. Rinse with clear warm water, squeezing out the excess soap.

• **BALLPOINT INK:**
Method 1, Washable Fabrics: Hair spray or rubbing alcohol will usually remove ballpoint ink from washable fabrics. Don't spray directly on the stain; lightly spot clean it with a cloth dampened with either solution. Keep paper towels under the stain and change them frequently because the ink bleeds when in contact with alcohol. Rub liquid laundry detergent directly into remaining stain and launder as usual.
Method 2, Washable Fabrics: Apply hair spray until wet or sponge stain with rubbing alcohol as in Method 1. Flush with solution of 1 teaspoon detergent to 1 quart warm water; rinse in cool water; launder as usual. Apply glycerine to tough stains before washing.
Method 3, Dry-cleanable Fabrics: To home treat, place a blotter under the stained area; drip a compatible dry-cleaning fluid through it; reapply if needed. As always, be sure to tell the dry cleaner what caused the stain and how you treated it if you attempted to remove it yourself.

• **BEER:** Apply hydrogen peroxide to dried stains on white cotton; sponge stains on colored fabrics with white vinegar.

• **BLOOD ON FABRIC:** Getting to this stain ASAP (as soon as possible or sooner than possible is the key). Always avoid hot water; heat sets blood stains.
Method 1, Washable Fabrics: Apply pre-wash stain remover. Or, soak in cold water for one-half hour. If stain is stubborn, rub with detergent and rinse. Really stubborn stains can sometimes be removed with a mixture of 1 tablespoon ammonia and 1 cup water applied to stain. Rinse well before washing with chlorine bleach. Avoid hot water, it sets the stain.
Method 2, Dry-cleanable Fabrics: If you can't get the garment to the dry cleaner immediately, try treating the stain with a solution of 1 ounce table salt to 1 quart cold water. The salt may help prevent color bleeding. Rinse areas and blot with towel. Warm water and

hydrogen peroxide may remove final traces of the stain on some white fabrics.

Method 3: Soak stain in cold water immediately. If stain remains, pour 3 percent hydrogen peroxide over stained area. Test first, peroxide removes color.

Method 4: Dampen stained area with cold water; sprinkle with unseasoned meat tenderizer and let set. You may need to repeat the method until all traces of the stain are removed; then wash as usual.

Method 5: If fabric is bleachable, douse with hydrogen peroxide or diluted ammonia before rinsing in cool water.

• **BRASS/COPPER TARNISH:** Rub into the stain a paste made as follows: Mix together equal parts salt and flour, then add white vinegar to make a paste. You may have to repeat applications.

• **BUBBLE GUM,** *Removing:* While bubble gum is not really a stain, it certainly is a blemish when it's stuck to clothing, hair, furniture, etc. Tried and true is to rub with a small amount of peanut butter and the gum slides off. However, the surface should be washable for this method. **Note:** Please see CHEWING GUM.

• **BUTTER, MARGARINE:** Please see GREASY STAINS and OIL STAINS.

• **CANDLE WAX AND CRAYONS:**
Method 1, Washable Fabrics: Remove surface wax with dull knife; place stain between paper towels and press with warm iron, replacing towels frequently to absorb more wax. Then place stain facedown on clean paper towels and sponge the back of the stain with dry-cleaning solvent. Let dry, then launder. If traces of color remain, wash again with chlorine bleach, if fabric is bleach safe. Otherwise soak in enzyme detergent or an oxygen bleach in hottest water safe for fabric; then launder.

Method 2, Washable Fabric: Rub with ice cube to harden wax before scraping it off with a blunt knife. Place stained area between paper towels or brown paper bags and iron, changing absorbent papers and repeating until all wax is melted off. Sponge away remaining stains with dry-cleaning fluid.

Method 3, Dry-cleanable Fabric: Same as above for washable items. Please see CRAYON entries for more crayon stain removal methods.

- **CANVAS SHOES,** *Stain Prevention:* Spray with stain-resistant fabric spray before the first wearing. They'll be easier to clean. Repeat spraying if they are washed.

- **CARBON PAPER:** Dampen area and rub liquid laundry detergent into the stain. Hand wash garment in warm, soapy water, rinse, and repeat steps if needed until stain is removed, then launder as usual.

- **CATSUP/TOMATO SAUCE:** Dab off excess and soak garment in cold water for 30 minutes. Rub liquid laundry detergent or white bar soap into remaining stain while still wet. Then launder in warm water and detergent.

- **CHEWING GUM:**
Method 1, Washable Fabrics: Rub with ice cube to harden gum before scraping it off with a blunt knife. Place fabric facedown on paper towels and sponge remaining stain with dry-cleaning fluid or treat with pre-wash spray, and then launder.
Method 2, Dry-cleanable Fabrics: Same as for washable items, except don't launder.
Method 3: Rub area with ice until gum hardens and can be removed as in Method 1, then place waxed paper over excess gum and iron lightly over paper; changing paper as gum sticks to it.

- **CHOCOLATE:**
Method 1: Soak garment for at least 30 minutes in cold water. Rub liquid laundry detergent into the stain while still wet. Rinse. If a greasy stain remains, sponge area with cleaning fluid, then rinse and launder in warm water. Bleach will remove some stubborn chocolate stains, but use only with colorfast clothing.
Method 2: Soak in warm or cold water. Brush area with a paste of detergent and hot water. Remove remaining grease stains with non-flammable dry-cleaning solvent.

- **CLEANING FLUID RINGS:** Sometimes, these can be steamed out if the garment is held over a tea kettle. **Caution:** Steam can burn; put the garment, not your hands, over the steam spout!

- **COFFEE OR TEA:**
Method 1, Washable Fabrics: Sponge with cold water. Simple washing will usually remove black coffee or tea stains. You can also

sponge the stain with dry-cleaning fluid if you've used cream in your coffee or tea.

Method 2, Dry-cleanable Fabrics: Treat the same as washables.

Method 3: Immediately rinse area well in cold water. Treat stain with pre-wash spray and launder in warm water and detergent. Allow garment to drip-dry to make sure all traces of stain are gone. (Dryer heat will set stains.) If necessary, repeat all steps.

Method 4: Wipe clean with a paste made from baking soda and water or non-iodized salt and white vinegar.

• COFFEE STAINS ON FABRIC, *When They Reappear:* Because they contain tannin, coffee and tea may cause a stain that seems to disappear after washing but returns later. When these stains set too long, they may be impossible to remove. It's best to take the garment to a dry cleaner and point out the stain so that a professional can treat it with special chemicals.

• COLORED GARMENTS, *Brightening Dull Colors:*
1. Black Clothing and Stockings: Rinse in clear water to which a couple of glugs of vinegar have been added.
2. Colored Fabrics and Embroidery Cottons: Set colors by soaking washables in a strong salt water before first laundering.
3. Avoid dulling Colors: Wash fluorescent colors separately and same colored clothing together. And always follow care directions for water temperature and bleach use or non-use.

• COSMETICS:
Method 1, Washable Fabrics: Dampen stain with detergent until outline is gone, and rinse well. If safe for the fabric, a few drops of ammonia, followed by a good rinse may work on stubborn stains.
Method 2, Dry-cleanable Fabrics: Sponge dry-cleanables with dry-cleaning fluid.
Method 3, General Spot Removal: Wet stain and rub bar soap into it. If the stain remains, use regular liquid detergent. Gently work it into the stain and then wash the garment as usual.

• CRAYON, *When Clothing Has Gone Through the Dryer:* Spray liberally both sides of the stain with petroleum-based pre-wash stain remover, and rub it into the fabric with your fingers. Let stand for a while and wash as usual. You may have to repeat the process two or three times. If stains remain on bleach-safe fabric, follow directions on the bottle or box for the amount to use for removing stains from that fabric. If there is any wax on the dryer drum, dampen a small cloth with the spray and wipe out the drum.

• CRAYON/CANDLE WAX, *General Stain Removal:* Scrape off excess wax with dull knife; sponge with non-flammable dry cleaning solvent; launder.

• CRAYON STAINS, *When a Crayon Has Gone Through the Wash Cycles in a Pocket:* Try this: Rub all crayon stains with waterless hand cleaner, then wash the garment in cold water with detergent but after the wash cycle, stop the machine and let the garment soak overnight. In the morning complete the wash cycle. If some spots still remain, repeat scrubbing the spots with waterless hand cleaner and a scrub brush.

• CRAYON STAINS, *Whole Load of Clothes:* First wash with hot water and laundry soap, such as mild baby-clothes soap, and 1 cup baking soda. If color remains, launder with chlorine bleach if fabrics are bleach safe. Otherwise soak in enzyme detergent or oxygen bleach in hottest water that's safe for fabric and then launder.

• CREAM, MILK, ICE CREAM: Sponge with non-flammable dry-cleaning solvent.

• DEODORANTS, Please see ANTIPERSPIRANT/DEODORANT and PERSPIRATION.

• DYE TRANSFER:
Method 1, Whites: Fabric color remover, used according to directions, may remove dye that has "bled" on white fabrics. Launder after treatment. If dye remains, launder again using chlorine bleach if safe for fabric.
Method 2, Colored Fabrics, Non-Bleachable Whites: Soak in enzyme detergent or an oxygen bleach, then launder.

• DYE TRANSFER, *On White Collar of Colored Sweater:* You can try a color remover just on the color but if it doesn't work, return the garment for replacement or refund.

• FABRIC SOFTENER SHEETS, *On Polyester Silk-Look Garments:* Wet the area, then rub stain with white bar soap or liquid laundry detergent. Rinse well, let air-dry. If necessary, repeat cleaning steps and launder in hottest water safe from fabric. Make sure all the stains are gone before placing the garment in the dryer because dryer heat can set them permanently. It's better to air-dry the garment to avoid having the dryer heat set the stain permanently. **Note:** Too few or too many clothes in the dryer can cause these stains, as well as too high a heat setting. If you are only drying one or two garments in the dryer with a fabric softener sheet, add some lightweight bath towels. **Hint:** Certain polyester fabrics seem especially prone to this problem. Try saving old softener sheets and using the old sheets instead of new sheets with fabrics you think might absorb the softener. Or, just avoid the dryer altogether!

• **FRUITS, FRUIT JUICES, BERRIES: Caution:** don't use soap to treat fruit stains; it sets them.
Method 1: Soak immediately for about 30 minutes in cold water. Rub some detergent into the stain while it's still wet. Wash as usual. If this treatment doesn't work, apply hydrogen peroxide if the garment is bleach-safe, then rinse well.
Method 2, Washable Fabric: Soak. If stain remains, apply white vinegar and rinse; stubborn stains may need application of hydrogen peroxide.
Method 3, Dry-cleanable Fabric: Apply a small amount of detergent on the stain and rinse if the fabric allows, or sponge with dry-cleaning fluid.
Method 4: Soak immediately in cool water; wash. If stain remains, cover area with a paste made from oxygen-type bleach, a few drops of hot water and a few drops of ammonia; wait 15 to 30 minutes; wash.

• **GENERAL STAINS IN HOTELS AND RESTAURANTS:**
Quick-Fix 1: Rub stain with bar soap and wash/rinse. Or, use hotel shampoo on the stain and for washing garments.
Quick-Fix 2: Some liquid hand soaps in restaurants can be used to quick clean a spill. (Spots are one reason to always carry a purse. If you want to conceal the wet spot, you can always hold your purse or a stole over it until it dries.)
Quick-Fix 3: Apply tried-and-true club soda, especially to wine stains. At home clean as usual for that fabric.

- **GRASS, FLOWERS, FOLIAGE STAINS:**
Method 1, Washable Fabrics: If you have no pre-wash stain remover, work detergent into the stain and rinse; then launder in hottest water safe for fabric.
Method 2, Washable Fabrics: Try sponging the stain with one part alcohol to two parts water and rinse. If stain persists try applying hydrogen peroxide.
Method 3: Apply rubbing alcohol liberally to stained areas before laundering as usual.
Method 4, Dry-cleanable Fabrics: If the garment is dry-cleanable only, you probably shouldn't be wearing it gardening but if you did, it may be safe to apply alcohol or sponge with dry-cleaning fluid.
Method 5, Acetate Fabrics: Sponge with non-flammable dry-cleaning solvent.

- **GREASE ON TABLECLOTH:** Sprinkle talcum powder or cornstarch over the stain. As the grease is absorbed, add more powder until no more grease is absorbed; brush it off. Treat the remaining stain with pre-wash spray and wash in the hottest water safe for the fabric. Before putting the cloth in the dryer, check the spot to make sure it doesn't need a second treatment.

- **GREASY STAINS** (Car Grease or Oil, Butter, Margarine, Lard, Salad Dressings, Cooking Oils):
Method 1: Pre-treat with heavy-duty liquid laundry detergent or pre-wash spray or liquid. Launder.
Method 2, Heavy Stains: Place stained areas facedown on paper towels. Apply dry-cleaning solvent to back side of stain, replacing towels frequently. Allow to dry, then rub in liquid detergent or dampen stain area with water, and rub with bar soap or detergent paste. Rinse and launder.
Method 3: Gently rub in talcum powder, cornmeal, or cornstarch and let set. Later, brush or sponge powder away. Please see OIL ON FABRIC.

- **GUM:** Please see CHEWING GUM.

- **ICE CREAM:** Soak garment in cold water; hand wash in warm soapy water and rinse. If a greasy stain remains or if the ice cream was chocolate, sponge the stain with cleaning fluid. After all traces of stain are gone, launder as usual.

- **INKS: Caution:** Regular laundering removes some types of ink but sets others. If you have doubts, take a good garment to a professional. Also, some inks require a color remover and some permanent inks can't be removed.

Method 1: Pre-treat first by placing stain facedown on paper towels and then sponging the back of stain with alcohol or dry-cleaning solvent. If some ink remains, rub with bar soap; rinse; launder.

Method 2: Dampen stain with water and rub with bar soap. Rinse. Soak in enzyme detergent or oxygen bleach in hottest water safe for fabric; launder. If stain remains, launder again with chlorine bleach if safe for fabric.

Method 3, Dried Ink Stains: Rub non-iodized table salt in and dribble lemon juice over the salt. Launder after stain is gone.

Method 4, Old Wives' Tale That Works on Some Fabrics: Soak ink spots in warm milk before they can dry. Then launder as usual.

- **IODINE:** Rinse from underside of stain with cool water. Soak in solution of color remover, rinse, and launder.

- **IRON RUST:** Moisten the stain with water, apply lemon juice, then rinse. You may have to repeat the treatment several times to get the stain out. Hanging a lemon-juice treated item out in bright sun sometimes makes the lemon juice work better. **Caution:** Lemon juice will lighten certain colors. Test the juice on an inconspicuous place on the garment before using it. Of course, if you can't wear the garment with the rust stain, a bleach spot isn't going to matter much.

- **LIPSTICK:**

Method 1: Place stain facedown on paper towels. Sponge back of stain with dry-cleaning solvent, replacing the paper towel underneath frequently so that color can be absorbed. Dampen stain with water and rub with bar soap, rinse, and launder.

Method 2: Immediately, place stained area over absorbent towel and saturate with rubbing alcohol, then rub area with cloth dipped in rubbing alcohol. (Test for color-fastness before using alcohol.) Rinse and launder after all traces of stain are removed.

Method 3: Try pre-wash spray before laundering as usual.

Method 4: Sponge with non-flammable dry-cleaning solvent; launder white fabrics with diluted chlorine bleach or launder colored fabrics with oxygen-type bleach.

- **MAKEUP/FOUNDATION:**

Method 1, Powdered or Water-based Makeup: It's non-greasy and so can be removed by dampening the area and rubbing stain with white bar soap. Rinse and launder.

Method 2, Oily Makeup: Treat with pre-wash spray, then dampen the area and rub to work stain out. After all stain is gone, rinse and launder in hottest water safe for fabric.

- **MASCARA:**

1. Oil-based Mascara: Apply pre-wash spray or stick directly to the stain and machine wash.

2. Water-based Mascara: Try liquid detergent or dampen the area and rub with a bar of soap until suds form. When the outline of the stain has disappeared, rinse thoroughly. You may have to repeat the process.

3. Waterproof Mascara: Some waterproof mascara is impossible to remove.

- **MATTRESS "ACCIDENT,"** *Removing Urine Stain:*

1. Immediately (before the area dries) try to absorb as much of the urine as possible with dry towels. Sponge the stained area with a solution of half vinegar and half water to clean the stain. Again, remove as much of the moisture as possible with dry towels, or dry with hair dryer on "Low" or "Cool."

2. If the stained area has dried, try to keep it from getting larger by rubbing the stain from the outside in toward the center with upholstery shampoo. If the outer ring is still present, repeat the process.

3. After the mattress has dried, spray it with an air freshener made for fabrics to help prevent a musty or urine odor. If you can, place the mattress outside in the fresh air and sunshine to air it out.

4. As with all stains, immediate treatment gets the best results. **Note:** If you fail to remove the stain but are able to remove the odor so that the mattress is still sleepable, cover the mattress with a zippered fabric mattress cover available in many catalogs.

- **MEAT-JUICE, EGG:** Soak in cold or warm water with enzyme presoak. Treat grease stains with non-flammable dry-cleaning solvent. Then wash.

- **MILDEW:** Old mildew stains are almost impossible to remove and mildew fungus can destroy or weaken fabrics. **Hint:** When brushing mildew off garments or items, take them outdoors to prevent the spores from becoming airborne and setting up housekeeping elsewhere in the house.

Method 1: Launder with chlorine bleach if it's safe for the fabric, if not, soak in oxygen bleach for 15 to 30 minutes, and then launder.

Method 2, Bleachable Fabrics: Brush with a stiff brush to remove mold spores and soak in solution of 1 tablespoon of chlorine bleach to 1 quart water for 15 minutes. Rinse and launder, adding ½ cup chlorine bleach to wash cycle.

Method 3, Non-bleachable Fabrics: Brush with stiff brush to remove mold spores. Flush the stain with solution of ½ cup lemon juice and 1 tablespoon of salt. Dry garment in the sun. After stain is removed, launder as usual.

Method 4, Walls and Floors: Scrub with a brush dipped in borax and water.

Method 5, Books and Papers: Dust with talcum powder, cornmeal, or cornstarch; let set two days; brush off.

- **MILK:** Albumin, a protein in milk, is the culprit.

Method 1, Fresh Stains: Soak clothing for several hours in water to which detergent containing enzymes has been added. Launder as usual.

Method 2, Milk, Baby Formula: Soak garment in cold water. Rub liquid laundry detergent into stain and then launder in hottest water safe for fabric with enzyme detergent. If a greasy stain remains, sponge area with cleaning fluid and launder again before drying in clothes dryer. **Hint:** When you have a baby, it's handy to keep a diaper pail for soaking stained clothing. Then you can use a no-hands approach—empty the pail into the washer, put it on "Spin" to remove excess water, then run the wash cycle as usual.

- **MUD:** Allow to dry, then brush off excess dirt and spot clean with detergent or shampoo, and launder in cold water.

- **MUSTARD:**

Method 1: Dampen area and rub liquid laundry detergent into stain. Rinse, then soak in hot water and detergent for several hours. Launder with enzyme detergent.

Method 2: Apply pre-wash spray or liquid, or dampen stain with water and rub with bar soap. Rinse and launder with chlorine bleach if safe for fabric. If not, soak in enzyme detergent or oxygen bleach in hottest water safe for fabric; then launder. You may have to repeat the process.

Method 3: Soak stained area with diluted ammonia before laundering.

Method 4: Immediately rinse in cold water. Wash with hot soapy water with chlorine bleach if fabric is bleachable. Use oxygen-type bleach for laundering colored fabrics.

• **MYSTERY STAINS:** Flush with cold water; apply pre-wash spray and rub into stain. After all traces of stain are removed, launder as usual. These stains are usually water soluble if caught in time.

• **NAIL POLISH:**
Method 1: Test garment for color-fastness and fabric safety for acetone use. If it's okay, sponge stain with pure acetone. After removing entire stain, launder. **Caution:** Acetone will dissolve acetate and triacetate in fabrics. Amyl acetate is safe for acetate fabrics.

Method 2: Place stain facedown on paper towels. Sponge back with nail-polish remover, frequently replacing the towels beneath the stain. Repeat sponging until stain is gone. Launder. **Caution:** Do not use nail-polish remover on acetate or Arnel fabrics. Send them to the dry cleaner.

• **OIL ON FABRIC:**
Method 1, Quick-Fix for Fresh Spots: Salad oil dribble on your shirt or blouse? Apply baby powder to the spots, wipe it off, apply more, and let it set a while. Wipe powder away before laundering.

Method 2, Oil on Washable Fabric, Quick-Fix When Away from Home: In an emergency, toothpaste will remove oil on polyester, cotton and blends but you must apply it carefully because too much rubbing can damage fabric or color. **Caution:** Don't try this on silks or dry-cleanables.

Method 3, Quick-Fix: Rub white chalk into the stain before laundering. Chalk's easy to carry in a purse or bag. **Note:** Please see GREASY STAINS.

• **PAINT:** Check label on the can for instructions.
Method 1, Oil Base: Generally, you can remove oil-base paint with a bit of turpentine or paint thinner if the fabric is color safe; rinse well. Then rub with detergent paste and wash as usual.

Method 2, Oil-base Paint, Varnish: Apply solvent recommended on the paint container. If container is not available, apply turpentine. Rinse, then rub with bar soap. Rinse again, then launder.

Method 3, Paint Thinned with Solvents: Dab solvent onto the stained area. After wetting stain with solvent, work liquid laundry detergent into the area and soak the garment in hot water. Launder as usual.

Method 4, Oil-base Paint: Scrape off fresh paint. Sponge with non-flammable dry-cleaning solvent. Launder.

Method 5, Water-base Paint: If treated immediately, water-base paints may wash out with soap and water. After it has set and dried, water-base paint cannot be removed. Rinse the stain well in warm water to flush out paint, and then launder as usual.

• PENCIL LEAD: Try to gently erase as much of the lead as possible with a pencil eraser. Then rub liquid laundry detergent into remaining stain and launder as usual.

• PERFUME: Please see ALCOHOLIC BEVERAGES and use the same instructions.

• PERSPIRATION: The International Fabricare Institute says that these stains result when you apply a large amount of deodorant and then wash the garment with cold "hard" water (high-mineral, low-alkaline water). Many deodorants and antiperspirants contain aluminum salts. When combined with laundry detergent and cold water, the salts cannot be easily dissolved and so they remain on the fabric. Please see ANTIPERSPIRANT/DEODORANT for removal instructions.

• PET STAINS:
Method 1: Soak stained area in warm soapy water. If stains remain after soaking, sponge with solution of equal parts water and white household vinegar which will also help to neutralize remaining odors. Rinse well and launder as usual.

Method 2: Dampen area with equal parts of white vinegar and water; blot dry.

• PLAY PUTTY: Remove putty by rubbing liquid detergent into the spot from the underside of the fabric; scrub well. While this should remove the putty, a stain may remain. Try sponging diluted hydrogen peroxide onto the area. Always test in an inconspicuous spot first because peroxide can remove color.

• **REDDISH-TINGED AREA ON GARMENT:** This can be an acid color change, usually due to perspiration or deodorants, fruit juices, and some beverages. These areas are not noticeable immediately; instead they develop gradually when the staining substance remains on the fabric. Clothing should be washed or dry-cleaned often to avoid this problem. Depending upon how long the stain has been on the fabric, a dry cleaner may be able to minimize or neutralize the discoloration. As with all stains, removal is more likely to occur if the garment is cleaned immediately.

• **RING AROUND THE COLLAR:** Rub ring with hair shampoo, prewash spray or liquid laundry detergent. Let set for 30 minutes and launder as usual. You may need hottest water safe for the fabric to remove collar rings. AVOID the problem—it helps if you wipe your neck with astringent (or rubbing alcohol) before dressing, especially if you are in a big city where the air is polluted from traffic and industry.

• **RUST ON LAUNDRY,** *When You Frequently Find Rust Spots on Whole Loads of Laundry:*
1. Sometimes laundry soap has a chemical reaction with certain local water supplies—usually due to iron or manganese in the water. Dirt and soil are washed out but a new substance—the detergent and the soil—is redeposited into the garment; it looks like rust spots. Change laundry detergent. When iron is in your water supply, use extra detergent plus a non-precipitating water conditioner. Dissolve the detergent and water conditioner in warm water before adding it to the washer to get best results. You may also want to consider installing a water softener, chemical feeder, or special filters to remove iron and manganese from the water supply. Also, avoid overloading the washer—clothes should move freely with enough water to rinse away all deposits.
2. Rust stains can also be caused by a rusty water heater or rusty water lines. **Note:** Your local water company or a water-quality company can test your lines for iron or manganese (rust) content.

• **RUST SPOTS,** *Removing:* **Caution:** Do not use chlorine bleach on rust; it spreads the stain and sets it. Commercial rust removers for fabric use are available in the fabric dye sections of the supermarket. But, never use rust remover inside a washer and be careful not to spill any on a washer; it removes the glossy finish on porcelain outside or inside the machine.

Method 1, Few Spots: Apply commercial rust-stain remover; rinse and launder.

Method 2: Dampen stain with lemon juice and sprinkle on non-iodized table salt. Lay garment in the sunshine and continue to dampen area with lemon juice until the stain is gone. Then launder.

Method 3, Rusty Discoloration on White Load: Wash in phosphate detergent, if available, with 1 cup enzyme detergent or an oxygen bleach. If stains remain, dissolve 1 ounce oxalic acid crystals per gallon of water in a plastic container. Soak clothes in this solution for 10 to 15 minutes. Rinse and launder.

• **SALAD DRESSINGS:** Please see GREASY STAINS.

• **SCORCH MARKS: Note:** Severe scorch marks cannot be removed.
Method 1: Launder with chlorine bleach if safe for fabric.

Method 2, Non-bleachable Fabrics: Soak in strong solution of enzyme detergent or oxygen bleach in hottest water safe for fabric; then launder.

Method 3, Color-fast Fabrics: 3 percent hydrogen peroxide fades light scorch marks. After testing fabric for color-fastness, dab 3 percent hydrogen peroxide on scorched area with clean white cloth. Apply until scorch mark fades.

Method 4: Alternate rubbing the area with a lemon slice, then wiping with a dampened sponge until the stain disappears.

Method 5, Delicate Fabrics: Rub scorch marks lightly with a clean white cloth dampened with white vinegar. Wipe the area (don't rub) with a clean, dry cloth. Press if needed.

• **SHOE DYE/POLISH ON OFF-WHITE HOSE:** Soak the discolored section of the hose in rubbing alcohol and wash as usual. You may need to use a color-remover; if so, treat the entire pair because it may change the overall appearance. **Hint:** To keep dye from bleeding onto hose, spray the inside of the shoes several times with a fabric-protector spray; re-spray occasionally.

• **SHOE POLISH:** **Note:** Some shoe polishes won't come out. Try dampening the stain with cleaning fluid, then wash in warm water and detergent.

• **SILK FABRIC STAINS:** **Caution:** Do not attempt to remove spill-stains from silk by rubbing the area with a damp cloth. Silk fibers break easily when wet; blot instead of rubbing.
1. Beverage spills may disappear when the fabric dries but sugar in some beverages may cause a yellow stain that appears later. To avoid problems, take silk garments to the dry cleaner as soon as possible and tell what was spilled where.
2. Perspiration and body oils are silk's worst enemies; wear dress shields or spray the underarm areas with fabric protector spray to prevent stains and maintain all silk garments with regular dry cleaning or hand washing.
3. If there is a chafed area that has lost its color or luster, point this out to the dry cleaner who may be able to then give the item a special restoration bath.

• **STICKY RESIDUE,** *From Gummed Name Stickers, etc.:* Carefully dab with rubbing alcohol, petroleum based pre-wash spray, or cleaning fluid—whichever is suitable for the fabric.

• **SUGARED BEVERAGES, COFFEE, FRUIT JUICE, TEA:** Must be treated when fresh because they become more difficult to remove as they age and almost impossible to remove when they are completely set. These stains often show up as brown or yellow spots after clothing is washed; I call them "mystery stains."

• **SWIMSUIT,** *Prevent Fading/Fabric Damage from Pool-Water Chlorine:* From a pet store, buy chlorine remover for aquarium water. Rinse your bathing suit after each swim in a solution of 1 drop anti-chlorine formula to 1 gallon water.

• **TENNIS SHOES, WHITE RUBBER:** Clean stains off with whitewall tire cleaner. Follow directions on the container.

• **TIES,** *Preventing Serious Stains:* Before ever wearing a new tie, spray it with fabric stain repellent; spills won't always become stains. This is a favorite hint for frequent flyers! And, why do airline edibles leap onto your clothing anyway?

- **TOBACCO:** Dampen stain and rub with bar soap. Rinse. Soak in enzyme detergent or oxygen bleach and then launder. If stain remains, launder again with chlorine bleach if it's safe for that fabric.

- **TOOTHPASTE ON FABRIC: Caution:** This method is not for silk or other delicate fabrics because the rubbing motion can break the fibers. Place a cloth underneath the fabric, then work with a damp cloth to remove toothpaste. After removing the toothpaste, blow-dry with a hair dryer. **Note:** Avoid the problem by getting dressed after brushing your teeth or by putting a hand towel "bib" over the front of your clothing to protect it.

- **TYPEWRITER CORRECTION FLUID:** Soap and water will not remove paint-based correction fluid. Most are latex-based and must be treated like a paint stain. Take the garment to a dry cleaner and be sure to point it out and tell the cleaner what it is.

- **URINE, VOMIT, MUCUS:** Remove solid residue from fabric. Then, soak with enzyme detergent and warm water. Launder with chlorine bleach if safe for fabric. If not, launder with oxygen bleach and detergent or all-fabric bleach and detergent.

- **WHITE FABRICS TURNED GREY:** Dissolve 1 tablespoon of borax in hot water and add the solution to the final rinse to make whites get white again.

- **WINE OR COFFEE SPILLS,** *Quick-Fix:* Blot the fresh spill with a cloth soaked with tried and true club soda. Or, apply club soda liberally, then sponge up soda and wine.

- **WINE, SOFT DRINKS,** *Washable Fabrics:* Soak with enzyme detergent or oxygen bleach with hottest water safe for fabric and then launder. If stain remains, launder with chlorine bleach if safe for fabric.

- **YELLOWING** (White Nylon, Polyester, Durable Press, Etc.) Soak overnight with enzyme detergent or oxygen bleach and then launder in hottest water safe for fabric with detergent and bleach safe for these fabrics. Or launder with enzyme detergent/oxygen bleach added to regular detergent and hottest water safe for fabric. **Hint:** Modern fabrics contain fluorescent brighteners which react to the sun; instead of bleaching them, sunlight may cause them to become permanently yellowed. Avoid yellowing by drying white fabrics away from natural sunlight.

• **YELLOWING OF STONE-WASHED JEANS:** When the residue from the stone-washing process has not been rinsed completely from the fabric, yellowing can result when the fabric is in contact with some chemicals and even sunshine. Although it's usually permanent, the yellowing can sometimes be removed by commercial laundering.

• **LAST-DITCH STAIN REMOVER FORMULA**

Here is my favorite last-ditch stain remover for white and bleachable clothes (no silk, rayon, etc.). I use it when all else has failed and I can't wear the garment anyway with the spot on it.

    1 gallon of hot water
    1 cup of powdered dishwasher detergent
    ¼ cup of household liquid chlorine bleach

Mix well in a plastic, enamel, or stainless steel container. (This solution should not be used in an aluminum container or come in contact with aluminum because it will discolor it.)

When a garment has an impossible-to-remove stain, let it soak in this solution for 5 to 10 minutes. If any stain remains, soak longer, then wash as usual.

• **OTHER LAST-DITCH SPOT REMOVERS:**

Note: Applying strong bleach to spots can weaken fabrics where they are applied and those areas can deteriorate with each washing, but again, if you can't wear the garment with the stain, and a professional cleaner can't get it out, a last-ditch method is an alternative to throwing the garment out or sewing an appliqué over the stain. Also, note that these two methods may bleach colors out with the stain.

1. Wet the stain and sprinkle powdered dishwasher detergent powder on it. Work the powder into the stain and let the garment set until the stain is gone. Don't scrub too hard, the fabric may get "pills." Rinse, then launder with whites.

2. Squirt full-strength liquid dishwasher detergent on the spot, and work into the fabric. Again, don't scrub too hard or the fabric will "pill." Let set until the spot is gone. Rinse, then launder as usual with whites.

• **CARE-LABELS HINTS:** Keep a file of hang-labels from your clothing and home furnishings so that if sewn-in ones get lost, you have a record of their proper care needs. Keep price tags, too, in case a restaurant has to replace a garment one of its employees has damaged with a spill or if you have to make an insurance claim for a guest's damage to home furnishings. This is what care-label terms mean:

1. Machine Wash, Warm—Use washing machine, warm setting; hot water should not be used.

2. Hand Wash, Cold—Wash only by hand in cold water. Machine washing with warm or hot water shouldn't be used.

3. Bleach When Needed—All commercially available bleaches are safe for regular use.

4. Only Non-chlorine Bleach When Needed—Non-chlorine bleach is safe for use. Regular use of chlorine bleach could harm the garment.

5. Tumble Dry—Hot, medium, or low dryer temperature settings are safe for use.

6. Tumble Dry, Medium—Medium or low dryer temperatures settings are safe for use. Don't use hot setting.

7. Warm Iron—Iron on medium-temperature setting. The higher setting should not be used.

8. Dry Clean—Item can be dry-cleaned by any commercial method that uses any of the available dry-cleaning solvents.

9. Professionally Dry Clean, Perchloroethylene—Item can be dry-cleaned by any commercial establishment using perchloroethylene. Petroleum or fluorocarbon solvents should not be used.

10. Machine Wash, Separately—This warning must be given if the garment could cause harm to another product being washed with it.

11. A garment with detachable pieces will have separate care labels for each piece if each needs different care but one label for all if all can have identical care.

12. Care labels include all parts of the garment, such as lining, trim, buttons, and zippers, and should note if special care is needed for some parts, such as a warning to "remove trim before cleaning."

13. When the label says to clean separately, it means that the garment has limited colorfastness and some dye-bleeding may

occur the first few times it's washed. This can cause fading as well as dye transfer onto other garments washed with it.

14. International symbols for care meet requirements of other countries, but garments sold in the U.S. must also provide written instructions.

• **LAUNDRY WATER TEMPERATURES:** As most couples who play "thermostat Ping-Pong" during air-conditioning season know, the difference between "hot," "warm," and "cold" is a very individual and personal opinion. Not so with laundry, where terms can be translated into temperatures.

1. HOT—130°F or above; for white and colorfast fabrics, heavily soiled loads, diapers.

2. WARM—90°F to 110°F; for noncolorfast fabrics, moderately soiled loads, man-made fibers, and permanent-press fabrics, knits, silks, and woolens. (Heavily soiled, colorfast, sturdy man-made fibers and permanent-press fabrics can be washed in hot water if you use a permanent-press cycle.)

3. COLD—80°F or colder; for dark or bright colors that bleed, lightly soiled loads.

ODORS

I get a lot of mail about annoying or unpleasant odors and a lot of good solutions from readers. I do believe that odors are second only to spots and stains on the list of "little things" that drive us balmy and add stress to our already stressful days. Baking soda is, of course, one of the best odor-removers of all time and it's environmentally safe, too. Lemon juice and vinegar are also safe and effective odor-removers. So is charcoal. However, my resourceful readers have found other remedies that will work in a pinch and some, like mouthwash or toothpaste for removing onion odors from your hands, are in the "of course, why didn't I think of that" category.

REMOVING ODORS AND/OR ADDING PLEASANT SCENTS

• **AIR FRESHENER,** *Controlling Output of Commercial Products:* If you tear back the foil halfway on small plastic air fresheners, the scent will last longer and won't be overpowering in a small room.

• **AIR FRESHENER IN A JAR:** Soak a cotton ball with peppermint oil and put it in a small jar with a lid. When you need to scent or "de-scent" a room, remove the lid. Peppermint oil works well in smoke-filled rooms and leaves them pleasantly fresh. Keep out of reach of children.

- **AIR FRESHENER IN A VACUUM:** Toss a handful of spiced tea into the vacuum bag and each time you vacuum, the house will smell spicy and nice.

- **AIR FRESHENERS:** Also see ROOM DEODORIZERS.

- **ASHTRAY:** If you still smoke, put a little deodorized cat-box filler in ashtrays. It keeps odor down and cigarettes will be immediately extinguished when poked in.

- **BABY BOTTLE,** *Sour Odors:* Boil bottles in a solution of baking soda and water for a few minutes to rid them of the sour milk smell. Take care with glass bottles so that they don't bump each other and crack. A bottle sterilizer or canner might help. You may need to repeat the process weekly.
Note: To avoid odors, right after baby finishes the bottle, rinse it with cold water, then put about a teaspoon or so of baking soda in the bottle, fill with water and allow to soak until you need the bottle again. (Yes, it's untidy to have a row of soaking bottles in the sink but babies are precious and only need bottles for a relatively short period of time compared to the eighteen or so years they spend with you.)

- **BASEMENT,** *Removing Stale, Musty Odors:* Hang a nylon net bag or a bag from onions or potatoes with some charcoal in a convenient place.

- **BED SHEETS, PILLOWCASES,** *Quick-Fix When Taking Musty Guest Linens from Storage:* Toss bedding into the dryer with a fabric softener sheet or two for ten minutes. Or, put a fabric softener sheet in with the guest linens on the shelf a few days before they arrive.

- **BOOKS,** *Preventing Musty Odors When They Are in Storage:* Store books in a dry place and put charcoal in an old sock and place the sock in the book boxes.

- **BREAD-BOX WOOD SMELL:** No washing or cleaning can remove this smell from some boxes and so many people either return them for refund or use them for non-edibles' storage.

- **CARPET DEODORIZER:** With a flour sifter, sprinkle baking soda over the entire carpet and let sit for 20 minutes or longer, then vacuum. Rub cornstarch into lightly soiled spots before vacuuming and you'll clean your carpet while freshening it.

- **CARPET DEODORIZER,** *Stretching Commercial Brands:* Mix equal parts of baking soda and commercial carpet deodorizer to double the volume and still get equal fragrance.

- **CARS,** *Musty:* A problem, especially in damp climates.
1. Clean upholstery with a "dry"-type upholstery cleaner found in most grocery or discount stores. Follow instructions on the container.
2. If floor mats are removable, scrub them with a solution of half vinegar and half water, rinse well, dry in sun if possible.
3. Shampoo or clean carpeting with a spray-type carpet cleaner, making sure not to let the backing get wet.
4. Spray the ceiling and trunk with a good commercial spray deodorizer.

- **CAT ACCIDENT ON CARPET,** *Quick-Fix:* Company coming and kitty did it again in the dining room? Use a thick towel to blot up as much of the liquid as possible and heavily sprinkle the area with either scented carpet freshener or baking soda. Vacuum up when ready.

- **CIGARETTE SMELLS IN MATTRESS:** Try an aerosol spray from supermarkets made for fabric and upholstery odor removal and then lay the mattress and box spring out in the fresh air and sunshine all day if you can. If odor persists, you may need to thoroughly clean the mattress or box spring with a rented cleaning machine—follow use instructions with the machine.

- **CLOSET DEODORIZER:** Put a tablespoon or two of fresh unused ground coffee in one or two old socks and place them in the closet to prevent musty odors.

- **CLOSET MILDEW ODOR,** *Healthy Planet:* Fill a one-pound coffee can or other container with charcoal of the type used in aquariums and put it in the corner of a closet.

• **CLOSET SCENT:** A walk-in closet will smell nice if you step into it when you spray yourself with cologne. **Caution:** Take care not to spray cologne on clothing; it can stain or damage some fabrics.

• **COOLER,** *Preventing Musty Odors When Stored:* Sprinkle some baking soda into it before closing it up. Then, when you get the cooler out for a picnic, dump the soda into the kitchen sink, run water and it will freshen the drain.

• **CORNED BEEF AND CABBAGE COOKING:** Add a bit of vinegar to the water while boiling it.

• **DOGGIE DEODORANT:** In between baths, dust your dog with baking soda, leave it on 10 minutes or so, brush it out and enjoy a sweet-smelling dog.

• **DOWN/FEATHER-FILLED COMFORTERS, PILLOWS, ETC. MUSTY ODOR:** If tossing them in the dryer for a few minutes with a tennis ball and a dryer sheet using air but no heat doesn't work, find a professional cleaner who has the proper equipment to clean feather pillows and comforters. Not all do, so call first.

• **FIREPLACE ODORS:** Causes include creosote deposit buildup, soot, moisture, or animals caught in the flue and can also be due to the type of wood burned. Have a professional chimney sweep inspect and clean the chimney to determine the cause and solution.

• **FIREPLACE SMOKY ODOR:** If cleaning out all the ash from the fireplace doesn't remove the odor, shampoo carpeting; wash or dry-clean draperies/curtains; change filters in the furnace or air conditioner; and spray furniture with a fabric deodorant.

• **FISHY SMELL ON HANDS:**
1. At Home—Spritz hands with lemon or lime juice and wash.
2. On a Fishing Trip—Soak small hand towels in a mixture of lemon juice and water, put the wet towels in plastic self-sealing bags (two per bag) and store the bags in the freezer. Take as many bags as you think you'll need and put them in a cooler when you go fishing. At the end of the fishing day, the towels are thawed and ready to wipe away fish odors from hands and freshen your face, too.

• **FLOOR SAFE,** *Getting Rid of Musty Odors:* If keeping an open box of baking soda doesn't prevent musty odors, try silica gel available at craft stores, which are installed in cement floors.

• **FOOT ODOR,** *Prevention:*
1. Scrub feet with soap and water at least once daily and dry well. Follow washing with antiperspirant foot spray or powder.
2. Buy shoes made from either canvas or leather so that feet can "breathe" and perspiration is absorbed. And/or try wearing sandals.
3. During the day when feet feel hot and tired, spray with a little cologne. They will feel refreshed. If you have no cologne handy, wipe your feet with a packaged moist towelette. You can do this with panty hose still on.

• **GARBAGE DISPOSAL,** *Deodorizing:*
1. If it's a sturdy model, freeze vinegar and water into ice cubes and run cubes through the disposal.
2. Run a handful of lemon or lime peels followed by lots of cold water. My favorite!
3. Pour leftover drops of peppermint or other extracts down the disposal. **Note:** Please see KITCHEN SINK.

• **GARBAGE PAILS:** Place a fabric-softener sheet in the bottom of the pail before putting in the plastic garbage bag.

• **HANDS,** *Onions and Other Odors:* Rinse hands with mouthwash or scrub with toothpaste. And, next time, wear rubber gloves to avoid the problem.

• **KITCHEN GARBAGE CAN:** Sprinkle floral-scented carpet deodorizer in the bottom of the indoor kitchen garbage can to control odors.

• **KITCHEN SINK,** *Persistent Odor Even After Cleaning in and Under It:*
1. Buildup of bacteria in the drain can make the sink area smell. Pour some bleach down the sink and let sit for several hours to kill any bacteria that may be thriving there. Then run hot water for at least 60 seconds.
2. If you have a garbage disposal, unplug the unit and remove the rubber splash guard located in the sink drain. Wash it thoroughly,

especially the underside. Then run a lemon or orange rind through the disposal for a sweet-smelling sink.

3. Sink stoppers and splash guards are inexpensive and you may want to buy new ones; sometimes the rubber in old ones gets very grungy and harbors musty odors.

• **LAUNDRY,** *Getting a Fresh Fragrance:* Add 1 cup of vinegar to the final rinse water and laundry will be soft and fluffy as well has have a fresh, clean fragrance.

• **LUGGAGE, MUSTY ODOR FROM STORAGE:** Place a shallow box filled with cat-box litter deodorizer in the suitcase, close the lid, and wait twenty-four hours or longer. The litter should absorb the musty odor. You may want to also let the luggage sit outside, opened so that Mom Nature can finish the job for you. **Hint:** Avoid the problem by stuffing the suitcase with newspaper and a handful of fabric softener sheets before storing it and don't store luggage in damp places like basements or garages.

• **LUNCH BOX:** Dampen a piece of paper towel or stale bread with vinegar and put it in the lunch box overnight. Wash in the morning and it will smell fresh.

• **MATTRESS "ACCIDENT,"** *Removing Urine Odor:* Please see MAT-TRESS "ACCIDENT" in the Spots and Stains section.

• **MICROWAVE:** To remove cooking odors like those from fish, put 1 cup water, 6 whole cloves and half a lemon into a microwave-safe dish. Cook on "High" for about 3 to 5 minutes.

• **MOTHBALL ODOR,** *Removing from an Antique Dresser:* Try spraying evergreen-scented spray left over from Christmas into drawers; take them outdoors and leave in the fresh air for a day.

• **MOTHBALLS,** *Removing Odor:*
1. From Clothing—Allow to air outdoors if possible but don't hang non-colorfast garments or fabrics in the bright sun.
2. From Furniture—Place the chest or its drawers outside in the sun for several days to dissipate the odor. If that doesn't work, clean the inside with a wood cleaner found in hardware or home-improvement stores. Make sure wood is dry before you replace clothing.

3. From the House: Send draperies, bedding, and carpets to professional cleaners. Mattresses, upholstered items, suitcases, and other movable items can be placed outside in the sun to air. Leave doors and windows open; ceiling and oscillating fans may help push the odor out. Air fresheners throughout the house can mask the odor until it goes away but no matter what you do, expect the airing to take a long time.

• **NATURAL GAS ODOR,** *Checklist for Safety When You Smell a Leaky Gas Source:*
1. Check for the source—such as pilot lights of stove, water heater, whatever runs on gas.
2. Turn off the gas supply and open all windows to allow some of the gas to escape. **Caution:** Do not attempt to light a pilot light without letting gas escape. One of my secretaries didn't ventilate the room enough when she re-lit the pilot on her oven; there was enough gas still present to flare up and singe her bangs, eyebrows, and eyelashes!
3. If the gas odor is strong and you can't find the source, shut off the main gas valve; open windows and doors to ventilate the area; leave the house and call the gas company from a neighbor's house. Do not use light switches, electrical appliances, or even the doorbell—even a slight electric charge could cause a gas explosion. Certainly don't light matches, lighters, or candles to look for the leak! Gas leaks are extremely dangerous and it's best to have a professional deal with them.

• **OIL ODOR IN CAR,** *Quick-Fix:* Tuck a fabric-softener sheet under one of the front seats. This is not a permanent solution but will work for a while for dirty oil and some other odors. Try having the upholstery cleaned and keeping a sockful of charcoal in the car.

• **ONION ODOR,** *Avoiding It on Hands:* When you grate onions, put your onion-holder hand into a plastic bag and then when you are finished grating, put the bag around the onion without touching it. The onion is ready to cook and leftovers ready to refrigerate and your hands don't smell!

• **ONIONS,** *Removing Odor from Hands:* After peeling of slicing onions, sprinkle a bit of salt on your damp hands, work it over and rinse.

• **OVEN-CLEANER ODOR,** *Removing/Preventing:* Here's how to remove all of the oven-cleaner residue so that you don't get a terrible whiff of it the first time you heat up the clean oven.
1. After cleaning an oven with oven cleaner, spread a thick layer of newspapers on the oven floor.
2. With a spray bottle, spray warm water on the top and sides of the oven wall.
3. Dry the inside of the oven with a clean cloth then roll up the newspaper carefully and discard it.

• **OVEN SPILLS,** *Eliminating Burnt Odors and Smoke:* When food baking in the oven boils over, sprinkle a little salt on the burned goo. In addition to killing odor and smoke, it will be easier to wipe up the mess when you have finished baking. **Hint:** Avoid mess by placing a cookie sheet or foil piece under foods that are likely to spill over.

• **PET DEODORANT,** *Homemade "Doggie Spritzer":* Mix 32 ounces of water with two capfuls of your favorite fragrant bath oil and put the mixture into a spray bottle. Spray on pet's coat between baths and rub it in. **Caution:** Always clearly label bottles of homemade solutions.

• **PILLOWS,** *Freshening:* Toss bed pillows in the dryer air cycle with a fabric softener sheet for about 20 minutes to fluff and freshen them.

• **POTPOURRI,** *Expensive vs. Bargain Brands:* While room fresheners mask unpleasant odors, potpourri's function is to add pleasant fragrance to a room. Generally, the more expensive potpourri is made only from botanicals—dried flowers, leaves, pods, seeds, and other plant parts. Less expensive potpourri can be a combination of pine cones, acorns, sweet gumballs from a woods, dyed wood chips and sawdust, with added fragrances, cinnamon, dried orange and lemon peels and or scented wax chips. If all you want is the scent and don't care where it comes from, you'll wonder why you should pay $10 for a bag of scented wood chips in a boutique when you can get a bag of scented wood chips for $3.95 at a discount store. Like everything else, you need to read labels to get your money's worth. And, like so many "designer" luxuries, you can make homestyle substitutes for pennies.

1. To the water in your potpourri, you can add the remaining drops of your favorite perfume (rinse out the bottle with alcohol and pour into potpourri water).

2. Or mix up combinations of orange or lemon peels, cinnamon sticks, allspice (or simmer some poultry seasoning for a Thanksgiving fragrance) according to "taste."

• **POTPOURRI,** *Heloise Formula for Wet Potpourri:* Gather 2 cups of rose petals, 2 cups of rosemary, 2 cups of mint, four cinnamon sticks, ½ cup of whole allspice, and two whole cloves. Place all ingredients in a large jar and cover with heated white vinegar. Let the jar sit for about a week, then place some of the potpourri in a simmering pot. **Hint:** Experiment with different mixtures to find your favorite fragrance.

• **POTPOURRI,** *Substitute "Cookers":*
1. Put potpourri in the portable vaporizer/humidifier water compartment.
2. Simmer potpourri in a mug or old gift cheese crock placed on a coffee-cup warmer.
3. Nuke a bowl of water and potpourri in the microwave.

• **REFRIGERATOR DEODORIZER:**
1. Keep a tried-and-true box of baking soda in the fridge and every few months, replace it. Pour the used baking soda down the sink to freshen it or put the baking soda into the bottom of a cat litter box.
2. When you move or put a refrigerator or freezer in storage even for a short time, place a sock filled with dry coffee grounds or charcoal to prevent musty odors.

• **REFRIGERATOR ODOR FROM SPOILED MEAT:** If washing the inside with baking soda doesn't work, put dry coffee grounds on a couple of paper plates and set them on different shelves. The odor should go away in two or three days.

• **ROOM DEODORIZER MUSHROOMS,** *Recycling by Renewing the Scent:* Put a few drops of a liquid deodorizer or your favorite perfume on top of the "mushroom."

• **ROOM DEODORIZER VACUUMING:** Place a scented fabric softener sheet between the inner and outer vacuum bags or into the bag of an upright vacuum cleaner to put a pleasant scent of fresh laundry in the room when you vacuum. The scented softener sheet can be used for several weeks.

- **ROOM FRAGRANCE FROM FIREPLACE:** Sprinkle herbs—fresh or dried—cinnamon sticks, or spices on a small, gently burning fireplace fire to make a room smell festive. Or you can buy bags of scented chips in hardware stores to make the house smell spicy and sweet.

- **RUBBER GLOVES,** *To Prevent Odors:* If you don't like to sprinkle talcum powder or baking soda inside, try this: After you've finished a chore, dry your rubber gloves (outside surface) while they are still on, then pull them off so they turn inside out. The fingers usually stay stuck in, so cuff the end of the glove and blow it up like a balloon. Hang the inside-out gloves on a towel rack to air-dry. To wear, "cuff and puff" again to blow them right-side-out.

- **RUBBER GLOVES,** *Sweet Smelling:* Sprinkle a bit of baking soda or talcum powder into rubber gloves to help them glide on and off and smell better.

- **SHOES:** Sprinkle a little baking soda in shoes at night after removing them and let it set overnight. In the morning, sprinkle the soda into the bathroom sink or commode to recycle this wonderful deodorizer.

- **SLEEPING BAGS:** To prevent musty odors in sleeping bags, lay fabric softener sheets on the bag and roll them up with the bag for storage.

- **TOBACCO SMOKE,** *Stale Room Odor:* Put about a capful of ammonia in a bowl of water and leave it out overnight (out of reach of children and pets) and the stale smoke odor will be gone in the morning.

- **VACUUM-CLEANER BAG,** *Healthy-Planet Air Freshener:* Add to the bag any of the following fresheners to prevent that stale musty odor that can come from the vacuum cleaner "exhaust"—a few whole cloves, carpet freshener or baking soda, a cotton ball sprayed with your favorite perfume or dabbed with peppermint or almond extract.

• **WATER BED:** If the plastic is the problem, try washing the "mattress" with baking soda and water. Bacteria growth in the water inside the mattress also can cause odors; ask at a water-bed shop for a commercial product to cure odors.

Heloise's column "Hints from Heloise" is syndicated in over five hundred newspapers internationally; in addition, she writes a monthly column for *Good Housekeeping*.

Indispensable home reference guides
from America's most trusted household-hints advisor.

All-New Hints from Heloise
A Household Guide for the '90s

An invaluable collection of advice tailored to working people for whom convenience is imperative, with special hints for new home technology, including computers, CD players, and more.

Heloise Hints for a Healthy Planet

Heloise's columns have always emphasized the three Rs—recycling, reuse, and resourcefulness. Now she explains how to make them a way of life, with tips for the kitchen, bathroom, laundry room, garage, basement, garden, schoolroom, office, and more.

Heloise from A to Z

By popular demand: the first book of Heloise's timeless wisdom for the home to be presented in a convenient, easy-to-use dictionary format.

These books are available at your local bookstore or wherever books are sold. Ordering is also easy and convenient. Just call 1-800-631-8571 or send your order to:

The Putnam Publishing Group
390 Murray Hill Parkway, Dept. B
East Rutherford, NJ 07073

		U.S. $	Canada $
_____All-New Hints from Heloise	399-51510-0	$9.95	$12.95
_____Heloise Hints for a Healthy Planet	399-51625-5	$7.95	$10.50
_____Heloise from A to Z	399-51750-2	$10.95	$14.50

Subtotal $ _____

Postage and handling* $ _____

Sales tax (CA, NJ, NY, PA) $ _____

Total amount due $ _____

Payable in U.S. funds (no cash orders accepted). $10.00 minimum for credit card orders.

*Postage & handling: $2.00 for 1 book, 50¢ for each additional book up to a maximum of $4.50.

Enclosed is my ☐ check ☐ money order

Please charge my ☐ Visa ☐ MasterCard ☐ American Express

Card # _____ Expiration date _____

Signature as on charge card _____

Name _____

Address _____

City _____ State _____ Zip _____

Please allow six weeks for delivery. Prices subject to change without notice.

28